Scotland

Manchester University Press

Scotland

The new state of an old nation

Murray Stewart Leith and Duncan Sim

with

Duncan McTavish and David Torrance

Manchester University Press

Published by Manchester University Press
Altrincham Street, Manchester M1 7JA
www.manchesteruniversitypress.co.uk

British Library Cataloguing-in-Publication Data
A catalogue record for this book is available from the British Library

ISBN 978 1 7849 9255 2 hardback

First published 2020

Typeset by Newgen Publishing UK
Printed in Great Britain
by TJ International Ltd, Padstow

This book is dedicated to two former political science colleagues,

Fiona Veitch and Duncan McTavish

Fiona Veitch was our colleague, who taught politics with us at the University of the West of Scotland for many years but died suddenly in September 2017.

Duncan McTavish taught at Glasgow Caledonian University. He has contributed a chapter to this volume but died in late 2018 before it was published.

Both are missed greatly and are, and will be, remembered within the Scottish academic community.

Contents

Tables

Acknowledgements

There are a number of people we would specifically like to thank for their help and support while we were writing this book.

First and foremost, we would like to thank the University of the West of Scotland for its continuing support over a number of years, and in particular those colleagues who provided us with advice, comments and feedback. We are also grateful to our undergraduate students who provided comments and feedback on the modules that we taught and that have informed much of the book's content. Our thanks, in particular, to five students – David, Holli, Kerry, Megan and Taylor – who read some of our draft chapters and gave us initial feedback.

We would also like to thank all the members of the Scottish academic community and those wider members of Scotland's civil society who have contributed to the debates surrounding the concepts, ideas and issues we discuss in this book. The old cliché of academic work is that we stand on the shoulders of giants; well, this work stands on the shoulders of many, many people over many, many years.

We are indebted to David Torrance and the late Duncan McTavish for contributing their chapters to the book. Duncan's death, just after he had completed the chapter, was a blow to us all.

Finally, our thanks to the staff at Manchester University Press, notably Tony Mason (who went along with our proposal) and Rob Byron and Jon de Peyer (who have seen it to fruition), as well as our anonymous reviewers.

Any errors in the text are, of course, entirely our responsibility!

Murray Stewart Leith and Duncan Sim

July 2019

Chapter 1
Introduction

Origins of the book

The idea for writing this book about Scotland arose as a result of many years teaching by the two main authors at the Universities of Glasgow, Stirling and the West of Scotland. We have, separately and jointly, organised and contributed to courses and/or modules on the sociology, policy and politics of Scotland but have sometimes been quite frustrated by the lack of adequate texts to recommend to our students. For a number of years, books were often written on a UK-wide basis with limited attention (if at all) paid to the position north of the border. Scotland, in most cases, became a kind of regional opt-out, rather like those television programmes that sometimes carry the rider 'except for viewers in Scotland'.

For a long time, the situation made a kind of sense in that many of the social and political issues with which our students were grappling were broadly the same north and south and west, as England, Scotland and Wales were under the same governmental system and facing and responding to socio-political issues in much the same ways. But as politics in Scotland began to change from the late 1960s onwards and, given that Scots law had always been different from English law and that many aspects of policy and socio-political views in areas such as education (which once again, had always been different in Scotland) were increasingly diverging, it became more difficult to find adequate coverage of Scottish issues in the mainstream UK-focused textbooks.

To be fair, there have been some honourable exceptions. In the field of sociology, we made extensive use of David McCrone's *Understanding Scotland* for many years, but the second edition dated from 2001 and so barely covered the devolution era. It was therefore a particularly welcome development when McCrone published a new, revised and much-needed text (McCrone 2017). He is also, like ourselves often working in close partnership with a long-term colleague, the author of a number of other texts on issues of nationalism and national identity (for example, McCrone 1998; McCrone and Bechhofer 2015), as well as large numbers of journal articles, so he has been an important figure in Scottish sociology. He and his colleagues at the Institute of Governance at the University of Edinburgh have conducted a range of important research studies in this field.

Within the wider policy field, there have been some important texts that have examined the changing landscape within Scotland in the period since devolution in 1999, particularly the edited volumes produced by Gerry Mooney and Gill Scott (2005 and 2012). But it is difficult to keep up with the pace of change – not just within Scotland but also in the context of the UK as a whole. Indeed, we expect widespread policy changes arising from Britain's exit from the European Union (EU) in 2019, just as changes have occurred as we write this text.

It is perhaps in the field of politics where events and outcomes have moved at a sometimes bewildering pace and where many insightful works have been produced within the last two decades in particular. There is a seemingly ever-increasing number of political scientists working within Scottish (and other) universities who have undertaken research and published on Scottish political and sociopolitical affairs (for example, Hutchison 2001; Ichijo 2004; McEwan 2006; Henderson 2007; Keating 2010; Mitchell 2014). In terms of more general texts for students of Scottish government and politics, the most recent books are perhaps Paul Cairney's (2011b) *The Scottish Political System Since Devolution* and his co-written book with Neil McGarvey, *Scottish Politics*, first published in 2008 but already in its very welcome, second edition (2013). In 2016, Duncan McTavish edited a valuable book, simply entitled *Politics in Scotland*, and he also very kindly contributed a chapter on Scottish politics to this present volume before his untimely passing in 2018.

However, it is easy to illustrate how difficult it is to keep pace with the social and political change in Scotland as most of these books were written before the referendum on Scottish independence in 2014. During the run up to the referendum itself, and since, numerous other works examining Scotland, with many seeking to address what the authors see as Scotland's deficiencies or problems, have been published. These works are often more prognostic than analytical, and sometimes just polemical, but they contribute thoughts and ideas and are a welcome debate to a society facing and dealing with significant issues and change. It can safely be said that today Scotland is therefore unsurprisingly a thriving subject in the wider realm of texts and articles.

Indeed, we should also make honourable mention here of the journal *Scottish Affairs*. Established by Edinburgh University's Institute of Governance in 1992, it is now published by Edinburgh University Press and has been and remains an invaluable source of material and we strongly recommend it to all students of Scotland and Scottish-related matters.

Yet, despite this cumulative scholarly activity there remain few texts that explore the wider aspects of Scotland – its society, culture, life and politics. Hence, our efforts within. Nevertheless, in this book, we should say straight away that we have not tried to write from the specific perspectives of sociology or political science. As we note above, there are many excellent works that have recently arrived that have done just that. Rather, we have sought to explore issues – identity, employment, gender, ethnicity, culture, heritage and so on – in such a way that we hope that this book will be of interest across the wider academic disciplines and social sciences. That said, it may be that our writing reflects our own different backgrounds. Murray Leith is a political scientist, Duncan Sim a social geographer by training who moved gradually into sociology and social policy. Our guest contributors are Duncan McTavish, whose academic career was also in political science, and David Torrance, who has a background in politics and public life from political history and public policy perspectives.

We are also conscious that we are writing at a time when, like some of its predecessors, this book may well be out of date on certain subjects and information by the time it appears, such is the pace of contemporary change. That, however, may well be its justification – to try and say something about Scotland in 2019, for the benefit of students who find it hard to keep up!

We move on now to provide some background to change in Scotland over recent decades and to explain how Scotland has become so different in many ways to other parts of the UK. We then end this introductory chapter by outlining a plan of the book.

Scottish society in the post-war period

The early 1950s are often regarded as a high point of Britishness in the UK, in the aftermath of the Second World War and before the disintegration of the British Empire (Devine 1999). But the UK emerged from the war almost bankrupt and had to be rescued by American loans. Scotland in particular appeared to be in bad shape and in desperate need of industrial reconstruction and diversification. The approach taken by the Attlee government after 1945 was the establishment of the post-war welfare state and the nationalisation of key industries such as coal, steel and the railways. While this allowed for reorganisation of these industries, they were all headquartered in England – usually in London – and so important decision-making, research and development were removed from Scotland. That said, however, during the 1950s, UK regional policy succeeded in encouraging new investment, such as motor manufacturing plants at Linwood and Bathgate, a new steel mill at Ravenscraig, near Motherwell, and a new aluminium smelter at Invergordon. But these developments only served to highlight how much of a 'branch economy' Scotland had become.

This was particularly true of the electronics industry, which expanded significantly in Scotland during the 1960s and 1970s. Although initially viewed as a major success story, with the term 'Silicon Glen' being coined to refer to the Scottish version of California's 'Silicon Valley', the developments were essentially branch plants of American companies. These included IBM, NCR, Burroughs and Honeywell, later joined by a number of Japanese firms (Payne 1996). By the end of the twentieth century, some of these plants had closed, as companies retrenched.

At the same time as Scotland was experiencing mixed economic fortunes at home, the decline of the British Empire was reducing opportunities overseas. During the 1950s and 1960s, the UK appeared unsure as to its future direction and it was not until 1973 that it joined the EU (then the European Economic Community). This allowed Dean Acheson, American Secretary of State in the early 1950s, to make his famous remark that Great Britain had lost an empire but not yet found a role. It is ironic that, at the time of writing, the future direction of the UK is again unclear as it negotiates its exit from the EU. Clearly that role is still to be found.

Scotland during this period was a somewhat conservative country, both socially and politically. Indeed, Brivati (2002: 238) suggests that it was not only socially conservative but authoritarian, with both the Church of Scotland and the Scottish education system particularly dominant. Both could be seen as progressive; the Kirk for example, had a strong sense of social responsibility. But both could also be viewed as oppressive and hierarchical, and Brivati suggests that Scotland emerged later than the rest of the UK from 'the long dark night of Victorian moralism' (2002: 238).

In writing about his own childhood in 1950s Scotland, Jack (1987) recognises the improvements in people's lives as they became better off – or as Prime Minister Harold Macmillan suggested, 'had never had it so good'. But Jack believes that this picture, for Scotland at least, lacked a historical perspective with many families experiencing only limited change: 'In our house we lived with old times, concurrently in the 1910s and Twenties as well as the Fifties. The past sustained us in a physical as well as mental sense. It came home from work every evening in its flat cap and dirty hands and drew its weekly wages from industries which even then were sleepwalking their way towards extinction' (Jack 1987: 5–6). Even where Scots had moved into white-collar employment and had become essentially middle class in terms of socio-economic classifications, they still tended to view themselves as working class. This continuing identification as a working-class society was far stronger in Scotland than in England (McCrone 2001).

Scottish families tended to be slightly larger than in England, partly due to a larger proportion of the population being Roman Catholic, but this had the effect of increasing the non-earning section of the population (Harvie 1993) and so many families were far from well off. As was the case in other countries, many women stayed at home to look after children and the labour-saving devices that would transform domestic work were only just beginning to have an impact. The wider availability of contraception that also impacted significantly on family size and the role of women did not occur until the mid-1960s. Families were generally stable in this period, however, and divorce was rare. In 1960, there were fewer than 2,000 divorces in Scotland, but within thirty years, the figure was 12,400, as the process was made easier by law (McIvor 1996).

The housing conditions in which many Scottish families lived were often very poor. Housing had begun to improve in the 1920s with the expansion of local authority house building, but conditions remained problematic well into the 1960s. The 1951 census, for example, revealed that over 45 per cent of houses in Glasgow consisted of only one room and over 130,000 houses were overcrowded; thousands of other houses were rendered substandard on a sanitary or piped-water basis (Gibb 1989). The post-war period was characterised therefore by massive house building and clearance and renewal programmes.

Outside the home, activities could also be described as fairly traditional. Just after the war, 43 per cent of Scottish children went to the cinema once a week and Scotland was one of the strongest cinema-going parts of the UK (Brown 1996). A study of Glasgow males in the mid-1950s suggested that their top leisure activities were watching or playing football, the cinema and dancing

(Ferguson and Cunnison 1956). In 1952, Glasgow had ninety-six dance halls. Pubs were significant places for socialising but were very male dominated and there was no elaborate pub society, as in England (Harvie 1993). As late as the 1970s, there were still many pubs that were divided into a public bar where the men drank pints of beer and from which women were excluded, and a lounge bar where women were able to drink but where pints were not allowed.

We should also note the importance of religion in post-war Scottish society and Scotland had a high level of church attendance. In 1960, almost 70 per cent of Scots over the age of fourteen were claimed as church members, very much higher than elsewhere in the UK (Harvie 1993). But this began to fall during the decade as both the Church of Scotland and the Roman Catholic Church lost members.

The social conservatism of much of Scotland may be seen perhaps in regard to shifts in social attitudes, which were generally slower north of the border. The 1960s may have been 'swinging' for many and was a period of significant social reform. But the changes were perhaps more obvious south of the border and not all reforms were enacted in Scotland. The decriminalisation of homosexuality for example, which occurred in 1967 in England and Wales, did not happen in Scotland until 1980.

Scottish post-war politics

We examine Scottish politics in detail in Chapter 8. But suffice to say here that politically too, Scotland embraced Conservatism in much of the post-war period, and indeed voting patterns were similar north and south of the border until the 1970s. In 1955, like the rest of Britain, Scotland voted Conservative and the party achieved a majority of both votes and seats, a feat unmatched since – although the Scottish National Party (SNP) came close in 2015 with 49.9 per cent of the vote (and all but three of the country's seats). In 1964 and 1966, Scotland voted Labour but the late 1960s saw the start of a significant growth in political nationalism.

In part, these changes may have owed their origins to Britain's post-imperial lack of direction and a feeling in Scotland that the Union was no longer working to Scotland's advantage. After the discovery of North Sea oil, with its potential to transform the country's economic fortunes and that would make an independent Scotland economically viable, the Union came under particular strain. By 1977, Tom Nairn could write of the likely 'breakup' of Britain (Nairn 1977).

The late 1960s saw significant advances by the SNP. It had been founded in 1934, following the merger of some smaller predecessors, but had had only limited political success (Lynch 1999). But its breakthrough came with the victory of Winnie Ewing at the Hamilton by-election in 1967 (Ewing and Russell 2004; Mitchell 2017), after which the party has had continuous representation at Westminster. Indeed, this period marked the start of shifts in political allegiances and voting patterns between Scotland and England. In 1979, when Margaret Thatcher swept to power, there was actually a swing to Labour in Scotland and the Shadow Secretary of State for Scotland, Teddy Taylor, lost his seat. By 1997, there were no Conservative Members of Parliament (MPs) left in Scotland and only in the 2017 general election was there something of a revival. Meanwhile, the SNP has won three elections to the Scottish Parliament – as a minority in 2007 and 2016, and with an unexpected overall majority in 2011. In the 2015 UK general election, they won fifty-six out of Scotland's fifty-nine seats and, although they lost seats in 2017, they remain the dominant Scottish party at Westminster, Holyrood and in local government. The last fifty years bears witness to the clear rise of the SNP from a party of the fringe to that of government.

Our references earlier to Britain's loss of empire and subsequent lack of direction are important. Many people in Scotland watched as a series of British colonies became independent and this process inevitably raised the question as to whether Scotland itself ought to be independent – or at the very least, have a measure of home rule. Thus:

> In a television programme in March 1998, Ludovic Kennedy said that he was present to report for the BBC at scores of hand-over ceremonies in former British colonies where the Union flag was lowered and the flag of the newly independent country was raised. 'I started to think,' he said, 'if these little places, and some of them very small and very poor, can have self-government, why can't Scotland?' (Scott 1999: 58)

The success of the SNP – and its equivalent, Plaid Cymru in Wales – led governments at Westminster to look in more detail at the ways in which Scotland was governed. Following the Hamilton by-election, Prime Minister Harold Wilson had established the Kilbrandon Commission to explore the possibilities for Scottish devolution but, although it argued for a directly elected 'assembly', its recommendations were not immediately acted upon. Part of the problem was the opposition of many Scottish MPs, not least in the Labour Party itself. The Scottish executive of the party actually voted against devolution at a poorly attended meeting in Glasgow in 1974 and, in a moment of supreme irony, had to be overruled by Labour headquarters in London (Harvie and Jones 2000). Internal Labour opposition dogged the progress of the subsequent Scotland Bill through Parliament and a Labour backbencher, George Cunningham, managed to insert an amendment, requiring a vote of 40 per cent of the total Scottish electorate (not merely those voting) to vote in favour of a Scottish Assembly for it to be established. Although there was a vote in favour of the Assembly in the 1979 referendum, it failed to overcome the 40 per cent hurdle (Devine 1999) and so the devolution proposals failed. The argument was that the Cunningham modification was a 'wrecking' amendment and it certainly slowed devolution for twenty years.

This failure to gain an elected Assembly, followed by the election of a Conservative government under Margaret Thatcher, had a considerable dampening effect on Scottish constitutional politics. But during the 1980s, the continuing success of the Conservatives in England, while losing votes and seats in Scotland, led to claims that the country was experiencing a 'democratic deficit' (Maxwell 2012). A cross-party Constitutional Convention was established to prepare for fresh devolution legislation once Labour regained power. In 1997, following the election of Tony Blair and New Labour to government, a new Scotland Bill was introduced into Westminster, along with a new referendum, and the Scottish Parliament was finally established in 1999.

Although there was an overwhelming 3:1 vote in favour of the Parliament in the 1997 referendum, there were still some who argued that it would, in the long run, help to destabilise the Union (Jeffery 2008). Indeed, the veteran Labour MP, Tam Dalyell, had always believed that devolution was a 'motorway without exits' on the way to independence (McGarvey 2008). Such fears may have appeared to hold some truth after the SNP won an overall majority in 2011 and began the legislation that led to the 2014 referendum on Scottish independence. At the time of writing, a second referendum remains possible, especially following the decision by the UK to leave the EU, despite Scotland voting by 62 per cent to 38 per cent to remain. Yet again, this illustrates the divergences in voting within the UK. Yet constitutional decision-making formally remains the purview of Westminster, and only with the agreement of the UK Government can the Scottish Government hold another legally binding independence referendum.

A more confident nation?

Devolution and the establishment of the Scottish Parliament have undoubtedly had a massive impact on Scotland's sense of itself, and the Parliament has been a significant 'engine of change' in terms of the legislation it has introduced (Pittock 2008). The introduction of free personal care for the elderly, the abolition of student tuition fees, the abolition of prescription charges, the introduction of a smoking ban in public places, minimum-pricing legislation to tackle alcohol abuse and a divergent income tax policy have all indicated a legislature determined to make its mark. As a result, Pittock suggested in 2008 that Scottish and English domestic societies were steadily diverging, and events since have continued to support his argument that the experience of living in the two countries is becoming increasingly different.

In fact, it is possible to look back to the 1970s and the first demands for devolution to find indications that confidence and attitudes in Scotland were changing. This was particularly noticeable in the country's largest city, Glasgow. In the 1960s, the city still had significant numbers of houses in poor condition and was experiencing industrial decline, particularly in its traditional industries of shipbuilding and manufacturing. In 1971, the Conservative government under Edward Heath had actually proposed the complete closure of shipbuilding on the upper Clyde but, after a spirited resistance by the workforce including a 'work-in' led by the shop stewards, a slimmed-down presence remained (Checkland 1981). At the same time, the 1974 Housing Act provided for the funding of housing associations as a 'third arm' of housing provision between local authorities and the private sector, and there was a significant growth in community-based associations in older parts of the city. Their main focus was the renewal and rehabilitation of the older tenemental housing stock, installing the modern amenities that had hitherto been lacking. In this way, the inner city was renewed (Keating 1988).

Interestingly, the City Council chose to acknowledge Glasgow's industrial decline, opting to reinvent itself as a post-industrial city, and changing its working-class, somewhat negative image under the slogan 'Glasgow's Miles Better'. In 1988, Glasgow hosted the UK's National Garden Festival, in 1990 it was the European Capital of Culture, in 1999 it was the City of Architecture and Design and it developed an important role as a conference location, opening the Scottish Exhibition and Conference Centre in 1985. Some have suggested that, while these developments have had important economic benefits for the city, they have not always 'trickled down' to the more marginalised communities (Damer 1990). But there is no doubt that the city's reinvention of itself is a prime example of 'civic boosterism' (Boyle 1997) and has ultimately been of national importance for Scotland.

The regeneration of Glasgow is indicative of other forms of regeneration within Scotland, particularly in the arts and culture. Glasgow's year as European City of Culture left a tangible legacy in the building of the city's Royal Concert Hall and the establishment of various cultural activities (we refer, for example, to the annual Celtic Connections festival and developments in Scottish theatre, such as the establishment of political theatre groups like 7:84 and Wildcat, in Chapter 12). The 1970s also saw an expansion of BBC Scotland and the establishment of a range of new independent radio stations such as Radio Clyde and Radio Forth, providing new voices for the country.

In literature, there were also new political journals launched. Some, like *Glasgow News* and *Clydeside Action* were local campaigning journals, while others such as the *New Edinburgh Review*, founded in 1969, had a more cultural focus. Journals with a more political focus included *Calgacus* and *Question*, the latter beginning in 1975, specifically in anticipation of the coming of a devolved Scottish Assembly; with the failure of the devolution vote in 1979, the journal folded. There was therefore a distinct feeling in 1970s Scotland that the country was finding its own voice, distinct from the rest of the UK.

There is no doubt that the failure to establish a Scottish Assembly in 1979 dented Scottish confidence and it was clear that the new Conservative Prime Minister Margaret Thatcher had no interest in devolution. But the Labour Party took the lead in setting up a campaign for a Scottish Assembly to continue to press for some form of elected legislature and this ultimately led to the cross-party Scottish Constitutional Convention in 1988. The public face of the Convention was the episcopalian cleric Canon Kenyon Wright and, recognising the opposition of the then government, he defiantly told the Convention: 'What if that other single voice we all know so well responds by saying "We say No, We are the State?" Well We say Yes and We are the People' (Torrance 2009: 191).

Changes in national identity

In terms of national identity, Scots in the 1950s and early 1960s appeared to feel both Scottish and British. The sense of Britishness permeated throughout society. As Spence recalls:

> How did I fit into it? How was my definition of myself shaping up? Well, I was a Protestant, I knew that. I also knew that I was Scottish. Scotland was my country, Glasgow my city. Sometimes being Scottish meant being British, sometimes British just meant English. But then sometimes Scottish and English were opposed, as in football internationals, as in great battles from the past ... It was all too confusing. (1977: 19–20)

But the growing sense of confidence in Scotland that was becoming evident in the 1960s and 1970s led to significant challenges to the whole notion of 'Britishness' as many Scots began to view their national identity as 'Scottish' more than or instead of 'British'. Important research on this issue was first carried out by Moreno (1988), seeking to explore the dual identity that most Scots appeared to feel, being both Scottish and British at the same time. In his research, he found that 39 per cent of his sample stated that they were Scottish-only, while a further 30 per cent prioritised their Scottishness over their Britishness. He noted that this sense of Scottishness did not, at the time, translate into significant political support for 'home rule', as was the case in his native Catalonia, where individuals had a similar dual identity (Catalan and Spanish) (Moreno 2006).

During subsequent years, there have been a number of studies of changes in Scottish identity and whether this has been affected by constitutional change more broadly. We explore this issue in more detail in Chapter 3, but suffice to say here that it certainly appears that an overall sense of a British identity has declined in all of the nations of the UK. Of course, there may be many different reasons for this and an individual's sense of identity is often a very personal thing. As the writer William McIlvanney has suggested, 'Having a national identity is like having an old insurance policy. You know you've got one somewhere but you're not sure where it is. And if you're honest, you'd have to admit you're pretty vague about what the small print means' (cited in Bechhofer and McCrone 2009: 7). While this quote may well hold validity for many, others in Scotland are clearly very aware of their national identity and the 2014 independence referendum may stand as a marker that that old insurance policy has been dusted off and mounted on the living room wall.

Most recently, questions on national identity were asked in the 2011 census and in their analysis of this, Simpson and Smith (2014) show that a sense of Britishness has declined across the UK, albeit more so in Scotland (Table 1.1). The table shows that country-only identity is strongest in Scotland while

Table 1.1 National identity within UK countries

	Scotland (%)	Wales (%)	England (%)	Northern Ireland (%)
Country identity only	62	58	60	47
British identity only	8	17	19	40
Country and British only	18	7	9	8
Other identities	11	18	11	5

Source: Simpson and Smith (2014).

British-only identity is weakest. For those individuals who were actually born in Scotland, 72 per cent claimed a Scottish-only identity.

It is clear therefore that there is a growing sense of a distinct national identity within Scotland, sometimes quite separate from 'being British'. This reflects the way the country has changed within the post-war period and indeed, the Scotland of the present day appears light years away from the 1950s nation that we described at the beginning of this chapter. Our main hope is that we have been able to reflect some of those changes in this book.

Plan of the book

In this introduction, we have therefore sought to show how Scotland has changed dramatically from a rather conservative country – both socially and politically – within the overarching context of the UK, to a more self-confident nation with its own legislature and contemplating, for the second time, whether to move to independence. The pace of change is fast and already many of the textbooks that we could recommend to our students are out of date. That fate will no doubt befall our own work but that is not a reason not to write it. Rather, it serves as the very indicator of why we felt we had to do so.

We begin the book by exploring some aspects of Scottish history – not because we are historians (we are not) but because it is necessary to provide some context for what follows. We need to have some idea of when Scotland became a national entity with which individuals could identify and with its own laws, politics and social structures. We then explore issues of identity in more detail and the imagery that is so often used to define Scotland.

The subsequent chapters deal in turn with a range of social and political issues, including employment, education, gender, ethnicity and class. We also look at the various groups that make up Scottish society, including in-migrants from Ireland, Europe and elsewhere in the world – both settled groups and more recent arrivals such as asylum seekers and refugees. Scotland itself is also, of course, a country of emigration as well as immigration and we deal with the Scottish societies that exist overseas, as well as within our nearest neighbour, England. Finally, we explore issues of art, culture, heritage and sport – all of which are key to the sense of identity of any country, and very much so in the case of Scotland.

Throughout the book, we have provided key references within each chapter and a consolidated bibliography at the end.

We are conscious that we have not, by any means, provided some kind of definitive text on Scotland. As we have stated earlier, Scotland – like the rest of the UK – is going through fast-moving times. But we believe it is important to give students some understanding of where things are at just now. Scotland is not a large European country but, as a stateless nation, it is a complex one in its relationships with other parts of the UK, with our near neighbours in Europe and with the rest of the world. We close with a nod to that complexity, as expressed by the poet Hugh McDiarmid:

> Scotland small? Our multiform, our infinite Scotland *small?*
> Only as a patch of hillside may be a cliché corner
> To a fool who cries 'Nothing but heather!'
> ...
> 'Nothing but heather!' – How marvellously descriptive! And incomplete!
> (1943: 255)

Further reading

In terms of a wide-ranging view of Scottish society, the best book to read is David McCrone's *The New Sociology of Scotland* (2017). There are also a significant number of books that explore aspects of Scottish politics, including Paul Cairney and Neil McGarvey's *Scottish Politics* (2013) and Duncan McTavish's edited volume *Politics in Scotland* (2016). James Mitchell's *The Scottish Question* (2014) ties many issues into a clear political thread.

For those with a broader interest in Scottish history and how we came to be where we are, then the work of Sir Tom Devine, Emeritus Professor of History at Edinburgh University, is to be recommended – especially *The Scottish Nation: A Modern History* (2012). Professor Dauvit Broun, of Glasgow University, has several works on earlier Scotland that show the deeper connections of history very well, such as *Scottish Independence and the Idea of Britain from the Picts to Alexander III* (2007).

Chapter 2

When was Scotland?

Introduction

As pointed out in Chapter 1, this is not a history book, nor does it seek to be. Yet, the importance of history, and the lessons that can be learned from it, echo through to many other academic disciplines, especially to politics and sociology. So much of the present is a result of actions of the past and, if we are to understand how things have come to be, we must understand what went before. It is important that we appreciate that many of the long-running sociopolitical tensions of the modern era that impact upon modern Scotland have their origins in the events and decisions of yesterday. This chapter therefore provides a short historical consideration of certain key periods and events of the past that helped form and inform contemporary Scotland.

We will consider the original formation of what would become Scotland and key events during history, such as when Scotland became a kingdom, when the people within it became 'Scots', how Scotland strove to remain an independent state, and how it came to assume its historical non-state status. We will specifically seek to consider the variety of factors during such events that acted to unify the country, as well as those that may have caused division. Obviously, this will include such politically and historically well-known events as the Battle of Bannockburn, the Union of the Crowns in 1603, the not so civil wars of the 1600s, the Treaty of Union in 1707 and Scotland as part of the new 'United' Kingdom of Great Britain and its place in the growing British Empire. It was these core events that gave rise to the more contemporary Scotland that we present throughout the rest of this work. Finally, as a conclusion, we will consider what these historical events portend for contemporary Scotland and how our understanding of history shapes the vision of Scotland today.

It is perhaps not initially obvious, yet one key recurrent theme throughout much of these considerations will be England, and Scotland's relationship with its only geographically connected neighbour. It is this geographic connection, and the subsequent social and political manoeuvrings that have arisen from it during centuries past, that have always served to link the two nations in more ways than one. Long before the formal political union of 1707, or the preceding regnal union of 1603, Scotland's history has often been shaped by the fact it shares a single land border – with England. Furthermore, today, hundreds of years after the political decisions and actions we are about to discuss, Scotland's relationship with England continues to dominate our socio-political activity. Across the field of scholarship, ranging from history to politics, to education and to literature, many works examine Scotland through the lens of the geographic, sociopolitical and historical relationship with England. The impact of England upon Scotland (and of course, Scotland upon England) cannot therefore be underestimated. Whether acting as friend or foe, ally or enemy, the history and development of the two nations are firmly intertwined.

Scotland is

Scotland is. This statement is, in itself a fairly non-contentious one. Scotland, for its size, limited resident population and location on the northern part of an island on the western edge of Europe, remains a well-known country. A small atlas to 'stateless nations' describes Scotland as 'a nation situated to the north of the British Isles' (Bodlore-Penlaez 2012: 44) and goes on to label it as a 'constitutive nation' of the UK.

Wherever one goes in the world, the statement 'I am a Scot' or 'I am from Scotland' (often delivered in English, given the usual monoglot nature of many modern Scottish residents) locates a person in the mind of others. While some remain confused about the status of Scotland as a nation, state or country (one of the authors was once asked exactly where in England, Scotland was!) there are few around the world that have not heard of it and the symbols of Scottishness, the identity of Scottishness, of being Scottish, can open doors and provide a different welcome than others might receive. But while Scotland may have a history that makes it one of the older nations of Europe, its beginnings may be slightly more modern that many people might initially assume.

It is important at this point to note that there is an ongoing academic argument about the actual modernity of nations, which is part of a wider debate about exactly when nations and the idea of national peoples can be placed. This is an aspect of the arguments that seek to understand the nature of nationalism itself, and thus are key to understanding Scotland. For example, Gellner (1983), a member of the modernist school of thought, argues that nations are a construct born out of the post-French Revolution and industrial era. However, Anthony Smith (1996), a founder of the ethno-symbolist school of thought, challenges such thinking, arguing that nations have a greater link to antiquity and pre-modern times than the modernists allow. Such arguments have great relevance to contemporary Scotland and a wider discussion of this, firmly linked to the discussions around Scottish identity, can be found in Chapter 3.

Pre-Scotland

Irrespective of the depth of any nation's roots, we should never make the mistake of thinking that Scotland has always been. Whatever the actual timing and origin, all nations, sovereign states or countries in general – and Scotland as an entity in itself – are sociopolitical constructs and have definite beginnings. It has been very insightfully argued that the nation is an imagined community of the mind (Anderson 1983) and so individual Scots may, in their own imagination, make connections far into the past and long before their own existence. Scotland, as a geographical, temporal or sociopolitical entity, does indeed, have a long historical presence, but it has not quite the historical pedigree that some modern imaginations perhaps like to envisage. While it is or has been commonplace for many to joke that Hadrian's Wall, a symbol of a military, if not legal, border of the Roman Empire, was built 'to keep the Scots out' (or for Scots to boast it was to keep the rest of that empire safe), it is highly unlikely that any such national (or tribal) entity existed, or that any individual perceived of themselves as *Scottish* during that time period. As Davies points out, in Roman Britain (he uses the term geographically but it could be extended to mean pre-410 AD), there was no, nor could there be any such entity as, Scotland, 'since the Scots had not even started to arrive' (2012: 44).

Furthermore, the Roman Empire did of course extend into what is modern Scotland, with formal control reaching as far as the Clyde valley, where the

Antonine Wall was constructed. However, this area would only be formally occupied between 142 and 161 AD, the Intervallum as this period is known. Later periods of greater or lesser Roman rule would exist in this lowland area of Scotland, and Rome would establish a number of small 'buffer' kingdoms in the general area in the fourth century (Davies 2012). Nonetheless, Rome never controlled the vast majority of Scottish territory, leaving that to tribes that followed pre-Roman rules and culture and stood distinct from other British tribes. These various peoples the Romans labelled *Picti*, and that is the name, Picts, that history has bequeathed to them.

So, while many upland tribes beyond Hadrian's Wall were partially Romanised, and Rome moved into and out of the lower part of modern Scotland during the third and fourth centuries, 'the "Picts" of the further North were virtually untouched' (Davies 2012: 44). Davies goes on to discuss that what we now call Scotland would, over the next few centuries, witness the rise (and subsequent fall) of several kingdoms. At the time of the withdrawal of official Roman control from the islands of Britain, there were between five and seven kingdoms stretching across what is now Scotland; some of them quite powerful in their own right.

It is not until the sixth century that 'changes occurred that were to transform the scene radically' (Davies 2012: 53). In this period, while the Angles (a Germanic tribe) were entering into southern British territory (and they would be the early forerunners of the people now referred to as the English, or Anglo-Saxons), they were also arriving in the north-east, from the Firth of Forth down to Hadrian's Wall. Around the same time period, on the opposite coast, just north of modern-day Dumbarton, Gaelic Scots were arriving from Ulster and establishing a client kingdom there. Thus, Scotland was then an area being contested by four groups: the native Briton and Pict tribes and incoming Angles and Scots. However, as Davies points out, it would be three centuries later before 'a fifth party, the Vikings, would act as a vital catalyst in the final phase of the contest' (2012: 53).

It is clear, therefore, that it was not until the late fifth and early sixth centuries that the people who gave their name to Scotland actually arrived and established a foothold in the territory. Furthermore, it would take the arrival of another migrating group of various peoples, the Vikings, to lead the previously competing Britons, Picts, Angles and Scots to coalesce into one kingdom. This is because those migrating groups, the Vikings, may have started out as seaborne raiders, but they established a significant presence across many parts of the British Isles and what is now Scotland (and England and Ireland) may well have developed into 'another Norse realm like Denmark or Norway' (Davies, 2012: 68). There are many social commentators today that seek to emphasise Scottish connections to Scandinavian culture and it has become an aspect of the contemporary independence debate, so such historical roots clearly retain their importance.

It was out of these major migrations and movements of tribes and the various battles and elite challenges that Scotland would become a kingdom, together with the emergence of the modern understanding of Scotland, as a country that stretches from the northernmost parts of the British Isles, southwards to the border with England. This southern border would, of course, shift backwards and forwards for some centuries to come.

The formation of early Scotland (1200–1300)

The historian Dauvit Broun has written extensively on the idea of when Scotland and the idea of the Scots came into being. He has argued that 'to insist that Scotland was not a meaningful concept ... before the end of the thirteenth century, would surely be to allow our modern idea of Scotland to take precedence over the view of contemporaries' (1994: 38). McCrone (2017) has considered this statement and examined the issue of whether we could draw a line between the Scotland of then and the Scotland of now. He is certainly correct to say that we cannot gauge what people then thought – and whether the idea of 'Scotland' meant anything to its peoples. He is also correct when he states it is usable for political purposes and it is most certainly usable for academic analysis and understanding.

Whatever the individual conceptions of Scotland and identity in the past, we always return to the fact that Scotland 'is'. It is, and has been for many decades, indeed, many centuries, a nation, although it is certainly the case that '[m]uch ink has been wasted on the question' (Edwards 1989: 13) and certainly by many individuals who love to argue for the opposing case. More important perhaps is to seek to understand the events that brought about the formation of the nation, how they are perceived today and how such perceptions of events, and the events themselves, influence contemporary Scotland. To understand contemporary Scotland, we must always recognise that our understanding (and interpretation) of past events changes and this applies to the events that resulted in a single Scottish king and resultant kingdom.

As we have seen, it was Viking raiders who acted as a catalyst to bring about a united Scotland. Their predatory activities forced the unification of the other elements that existed within what would become Scotland. Harvie states the classic argument:

> Cinead (Kenneth) I. Mac Alpine (reigned 841–858), was claimed as the unifier of Alba, 36th king of the Scots, and dominator of the Picts. He established himself at Scone and Dunkeld, married his daughters into two Irish houses and one British and absorbed his forebears into the ritual histories of the Scots kings. So, anyhow, said his grandson ... claiming a precedent for being the real founders of the kingdom of the Scots. (Harvie 2002: 29)

This generally long-held view has, however, recently come under challenge. Broun argues that there is no longer a consensus around the role of Kenneth Mac Alpine, 'or about whether he was a Gael or a Pict. Some have abandoned the notion of Cinead as founder but have still retained the idea that a new, united kingdom emerged in the end of the 9th century' (Broun 2015: 107–108). Nonetheless, irrespective of Mac Alpine's role, Broun emphasises that what is not disputed is that by the end of the tenth century the inhabitants of the previously Pictish area of Scotland now spoke Gaelic.

Therefore, while it is often considered that Scotland was unified in the tenth century, the idea of a united Scotland existing around that period would not emerge until much later. The evidence is found in documents such as John of Fordoun's *Chronica Gentis Scottorum*, itself produced in the 1380s. This is one of the earliest histories of Scotland, a forerunner of the numerous academic histories of Scotland to come. While the contents of the *Scottorum* may be challengeable in some respects, what is of little doubt is that the outcome of the Viking invasion was to 'make Alba the minor of two great powers within the Island of Britain, with various smaller regional monarchies between and to the north of them' (Harvie 2002: 31).

When Harvie refers to Alba, he may be using the term to mean 'Pictland' as it was employed from the tenth century onwards (Broun 2015: 129), or he may be using it to refer to Scotland itself. However, at that time Scotland was not the geographical entity we consider it to be today. The idea of a united and single Scotland was still some time away. In the twelfth century, 'Scotland' was the area between the rivers Forth (southern boundary) and Spey (northern boundary). It would not be until the 1280s at best that the 'kingdom and country become one' and all the people within were considered 'Scots' (Broun 2015: 110). The current geographical entity that is Scotland is much larger and would not form the shape, with the current legal borders assigned to it, until much later.

How these disparate groups and kingdoms became one was due partly to what Harvie (2002) calls the 'centripetal pattern of authority' that existed in Scotland and partly to the influence of two dominant monarchs, Malcolm III Canmore and David I, his son. Harvie argues that, through their military and administrative actions, they would create a unified and established kingdom. However, as Broun notes, the emergence of Scotland was part of a broader European pattern and furthermore it was one that allowed Scotland to frame itself in a manner that was 'obviously distinct from Britons or English' (2015: 130). It is important here that the overall British dimension inherent in the creation of a unified Scotland is acknowledged and understood. Scotland sought to mould itself and to present itself, politically and internationally, as a distinct entity. The creation of a unified Scotland occurred with a primary driving force being the need to differentiate the nation from the rest of the British Isles and to particularly highlight 'Scotland's separateness from the south' (Broun 2015: 131).

What is clear is that when the Normans had established their control over England after 1066, the kingdom to the north had a clear identity as Scotland (Trevor-Roper 2008). Nonetheless, as many scholars of history have noted, Trevor-Roper, Broun and Harvie among them, Scotland was not a society dominated by a single 'race' or tribe. The various tribes and invaders who had dominated their own distinct territories and kingdoms may have coalesced into a single political entity and one people, but they remained a 'mixture'. Although found throughout Scotland, particular groups were heavily located in specific areas, with the Picts and Scots in the north and the Vikings on the coasts and in the islands. There were also Angles and Saxons and soon there would be more Normans, with the latter 'establishing new forms of power and particularly creating a modern feudal monarchy' (Trevor-Roper 2008: 8). Nonetheless, while the monarchy may have been as much Norman as it was Scots and heavily influenced by English trends and culture, it publicly traced and linked its heritage to the Scots and Picts; once again emphasising the distinct nature of Scotland.

The wars of independence (*Braveheart et al.*)

The period covering the late 1200s through to the early 1300s covers a period of time that is 'one of the most emotionally charged issues in Scottish history' (Watson 2006: 33). Indeed, with the Hollywood blockbuster of 1995, *Braveheart*, the story of William Wallace (long a staple of Scottish storytellers) became a legend known worldwide and the '*Braveheart* phenomenon' (Edensor

1997) has a significant impact on how people view contemporary Scotland, not to mention its relationship with England and its position within the UK. Unfortunately, like many a Hollywood film, it was, to say the least, historically inaccurate on any number of counts. However, American artistic licence aside, this period of history remains highly influential in terms of modern myth and memory and it did indeed give Scotland two of its greatest historical heroes – the aforementioned William Wallace and the man who would be king, Robert the Bruce.

When King Alexander III of Scotland died suddenly without a male heir in 1286, the somewhat convoluted relationship that existed between England and Scotland was thrown sharply into focus. While Scottish kings and lesser nobles swore fealty to the King of England for lands they held in the south, they did not, they argued, see how this extended to Scotland being a subordinate kingdom. However, the English kings, drawing on their Norman heritage, saw these oaths are far more binding. Furthermore, when Alexander's young granddaughter, Margaret, having grown up in Norway, died on her way back to Scotland and left the immediate line of succession in doubt, the throne became contested – with two strong claimants ready to become king – Robert Bruce and John Balliol.

In order to avoid a civil war, which would have left the kingdom even more weakened and divided than it already was, John Balliol was appointed king, a decision arbitrated by Edward I of England, a man who clearly had designs upon Scotland – including the idea that it was indeed subordinate to England. However, John Balliol, while his position was initially approved by Edward, had a clear view that Scotland should remain a country independent from England. As a result, Edward felt compelled to invade, subjugate Scotland and take prisoners south to ensure that continued subjugation; said hostages included King John Balliol himself.

Threatened by England and wishing to preserve Scotland's independent status, a number of local rebellions took place against English invaders, eventually coalescing around William Wallace and Andrew Murray, who successfully led the battle of Stirling Bridge in 1297. In one of those amusing coincidences of history, it would be 700 years later to the very day (11 September), that Scotland would vote for a devolved parliament in a national referendum. Appointed guardian of Scotland as a result of his military prowess, Wallace actually fell from favour fairly quickly when he was defeated by the forces of Edward during 1298. Henceforth, it would be two nobles, John Comyn and another Robert Bruce (the grandson of the man who was passed over in favour of John Balliol) who would take up the guardianship, and fight for Scottish independence, both militarily and diplomatically.

Without going into the intricacies of the period, both men made their peace with Edward at different times (while William Wallace was taken to London in chains and executed). Initially, it appeared that Comyn would emerge victorious from the elite power struggle. However, at an arranged meeting in a church in 1306 Comyn was stabbed to death, and Bruce (probably the perpetrator of the act) was then declared King of Scots at Scone, only six weeks later. A more inauspicious start to any reign would be difficult to imagine. Bruce had murdered his more popular opponent in a church and broken his fealty to Edward by having himself declared king. Unsurprisingly, most Scottish nobles believed it safest to keep their oaths and side with Edward!

This is not the place to consider the strengths of oaths and elite relations in the Middle Ages. Nor do we have the time to consider the reign of any Scottish king, and particularly that of Robert Bruce as it is 'perhaps one of the most difficult to analyse subjectively because it started so inauspiciously and ended in almost unbelievable success' (Watson, 2006: 41). What we should note is that by 1309 Bruce had taken such control of Scotland that he could call his first parliament and he had begun formally seeking international legitimacy as King of Scots. One of the documents from this propaganda war would be the 1320 Declaration of Arbroath, which would become historically significant and quite famous, even if it was not so at the time. The Declaration was just one of several documents that represented over a decade of fierce diplomatic lobbying by Robert, his adherents and the Scottish nobles who sought to keep their nation independent.

Alongside the diplomatic war, a military war was also being fought and the battle of Bannockburn in 1314, which ended the English campaign to relieve Stirling Castle from siege, has become legendary as the event that ensured Scottish independence. This is an idea that remains so popular that the site, currently in the care of the National Trust for Scotland, has a fully dedicated 'battle room' where modern generations can refight the battle several times a day, to the delight of visitors, children and adults, alike. However, this idea is in itself a very challengeable assertion. In fact, the battles and wars dragged on for decades and while Bruce secured a thirteen-year truce in 1323 and a peace treaty was formally signed in 1329, this peace only lasted four years before Edward II invaded Scotland, seeking to put Edward Balliol (son of John) on the Scottish throne – even though it was already occupied by David II, Robert Bruce's very young son.

Such were the convoluted affairs of the Scottish wars of independence – wars that would continue well beyond the early 1300s. Indeed, English kings would claim higher authority over Scotland for several more centuries; several Scottish kings (James II, IV and V) would die in battles around the very issue of Scottish independence. Furthermore, these events still echo today, especially in film and song. Whatever the actual outcome of the Battle of Bannockburn in 1314, it stood, and still stands, as a symbol of Scottish identity, nationhood and, for a while, independent statehood. While there were agreements and treaties and payments and counterclaims aplenty, the wars of independence would carry on in some fashion or another until the Union of the Crowns between Scotland and England in 1603. Even this regnal union did not lessen the competition between the two countries and the (somewhat inaccurately named) English Civil War would see Scotland playing a full part. Thus, war between the two nations would break out again, although this would be as much because of religion as national identity.

Religion, (English) Civil War and the Interregnum

Any history of Scotland cannot downplay the importance of religion. Scotland today can be considered a highly secular country. According to the 2011 census, 32 per cent of the population claim affiliation to the Church of Scotland, but only 7.5 per cent attend church services. Likewise, the Catholic Church in Scotland claims a large number of adherents, but regular church attendance is much lower. This was not always the case, however, and the importance of religion in past Scottish life and the implications of religious belief in shaping modern Scotland, politically and geographically, should not be underestimated. Nothing illustrates this more than the series of wars fought during the middle 1600s and into the 1700s. While sometimes portrayed as representing loyalty to one royal house or another, it was often intermixed with the issue of religion and specific religious adherence; whether of the monarch himself or on a more individual or group basis.

The history of the Scottish nation is, in many ways, reflected in that of the Church of Scotland. Just as the status of Scotland as a sovereign state and nation has undergone significant change, so too has the church. Protestantism was firmly established in Scotland with the Reformation Settlement of 1560; which the reigning monarch, Mary Queen of Scots, refused to sign. She was, after all, a Roman Catholic. Yet Scottish history has seen numerous events stemming from discontent surrounding the involvement of the state in church affairs, or vice versa. With major and minor schisms, it would not be until the Church of Scotland Act in 1921 that the (UK) state formally recognised the independence of the church in spiritual affairs. However, the church was firmly caught up in the affairs of state during the 1600s, which would see the monarchy swing back and forth from Catholicism to Protestantism. Many events, such as the National Covenant of 1638 (that saw Presbyterianism established as the main religion) rapidly descended into violence and civil war of one kind or another.

The involvement of England in these wars (and Scotland in the subsequent English Civil War) was always likely due to the simple fact that not only did the two countries now share a monarch, but also because England and Scotland shared a land border. They also shared similar cultural and, more importantly, religious beliefs. Both had witnessed the rise of Protestantism, and this brought significant discord in terms of wars within Scotland and between Scotland and England (and Ireland). Protestantism was widespread in Scotland; with Presbyterians being committed to making theirs the national religion of the country. Nonetheless, in some areas, such as the Highlands and certain other northern parts of Scotland, significant numbers of Roman Catholic and episcopalian adherents remained. These areas also tended to be culturally distinct in other ways, with language (Gaelic) and more traditional clan forms of relationships holding sway. Such groups firmly disliked and distrusted the lowland dominated Covenanter government (so named due to the agreement that they undertook with God and their faith and to which all within the kingdom of Scotland were bound).

In the late 1630s, the Covenanters firmly opposed King Charles I's ideas of religion, especially his imposition of a 'new' prayer book, and his preference for appointing bishops. However, in many ways, the outbreak of open hostilities was part of a wider dissatisfaction with the seeming lessening of Scottish influence on the King, since the Union of the Crowns. His father, James VI and I, had departed to England to take up the English Crown upon the death of Elizabeth I of England, but had promised to come back to Scotland regularly. He returned only once, after a period of fourteen years.

The ultimate result of this dissatisfaction was war in Scotland, then Ireland and then a full civil war in England from 1642. Senior Scottish figures battled among themselves over matters of religion and loyalty to the King and even switched sides on several occasions; individually, or in groups, during the 1630s to 1660s. For instance, while the Scottish Covenanter Army handed Charles

I over to the English parliamentarians in 1646, it also invaded England in his favour in 1648, and then the members of that army fought among themselves over that invasion. In fact, Scottish Covenanters fought in all three kingdoms, and formed an alliance with the parliamentary side of the English Civil War. Nonetheless, they would later fight for Charles II, but were heavily defeated. Scotland was then annexed by Lord Protector Oliver Cromwell, who created a Commonwealth of the three kingdoms. This period, known as the Interregnum, is a somewhat under-recognised historical event in many ways. Interestingly, it was the first formal political union of England and Scotland (and Ireland and Wales, of course) but it was very hastily dissolved with the restoration of the Stuart monarchy under Charles II.

However, the issue of religion had not gone away and once again played a major historical role when Charles II died childless in 1685, and his openly Roman Catholic brother James became James VII of Scotland/James II of England. This clearly untenable state of affairs (in the eyes of certain Protestant elites anyway) would eventually result in the 'Glorious Revolution', where the thrones of both England and Scotland were offered to William and Mary of Orange, although under distinctly differing circumstances. Mary was the daughter of James VII and II and both she and her husband were firmly Protestant. James sought to retain his throne in Scotland through political machinations but all he achieved was to alienate potential support and force his faction to withdraw from the Scottish decision-making body, which then resulted in an outcome that firmly supported placing Mary and William on the Scottish throne.

Thus, the last decade of the seventeenth century saw the Stuart dynasty firmly out of power, and a 'Scottish' king removed from both the English and Scottish thrones. This is not to say that they had had their last turn on the Scottish stage though. The Stuarts would continue to impact on Scotland's sense of self and identity for some time, and certainly influence the relationship between Scotland and England for many decades. The Jacobite Risings, especially those of 1715 and 1745, have long morphed from purely history into myth and legend. The stage was now set for the next distinct event of Scotland's development into the political form it still retains today (albeit with a devolved parliament in these modern times – see Chapter 8). The next steps would be the establishment of a formal political union with England and, whatever the motivations of such a move (and these were as much social as they were economic and/or political), Scotland entered that union as, in its view, an equal partner in the relationship.

The Treaty of Union

In another quirk of historical coincidences, May 2007 was the three hundredth anniversary of the Act of Union of 1707 (properly known as 'The Treaty of Union of the Two Kingdoms of Scotland and England'). May 2007 was also the first time that the SNP formed their first (minority) government of Scotland. This placed the Union, which had not been seriously under sociopolitical pressure since the first decades of the 1700s, under a much harsher political microscope and it would ultimately lead to the first real democratic challenge to the Union, namely the 2014 referendum on whether Scotland should be an independent sovereign state. While nationalist opposition to the Union had been growing in Scotland during the latter part of the twentieth century, for much of the preceding three hundred years, the Union had seemed not only accepted as the normal political state of affairs, but firmly entrenched in the Scottish psyche. However, as Devine (2008) notes, when 1707 and the following period is examined more closely, the longevity of the Union becomes quite remarkable. Other formal unions between European nations rarely lasted as long, and in both historical and more contemporary periods, political divorces have been the usual result and long, if not happy, relationships, the exception.

The roots of and reasons for the union between the two nations (and sovereign states up to 1707, of course) are numerous and varied. The shift in the relationship between the Crown and the Scottish Parliament, with the King and Queen having been chosen, brought about a period of political instability for Scotland, as the elites sought to understand and control this new dynamic. In addition, the wider Scottish economic scene was not at all healthy. An attempt to establish a colony and provide a base for a potential Scottish empire, the Darien scheme, had come to a disastrous and ruinous end. While a number of factors had led to the debacle, the blame as far as Scotland was concerned was clear – England. This may well have been unfair, as there were many other factors involved. Nonetheless, England had pressured London-based capital not to support the Darien idea financially and also because of wider international diplomacy at the time, refused any form of support in terms of provision or rescue when the colony ran into trouble. The economic impact of the catastrophe was felt across Scotland and this brought about a significant anti-English feeling in sociopolitical circles. In addition, Scotland not only suffered as a result of the Darien scheme, but the 1690s also witnessed several very poor harvests and also saw Scotland, through its royal union with

England, on a war footing against France, further limiting international trade possibilities.

With all of these factors adding up to a significant level of anti-English feeling, the political union that created the UK was never a certainty by any means. The Scots had quickly and firmly separated themselves from the Cromwellian Union and in the first decade of the 1700s the Scottish Parliament had passed acts that seemed clearly to diverge from England in the areas of political rule and foreign policy. Furthermore, when the Union came about there was significant popular unrest, and while it has been argued that the level of this unrest has sometimes been overemphasised, it was very much present, especially due to all the factors discussed above. However, the idea that Scotland was 'sold out' and the people 'helplessly betrayed' is subject to question (Bowie 2008), as the nuances of religion, a strong sense of Scottish national identity and resentment of English influence and power were not enough to successfully unify the potential opponents of the Union. Likewise, the numerous and yet ultimately unsuccessful Jacobite Risings during the next few decades indicated the same divisions remained at both the mass and the elite level too. Hence, despite a number of potential and immediate military and political challenges (one vote in the House of Lords to end the Union of 1707 came very close to success in 1713), the Union endured.

As Devine (2008) points out, the Union saw the distinctive aspects of the nation – the church, the legal system and the education system – supported and maintained. The nobility of Scotland also saw several advantages in the Union as their traditional privileges were also maintained. Politically, post-Union Scotland operated a continuing semi-self-functioning political system, one of almost benign neglect from Westminster, as long as Scotland could guarantee internal stability. The endurance of the Union and its successes can be firmly linked to the positive economic and social impacts, such as the emergence of opportunities for Scots in the (now) British Empire and also in England itself. From the mercantile trade of the West Indies, the administrative staffing requirements of imperial activity and the soon to be raised Highland regiments of the British Army, the Scots quite rapidly became central to the operation of the British state, especially within the imperial domain.

It is important to remember that the actual action of Union was carried out by the political elites of the day, even though they stood divided on many elements and aspects of the idea. Democracy remained a faint glimmer for the future. Thus, while rioting occurred in Glasgow and scenes involving angry mobs were witnessed across Scotland, the wishes of the everyday folk of

Scotland mattered little, if at all. The choices of the elite, whether religious, noble or mercantile, were what decided the event and with their particular interests protected and the remaining elite opposition divided among themselves, the result was clear.

With the Union, Scotland had now taken on the broadly political and geographical form that it has today. It remained a nation, but had ceased to be a sovereign state – it was now a part of a larger, multi-nation sovereign state and while we have noted that Scotland saw itself as a partner in the new Union, the English-based majorities of population, the elected elements of the House of Commons and the House of Lords at Westminster clearly illustrated that it was very much a junior partner in many respects. This was especially so from the English perspective. As a nation, Scotland's population was much smaller than its southern neighbour and its economic and mercantile activity much more limited. Nor did the start of the Union witness the whole of Scotland firmly united behind this new political and social enterprise. Yet, this reticence about, and resistance to the Union was to change. Once the *ancien régime* began to give way to a slightly more democratic Scotland in the 1800s and then a clearly more democratic one in the 1900s, the support for the Union was actually much firmer and it became an entrenched aspect of Scottish society and politics. The Union clearly seemed to have provided Scotland with benefits and Scotland seemed to prosper within it for much of the 300 plus years that followed.

Scotland and Union: then to now

While the Union got off to a less than auspicious start in terms of widespread support, it embedded after the first few decades and continued, initially due to the perception that Scotland did well from it, although whether that is the current perception is open to challenge. In the early twentieth century, the general perception within Scotland was that Scotland had played a significant role in the building of the British Empire, above and beyond its size, and that this reflected the strength of Scotland as much as it did the benefits of the Union. It was not until more recently, during the latter part of the twentieth century that an alternative narrative, in which Scotland was presented as a casualty of a colonial power (England) emerged as part of the wider academic, and subsequent sociopolitical, discussion (see, for example, Nairn 1977; Hechter 1975). However, there can be little doubt that Scotland maintained a strong sense of self within the Union; holding on to the idea of 'Scotland the nation', even while there was no formal 'Scotland the state'. Finlay (2011) illustrated that even while official and elite narratives tended to emphasise a sense of 'England' rather than 'Britain', it was the sense of multiple identities, from regional to imperial, but also how they linked to Scottish national identity, that allowed Scotland to maintain a sense of self. By firmly engaging in empire, and perhaps conflating the national input with the individual input of prominent Scots-born individuals, Scotland came to the twentieth century as a nation that stood proud on its imperial and Union-based roots.

The events of the twentieth century, two major world wars, a shedding of the empire by the British state and the massive social and political change that took place alongside such events, has also led to a redevelopment of Scotland and the emergence of differing interpretations of Scotland's place within the Union – and whether it should have one at all. We will not go into such discussions in great depth here – as they are linked to the idea of change and national identity, which is considered in the next chapter. There can be no doubt that one of the main links holding Scotland to the Union was the firm part played in it by individual Scots and also the role of such institutions as the Scottish regiments in the imperial project. Even when the empire waned in the aftermath of the Second World War, 'the imperial dimension was replaced by an alternative British institution; the Welfare State' (Finlay 2011: 311). These clearly prophetic words were held up by much of the discussion about the benefits (or not) of Union during the 2014 independence referendum.

What can be of little doubt is that, towards the later decades of the twentieth century, there was a growth in nationalist challenges to Union, predicated upon the idea of the Union itself as a form of imperialism. This did not, however, immediately lead to a significant decline in any sense of support for the idea of Union or Britishness as an identity for Scots to hold. While today the people of Scotland, and certainly the elites of Scotland, are divided upon the positives that the political union brings and whether it should continue, this is in many respects a reflection of the situation that Scotland was in when it first entered the Union. Scotland has witnessed significant changes and challenges in the last three hundred or so years of the Union, and the support for the Union has waxed and waned. Many of the arguments that were predicated at the beginning of the Union are still being argued today; the economic well-being of Scotland and the people within it, the domestic standards of living, Scotland's role in the wider world, and of course, Scotland's social and political relationship with England.

Conclusions

As we stated at the beginning of this chapter, we are not historians and we have not sought to encompass the full breadth of Scottish history as there are many excellent texts that do just that. What we have provided is an examination of certain major periods and specific events that brought about the general shape and structure of contemporary Scotland. What we did seek to do, above all, is indicate that among all the tensions and challenges to the existence of Scotland as a society and nation there have been certain themes that have become evident.

Key among these is that Scotland, and also the people of Scotland, while often considered as a singular entity, has long been a meeting, and oftentimes a clash, of different groups, cultures or ideas. Whether we are discussing the formation of Scotland as an idea in the eighth to tenth centuries, the formation of the Kingdom of Scotland in the thirteenth to fourteenth centuries or the development of the early parliamentary Scottish state in the seventeenth century (and not to mention the eighteenth to twenty-first centuries), we can witness the contending ideas and arguments and the coming together of differing groups that have resulted, through the formation of Scotland and Scottish society in each period, to the nation of today. Throughout the past, just as now, contending elites have sought and seek to direct Scotland down a path they envision and proclaim as 'the best' for Scotland. This is a story that has occurred time and time again. It is a story openly playing out today.

Perhaps the most prominent theme during this analysis of the development of Scotland has been the idea of a sense of nation and identity and Scotland's relationship with, to and alongside that of England and Britain. Long before the formal union of 1707 there was an element of Britishness to be considered – and certainly that has echoed throughout. During the period of Union and Empire, for a wide variety of reasons, Scotland embraced the idea of dual identity, combining a strong sense of itself, with a sense of Britain, and it has retained that dual identity, long after the imperial emphasis has dissipated. Whether such a sense of identity exists today because of such general ideas as the welfare state or even more specific or personal reasons, is part of a wider debate. What we can state is that there has always been a key drive to illuminate, whatever the formal political relationship between the two nations, clear elements of Scotland's distinctiveness. This has often resulted in moves to legally, politically or socially emphasise that distinctiveness from England throughout Scottish history. This has been the case whether Scotland was seeking to remain firmly independent from, or politically entering into union with, England.

As we move to our wider analysis of contemporary Scotland it is also important to remember that our study here will illustrate that the myths and legends of Scotland are as powerful as any facts or material presented as 'truths'. Scotland the nation continues to develop and change, and as it does it is important that we understand the role that the past plays, or is employed to play, and the reasons as to why.

Further reading

Probably the most accessible book on Scottish history is Tom Devine's *The Scottish Nation: A Modern History* (2012). There are also books by T. C. Smout, including *A History of the Scottish People 1560–1830* ([1972] 1998), *A Century of the Scottish People 1830–1950* ([1986] 2010) and *Scottish Voices* (1991).

Also, Richard Finlay's *National Identity, Union, and Empire, c.1850–c.1970* (2011) and for twentieth-century Scotland, Catriona Macdonald's book *Whaur Extremes Meet* (2009) is excellent.

For those interested in earlier Scottish history, we would recommend Dauvit Broun's *Scottish Independence and the Idea of Britain from the Picts to Alexander III* (2007) and Fiona Watson's *Under the Hammer: Edward I and Scotland 1286–1307* (2006). For an excellent consideration of Scotland among the general pattern of European history, Norman Davies's *Vanished Kingdoms: The History of Half-Forgotten Europe* (2012) provides a fascinating picture.

Chapter 3
Scotland's identity

Introduction

While the previous chapter provided a brief consideration of key aspects of Scottish history, what it also provided was a clear sense of the importance of Scotland's identity throughout that history. We established that, academic arguments about reification aside, Scotland is a nation and the people who feel they belong to that nation hold a strong sense of national identity. Therefore, our discussion now moves to consider the nature of that sense of Scottish identity. Drawing upon a number of leading theorists and ideas about national identity, this chapter will look at how the Scottish nation and Scottish national identity is defined. Then, employing social research data results from the last few decades, we will consider how individuals within the Scottish nation define themselves and are defined by others. Within our discussion, we will consider the various layers and aspects of identity that exist and interact and, bearing in mind the sociopolitical changes of recent years, such as devolution, the independence referendum and Brexit, we will consider the main issue of whether the Scottish sense of national identity is growing at the expense of the Scottish sense of British identity and the potential longer-term implications of such a result.

What is the Scottish nation?

Scotland is a nation. We have discussed and established that. However, this leaves us with the question, what is the Scottish nation? There is also a related, interesting and, to many historians, somewhat amusing debate among the wider social sciences as to what came first – nations or nationalism? As a result of much discussion on these topics, there are widely differing theoretical approaches that seek to explain nations, nationalism and the related idea of the antiquity (or not) of nations. It is the latter aspect that drives much of the underlying debate among and around those approaches. We will discuss the core of these in depth in this chapter as we consider the nature of Scottish national identity, and to do that, we must discuss the nature of the Scottish nation.

So, the wider question is, what is a nation? In the nineteenth century, the French historian Renan posed that very question in his book titled *Qu'est-ce qu'une nation?* and he concluded that it was 'a soul, a spiritual principle … To have had glorious moments in common with the past a common will in the present, to have done great things together and to wish to do more, those are the essential conditions for a people' (1996: 52). This was quite a visionary statement in many respects. It foresaw significant components of the debates that would occur during the twentieth century (and into the twenty-first) about the nature of nations and national identity. Furthermore, it poses challenges in particular to the nature of being Scottish. On the face of it, the statement above certainly applies to the Scottish people, who often speak of 'glorious' past moments and reflect on the great things fellow Scots have done. Yet, it could also apply to the British people in the same manner. Therefore, defining the nation and national identity is more than a purely theoretical exercise that keeps academics happy, employed and argumentative. The nature of Scottish nationhood and national identity has clear ramifications for the future shape and outcomes for the wider UK union, as illustrated by the 2014 referendum. In that very public and clearly national debate, 55.3 per cent of voters (from a total vote by 84.6 per cent of the registered electorate) indicated they wished to be 'better together' as Britons, whereas 44.7 per cent did not. So, what can the study of nations tell us about Scottish identity, its relationship with British identity and help us make sense of Scotland today?

Renan was not speaking alone in 1882; he was part of a wider interest in the nature of nations and identity and many famous theorists, such as Kant and Rousseau, have contributed their philosophical thoughts. The birth of the United States in 1776, or modern France in the subsequent decades were forerunners of the birth of many nations we take for granted today – Germany, Italy and Austria. Yet, while these nations continue to exist, others, such as Yugoslavia and Czechoslovakia, have been consigned to the historical dustbin. Throughout that period, Scotland has existed, but it ceased to be a state in 1707. It has, however, remained a nation, when others have not.

Perhaps because of its antiquity and status, it has often been a problem for the study of nations and nationalism, simply because it has not followed the more general pattern exhibited (Leith and Soule 2011).

Indeed, for much of Scotland's history, nationalism was not a focus of wide academic study and it would not be until the twentieth century that the study of nations would move beyond description or discussion and into serious academic analysis. Leaving aside the formation of states across Europe in the nineteenth century, it would be the massive decolonisation and the birth of new states across Asia and Africa that would lead to the emergence of a deeper academic analysis (Özkirimli 2010). Scholars such as Kedourie (1960) and Gellner (1972) would generate a wider debate over the next decades, with many emerging works and theories being specifically applied to Scotland (see Hechter 1975; Nairn 1977). These sought to explain Scotland's seemingly 'anomalous' status as a nation with a strong sense of national identity, yet one subsumed within a larger state. While we have ourselves previously undertaken a considered analysis of the debate around Scotland and Scottishness (see Leith and Soule 2011; Leith and Sim 2014), we do need to consider the various differing camps, in order to illustrate the Scottish nation's understanding of itself, today.

Approaches to understanding nationalism and national identity

There are differing schools of thought, which are roughly predicated in understanding the date and source of nations, and the nature of nationalism as a sense of belonging. The major school of thought prior to the twentieth century is often grouped under the title of primordialism (although Smith (2000) differentiates this into two strands, adding perennialism as a variant). As the oldest school of thought on nationalism, primordialism takes nationalism and nations as an everyday aspect of the human condition. To a primordialist, having a nationality is as normal as having 'a nose and two ears' (Gellner 1983) and nations are an historic product of humanity created through kinship, blood and ethnic connections. Thus, this is perhaps the most appealing theory to many political nationalists and national movements around the world for rather obvious reasons. It creates a clear divide between their 'nation' and the ubiquitous 'others' who provide an exclusive sense of belonging, built around the ideas of homeland, ethnicity and tribe.

However appealing any sense of tribe that primordialism so easily seems to offer, it fails the test of explaining nations such as the United States or

Switzerland and it has been strongly dismissed as explaining Scotland too. The major challenges to primordialism arose during the latter part of the twentieth century, with scholars such as Gellner (1983), Anderson (1983) and Hobsbawm and Ranger (1983). Their combined efforts all strongly advocate the modern nature of nations, as constructs of the modern world, developed in the industrial (and now post-industrial) era, with little relation to any sense of historic, ethnic kinships. Loosely grouped under the title of modernism, scholars employing this approach dismiss the antiquity of nations, limit the applicability of ethnicity and emphasise the influence of urbanisation and industrialisation as creators of nations. Advocates of modernism, although they constitute a very broad group with differing strands, often emphasise the invented (Hobsbawm and Ranger 1983) or imagined (Anderson 1983) aspect of contemporary national belonging.

Many adherents of the modernist approach have been very influential on approaches explaining Scottish nationalism and Scottish national identity. The study of the nation and identity flourished alongside that of modernist thinking, being more deeply developed from the 1960s onwards. One of the first major studies of the Scottish nationalist movement was Hanham (1969), while Kellas (1973) and then Miller (1981) examined the more political behaviour of Scotland and the Scottish people. Many of the contemporary leading thinkers on Scottish society, identity and politics, such as Keating, McCrone and Mitchell, draw inspiration from the modernist school of thought, with Keating seeing Scotland as 'one of the least romantic of nationalist movements' (2001: 221). Likewise, both McCrone (2001) and Mitchell *et al.* (2012) have long emphasised the civic nature of Scottish nationalism and Scottishness, while downplaying or rejecting any ethnic-based interpretation or approach.

However, while primordialism has been challenged and strongly dismissed across the majority of more contemporary thinking, and modernism has presented many strong and compelling considerations, it has also been challenged in some key aspects by the ethno-symbolist school of thought. Drawing heavily upon the works of Anthony Smith, among others, ethno-symbolism crosses the divide of primordialism and modernism, emphasising the importance of both historical and cultural experiences on contemporary nations. Using the phrase, *la longue durée*, Armstrong (1982) and Smith (2000) have sought to argue that nations must be considered throughout a wider range of time and space and that modern nations have a more direct connection to pre-modern societies and kinship groups than the modernist approach allows for.

Ethno-symbolism accepts that nationalism is not an inherent product of nature (thus clearly rejecting primordialist thinking) but does point to the ability to document nations, and the idea of national identity, long before the industrial revolution began. This can clearly be seen in the case of Scotland. Thus:

> All historians agree that ethnically the Scottish landmass was occupied by at least five linguistically separate and distinct groupings in the middle ages. Most historians also agree that by the eleventh to thirteenth centuries at least four of these groupings had fused together into a nation that identified itself as Scottish; long before any moves towards modernisation and at a time when Scots society was decidedly uncivil. (Foster 1989: 35)

The Declaration of Arbroath, signed in 1320, saw the signatories append their names to a document that referred to the 'people of Scotland' and did so in relation not only to being distinct from the English, but also in a manner that was not purely territorial, reaching beyond the idea of Scotland, to the idea of 'Scots'. Nonetheless, while some have seen this as a 'supreme articulation' (Cowan 2008) of a sense of Scottish nationhood and identity, it has also been subject to challenge as indicative only of elite powerplays (Kerevan 1981; Davidson 2000). Scotland was a case study for Smith (2003) in which he considered the need to understand history as a tool in understanding national identity.

Among the ongoing arguments about the efficacy of one approach versus another, there is the need to better understand the political aspects of nationalism, as well as gain a firmer understanding of the civic versus ethnic debate as a means to understanding Scottish national identity. It has been argued that the focus on civic versus ethnic forms of national identity, an often used means of comparison, is insufficient as a means to gain insight into public discourse and opinion on the subject of national identity (Zimmer 2003). The symbolism of belonging has often been identified as a means to better understand the disjunction between Scotland's strong sense of national identity and substate status as a non-sovereign nation.

For decades it has been argued that Scottish national identity was predicated around a much greater inclusive, and less ethnic sense of belonging. The historian T. C. Smout (1994) argued that Scottish identity was based on a 'sense of place' rather than that of a 'sense of tribe' and this has often been employed to support the modernist approach. McCrone employed this approach to illustrate the understanding of Scottishness as a civic and democratic national identity, in direct contrast to those movements that hold to a more primordial sense of identity and that 'may flourish in the short term, but ultimately are doomed to fail' (2001: 188).

Certainly, one of the most influential thinkers on Scottish nationalism in the late twentieth century, Tom Nairn, saw nationalism as a 'janus-faced' movement in that while many social and political goals were progressive, they tended to be 'looking inwards, drawing more deeply upon their indigenous resources, resurrecting past folk heroes and myths about themselves' (1980: 348). He saw clearly that nationalism had long been an aspect of Scottish politics (Nairn 2000), but for him it remained very much a by-product of modernity.

Nairn's *The Break-Up of Britain* was first published in 1977 and this work has been hailed as the 'key political tract' of the Scottish nationalist movement (Davies 1996). Nairn presented the argument that Scottish identity was a dual one, with both a British and a Scottish aspect. Employing similar concepts as Gellner, Nairn considered the economic development of the UK, and specifically Scotland. He argued that, with the decline of the British Empire, and the associated economic and political benefits that it brought to Scotland, Britishness had become less appealing as a sense of identity.

Nairn's analysis helps us understand how Scotland could have been both a strong nation, and yet remain a substate component of the UK. Scotland's development was somewhat unique because as a 'first nation' of the empire it did not suffer, but actually profited. In addition, while it developed economically within the UK, it continued to develop a distinct civil society that was outside of an anglicised framework. In other words, the nationalism that did develop in Scotland during the nineteenth century was a cultural form of 'sub-nationalism'. Nairn holds this form of nationalism somewhat in contempt (Leith 2006).

Nairn is one example of an explanation that seeks to understand Scottish nationalism and national identity within the framework of the UK. This is perhaps one of the most important aspects of the debate that is often overlooked. Since the inception of democracy as an aspect of modernised societies, Scotland has been a part of the UK. The decision to join with England was taken prior to democratic voting as a norm, and whatever the public reaction, it rapidly became an established part of the sociopolitical order. There can be little doubt that this had an influence on the Scottish sense of identity, both historically and more importantly, contemporarily, so let us now consider discussions on Scottish identity more closely.

The nature of Scottishness

Our conversation has focused upon Scottish nationalism and national identity from a number of approaches and while each disagrees on the specific nature of identity, there is a strong agreement about the strength of that identity, and its resonance and influence within modern Scotland. Furthermore, we recognise that it has arisen in a society that had a differentiated political (UK) and civic/social (Scotland) component. Even on this front, academics disagree about the ability of individuals to grasp the boundaries between their Scottishness and Britishness.

A common claim is that Scottish nationalism is civic in nature, with an inclusive and open sense of identity (Keating 2001; McCrone 2001, 2017). However, this claim has come under challenge. Several studies have illustrated that the emphasis on the civic and open aspects of Scottishness, a key component of the modernist interpretation of identity, and certainly a common element of contemporary political understanding of Scottishness across the mainstream political spectrum, were not always so clear when applied to general, or public discourse (Leith 2006; Henderson 2007).

In more recent studies, the limitations of the modernist interpretations of identity have also been recognised (McCrone and Bechhofer 2010) and it has been noted that 'politicians (and academics) may explicitly affirm their commitment to civic and inclusive criteria of national identity, they do so laden within a discourse of atavistic tendencies, historical references, and irrational collectivism' (Leith and Soule 2011: 143). Clearly the Janus-faced nature of nationalism highlighted by Nairn is still evident.

What our consideration of the theoretical approaches to understanding Scottish identity has illustrated is that there is no one approach that explains or grasps the full intricacies of the Scottish case. Attempts to limit Scotland to a particular theoretical model risk losing sight of the importance of aspects of Scotland itself. Certainly, Scotland can be considered to have seen itself as a nation in the pre-modern era (unquestionably the elites of that nation did; there is less evidence about what the masses thought – no one was asking them). Furthermore, a sense of Scottish national identity was not diminished by the Treaty of Union in 1707 and certainly civic Scotland maintained a strong sense of self throughout the next three hundred or more years. Yet we are left with questions about the foundational nature of contemporary Scottish national identity. Is it inclusive, or is it exclusive? Does it contain a larger ethnic component than the political or social discourse allows for? Has it, as Nairn argued, suffered due to a decline in the benefits of the relationship that is the Union?

Also, what is very clear is that the contemporary era has brought about political challenges in relation to Scotland's understanding of its identity and the strength and depth of the associated duality of that identity. The independence referendum of 2014 was not the result of any instantaneous decision on the part of contending Scottish political elites to take their argument public, but the result of a shift in mass voting behaviour and preferences over time. It was the increasing support for the SNP, who seek independence as a political and social goal, and the party's political victory in the 2011 Scottish Parliament elections that allowed it to negotiate for a referendum on independence for Scotland. Yet, as Miller (1981) indicated, Scotland had begun to diverge in terms of voting behaviour and preferences long before devolution.

Yet, can we relate these events and changes and shifts of sociopolitical behaviour to Scottish identity? What is the nature of Scottish national identity? Is it inclusive, exclusive, civic, ethnic or a mixture of all of these? What does this tell us about our understanding of Scottishness and the implications for the future of Scotland and the UK? Is it the case that people in Scotland are increasingly Scottish when choosing their identity, or are they still just as British, or is it perhaps they are simply 'Not English'? It is to those questions we now turn.

Mass data on identity[1]

There can be little doubt that the sense of national identity is important to people in Scotland. A less recognised aspect of national identity is that it is vital in creating a sense of connection between the individual and the institutions of the state and society; 'a sense of nation and national identity … as portrayed by the political system, serves to connect individuals … for political purposes' (Leith 2009: 298–299). The legitimacy gained and held by political institutions is due to the connections that can be made via this identity. There have only been five elections to the Scottish Parliament and as Scotland has begun to develop the organs of legislative government, it has had to ensure that the people of Scotland see those organs as being important to, and for, them. Turnout for elections to the Scottish Parliament since devolution in 1999 has averaged 53 per cent, while Westminster elections have averaged 64 per cent during the same period. While this is a somewhat crude measure, it does indicate a potential difference in the perceived efficacy of each institution in relation to the other.

Mass surveys and 'big data' are a feature of contemporary society – but that has not always been the case. As previously noted, no one asked the majority of the residents of Scotland who they wanted to be king in the early 1300s. Likewise, no one asked Scotland's population what they thought about the Treaty of Union in the early 1700s. However, the combination of democracy (which requires such questions to be put before the people) and modern data collection and analysis methods have allowed for significant advances. Not only are the questions asked at key political junctures, they are revisited on a regular basis. We now have an increasing understanding of the sophistication required to ensure that data is being collected, measured and analysed in a manner that ensures it is as reliable and valid as possible. While this revolution in social sciences has been occurring, Scotland has embarked upon significant sociopolitical changes and the ability to track those changes and any resultant impacts over time has been available. This has resulted in a capability to measure social and political attitudes at key times, and especially during such times as the 2014 referendum on independence and the Brexit campaign that closely followed. There are also several long-standing measures of social and political opinion, such as the Scottish Social Attitudes Survey and surveys carried out for Scottish Parliament and UK Parliament elections. Society and political leaders not only ask the people about key decisions, but academics now regularly ask the people why they support such key decisions.

The importance of having such data cannot be underestimated. An ability to measure not only contemporary attitudes and behaviours, but to track changes over time, in the short and longer term, is invaluable. Not only will an analysis of such data allow us to gain insight into how the people of Scotland express their sense of identity, but it will also allow us to gain a better understanding of the potential impact of recent sociopolitical events on the Scottish population and the implications for the future.

Our analysis begins with a reflection on attitudes towards a sense of Scottish versus British identity, and the changes over the period since the devolution referendum in 1997. We will then shift to a consideration of certain key elements concerning the perception of Scottish national identity and belonging. This will allow us to consider the relationship between the theoretical considerations of national identity that we have just discussed, and the perceptions of the people of Scotland today.

Scottish or British?

We have previously discussed the difficulty of considering national identity in a territory like Scotland, where the nation exists on the substate level. While academics often use different terminology to relate to the status of Scotland (substate, regional, territorial, etc.), the issue remains that Scotland is a nation, but the people who are nationals of Scotland are also citizens of the larger, UK state. Therefore, we have the ability to examine the distinctions that people in Scotland draw between their state and national level of belonging and how this has shifted since 1997; a period during which we have seen devolution introduced, witnessed a referendum on the possibility of Scotland leaving their union with the UK and then another on the UK leaving their union with the EU.

It was during the 1980s that a Spanish political scientist called Luis Moreno (1988) began undertaking regular measurements of the nature of national identity within a variety of substate territorial/national areas. The approach he employed was built around the idea that individuals could (and do) hold more than one possible identity in relation to both the nation and the state. It allows for a more sophisticated consideration of the binary relationship. Since then, the question has become synonymous with his name, and has been employed in a variety of settings. The question matrix employed allows an individual respondent to choose between two distinct identities, and the relative value individuals hold of those identities.

As Table 3.1 clearly illustrates, there has been some movement but, overall, a continuation of a general sense of belonging since the vote to create a devolved Scottish Parliament was taken in 1997. What an initial consideration clearly provides is that a majority of respondents, when asked about the relative values of their sense of identity, prioritised Scottishness over Britishness. In 1997, voters in Scotland voted by 74.29 per cent (on a turnout of 62 per cent – significantly lower than that recorded in the independence referendum of 2014) to create a devolved Scottish Parliament. At the same time, almost one-third of people living in Scotland (32 per cent) stated they felt Scottish and not British. This was equalled by the same figure who ranked their sense of Scottishness more importantly than their sense of Britishness.

At the same time as two-thirds rated Scottishness as their only or primary sense of identity, 28 per cent rated themselves equally Scottish or British. So, overall 92 per cent rated themselves as firmly Scottish. This is a significant figure and points to the overwhelmingly significant sense of Scottishness that

Table 3.1 *National identity in Scotland 1997 to 2016*

	1997 (%)	2000 (%)	2001 (%)	2003 (%)	2005 (%)	2006 (%)	2007 (%)	2009 (%)	2010 (%)	2011 (%)	2012 (%)	2013 (%)	2014 (%)	2016 (%)
Scottish not British	32	37	36	31	32	33	26	27	28	28	23	25	23	28
More Scottish than British	32	31	30	34	32	32	29	31	30	32	30	29	26	28
Equally Scottish and British	28	21	24	22	21	21	27	26	26	23	30	29	32	29
More British than Scottish	3	3	3	4	4	4	5	4	4	5	5	4	5	4
British not Scottish	3	4	3	4	5	5	6	4	4	5	6	6	6	6
Other description	1	4	3	4	5	4	6	6	8	6	5	6	7	4
None of these	1	1	1	1	1	2	0	2	0	1	1	1	1	1

Sources: McCrone *et al.* (1997) and whatscotlandthinks.org.

pervaded the population of Scotland in 1997. This result is, in itself, far from surprising. Almost all academic studies of Scotland have always noted that Scots consider their identity as a nation and individually as members of the Scottish nation, very significantly. In 1997, when Scotland was, after almost three hundred years without a parliament of its own, and when it voted three to one to establish just such a body, a clear sense of national identity and the strength of that sense of national identity was very evident.

Undeniably, perhaps the most surprising figure from the 1997 vote was that only 3 per cent rated themselves more British than Scottish, and likewise, only 3 per cent rated themselves as British not Scottish. So only 6 per cent of respondents prioritised Britishness over Scottishness. At the same time, 25 per cent voted against the establishment of a Scottish parliament, which clearly supports the argument that wider constitutional preferences and national identity are not always easy to align within Scotland.

In addition to the 1997 figure, we can see that by the establishment of the Scottish Parliament (in 1999) a clear impact is taking place. Those who identify as holding a singular sense of Scottish identity, and reject a sense of Britishness, had increased in 2000 to 37 per cent of respondents, a shift of 5 per cent. At the same time, this move had also evidently taken place within those who had previously held a dual sense of identity. Those who prioritised their Scottishness over their Britishness remained very roughly the same – the 1 per cent difference being well below any significant numerical shift. However, the group who had previously considered their dual identity to be equally both Scottish and British had declined quite strongly. Having been 28 per cent in 1997, only two years later that figure had dropped to 21 per cent. Furthermore, while there would be a slight increase in the results during the 2001 Scottish election period, this figure of 21 per cent of 'equal identity' holders would be repeated in 2005 and 2006, illustrating that there had been a clear movement. This movement among the residents of Scotland was very much in favour of Scottishness, and not in favour of any increased sense of Britishness. As we noted, in 1997, 64 per cent rated being Scottish above British in a sense of identity, but by 2000, this was 68 per cent and in 2001 it remained 66 per cent. At the same time, the group who prioritised British identity over Scottish identity remained very stable; it was 6 per cent in 1997, 7 per cent in 2000 and 6 per cent in 2001.

However, while the 'dual identity' group declined, the primarily Scottish group increased and the British identity group remained stable, it was the 'other description' group that increased; only 1 per cent of the sample in 1997,

4 per cent in 2000 and 3 per cent in 2001. This may reflect Scotland's shifting population, a willingness to embrace different minority identities or Scotland's increasing immigrant numbers (see Chapter 7 for a discussion on immigration and ethnicity).

Once again, what we witness is an extremely strong sense of Scottish identity and an increasing shift towards prioritising Scottishness over Britishness during the early devolution period. At the same time, however, this 'Scottish Parliament bounce' clearly did not last. In fact, it has been argued by numerous academics that the expectations for a 'new' kind of Scottish politics and a 'different' sense of politics in Scotland were so high that they could only lead to disappointment. There can be little doubt that the public expectations were high, and that they have, with regard to a different manner and style of politics, failed to materialise. Whatever the position on this argument, there was an impact on the sense of Scottishness and the prevailing pattern towards emphasising Scottishness, as the next decade from 2006 onwards illustrates. Table 3.1 clearly provides evidence of another shift and this time it is a decline in the first two categories, a rise in the 'equal' identity group and a similar rise among those identifying as or ranking British identity first.

In 2006 the figures were broadly similar to those of 1997, although we can witness an increase among those who hold an equal sense of identity and those who consider themselves British only. What we can also see is that during the next ten years all of these groups would (with 2011 being an exception) see an increase – an increase that would be at the expense of those within the Scottish-only group and, to a lesser extent, those who identified as emphasising their Scottish identity over their British identity.

Form a high of 37 per cent in 2000, the group who considered themselves Scottish only would witness a decline from their 1997/2005 strength of 32 per cent to a low in 2014 of 23 per cent. The average result from these figures, between 2007 and 2016, was 28 per cent and this would be the figure that was recorded in 2010, 2011 and 2016; it remains well below, the average of 33.5 per cent for 1997–2006. It may well be that the 2014 independence referendum caused some reflection on the part of those who had rejected any sense of Britishness, but whatever the driving influence, the figure during the past decade illustrates a drop of 5 per cent.

At the same time, the shift is evident among those who hold a dual sense of identity, and only very slightly towards those who prioritise Britishness or reject Scottishness. While the British-only identifiers have averaged 6 per cent during the last decade (a doubling of recorded support for this category when compared to 1997/2001), the support for those who prioritise being British over Scottish has shifted between 4 per cent and 5 per cent, a modest increase from the 3 per cent recorded from 1997–2001. It is among the equally Scottish and British group that we see the positive gains. The recorded low support of this group, witnessed in 2001, 2005 and 2006, saw a clear upward trend that started in 2007 and apart from 2011, would continue. Reaching a high of 32 per cent in 2014 (again, perhaps illustrating a 'referendum' effect) it would stand at 29 per cent in 2016. This closely reflects the average figure of 28 per cent for the decade between 2007 and 2016.

Thus, our consideration of the Moreno question, within a Scottish context, clearly illustrates a number of conclusions. First, a majority hold a strong sense of Scottish identity, clearly illustrated in Table 3.1, throughout the last twenty years and is a consistent and regular finding among academic studies and considerations of Scottish national identity. Second, and very much related to our first conclusion, the majority of individuals who hold a strong sense of Scottish identity either prioritise their Scottish identity over a British identity or reject a British identity altogether. These groups today represent about one-third each of those who hold a sense of Scottish identity. The remaining third is a group who equally identify Scottishness with Britishness. Third, there has been an identifiable, if limited, shift over the last decade from the first two groups towards the group who equally identify their sense of identity. While this has been subject to movement, it is the general trend and reflects a shift from the exclusive or Scottish prioritised groups. Our final conclusion is that only a small percentage, about 10 per cent, either prioritise Britishness over Scottishness or reject Scottish as an identity.

However, it should be noted that the Moreno question allows for a consideration of a more nuanced form of identity, one that is not often found among more political questions of the day (such as whether Scotland should remain part of the UK or of Europe). While both of these questions have very recently been asked of the population in Scotland, attempting to map a relationship between the results of those two referenda and the national identity choices in Scotland is not recommended. It has been clearly illustrated that the constitutional preferences of voters in Scotland do not clearly align to choices and statements of national identity.

To illustrate this, we only have to examine Table 3.2. As we can see from the table, when presented with a binary choice between a sense of British and a sense of Scottish identity, the result is, while not overly surprising, not as clear-cut as could be expected, given our analysis above.

Table 3.2 *Forced-choice national identity question*

	Dec. 2014 (%)	Mar. 2015 (%)
British	36	31
Scottish	58	62
Other	5	6
Don't know	1	2

Source: whatscotlandthinks.org.

While the results from Table 3.1 clearly show overwhelming support for a sense of Scottishness, it recorded that a significant minority clearly hold a sense of British identity. This is also evident in Table 3.2, where when forced to choose, almost one-third choose British identity over that of Scottish. While a minority, this still represents a significant proportion of those within Scotland who, when faced with a binary choice, chose a sense of British identity. This puts our previous finding of a strong sense of Scottish identity (which we stated above as being 92 per cent) into a wider context. Most significantly, it does not easily map on to the results of the 2014 independence referendum, where a clear majority voted to remain within the UK. Once again, the link between national identity and constitutional preferences is not clear. However, what is clear is that the results above do indicate a strong affinity for a Scottish identity in contemporary Scotland, at a rate of almost two to one.

What is Scottishness though?

While we have established that Scotland holds a strong sense of national identity, we have not established an underlying nature to that identity. As we discussed above, there are contending approaches to understanding Scottish nationalism and national identity. The majority of scholars within Scotland perceive of the Scottish nation as a modern, civic and inclusive nation (McCrone 2001, 2017), an argument that is also projected by all the major political parties (Leith and Soule 2011). In 2001 McCrone argued that while birth and ancestry were important aspects for being considered Scottish, Scottishness could also be conferred through residency. Likewise, leaders and spokespeople for the SNP, the leading nationalist political party in Scotland, who have formed the Scottish Government since 2007, have argued on numerous occasions that if a person lives in Scotland, believes in Scotland and wishes to be considered a member of the Scottish nation, then they are. It is also argued that this conception of Scotland as a civic and inclusive sense of identity is the finding among the membership of the SNP (Mitchell *et al.* 2012).

However, there have been those who have challenged this perception of Scotland as a civic and inclusive nation, by drawing upon mass survey data to investigate the borders that the Scottish masses place around membership of the Scottish nation (Leith and Soule 2011). Therefore, we will now consider such findings with questions that specifically focus on who can, and cannot, be considered members of the Scottish nation by those living within contemporary Scotland.

In 2003, when asked how they responded to the statement that 'to be truly Scottish you have to be born in Scotland', 54 per cent of Scottish respondents in the Scottish Social Attitudes Survey agreed, while 35 per cent disagreed (Leith and Soule 2011). In the same survey, non-Scots (living in Scotland) agreed with that statement 41 per cent of the time, while 47 per cent disagreed. In their analysis of these findings, Leith and Soule stated that it was clear that to 'be a member of the Scottish nation, according to those who identify themselves as belonging to it, birth plays an important role' (2011: 94).

As we can see from Table 3.3, a similarly worded question in 2016 gained a much more exclusive, and distinctly one-sided answer. It should be noted that these questions are not the same nor do we have a similar breakdown of respondents, but what we can see is a clear feeling that birth in Scotland is a key aspect of making an individual Scottish. There can be little doubt that in contemporary Scotland, mass feelings consider place of birth an important aspect of national identity.

In modern states, citizenship (which, of course, does not apply to Scotland, as Scotland is not a sovereign state, but a nation within a multinational state, the UK) is often derived from parentage. Being born with a parent who is a UK citizen immediately confers citizenship on that child, by virtue of that parent. While we are discussing membership of the nation, we have already established

Table 3.3 Do you think being born in Scotland makes a person Scottish?

	Aug. 2016 (%)
Does	87
Does not	10
Don't know	3

Source: whatscotlandthinks.org.

Table 3.4 Do you think having one Scottish parent makes a person Scottish?

	Aug. 2016 (%)
Does	50
Does not	40
Don't know	10

Source: whatscotlandthinks.org.

that being born in Scotland is strongly considered to be a key aspect of being Scottish. Therefore, a related question to birth would be that of parentage, and whether having a Scottish parent would automatically make one Scottish.

Here, unlike the location of birth, the answer is much less clear. While half of respondents to the question would argue that having a Scottish parent makes one Scottish, 40 per cent disagreed, making the decision much less clear-cut. Again, while birthright clearly holds significance for membership of the Scottish nation, there are a substantial number who would place firmer barriers on membership of the Scottish nation. Indeed, when asked in 1999 if not being born in Scotland, and not living there, but having a Scottish parent made one Scottish, only 34 per cent of respondents agreed (Leith and Soule 2011: 89). Unlike the question asked for the results in Table 3.4, the 1999 question linked birth, territory and parentage and it may well be that that the 'living in Scotland' aspect of the question had an impact upon the positive responses. Therefore, let us consider the issue of living in Scotland.

There are a number of issues related to the idea of residency. Time is clearly a factor. It may well be that a person has to have been resident in Scotland for a substantial period of time, for people to consider them Scottish, or there may also be the issue of when the time was spent, if a person was resident in Scotland for their childhood, would this be a more powerful factor to being considered Scottish than spending time in the nation as an adult? As we can see from Table 3.5 through to Table 3.8, there are clear differences in attitude to these questions.

Residence during childhood is clearly a factor for a majority of respondents. Being socialised into the nation and the culture of Scotland obviously carries weight in terms of being considered a member of the nation. A clear majority, over two-thirds, consider childhood an acceptable aspect of being Scottish. This indicates a potential clash between the data presented in Table 3.5 and the data discussed in Table 3.3, but it is clear that 'growing up' in Scotland has an impact.

Table 3.5 Do you think growing up in Scotland makes a person Scottish?

	Aug. 2016 (%)
Does	69
Does not	26
Don't know	5

Source: whatscotlandthinks.org.

Table 3.6 Do you think living in Scotland for five years makes a person Scottish?

	Aug. 2016 (%)
Does	16
Does not	75
Don't know	9

Source: whatscotlandthinks.org.

Table 3.7 Do you think living in Scotland for five to ten years makes a person Scottish?

	Aug. 2016 (%)
Does	21
Does not	70
Don't know	10

Source: whatscotlandthinks.org.

Table 3.8 Do you think living in Scotland for over ten years makes a person Scottish?

	Aug. 2016 (%)
Does	35
Does not	58
Don't know	8

Source: whatscotlandthinks.org.

Nevertheless, the same cannot be said for residency alone. As we can see in Tables 3.6, 3.7 and 3.8, there is no majority opinion that supports the idea of residency alone being an option for establishing membership of the Scottish nation. This clearly places this mass data at odds with academic and political elite interpretations of national belonging.

While 16 per cent agree that five years would make a person Scottish, this is rejected by three-quarters of respondents, illustrating that residency alone is a weak factor for establishing oneself as a member of the Scottish nation. This is broadly in line with similar analysis carried out in 1997. Then, 30 per cent considered residency very important, while 35 per cent considered it fairly important (McCrone 2001, cited in Leith and Soule 2011), but the question was linked to a general set of criteria, including birth and ancestry. When isolated as a distinct question in 2016, it clearly carried less weight as a factor.

The addition of extra time to the residency question does not seem to produce a majority that support it as making a person a member of the Scottish nation, although it clearly has some impact. As Table 3.7 illustrates, only an additional 5 per cent agreed that up to ten years would confer national belonging. Even with over ten years residence, only 35 per cent agreed that a person could be considered Scottish, although this does reflect similar figures to the 1997 data. Nonetheless, what is clear is that while political elite arguments may consider residency an appropriate basis for being Scottish, such findings are not supported by mass survey responses.

Leaving aside arguments about birth, ancestry and residency, there is also the issue of self-selection. Simply put, one of the main arguments put forward by those who argue for a civic and inclusive sense of Scottishness is that a person can see themselves as being Scottish for any number of reasons. Yet when we consider mass responses to self-selection, we do not find differences with the majority opinion previously examined.

As with previous arguments, Table 3.9 clearly illustrates that self-selection of the nation is not supported by mass opinion within Scotland. While 31 per cent makes the response rate more positive than a number of criteria measured above, it remains a minority opinion, with a clear majority putting clear boundaries around the idea of Scottish national identity.

Table 3.9 Do you think someone considering themselves to be Scottish makes a person Scottish?

	Aug. 2016 (%)
Does	31
Does not	59
Don't know	10

Source: whatscotlandthinks.org.

Conclusion

In this chapter we have considered the main theoretical approaches to understanding Scottish nationalism and Scottish national identity. We have seen that, while Scotland is a nation with a long and established history, many academics consider nations to be a more modern construct, which came about during the sociopolitical changes involving the Industrial Revolution and the creation of the modern world. We have considered alternatives to this argument, which highlight the links between yesterday and today and illustrate the connections that can be made, especially in relation to nations such as Scotland. Whatever the school of thought that appeals most, what can be seen is that Scotland has not always been an easy nationalism or national identity for academics to understand or explain. Yet the last few decades have witnessed several works that have helped us understand the drivers behind national understanding and the framing of national identity. As Scotland continues to examine and consider its place in the contemporary era, these arguments and ideas will help us understand the Scottish nation and the nature of Scottish national identity.

Likewise, previous academic work has discussed how and what makes people Scottish, with some academics arguing that the boundaries to membership of the Scottish nation are quite permeable, while others have indicated that there are much clearer boundaries to belonging. While mainstream Scottish political parties have often argued that Scotland is an inclusive nation with a civic-based sense of belonging, this has also been challenged within previous findings and the findings presented here. These findings also challenge some of the previously established ideas around the nature of Scottish national identity. In 2011, Leith and Soule argued that a strong sense of Scottishness clearly existed, yet the idea of being a member of the Scottish nation was 'highly complex'. Drawing upon survey material from the late 1990s to the early 2000s, they argued that the responses indicated that many people within Scotland put clear limits around who could be Scottish. They argued that English people, and others born outside Scotland, would be excluded as place of 'birth remains influential to attributing national belonging' and that 'some non-civic and exclusive criteria of national belonging seem at play' (Leith and Soule 2011: 99).

It is important to note that they, and others such as Bechhofer and McCrone (2009), did not refute that civic and pluralistic elements were not in play in Scotland – they were, and they are. Yet, what previous work has illustrated is that the strong sense of identity in Scotland is allied to a strong sense of who is, and who is not, Scottish. Furthermore, this mass understanding and expression of Scottishness is often at odds with the more elite and political expressions. Although in this regard, Scotland may not differ from other Westernised nations and cultures, where elites are often more cosmopolitan in expression than the wider population. What we can assert today is that Scottish identity remains strong, clearly distinguishes itself from other identities and yet is clearly intertwined with a sense of Britishness. This intertwining may shift and fluctuate, as we can witness above, but it remains a key competent of that identity for a majority of the Scottish population.

Further reading

Issues of Scottish identity have interested scholars for some time and so there are numerous texts that could be consulted. Among the most important are Murray Leith and Dan Soule's *Political Discourse and National Identity in Scotland* (2011) and the various publications by David McCrone and Frank Bechhofer from Edinburgh University. These include their books *National Identity, Nationalism and Constitutional Change* (2009) and *Understanding National Identity* (2015). Their paper on 'Claiming National Identity' in *Ethnic and Racial Studies* (2010) is also useful.

The journal *Scottish Affairs* has a wealth of articles throughout the past decades and remains one of the first and best places to stop for discussion and debates around key concepts of identity, belonging, Scottishness (and Britishness) and civic/ethnic identity in relation to Scotland. You can find it at www.euppublishing.com/loi/scot. For an analysis of core theories and central concepts involving nationalism and national identity on a wider scale there are numerous texts, but we recommend the excellent insights found in Umut Özkirimli's *Theories of Nationalism: A Critical Introduction* (2017), which is a very welcome third edition.

Key texts on other major concepts such as nationalism and national identity are Benedict Anderson's *Imagined Communities: Reflections on the Origin and Spread of Nationalism* (1983), Eric Hobsbawm's *Nations and Nationalism since 1780* (1990) and Anthony Smith's *Nationalism and Modernism* (1998). To gain a good understanding of the 'Moreno question' the originator of the question has written a recent paper, 'Scotland, Catalonia, Europeanization and the "Moreno question"', in *Scottish Affairs* (2006).

Finally, many of the tables in this chapter are taken from the very useful and always contemporary website 'What Scotland Thinks', which provides access to the Scottish Social Attitudes Survey and can be accessed at http://whatscotlandthinks.org/ssa.

Chapter 4
Images of Scotland

Introduction

A popular musical duo in the 1960s were Michael Flanders and Donald Swann, who wrote and performed a series of comic songs. One of their most famous was entitled 'A Song of Patriotic Prejudice' in which the pair exalted the English, while at the same time dismissing the Scots, Welsh, Irish and a host of other European peoples on the basis of a series of national stereotypes. The song, while entertaining in itself, also lampooned the kind of unthinking nationalistic prejudice that fails to look beyond surface stereotyping.

For Scotland, such stereotypical images, of course, are usually associated with tartan, with a smattering of heather and haggis thrown in for good measure. Ironically, however, such imagery has often been constructed by Scots themselves. Craig (1996), for example, describes in some detail an exhibition entitled 'Scotch Myths' that was staged at the Edinburgh Festival in 1981 by film-makers Murray and Barbara Grigor. A film followed in 1982, in which they parodied television's annual Hogmanay Show. The exhibition itself contained a large collection of the tartan kitsch that so often passes for Scottish national identity.

> The material which the Grigors have assembled matters, profoundly and disturbingly. It matters obviously to anyone concerned with the development of a healthy Scottish identity ... Distorting, frothily romantic, escapist and trivialising, the Myths have concealed our history and our social reality. They have created a national identity that cringes in the face of radical change. The enemy of national development is, in short, not the English, not the Americans, not the EEC, not even, simply Westminster; it is far more acutely, our own perverted self-image. (Craig 1996: 106)

Thus – and perhaps uncomfortably – as Craig points out, Scots themselves have colluded in the development of this tartanised identity, rather than having it imposed from elsewhere.

The development of a sense of a national identity and a national consciousness is traced by Anderson (1983) to the convergence of capitalism and print technology around the sixteenth century. These developments helped to create national languages of administration and the possibility of new forms of imagined communities. This in turn set the stage for the establishment of modern nations. The heyday of nation-making, according to Billig (1995) was the eighteenth and nineteenth centuries and new nations were often accompanied by the invention of seemingly ancient traditions and rituals, national histories and interpretations of themselves. Billig refers to the various ways in which the nation is symbolised, such as the use of flags, banknotes with national emblems and so on. But of course, the nation is 'flagged up' using a whole array of different imagery.

Scotland is interesting because it is, in some ways different to other nations. First of all, it is not a nation created in the 'heyday' of nation-building but (like England) dates from early medieval times. But the UK as a whole does date from the eighteenth century and so many of the symbols and images associated with Scotland are not an attempt to manufacture an identity for a new nation. Rather, they represent an attempt to *maintain* a national identity within a newly created multinational state. Black *et al.* (2015) highlight Scotland's position as a 'stateless nation' as one of the main elements that has created the country's brand imagery. The other two elements are the writings and actions of Sir Walter Scott (who we deal with later) and the romanticised influence of the Scottish diaspora.

> The need for a distinctive Scottish identity in the period after the Union of the Parliaments, and especially around the time of Sir Walter Scott (at a safe distance in time from the end of the Jacobite rebellion) perhaps explains why the imagery adopted is that of the Highlands. The Lowland Scots … embraced the romanticised and non-threatening version of the 'noble savage' portrayed by Scott – and one consequence was to underline their distinctive Scottish identity and their separateness from England. (Black *et al.* 2015: 52–53)

This need to see England and the English as 'the other' and to differentiate Scotland from England within the overarching umbrella of the UK is a strong theme throughout the development of Scottish identity (as we have illustrated in the previous two chapters) and the country's view of itself. Billig (1995) understands this, pointing out how English people have allowed the term 'England' to speak for the whole of Britain, to the exclusion of Scotland, Wales and Northern Ireland. Much of the so-called 'national' imagery evoked by politicians from Stanley Baldwin to John Major is in fact 'English' rather than 'British'.

Lindsay (1997) sought to unpick the Scottish and English stereotypes by asking individuals (in Scotland) to list what they believed were the characteristics of Scottish and English people. The Scots were believed to be a friendly, warm, down to earth, patriotic and humorous people, while the English were thought to be more arrogant, reserved, materialistic and xenophobic. Lindsay suggests that the negative image of Englishness reflects the fact that the smaller partner in any relationship has to assert itself more strongly to maintain identity and that means emphasising differences. The strong stereotypes of Scottishness and Englishness displayed are to a large extent constructs that serve to protect identity and values that may be seen to be threatened. National stereotyping was also present in McIntosh *et al.*'s (2004) study of English people living in Scotland. Their experiences suggested that English people were often viewed as middle class and rather arrogant, whereas Scots saw themselves as being much more proletarian and down to earth in nature and outlook.

This preservation of national difference within the UK state is demonstrated in many other ways. Cooke and McLean (2002), for example, demonstrate the importance of national museums in helping our understandings of national identity. They explore the ways in which the National Museum of Scotland in Edinburgh presents the nation to the visitor. McCrone and McPherson (2009) point out how, unlike many other states, the UK has no 'national day', whereas each of the four constituent nations has its own national saint's day. In the case of Scotland, Hogmanay on 31 December and Burns Night (the birthday of Robert Burns, the national poet) on 25 January, are also national days of celebration. Such days are global tourist events, so how much do they 'self-reflect who Scots are, and how much reflect how they present themselves to others?' (McCrone and Mcpherson 2009: 8).

Certainly Scotland's iconography is reflected worldwide and is almost universally recognised, be it tartan, kilts, heather, haggis, whisky or misty landscapes. This sometimes leads to disappointments among visitors when they discover that the imagery and the reality do not always coincide. The most famous example of this is MGM's film producer Arthur Freed who travelled to Scotland in 1954 to identify locations where he could film the musical *Brigadoon*. After several weeks, he gave up and went back to America.

> Scotland, he remarked, no longer looked like Scotland. Instead the production team back in Hollywood constructed studio-sets to represent the thatched Highland village that only stirred for three weeks each century and the bridge that bounded its area of enchantment. Painted backdrops served to illustrate the tree-fringed loch and the heather on the hills. These, after all, provided imagery more in keeping with popular expectations. (Gold and Gold 2002: 261)

The story is a revealing one because, on the one hand, it demonstrates how the imagery associated with Scotland is not necessarily rooted in reality, while on the other, it illustrates how Scots themselves have allowed such imagery to persist, and how they have often colluded in the process.

Exploring the imagery

We move on to discuss various elements of Scottish imagery, beginning with what might be termed 'Celticity' before exploring the more generally recognised symbols of Scottishness such as tartan.

Celticity

The image of Scotland is often bound up in a wider Celtic imagery, in which the 'Celt', whoever he or she may be, is seen as a rather romantic and noble figure. The origins of this Celtic imagery lie in the romanticising of the Scottish Highlands during the eighteenth century, leading to a widespread fiction about how people in the area actually lived. An example of this fiction is the publication by James Macpherson in 1760 of poems purporting to be by the legendary bard Ossian; the works were later proved to be forgeries (Trevor-Roper 2008).

But the public were enthusiastic to embrace the idea of a 'Celtic' Scotland, not least as a way to distinguish it from its Anglo-Saxon neighbour. Chapman summarises this neatly:

> The Anglo-Saxon … appears a brutal soulless figure, disfigured by every wart and sore that industry, cities, pollution, capitalism and greed can cast upon the countenance. The Celt, by contrast, is a magical figure, bard, warrior and enchanter,

> beyond the reach of this world, and an object of love and yearning for those doomed to wander among material things in the cold light of reason. (1992: 253)

He goes on to argue that this Celticity is essentially an ethnological fiction, in which Celtic symbols, Gods and language are used to demonstrate how Scotland is somehow *different*.

The concept of a modern Celtic identity evolved during the nineteenth century into a Celtic revival. Partly this was political, with some nationalist movements, for example in Ireland, embracing Celtic imagery. But more recently, it may be seen in terms of linguistic revival (the Gaelic language in Scotland) and a growing interest in Gaelic/Celtic music and the arts. A number of bands and singers have emerged in recent years, for example, performing in Gaelic – some of whom, like Runrig and Capercaillie, have been internationally successful. And each January since 1994 Glasgow has played host to a major international music festival – 'Celtic Connections' – that has brought together musicians and artists from Scotland, Ireland, parts of Europe, North America and indeed anywhere with a 'connection' to Scotland.

As far as the Gaelic language itself is concerned, the Scottish Parliament has now taken a number of steps to promote it and to seek to reverse its decline. A new body, Bòrd na Gàidhlig, was established in 2003 to promote the language and this was given statutory status in the Gaelic Language (Scotland) Act of 2005. The BBC began Gaelic broadcasting many years ago but in a relatively limited way; now a full Gaelic television channel, BBC Alba, launched in 2008, is available on Freeview. And there has been a considerable growth in Gaelic-medium education with a number of schools in the Highlands and also in several central belt locations opting to teach in the language.

The Celtic idea is still very prevalent within the Scottish diaspora. Ray (2001), for example, describes a growing interest in the United States in Gaelic language learning, Celtic folk music, 'Celtic' artwork in the style of medieval illuminated manuscripts, Celtic folklore and archaeology, while Basu (2007) notes that many members of the Scottish diaspora returning to the homeland have a keen interest in things Celtic, or believed to be so.

In his research on Scots in America, Sim (2011a) notes how, in the South in particular, Celtic imagery is used within a construction of a distinctive Southern cultural and ethnic identity (Hague and Sebesta 2008). In addition, a significant number of his interviewees referred not just to Scotland but to a 'Celtic' heritage, particularly in relation to music and the Gaelic language, and some made connections between Scotland and Ireland in this respect. Such individuals were perhaps 'cardiac Celts' in Bowman's (1995) phrase; that is, they felt 'Celtic' in their hearts.

The use of a Celtic imagery to represent Scotland is interesting as the Gaelic language and traditions have, for many years, been confined to the Highlands and Islands. But, like tartan, things Celtic have often come to represent Scotland as a whole.

Tartanry

Maybe nowhere is Scotland's discomfort with some of its associated imagery more obvious than in relation to tartan. For many, it is seen as a romantic and backward-looking image, completely at odds with the idea of a modern, twenty-first-century nation. Yet it remains a powerful image and one beloved of the tourist industry and marketers, because of its universal recognition and association with Scotland. Brown (2010b: 3) remarks that it is striking 'that such an intriguing aspect of Scottish culture should at various times and in various ways have attracted the levels of hostility that it has'.

There has been much debate as to the original appearance of tartan. It seems to be generally accepted that, in the Highlands, individuals wore clothing made of woven fabric, often coloured with vegetable dyes and colouring would vary geographically, reflecting the dyes available in a particular locality. The term 'tartan' appears to be derived from the French *tiretaine* or *tertaine*, meaning a blend of linen and wool (Faiers 2008). The link between certain colours and patterns and the areas in which they were woven has, over time, given rise to an assumption that patterns and designs in clothing represent the family or 'clan' residing in that area.

Whatever the truth of the origins of tartan, it was essentially confined to Highland areas although some early forms were in use by members of the Scottish royal family in the fifteenth and sixteenth centuries. Some regiments began to use tartan as part of their uniform, such as the Royal Company of Archers founded in 1676 and the Black Watch, the first Highland regiment to use tartan in 1739 (Faiers 2008). But the association of tartan with the Highlands led to the British Government proscribing its use after the defeat of the Jacobites at the battle of Culloden in 1746. As a result, Highland dress had virtually disappeared by 1780.

As in so many things, the pressure to repeal the ban and to embrace 'tartanry' came from outside Scotland and, following pressure by the Highland Society of London and from members of the aristocracy who wanted to wear tartan, the legislation was repealed in 1782 (Pittock 2010). Clan chiefs began to commission portraits of themselves wearing tartan (Nicholson 2005) and subsequently, the Highland Society began to compile a register of tartans that could be associated with particular chiefs. It should be noted that tartan had now become a fashion that was embraced by the Scottish/British 'Establishment' but would not have been in common use in Scotland. The trigger for widening its appeal came from Sir Walter Scott.

Scott was a highly successful novelist by the 1820s and much of his writing consisted of historical novels such as *Waverley* and *Rob Roy*, in which Highlanders were often portrayed in a noble and romantic way. He was given the task of choreographing the visit by King George IV to Edinburgh in 1822 (McCrone *et al.* 1995), a hugely significant event as it was the first visit to Scotland by a reigning monarch since 1650.

Scott used the Highland Society of London's tartan register and persuaded the various clan chiefs to wear their different tartans and he took advice from William Henry Murray, an actor-manager friend, who helped to choreograph and stage-manage the whole pageant. The King himself was persuaded to wear a kilt and his visit was marked by a series of balls and social events where most participants wore kilts. This royal association with tartan was subsequently enhanced by Queen Victoria when she purchased the Balmoral estate in 1852 (Butler 2007).

But although tartan was embraced by the elites within Scotland, it was not commonly used outside certain occasions such as the Highland Games. It was, however, used extensively in the theatre and particularly by music hall performers. Perhaps the most significant of these was Harry Lauder, who used his kilt, crooked walking stick and jokes about Scottish thrift to portray a stereotype of Scotland that has subsequently been comprehensively rejected. Goldie (2000) refers to him as an 'archetypal Uncle Tam' figure. Yet tartan music hall was as popular at home as it was abroad and UK television featured shows like *The White Heather Club* well into the 1970s. Tartan was also embraced by a number of popular singers and bands such as Rod Stewart and the Bay City Rollers.

Such tartan stereotyping was dubbed 'subcultural Scotchery' by Nairn (1977) but tartan remained exceptionally popular within the Scottish diaspora where Scots donned it a means of expressing their Scottish ethnic identification (Crane *et al.* 2004). Indeed, Strathern and Stewart (2001) have suggested that the diaspora, in promoting tartan and the kilt as symbols of Scotland abroad, have actually done much to strengthen them at home. This represents a significant shift from the experiences of Scottish-Americans returning to

Scotland for a clan gathering in 1977 and being met with some ridicule, not least for their devotion to the kilt and the bagpipes (Steinberg 1981).

It is not clear when Scotland itself began to reclaim tartan from the music hall stereotype and become more comfortable with wearing it. It may reflect the strengthening of Scottish identity and self-confidence associated with the establishment of the Scottish Parliament in 1999. But there is no doubt that the kilt has grown enormously in popularity within Scotland itself in recent years, becoming de rigueur for weddings, graduations and other formal and informal occasions. Scottish football fans have also adopted the kilt as a kind of uniform, especially for fixtures outside Scotland and this may be a useful way of distinguishing themselves from other (mainly English) supporters (Giulianotti 2005). We explore this further in Chapter 14.

The Scottish Parliament itself passed legislation in 2008, establishing a formal Register of Tartans and so there is now a desire for the country not only perhaps to be more at ease with the imagery associated with tartan but actually to take control of it. There remain, of course, many who are uncomfortable with tartan being seen as synonymous with Scotland – as in Tartan Day in the United States for example, when American Scots celebrate their heritage. As Brown notes, 'The issues discourses of tartan and tartanry raise for Scottish culture, the interaction of history and myth and any concept of what is "Scottish" proliferate and will remain unfrozen and lively for many years to come' (2010b: 11).

The kailyard

One of the major criticisms that has been levied at Scottish culture over the years is that it has sometimes been too parochial and uninterested in broader themes and, as Craig (1996) has suggested, those who did succeed on an international stage were dismissed as somehow losing their distinctive 'Scottishness'. While Scotland has undoubtedly produced its fair share of internationally recognised poets and writers – including for example Robert Burns, Robert Louis Stevenson, Hugh McDiarmid, Naomi Mitchison and Muriel Spark among others – there are many writers whose concerns are at a much more local, 'parish-pump' level. Within Scotland, this genre of literature has been referred to as the 'kailyard' or 'cabbage patch', literally a preoccupation with one's own back yard.

The period when this literature was at its most popular was the nineteenth century and it includes such authors as J. M. Barrie, Ian McLaren and S. R.

Crockett. At a time when central Scotland was a highly industrialised society, kailyard authors instead wrote of a country

> consisting wholly of small towns full of 'small-town' characters given to bucolic intrigue and wise sayings. At first the central figures were usually Ministers of the Kirk … but later on schoolteachers and doctors got into the act. Their housekeepers always have a shrewd insight into human nature. Offspring who leave for the big city often come to grief, and are glad to get home again. (Nairn 1977: 158)

Kailyard novels were therefore very backward-looking, obsessed with rurality and represented a very cloying, sanitised and sentimental image of Scottish working-class life. They were guaranteed to be popular with readers who wanted some form of escapism.

The output of many of these writers was specifically aimed at a wider British and even American audience and, as some of them were based outside Scotland, they often failed to have a realistic view of the country. Ian McLaren, for example, was born in Essex and lived in Liverpool. His novel *Beside the Bonnie Brier Bush* was published in 1896 and within ten years had sold almost three-quarters of a million copies (Cook 1999). J. M. Barrie, of course, relocated from Kirriemuir to London. Although best known as the creator of *Peter Pan*, he wrote a number of novels set in the fictional town of 'Thrums', representing the small-town Scotland he had left behind.

Although the kailyard originated in the nineteenth century, this narrow and parochial image of Scotland has remained significant to the present day. The advent of cinema led to films on kailyard themes such as *The Little Minister* (1934) and later *Whisky Galore* (1949), *The Maggie* (1954) and *Rockets Galore* (1958). A common theme in all these films is the impact of modern life on a small Scottish community and the ways in which the plans of big business are foiled by canny locals. From 1994 to 2003, Scottish Television broadcast a soap entitled *Take the High Road* (later just *High Road*), which was set in a fictional Scottish village of Glendarroch and was very much in the kailyard tradition.

In the publishing field, perhaps the most obvious example of the kailyard today can be found within the *Sunday Post*, published by D. C. Thomson of Dundee, who also publish the *People's Friend* and the *Scots Magazine*, the latter with a significant following overseas. The writer Tom Nairn, who deplored the kailyard imagery, stated that he looked forward to the day when the last minister had been strangled with the last copy of the *Sunday Post* (MacInnes 1992).

Although 'kailyardism' is essentially associated with small-town life, there is also a form of urban kailyardism, a genre of writing that focuses in a rather rose-tinted way on the warmth and closeness of city life while ignoring all of its hardships. Writers like Molly Weir, who has written a series of childhood reminiscences about Glasgow (*Shoes Were for Sunday* and the like) is a good example of this, while the poet Adam McNaughtan writes of 'The Glasgow That I Used to Know', in which doors are left unlocked, all neighbours know each other and children play happily in the street. This nostalgia is satirised by Jim McLean in a rejoinder poem that draws attention to the slum conditions in which many Glaswegians were living at the time (McLay 1988).

It is perhaps the unrealistic nostalgia of the kailyard that has, in turn, led to the development of a more realistic and certainly grittier image of Scotland. This is often referred to as 'Clydesidism'.

Clydesidism

At one level, Clydesidism may be seen as a more authentic image of many parts of Scotland than the kailyard. It provides a greater sense of reality and is generally more historically accurate in its depiction of the employment and living conditions of many working-class families in urban Scotland. The Clydeside tradition is one that prizes manual work and recognises the skills of the workers, while acknowledging the exploitation of the workforce and the appalling slums in which many people lived.

As with some of the other images of Scotland, however, some writers have taken it to excess. In terms of housing, for example, it is certainly true that conditions in Glasgow in the early twentieth century were appalling. In 1903, the Glasgow Municipal Commission on the Housing of the Poor found that much of the city's tenement housing was poorly managed and in severe disrepair. After the First World War, when the country was thinking about building 'homes fit for heroes', the journalist William Bolitho published a tract in 1924, drawing attention to the city's continuing poor housing conditions, entitled *Cancer of Empire*. Things were by that time beginning to improve, however, thanks in part to early housing legislation promoted by John Wheatley, a Glasgow MP in Ramsay MacDonald's first Labour government.

There were a number of novels written during the interwar period that focused on the harshness of life on Clydeside, portraying it not merely as a place of poverty but as one in which violence was able to flourish. Perhaps the most famous of these was *No Mean City* by Alexander McArthur and Kingsley

Long, published in 1935. The title was used for many years thereafter to describe Glasgow and surfaced as recently as the 1980s in the theme song used for Scottish Television's *Taggart*. This police drama series, which continued until 2010, was popular across the television network but promoted a particular image of Glasgow with which the city was perhaps not always comfortable. Other authors who may be considered to be part of the Clydeside genre are George Blake, whose most famous novel *The Shipbuilders* was also published in 1935, and in the post-war years, Jeff Torrington and William McIlvanney. McIlvanney has also been regarded as the key figure in the establishment of the 'tartan noir' tradition of crime writing (Wanner 2015). Usually set in urban Scotland, other writers in this genre include Denise Mina (who generally focuses on Glasgow), Ian Rankin (Edinburgh) and Stuart MacBride (Aberdeen).

While there are elements of truth in the images of Glasgow and other parts of central Scotland as harsh places in which to live, the position is, of course, much exaggerated. It is certainly true that the existence of slums like the Gorbals often led outsiders to view Glasgow in a negative light (Damer 1990). But the city has reinvented itself as a post-industrial city and cultural destination with some success (Tucker 2008), becoming a venue for the National Garden Festival and European Capital of Culture in 1990 (Garcia 2004; Mooney 2004). And, while it was possible for researchers such as Patrick (1973) to seek to analyse Glasgow's gang culture in the 1970s, urban redevelopment and population dispersal and overspill have broken up many of the poorer communities in which such gangs existed.

Clydeside in the early twenty-first century is a world away from what it was a century earlier. The gritty image of the area may have held some truth at one time, but it was always somewhat exaggerated and, as Scotland moves away from heavy industry into a more post-industrial phase, the imagery is increasingly outdated.

Miserablism

Although the imagery associated with Clydesidism was frequently negative, it did nevertheless prize working-class skill and manual work. But there was also a much darker, more nihilistic side to it and this has sometimes been referred to as Scottish miserablism (Yule and Manderson 2014).

Miserablism may be seen perhaps to have its origins in the original Calvinist belief in predestination and the thinking that some believers would be saved while others would suffer eternal damnation. This fatalistic view was well illustrated in the comic television serial *Dad's Army*, where the character Private Frazer (played by Scots actor John Lawrie) would greet any adversity with a cry of 'We're doomed!' In literature, there are a number of miserablist texts, such as Irvine Welsh's *Trainspotting* (1993), while in the cinema there have been a number of films like *Ratcatcher* (1999) and *Sweet Sixteen* (2002) that have a sense of hopelessness about them, with the key characters caught in a downward spiral of drink, drugs and personal crises.

To some extent, the miserablist approach has reflected a lack of confidence within Scotland itself. It is no coincidence that many of these books and films appeared during the 1980s and 1990s at a time when Scotland had been denied a devolved Assembly in 1979 because of an insufficiently large 'Yes' vote and when Margaret Thatcher was in power. A phrase often employed at the time was 'democratic deficit' because the Conservatives were in power at Westminster and governing Scotland, when only a minority of voters in Scotland supported them. Politically, many in Scotland felt disempowered and this undoubtedly led to expressions of negativity.

'England' or 'the English' were often blamed but, in fact, it was simply seen as important to blame *somebody* for Scotland's state of affairs. Hence,

> Something or somebody else must be to blame. The boss. The rich. The poor. The central belt. Lairds. Edinburgh lawyers. Subsidy junkies. Catholics. Protestants. The poll tax. The current Scotland football manager. Men. Wummin. Lanarkshire politicians. People who blame other people.
>
> But mainly, we like to blame the English. We define ourselves by what we're not. And above all, we're not English. (Fraser 2002: 77)

This sense of negativity is well illustrated in a key miserablist speech delivered by Mark Renton, the anti-hero of *Trainspotting*:

> It's nae good blamin it oan the English fir colonising us. Ah don't hate the English. They're just wankers. We are colonised by wankers. We can't even pick a decent, vibrant, healthy culture to be colonised by. No. We're ruled by effete arseholes. What does that make us? The lowest of the fuckin low, the scum of the earth. The most wretched, servile, miserable, pathetic trash that was ever shat intae creation. Ah don't hate the English. They just git oan wi the shite thuv goat. Ah hate the Scots. (Welsh 1993: 78)

Yule and Manderson (2014) end their review of Scottish miserablism in a more hopeful tone. They draw attention to the way in which Scottish confidence has grown, partly as a result of the establishment of the Scottish Parliament and partly as a result of the political empowerment generated by the independence referendum in September 2014. There are also now a number of Scottish 'heroes' dominating the stage, like tennis player Andy Murray and actors like Gerard Butler, Ewan McGregor and David Tennant. Images associated with Scotland may therefore be becoming more positive and markedly less 'miserablist'.

Heather, glens and bens

We have already referred to the experiences of Arthur Freed, the producer of *Brigadoon* in 1954, who could find nowhere in Scotland that looked like Scotland – as he imagined it to be. What Freed was essentially looking for was some kind of romantic and picturesque landscape, with heather-clad hills, which would form the backdrop to his film.

Scotland's scenery is undoubtedly a great tourist attraction and the Highlands are often marketed as Europe's last great – and almost peopleless – wilderness. Hence, 'the landscape … is the stuff of Romantic representations with "nature" presented as wild, rugged, barren, beautiful. The dominant colours are blues, browns, white. The lochs are deep, calm and always brooding' (McCrone *et al.* 1995: 80). Gold and Gold's (1995) analysis of Scottish Tourist Board publications reveal similar approaches to marketing with the hills and distant mountains presented in warm colours and accessible to the walker; the terrain, they suggest is always portrayed as inviting and never menacing. Occasionally, walkers are posed in photographs while thistles in full bloom are sometimes an optional extra. And this imagery is also employed as part of the second homes market with various agencies emphasising both views and remoteness as selling points.

Of course, while much of the Highlands is underpopulated and is a major tourist destination, the landscape is not a wilderness by accident. Before the eighteenth century, the Highlands were much more heavily populated, and the land was used for raising cattle and growing crops to a much greater extent than is the case today. After the Jacobite rising of 1745–6, however, the Highland way of life was suppressed and many families emigrated. By the early nineteenth century, the Highland Clearances were under way, with crofting households cleared from the land to allow for the grazing of sheep, which were deemed to be more profitable for landowners (Smout [1972] 1998; Devine 2018). Many crofters emigrated to places like North America while others were resettled in planned settlements like Wick and Ullapool, where they were encouraged to move into the fishing industry. The wilderness landscape that we see today is therefore man-made and is not especially romantic; rather it reflects a great many experiences of hardship and emigration.

Few writers in the nineteenth and early twentieth century really explored these aspects of Highland history. Byron simply wrote of the grandeur of the scenery, while Sir Edwin Landseer painted it. Authors like Compton Mackenzie wrote affectionately comic novels about landowners in books like *Monarch of the Glen* (1941), later serialised on television. But writers like Iain Crichton Smith, whose *Consider the Lilies* (1968) is now regarded as a modern classic, wrote more seriously of the Highland experience and the impact of landownership on the Highland way of life was explored by the 7:84 Theatre Company's *The Cheviot, the Stag and the Black, Black Oil*, written by John McGrath in 1973.

Since the advent of the Scottish Parliament, there has been legislation to encourage community land ownership (the Land Reform (Scotland) Act 2003), whereby local crofting communities take control of the land themselves, and there have been a number of successful buy-outs in Assynt, the Outer Hebrides and the islands of Eigg and Gigha (Bryden and Geisler 2007; Hunter 2012). During 2012–14, the Scottish Government undertook a consultation on extending this legislation (Land Reform Review Group 2014) and the recommendations were implemented in the Land Reform (Scotland) Act 2016. The Act establishes a detailed register of landownership, sets up a Scottish Land Commission to progress land reform and reintroduces business rates on sporting estates, an exemption that they had enjoyed since 1994.

The Parliament also legislated to introduce national parks to Scotland in 1999 and, in contrast to the position in England and Wales, has encouraged sustainable development in the parks, to try and redress the previous decline in population and economic activity in these areas (Barker and Stockdale 2008).

In summary, this image of Scotland as a land of scenic and deserted hills and glens is certainly an accurate one but it takes little account of how the present landscape came about and how it is, in many ways, an artificial creation.

Other images

There are of course, many other images by which Scotland is known and recognised. We have already referred to 'tartanry'; some have in turn branded this a 'shortbread tin' image of Scotland, in recognition of the ways in which such tins are usually decorated. Foods and drinks like haggis and whisky are also used as marketing tools and help to reinforce a particular external view of the country (Scarles 2004).

Another common Scottish stereotype is that of the Scots as a mean and thrifty people. This image may have its origins in the significant employment of Scots in financial affairs and the position of Edinburgh as the home of a number of significant financial institutions. Music hall performers like Harry Lauder played to this stereotype, with jokes about mean Scots and was famous for tipping people with a solitary penny (Goldie 2000). Such stereotypes have become a modern-day irritation for most Scots and Hopkins *et al.* (2007) show that, first, Scots are only too well aware of how they are sometimes viewed, especially by people from England, and resent it. Second, they show how Scots seek to refute this image by becoming measurably more generous and adopting behaviours aimed at helping others.

Conclusion: does imagery matter?

Writing in 1980, the American Scot Geddes MacGregor neatly summarised the occasional tensions that appear between the 'real' Scotland and the imagined one, and whether or not the imagery is important. He suggested that there are, in fact, three Scotlands, which he distinguished as:

> (1) the never-never land of *Brigadoon*, where kilted Rockettes dance in the moonlight on heather hills, and men, having greeted the dawn with a quaich of Scotch, sally forth to shoot a deer or two for breakfast; (2) the Scottish Homeland, an area of just over thirty thousand square miles inhabited by five or six million people on the northern part of the island we call Britain; and (3) the Scottish Diaspora, consisting of the vast millions of people of Scottish birth or ancestry dispersed throughout the world (in the United States alone an estimated five times as many as in the Homeland) who look to the Homeland with that deep affection and occasional exasperation that people never bestow on anyone but their mother. (MacGregor 1980: v)

Clearly the images of kilts and heather still have some traction, particularly in the diaspora. The question is whether this imagery is significant in terms of how Scotland is perceived – or indeed wants to be perceived.

VisitScotland, the national tourist body, has sought to tread a fine line between promoting artistic, cultural and economic aspects of Scotland, while also paying close attention to the country's heritage, with which many from outside Scotland would wish to engage. The agency's strategy for tourism has been on a themed approach, with each year being given a different theme. Hence 2014 was the Year of Homecoming (see Chapter 10), 2015 the Year of Scotland's Food and Drink, 2016 the Year of Innovation, Architecture and Design, 2017 the Year of History, Heritage and Archaeology and 2018 the Year of Young People. There was no theme in 2019 but 2020 will be the Year of Scotland's Coasts and Waters.

In fact, both 2009 and 2014 have been Years of Homecoming in which the Scottish diaspora has been invited to return 'home'. The 2009 event, for example, was timed to coincide with the 250th anniversary of the birth of Robert Burns, the national poet, and there was also an emphasis on Scotland's contributions to the world, including golf, whisky, invention and innovation (the Scottish Enlightenment) and the country's culture, heritage and people. But the centrepiece event of the year, reflecting a strong heritage focus, was the Gathering, which took place in Edinburgh. This was a clan gathering that included Highland Games, a parade up the city's Royal Mile and a clan pageant on the Castle Esplanade, so the tartan imagery was well to the fore (Sim and Leith 2013).

There may not in fact be an image that is uniquely Scottish. Rather there are several different images, all of which may have a degree of truth in them. As individuals, we all negotiate our identities and this is a particularly complex process within the UK, with its multiple layers of being Scottish, British – and perhaps European – all simultaneously (McCrone 2002). As part of these identity negotiations, Scots may choose to reject certain aspects of a nation's culture or iconography, while accepting others. They may embrace the arts and music in Scotland, for example, while rejecting the tartan *Braveheart* imagery. There are signs that Scots are increasingly comfortable about making those choices.

Further reading

For a general exploration of national imagery and the way in which the nation is 'flagged' we would recommend Michael Billig's *Banal Nationalism* (1995).

For a more specific focus on Scotland, then *Scotland – the Brand: The Making of Scottish Heritage* by David McCrone *et al.* (1995) is excellent. There are also a number of excellent contributions to Ian Brown's edited collection *From Tartan to Tartanry: Scottish Culture, History and Myth* (2010a).

An older publication but a very useful exploration of national imagery and stereotypes is Isobel Lindsay's paper 'The Uses and Abuses of National Stereotypes', in *Scottish Affairs* (1997). And finally, Hugh Trevor-Roper does some interesting, and challenging, debunking of Scottish myths and imagery in *The Invention of Scotland: Myth and History* (2008).

Chapter 5
Learning and working Scotland

Introduction

Both education and employment are essential elements in any society. In this chapter, we explore the ways in which, first, the Scottish education system has been particularly valued over time and assess its current state. Second, we explore how a sense of national pride has existed in regard to Scottish industry and the contribution that the country has made through its manufacturing, while looking at the changing nature of Scottish employment over the years and the shift from a manufacturing to a service economy. There is perhaps a mythology surrounding both education and work within Scotland and we try to drill down into the reality, casting aside a few myths on the way.

In the Treaty of Union of 1707, Scottish education remained largely untouched and so, along with the Kirk and the legal system, it remained as one of the key pillars of Scottish distinctiveness. Devine (1999) notes how the Scottish system of schooling from the Reformation to the Industrial Revolution had attracted lavish praise from both contemporary commentators and later observers, although gaps exist in source material, making it difficult to substantiate all the claims made. Nevertheless, education played a central part in the nation's sense of itself.

This pride in Scottish education stemmed in part from the system of parish schools established during the seventeenth century. The parish school was seen as

> the cradle of the 'democratic intellect' where, it was said, the children of lairds rubbed shoulders with the offspring of ploughmen. This mixing of the classes produced, so it was argued, a more egalitarian society than England and was a way of asserting distinctive Scottish values in the one area where Scots believed themselves not simply the equal but the superiors of the English. (Devine 1999: 91)

Higher education too was highly valued and Scotland had four universities by the sixteenth century, when England had only two. We explore this further below.

Work was also seen as a crucial element in the country's sense of identity. Scots took a pride in their inventiveness, as the country of Alexander Graham Bell, John Logie Baird, John Dunlop, Kirkpatrick Macmillan, John Loudon McAdam and a host of other inventors and industrial pioneers. Scots were proud too of advances in employment practices espoused by Robert Owen and David Dale in model villages like New Lanark. And they were proud of the country's engineering and manufacturing tradition, which saw Glasgow regarded as 'the second city of the Empire' (Mackenzie 1999). Phrases such as 'Clydebuilt' passed into everyday vocabulary. Scotland took a pride in the 'dignity of labour' and the country was at the forefront of the development of both the Labour Party and the trade union movement.

Education and work are therefore important elements in Scotland's sense of itself and we consider each in turn.

Education in Scotland

As a small country in the shadow of a much larger neighbour, Scotland has prized its educational system as an important element in the maintenance of a distinct national identity (Anderson 1985). Various myths have grown up around Scottish education regarding its egalitarian tradition – the 'democratic intellect' as it became known (Davie [1961] 1999) – and these myths and traditions have usefully been invoked against threats of assimilation or 'anglicisation'. As McCrone (2001) has pointed out:

> The myth of egalitarianism … is not dependent on 'facts', because it represents a set of social, self-evident values, a social ethos, a celebration of sacred beliefs about what it is to be Scottish. It helped to underpin a social and cultural order which placed a premium on collective, cooperative and egalitarian commitments. It is an ideological device for marking off the Scots from the English, which seems to grow in importance the more the two societies grow similar. (McCrone 2001: 102–103)

This idea of egalitarianism springs from the system of parish schools that were developed in Scotland in the wake of the Reformation. The newly established Calvinist Kirk placed schooling and literacy 'at the very heart of its programme for religious revolution. It was the means by which the essential precepts of religious belief were to be instilled in the young' (Devine 1999: 91). If everyone was to have access to the word of God, then education gained a new importance. Indeed, religious education advanced enormously when the Scottish King James VI, the year after he became James I of England, convened the conference that led to a new translation of the Bible. Published in 1611, the 'King James Bible' became the authorised version for use throughout the English-speaking Protestant churches.

The means by which mass education was to be achieved was through the establishment of a network of parish schools. Through a series of Acts of the Scottish Parliament during the seventeenth century, local landowners were taxed to maintain both a school and a qualified teacher and this national system of education was a significant achievement. The position within smaller burghs was broadly similar, but in the larger towns and cities the provision of schools failed to keep pace with industrialisation during the late eighteenth and nineteenth centuries and there were high levels of illiteracy (Devine 1999).

The wide availability of education across the country gave rise to the notion of the 'lad o' pairts' or 'lad of parts' (Anderson 1985). Essentially, this was a convenient shorthand term for the idea that, through the acquisition of knowledge and the encouragement of ambition, a lad (never a 'lass' in those days) from the humblest background could become socially mobile and secure a career. The parish schools represented a meritocratic system of education that 'offered a ladder of opportunity leading to the universities and on to the professions' (Devine 1999: 91).

Although one can perhaps overstate the impact of education, particularly in relation to social mobility, nevertheless Scotland was in many respects a more literate nation than England, 'a consequence of its many schools (religious and secular), its universities and a civil society bulked and developed by early urbanisation' (Morton 2012: 2). The development of a large and significant publishing industry provides some evidence of this.

In terms of post-school education, Scots have traditionally been proud of their universities and the country had four established institutions (St Andrews, Glasgow, Aberdeen and Edinburgh) by the late sixteenth century, at a time when only Oxford and Cambridge had been established in England. Importantly, the Scottish universities saw themselves as public institutions and academic work was viewed as a public service (Paterson 2003b). Knowledge itself was public and was a means of clarifying and making sense of society, part of the notion of 'democratic intellectualism' (Davie [1961] 1999). Scotland in many respects resembled many other European countries rather than

England, in terms of university provision. Many countries such as Germany, Italy and the Netherlands had established universities before the 1600s and it was not uncommon for Scottish students to travel abroad to study law, divinity and medicine. Between 1575 and 1800, for example, 1,460 Scottish students matriculated at Leiden University in Holland (Smout 1995), while others studied at Franeker, Groningen and Utrecht. Graduates from Leiden helped to found the Medical School at Edinburgh in 1726 and this was one of the earliest such schools in the English-speaking world (Guthrie 1946).

Edinburgh and Glasgow universities in particular were significant centres of learning during the period of the Scottish Enlightenment in the eighteenth century, as evidenced by the writings of Adam Smith and David Hume – although ironically Hume was denied a chair at both institutions. Smith argued very strongly in *The Wealth of Nations* for mass education, the need to overcome ignorance in society and for individuals to make use of their intellectual faculties. He saw education as a necessary social insurance in that the state was safer if people were educated. They would then feel valued, respected and would be more likely to form an 'intelligent consensus'. He claimed that 'an instructed and intelligent people are always more decent and orderly than an ignorant and stupid one' (cited in Reay 2006: 293).

As far as those partaking of a university education were concerned, by 1872 the ratio of those at university in Scotland was five times greater than in England and, importantly, Scottish universities were open to all levels of society without entrance qualification, allowing for more working-class entry. The degree structure was also distinct and Morton (2012: 186) has argued that this lends support to the notion of the Scottish democratic intellect. Another important distinction between Scotland and England relates to the idea of 'vocational' education. While education in the arts and sciences could be pursued for its own sake, Scottish universities were particularly strong in vocational and professional studies such as law, divinity and medicine.

The pace of industrialisation during the nineteenth century imposed significant challenges to the educational system in urban areas. But by 1872, elementary education had become compulsory, eight years earlier than England. In 1889, primary education was made free for all and in 1901, seventeen years before England, the Scottish school leaving age was raised to fourteen. In 1918, free secondary education was made available. In 1901, 95 per cent of Scottish children aged between six and twelve attended school (Macdonald 2009).

Scottish education today

So what is Scottish education like today? First, state school education is administered within a national system by the thirty-two local authorities. Roman Catholic schools have been part of the state system since 1918 and the range of 'faith' schools that exists in England has no equivalent north of the border. Similarly, there are no 'foundation' schools or 'academies'. There is an independent sector, but this is responsible for educating only around 4 per cent of school pupils, compared with 7–8 per cent in England. The independent sector is perhaps more significant within the two major cities – particularly Edinburgh – than in other local authorities (Paterson 2003a). This, it might be argued, makes the education system in Scotland more 'democratic' than in England, although Denholm and Macleod (2002) suggest that this might be exaggerated. While it is true that devolution has meant that Scottish schools have avoided the levels of private sector involvement, testing and target setting that have occurred in England, this has not necessarily resulted in superior academic attainment and they draw attention to continuing challenges in ensuring improved rates of literacy and numeracy within Scotland. Indeed, such challenges continue, although there have been some improvements.

In terms of overall academic performance, 61.2 per cent of school leavers in 2017 gained one or more qualifications at higher level or above; before 2010, the figure was below 50 per cent (Scottish Government 2018). There remains, however, an attainment gap between leavers from the most and least deprived areas of the country. Sosu and Ellis (2014) found that the gap between children from low-income and high-income households starts early and is linked to deprivation throughout primary school. By age sixteen, attainment has risen overall, but a significant and persistent gap remains between groups. Children from deprived households leave school earlier and low attainment is strongly linked to post-school destinations, with long-term effects on job prospects.

In March 2018, approximately nine months after leaving school, 94.3 per cent of the summer 2017 school leavers were in 'positive' destinations, with 67.6 per cent entering further or higher education and 22.7 per cent in employment. Just 5 per cent were unemployed.

The Scottish Government has long been concerned about standards in the country's schools and, following a national debate on education set up by the then Scottish Executive in 2002, the government developed what it called the 'Curriculum for Excellence'. Essentially, this approach

> privileges learning and a holistic understanding of what it means to be a young Scot growing up in today's world. At its heart are the four fundamental capacities: (i) successful learners, (ii) confident individuals, (iii) responsible citizens, and (iv) effective contributors. Up to around age 15, the aim is to lay the foundations for lifetimes of learning through Broad General Education (BGE), incorporating primary and the first stages of secondary schooling but also early learning from age 3 onwards. (OECD 2015: 9)

The Organisation for Economic Cooperation and Development (OECD) undertook a review of the new approach in 2015 and found that there was much to be positive about, with achievement in Scottish education being above international averages. But gaps were narrowing and the report, in making a number of recommendations for improvement, warned against complacency.

Indeed, in 2016, a study of Scotland's Programme for International Student Assessment (PISA) scores suggested that all was not well. The country's scores were similar to the OECD average in science, maths and reading, but in the equivalent previous survey in 2012, Scotland had been above the OECD average in reading and science and at the average in maths. There had therefore been a decline in performance in both science and reading with a number of other countries overtaking Scotland. Within the UK, both England and Northern Ireland scored higher than Scotland (Social Research 2016). The results have led to criticisms that the Scottish Government is not prioritising education sufficiently and it was significant that, following the 2016 Scottish parliamentary elections, the education portfolio was taken on by Deputy First Minister John Swinney. This was perhaps an indication that the government realised it needed to do more to raise educational standards. At the time of writing, the government is consulting on identifying the milestones towards closing the attainment gap and its 2019 Improvement Plan stresses the need to ensure high standards in numeracy and literacy as well as a focus on inclusivity, health and well-being.

For those Scots who leave school and move on to further education, Scotland has a large network of colleges, although there have been a significant number of mergers in recent years, to create larger institutions. The overall number of colleges therefore decreased from thirty-seven to twenty-six between 2011 and 2015. There has been some political debate regarding the numbers of students attending further education, which have fallen substantially between

2007 and 2016, from 379,000 to 227,000. Essentially, the Scottish Government has sought to prioritise full-time learning over part-time and this has led to the closure of a number of part-time courses (Denholm 2016).

In contrast, higher education has expanded in Scotland, as in other parts of the UK and there are currently nineteen higher education institutions. This figure is made up of fifteen Scottish universities, plus the Open University in Scotland, Glasgow School of Art, the Royal Conservatoire of Scotland (based in Glasgow) and the Scottish Rural College based on six campuses across the country. In 2016–17, there were 292,620 students in higher education in Scotland. Of these, the majority (57 per cent) were female, with that proportion steadily increasing; 162,130 (55.4 per cent) were at first degree level, 72.5 per cent were Scottish-domiciled and 19.6 per cent were from outside the UK (Scottish Funding Council 2018).

Scottish higher education has always had its distinctive features, notably its traditional system of four-year honours degree programmes in contrast to the three-year programmes in England. But recently, perhaps the greatest difference between universities north and south of the border has been the absence of tuition fees in Scotland. Within the UK as a whole, higher education tuition fees were first introduced for full-time undergraduate courses in 1998, initially at £1,000 per annum. The following year, maintenance grants were abolished and replaced with maintenance loans. From 2006, all full-time UK students at English, Welsh and Northern Irish universities have been charged a variable tuition fee, initially capped at £3,000 per annum but that now stands at a cap of £9,250 per annum. However, in sharp contrast, the Scottish Government decided that from 2007, undergraduate students domiciled and studying in Scotland would not have to pay any fees towards the cost of their tuition (Wilkins *et al.* 2013). Students from the EU have studied in Scotland on the same basis as 'home' students, but students from England, Wales and Northern Ireland studying in Scotland must pay tuition fees similar to the levels in their own country. The Scottish Government has confirmed that EU students will continue to benefit from free tuition on courses beginning in 2020 but thereafter, the effects of Brexit are very unclear.

The Scottish Government has argued strongly against the introduction of tuition fees as it sees them as a barrier to widening participation within higher education. In that sense, they are perhaps seeking to reinforce the historic attachment to the democratic intellect and the availability of education for all – or at least for as many as possible. Indeed, the existence of free tuition in Scotland was fiercely championed by former First Minister Alex Salmond and has become something of a touchstone for the current Scottish Government in emphasising Scotland's distinctiveness.

This inclusive approach would seem to find an echo within the attitudes of university academics themselves and Paterson (2003b) has undertaken interesting research in this area. In a study covering both Scotland and England, he found that Scottish academics were more in favour of a 'civic' role for universities than their counterparts in England, with students learning to contribute to the life of their communities and universities providing 'socially useful' knowledge. Scottish academics were also more likely to view their institutions as having an important community role and favoured providing access courses to local people. Finally, they were more inclined to view universities as having an important contribution to make to national culture.

The Scottish Government has (through the 2016 Higher Education Governance (Scotland) Act) made important changes to the governance of universities, with legislation now requiring universities to have elected chairs of the university court and to provide places on the university court (the governing body) to students, staff and representatives of campus trade unions. It might be argued therefore that Scottish universities are becoming more 'democratic' than institutions elsewhere.

The Scottish economy

We have already touched on the issue of school leavers and entry into the labour market. We move on now to look in more detail at the Scottish economy and at Scottish employment.

Scotland became a highly industrialised country in the nineteenth century, with Glasgow often referred to as the 'second city of the empire', supporting the British economy with its large manufacturing base. Reflecting this, the city hosted two large international exhibitions in 1888 and 1901 and Devine refers to the great 1901 exhibition, held in the city's Kelvingrove Park: 'The Machinery Hall and the Industrial Hall were particularly dedicated to Glaswegian prowess in the arts of engineering and science', prowess that had made Glasgow 'one of the great cities of the world' (1999: 249).

Glasgow and the wider Clydeside area were major centres of iron and steel working, metal manufacturing, locomotive building and, of course, shipbuilding. Shortly before the start of the First World War, almost one-quarter of the world's shipping tonnage was built on the Clyde and even in 1947 the figure was 18 per cent (Devine 1999). Elsewhere in Scotland, the textile industry was significant in towns such as Paisley, while Dundee was famous for 'jute, jam and journalism' (di Domenico and di Domenico 2007). Brewing was a major employer in Edinburgh, fish-related industries in Aberdeen, linoleum manufacturing in Kirkcaldy and sugar refining in Greenock. Each town and city appeared to have an industrial specialism.

But cracks began to appear in the Scottish economy, particularly in the interwar period. In part, this reflected weaknesses in the UK economy as a whole, a situation made worse by the British Government's adherence to the gold standard and the overvaluation of sterling. But Scottish entrepreneurs were less responsive than they might have been to the rise of a consumer society and Scottish industries proved unable to compete effectively in an increasingly challenging international market (Peden 2005). In shipbuilding, for example, the industry's problems were very clearly illustrated by the cessation of work at Clydebank on Cunard Line's *Queen Mary* in 1931. Although the industry, like many others, recovered as a result of demand created by the Second World War, the situation did not last and Clydeside's share of world tonnage had slumped to 4.5 per cent by 1958. High-profile events such as the launch of the *Queen Elizabeth 2* in 1967 only served to disguise the underlying decline.

Central government had initially failed adequately to address the issue of Scottish unemployment, which was persistently higher than the UK average (Peden 2005). In 1922, for example, it had passed the Empire Settlement Act, which assisted emigration to the dominions and colonies. Thus many individuals were encouraged to leave Scotland (and the UK) rather than being helped to find work at home. But during the Second World War, the Secretary of State Tom Johnston, concerned at the concentration of industry in the South and Midlands of England, launched a Scottish Council of Industry to attract new businesses to Scotland. Perhaps his most successful initiative was to establish a system of hydroelectricity using water power in the Highlands. By providing jobs in this area, he helped to reverse the long-term emigration problems of the Highlands (Torrance 2006).

In the post-war period, central government pursued a regional policy (McCrone 1969) and this led to significant industrial development in Scotland in an attempt to diversify the economy. The country gained a share of the British motor industry for the first time, with the establishment of the Rootes car plant at Linwood, near Paisley in 1963 and a British Leyland truck plant at Bathgate the following year. In 1958, a new state-of-the art strip mill had been built at Ravenscraig in Motherwell to boost the country's steel industry (Devine 1999). In the Highlands, a new pulp and paper mill was opened at

Fort William in 1964 and British Aluminium established a new smelter at Invergordon in 1971. Scotland was also very successful in attracting electronics companies. NCR, Honeywell, Burroughs and IBM all established plants and firms began to refer to 'Silicon Glen' as a Scottish version of California's 'Silicon Valley' (Macdonald 2009).

The weakness in all of this was the 'branch plant syndrome'. A number of older traditional industries such as coal, the railways and iron and steel had been nationalised after the Second World War and, as a result, senior management and decision-making was transferred from Scotland to head offices, usually in London. Although the establishment of new industries undoubtedly helped to address employment issues in Scotland, most of them were branches of businesses headquartered elsewhere. Many of the 'Silicon Glen' plants were simply branches of American businesses, for example, and this left the Scottish plants vulnerable in the event of company downsizing or retrenchment. In exploring this problem of external control, Firn (1975) showed that branch plants employed over one-quarter of total manufacturing employment in Scotland. Some 16.8 per cent (96,000 employees) were in English-owned enterprises and 8.6 per cent in American-owned. An interesting insight into the distribution of economic power within the UK could be gained by looking at the headquarters of the 318 branch plants operating in Scotland. No less than 184 of them were located in south-east England.

It was perhaps inevitable that many of these plants would close at some point. The motor manufacturing plants, for example, were a long way from the car components industry in England and proved to be expensive to run. There were also long-term trade union problems. During the period of the Conservative government in the 1980s, when there were significant industrial closures, Scotland suffered badly. Linwood closed in 1981, Invergordon in 1982, Bathgate in 1985 and the Fort William pulp mill in 2005. The closure of the Ravenscraig steel mill in 1992 was seen as being particularly significant, given its size as the largest hot strip steel mill in Western Europe and its somewhat iconic status in Scottish industrial history. These closures were marked in popular culture by the Proclaimers' song 'Letter from America', with its chorus of 'Bathgate no more, Linwood no more, Methil no more, Lochaber no more'.

On the Clyde, mergers took place to improve the productivity of the shipyards but in 1971, the Heath government sought to close the Upper Clyde yards due them being insufficiently profitable. This led to a famous 'work-in' led by shop stewards Jimmy Reid and Jimmy Airlie, which received widespread public support, perhaps reflecting the iconic status of Clyde shipbuilding (Foster and Woolfson 1986). The government backed down and shipbuilding survived. At the time of writing, most orders on the upper Clyde are secured for warship building through the Ministry of Defence. On the lower Clyde, Ferguson's yard at Port Glasgow survives, constructing smaller vessels such as ferries.

It would be quite wrong to portray the Scottish economy as one of failure, however. The greatest changes in Scottish industry from the 1970s onwards have been in the energy sector. The first commercial Scottish oilfield – the Forties – was located in 1970 and came onstream in 1977. Also in the 1970s, further oilfields were developed – the Brent and Ninian fields – and oil companies began to establish offices and research and development bases in Aberdeen, the city rapidly becoming the oil capital of Europe. By 1981, UK oil production exceeded 87 million tonnes (Macdonald 2009). By the mid-1980s, fifty thousand jobs in the north east of Scotland were oil-related (Macdonald 2009), but the industry was prone to booms and slumps as the oil price varied over time. The UK, unlike Norway, failed to establish an oil fund that could have been used to offset periods of slump and, in the long term, the Scottish economy failed to benefit from the oil industry as much as had been hoped. Indeed, the failure to capitalise on the benefits of oil proved a major boost to political nationalism during the 1970s.

Over time, the oil industry has experienced periods of boom and slump as the price of oil has varied. At the time of writing (July 2019), it is around $67 per barrel, a significant increase over the previous four years but much lower than the $125 in early 2012. There has been some retrenchment in the oil industry as some North Sea fields have become exhausted and, although in 2018 the industry supported over 300,000 jobs, this was a significant fall from 460,000 only four years previously (Oil and Gas UK 2018). There have been a number of recent discoveries of large oilfields that suggests that the industry still has a prosperous future, but some fields are in deeper water west of Shetland and the conditions for oil extraction will be challenging.

For some, the decline of oil represents an opportunity for Scotland to move into renewable energy and the country has taken a lead in this area in recent years. Hydroelectricity has been part of the energy mix since the Second World War but there is now a growing use of wind and wave power (Warren and Birnie 2009). Before 1995, no wind farms existed in Scotland but by 2018 there were around 750. As a result of this dramatic growth, onshore wind overtook hydro power as the most common source of renewable energy in

Scotland. Thus 'from being a rare novelty, wind farms have rapidly become a common sight in many parts of the country' (Warren and Birnie 2009: 105).

Wave and tidal energy developments are at a much earlier stage in Scotland. Wave testing began in 2004 in Orkney and tidal in 2007 and the Orkney/Pentland Firth area has seen most of the initial experiments because of its strong tidal currents (Scottish Government 2011). The Scottish Government has adopted ambitious targets in relation to renewables, stemming from the Climate Change (Scotland) Act 2009. The original aim was to ensure that all the country's electricity came from renewables by 2020 with an interim target of 50 per cent by 2015. According to Scottish Renewables (2018), 70 per cent of Scotland's electricity now comes from renewables, suggesting that the target may be met, although there may well be some slippage. Nevertheless, it is clear that the government remains determined to promote this form of energy in order to meet the challenges of climate change and the direction of travel remains firmly in favour of renewables. The aim is for 50 per cent of the country's total energy needs to come from renewables by 2030 and the government has now introduced a new Climate Change Bill to set even more ambitious targets and to improve transparency in regard to their measurement. The government sees this as being very much in the spirit of the 2016 Paris Agreement on Climate Change. To illustrate the shift in priorities, Scotland's last coal-fired power station at Longannet in Fife closed early in 2016; at the same time, employment in renewables is increasing and in 2018, renewable energy supported 17,700 jobs.

The current employment situation in Scotland

Much employment data originates in the census and, although 2011 data are now very out of date, the census remains a comprehensive information source and allows comparisons over time. The 2011 census showed that there were 2.5 million employed people in Scotland, aged between 16 and 74. The two largest industry sectors were 'health and social work' and 'retail activities', each employing 15 per cent (377,000 people). The third largest sector was education with just over 8 per cent, so a large proportion of Scots were employed in services. Despite Scotland's historical manufacturing tradition, only 8 per cent were employed in manufacturing and this had declined from 13 per cent in 2001.

Census analysis showed that during the century from 1911 to 2011, the numbers employed in both manufacturing and in agriculture and fishing had declined substantially. In 1911, these two sectors had accounted for 47 per cent of the workforce, but by 2011 they accounted for 10 per cent. The service sector in contrast had increased from 38 per cent to 79 per cent during the same period (National Records of Scotland 2013). It is important to note that only a part of this employment is in the public sector. There has been a marked growth in employment in private sector 'white-collar' jobs in Scotland, notably in the banking and finance sectors (about 16 per cent of the total workforce), and Edinburgh developed as a significant financial centre, although it was badly affected by the banking crisis and recession of 2007–8.

The Scottish economy has expanded in recent years – an expansion of 2.7 per cent during 2014 – but more recent data suggests a slowing down in 2015–16 and a great deal of economic uncertainty following the EU referendum (Gillespie 2016). The main drivers of growth, however, have been in consumer spending and construction, with the latter fuelled by a large number of public sector contracts in roads and in the building of the new Queensferry Crossing over the Firth of Forth, all publicly funded. This suggests that the private sector alone may not be sufficiently strong to grow significantly in the future and Gillespie (2016) notes the challenges to growth posed by the fall in oil prices and fiscal tightening at UK level.

In terms of economic activity, the 2011 census shows that 69 per cent of the 4 million people in Scotland aged between sixteen and seventy-four were economically active and this had increased from 65 per cent in 2001 (a rise from 2.4 million to 2.7 million). Some 7 per cent of the economically active population were unemployed and this had risen from 6 per cent in 2001 (National Records of Scotland 2013). By the end of 2018, the Labour Force Survey was indicating an unemployment rate of 3.5 per cent, lower than the UK figure of 4.0 per cent (Aiton 2019), although this varied slightly by age. Although the unemployment of young people aged between sixteen and twenty-four remained a concern, the rate of 7.6 per cent was much better than the UK average of 11.5 per cent. Although unemployment in Scotland therefore remains slightly high, employment activity (people in work) has risen and the number of people aged sixteen and over in employment in Scotland was 75.5 per cent at the end of 2018, just below the UK figure of 75.8 per cent (Aiton 2019). These increases may be due to increases in the population as a whole and a significant number of those in work will be working only on a part-time basis. Within Scotland, the highest employment rate was 87.5 per cent in Orkney and the lowest was 54.6 per cent in north Glasgow.

Data from Scottish Enterprise (2016) and from the Scottish Government (O'Connor 2017) provide a picture of employment and sector profiles (see

Table 5.1 Employment by broad industry group

Group	Numbers employed (000s)
Health	411
Retail	245
Accommodation and food services	190
Business administration and support services	188
Education	188
Manufacturing	180
Professional, scientific and technical	178
Public administration	154
Construction	141
Arts, entertainment and other services	136
Transport and storage	108
Finance and insurance	86
Wholesale	77
Agriculture, forestry and fishing	76
Information and communication	74
Mining, quarrying and utilities	68
Motor trades	49
Property	39

Source: O'Connor (2017).

Table 5.1). In terms of numbers employed, the largest sectors are in the retail trade and in the public sector, including health and education. Manufacturing remains significant but the numbers employed in this sector have declined over the years.

However, the value of the different business sectors to the Scottish economy do not always mirror the numbers they employ. Hence, although manufacturing has declined in terms of employment, it is the second largest contributor to Scotland's gross domestic product (GDP), after the energy sector. The third most valuable sector is finance, reflecting Edinburgh's position as a major banking and insurance sector, albeit somewhat tarnished after the 2007–8 financial crisis. Scottish Government data indicates that the total number of private sector enterprises in Scotland was 345,915 in 2017 but this had fallen by 2.5 per cent from the previous year. All but a handful employed fewer than 250 employees, so the number of large firms was small but they nevertheless accounted for 45 per cent of private sector employment and 59 per cent of turnover.

It is not possible within the confines of this book to explore all the different industrial sectors but it is of interest to look at some in more detail, notably those where the Scottish Government believes that the country has a comparative advantage.

Energy

We have already referred to the importance of the oil and gas industry to Scotland and it employs just over three hundred thousand people, although this number has fallen because of the fall in oil prices during 2015. The largest expansion is in renewables and Scottish Enterprise (2016) estimated that employment in Scotland's renewable energy and low carbon sector is around sixteen thousand. The numbers are forecast to grow, following the Scottish Government's policies set out in the Climate Change Act of 2009 and its current Climate Change Bill.

Creative industries

This sector is estimated to employ almost seventy thousand people and one of the areas in which Scotland has taken an international lead is in the gaming industry. The country has developed centres of research excellence – particularly in Dundee – and these can develop next-generation technologies to support growth in the sector. Two of the most internationally successful games, *Minecraft* and *Grand Theft Auto* have been developed in Dundee and there are a number of university courses linked to the industry. The Scottish Parliament (2015) found that there was little accurate data available on the industry, but one estimate suggested that over 11 per cent of the UK's games companies are now located in Scotland. Also, within the creative industries, there are currently (as of time writing in 2019) proposals to construct one or more large film studios in Scotland and this would enable the country to gain a greater share of the international film industry.

Food and drink

Although the contribution of this sector to Scotland's GDP is less than other industries, it is growing, based partly on a focus on high-quality food products such as salmon, game and meat, but also on the alcohol industry. The whisky industry has expanded, with a growing interest in malt whiskies, and many distillers are moving into the production of gin.

Tourism

Underpinning the Scottish economy and linked to many of the other industries, tourism contributes significantly to the Scottish economy. The country's five largest international markets are the United States, Germany, France, Australia and the Netherlands (Scottish Enterprise 2016). The sector employs almost two hundred thousand people and the sector is particularly significant in rural Scotland, although its seasonality remains a problem for those seeking full-time permanent employment in these areas. Scotland has moved to develop heritage tourism, linked to those seeking to undertake genealogical research and this is forming an increasingly significant element within the industry (Timothy 2011).

Challenges

It is clear that the economy of Scotland is in reasonable shape, has a number of buoyant sectors and, in many respects, is 'holding its own' in comparison with the rest of the UK. Nevertheless, there remain significant challenges.

Perhaps the most significant relate to the nature of the population as a whole. For young people seeking to enter the labour market, we have already noted the problems of the attainment gap, with many young people, particularly from deprived backgrounds, leaving school with few, if any, qualifications. Finlay *et al.* (2010) argue that the social and economic disengagement of many young people has its background in histories of poor housing, drugs, parenting, alcohol and offending behaviour and these are not issues that can be dealt with wholly in the education or training sector. Their research suggests that many young people in Scotland possess skills and have normal *aspirations* but end up with low *expectations* in regard to their employability and life chances. These expectations were based on young people's empirical observations of the experiences of others like them. Finlay *et al.* (2010) argue that there need to be greater opportunities in training, education and employment for such individuals.

Thus the employability of individuals is closely bound up with the jobs that are available and that they are offered. We have already referred to the changes in the Scottish economy and the shift from a manufacturing to a service sector base. Trebeck and Stuart believe that this shift has been a problematic one: 'Retail and call-centres have expanded to (partly) fill the void left by the demise of manufacturing. Service jobs have replaced skilled trades. Yet these new jobs do not necessarily offer a route out of poverty: many roles simply do not pay enough to live on, far less build for the future' (2013: 4). They believe therefore that, while numbers in employment have risen and the economy appears to prosper, the prevalence of poorly paid, low-skilled jobs is perpetuating a cycle of poverty in many of Scotland's communities. This in turn leads to the low expectations of many school leavers.

At the other end of the age range, Scotland has a possible problem with an ageing population. Although the Scottish birth rate is now rising and there have also been population gains from inward migration, low levels of fertility for a number of years have left the country's age structure with over one million people aged over sixty-five. Future immigration levels will also be affected by Brexit. Population projections based on the country's 2016 population (National Records of Scotland 2017) suggest that the dependency ratio – the ratio of people aged under sixteen and of pensionable age and over to those of working age – is projected to rise from around 57 dependants per 100 working population in 2016 to 64 per 100 in 2041. This rise is mainly due to the increase in the population of state pension age and over.

It is increasingly recognised that many of those of state pension age are not 'dependent' in the sense of requiring support but can continue to make a valuable contribution to the economy. A number of employers have widened their recruitment processes to take on older staff and the Scottish Government (then the Scottish Executive) recognised this in 2007 in its Strategy for an Ageing Scotland (Scottish Executive 2007); one of its sub-strategies was to improve and increase older people's participation in the labour market. But employers also need to examine their practices in relation to training, promotion and retention of older workers to allow, for example, greater flexible working and flexible retirement (Hollywood *et al.* 2007). Such challenges relating to older workers are reflected in many other Western societies of course, but the issue appears to be particularly acute in Scotland.

A third challenge for the Scottish economy relates to inward migration. Because the country has an ageing population relative to the numbers of those who are economically active, there has been a recognition that Scotland benefits from inward migration with 'new Scots' helping to grow the economy. Within the Scottish Parliament, there has been cross-party support for this policy and, between 2005 and 2008, the country pursued a Fresh Talent Initiative (Cavanagh *et al.* 2008), whereby international students were allowed to stay in Scotland to find work after graduation. There has also been substantial EU migration into Scotland. The EU referendum of 2016 and the UK Government's pursuit of 'Brexit', however, has profound implications for the movement of labour into Scotland in the future and this has led to considerable economic uncertainty at the time of writing, particularly in the tourism and agriculture sectors.

Conclusions

As has become clear in the discussion in this chapter, the Scottish economy has changed dramatically over the last fifty years or so, from one dominated by manufacturing to one dominated by service activities. The structure of the economy as a whole, levels of unemployment and employment activity are not significantly different from the rest of the UK.

Like other Western economies, Scotland suffered from the banking crisis and the resultant recession from 2007 onwards. Indeed, Scotland suffered particularly as a result of the near failure of its two largest financial institutions, Halifax Bank of Scotland and the Royal Bank of Scotland, both headquartered in Edinburgh. While both banks were rescued with UK Government support, there was significant damage done to Scotland's reputation as a financial centre (Kerr and Robinson 2016).

The economy has, to some extent, moved on, although we remain in a period of austerity. But it is important to look forward and explore the prospects for the Scottish economy in the future. Ashcroft (2015) suggests that both the Scottish and UK economies are recovering reasonably well and that the jobs market is buoyant but he points out that it is biased in favour of part-time employment, self-employment and temporary employment and this may not necessarily provide a strong foundation for the future. Scotland's GDP is rising, albeit slowly. Ashcroft is cautious about making predictions about the future of the economy but states that 'there are now reasonably strong indications that the recovery of GDP, jobs and unemployment in Scotland and the UK is set fair' (2015: 20).

Allan (2015) is also relatively optimistic. He notes that, although growth has slowed, nevertheless the Scottish economy grew in 2014 at a faster rate than in any year since the recession began in 2007. Exports were strong, particularly in the oil and chemicals, computing and food and drink sectors. He notes, however, that over 55 per cent of Scotland's international exports go to European markets and this has obviously been affected by the sluggish nature of other

European economies and problems in the Eurozone. Indeed, Scotland is a country whose economy is highly integrated with the rest of the UK and with the wider EU and so is crucially affected by events beyond its borders. The vote to leave the EU in 2016 has only added to this uncertainty.

Challenges remain, not least in relation to those who find it difficult to break into the jobs market in the first place and who may then only secure temporary, part-time or low-skilled work. As elsewhere in Europe, the challenge must be to grow the economy.

This in turn, brings us back to education and the importance of equipping young Scots for their future careers. Although education remains a priority for politicians, there remains an attainment gap, particularly affecting children from deprived backgrounds. Bloomer (2015) believes that one of the problems facing Scottish education is complacency. He points out that there was undoubtedly a time when Scotland was a world leader, contributing to the development of the modern world at the time of the Enlightenment and the Industrial Revolution. However, recent international surveys show Scottish schools as performing above average but not among the best, yet the country has sometimes been unwilling to acknowledge this. He believes that there are signs of a more self-critical stance emerging and notes that the Scottish Government is more obviously displaying a desire 'to create a system that learns, rather than resisting any suggestion of a need to improve' (Bloomer 2015: n.p.).

If this is indeed the case and we are able to meet the challenges of tackling shortcomings in the education system, then this should in turn produce a labour force equipped to take the Scottish economy forward.

Further reading

For some historical background on the Scottish education system, we would suggest George Davie's *The Democratic Intellect: Scotland and Her Universities in the Nineteenth Century* ([1961] 1999). There is also good coverage in Tom Devine's *The Scottish Nation: A Modern History* (2012). A study of the modern Scottish education system is Lindsay Paterson's *Scottish Education in the Twentieth Century* (2003a), while the best overall textbook is Tom Bryce *et al.*'s *Scottish Education* (2018).

For material on the Scottish economy, a useful book is the edited text by Tom Devine *et al.*, *The Transformation of Scotland: The Economy Since 1700* (2005). And there are chapters on both education and the economy in Catriona Macdonald's *Whaur Extremes Meet: Scotland's Twentieth Century* (2009) and in Gerry Hassan and Chris Warhurst's edited *Anatomy of the New Scotland: Power, Influence and Change* (2002).

Scotland

Of course, for up-to-date data on education and the economy, websites are the most useful. See www2.gov.scot/Topics/Statistics/Browse/School-Education for data on school education and see the Scottish Funding Council for data on colleges and universities at www.sfc.ac.uk/publications-statistics/reports-publications/reports-publications.aspx. Data on the economy can be found on the Scottish Government's website at www2.gov.scot/Topics/Statistics/Browse/Economy.

Chapter 6
Scotland and gender

Introduction

An understanding of gender is integral to appreciating how society operates and studies of gender have their roots in the historical invisibility of women in many aspects of society. Studies of the role of women can probably be dated back to the work of Mary Wollstonecraft in the late eighteenth century but are more commonly rooted in the feminist movements of the 1960s. We do not seek here to present an exhaustive study of gender, feminism and related research, but rather we explore how gender issues have affected the way Scotland is portrayed as a country and the position of women within it.

In this chapter, we begin therefore by asking if Scotland may be viewed as a somewhat masculine country and we also examine gender attitudes within a possibly rather 'macho' society. We explore the position of women in relation to employment, education, politics and public life and note how changes in fertility and family life have empowered women and made them more able to play an equal role within society. We look at specific changes that have taken place in Scotland post-devolution and ask if this has led to Scotland adopting approaches that may be different from other parts of the UK or indeed from other Western countries.

A masculine country?

Scotland may perhaps be viewed as a rather masculine country. Many of the symbols associated with Scotland – the Lion Rampant, the Scottish soldier, the Glasgow 'hard man' immortalised in novels like *No Mean City* (McArthur and Long 1935) – appear to be very male and virile symbols, while many of the key figures in Scottish history are male, ranging from William Wallace and Robert Bruce during the Scottish wars of independence, through to more recent literary figures like Robert Burns and Sir Walter Scott, who have had important influences on the nation's sense of identity. Writing about her experiences of moving to Scotland to attend the Glasgow School of Art, Patrick notes that 'Glasgow's culture was represented in the English press … as industrial, working-class, left-wing, sectarian, violent, hard-drinking and its culture, almost entirely represented by men – Billy Connolly, William McIlvanney, Rab C. Nesbitt, Jimmy Reid and Jimmy Boyle' (1997: 7). That is not to say, of course, that women have not played a significant role in the country's history but many of those with whom we are most familiar – for example Mary Queen of Scots and Flora MacDonald – sometimes appear as 'romantic and doomed as participants in history's lost causes' (Breitenbach *et al.* 1998: 45). This focus on women as rather romantic figures in history is criticised by Nenadic (1994), who argues that women's role is poorly served by Scotland's museums that focus overmuch on the male contribution.

The more recent contribution by women may be illustrated by figures such as Elsie Inglis, the Scottish doctor and suffragist, who helped to develop medical services for women in Edinburgh in the 1890s, or the work of the missionary Mary Slessor in Africa around the same time. But we can see how women's contributions were often marginalised by looking at the early years of the twentieth century, including the First World War, the period of early left-wing activism known as 'Red Clydeside' and the Glasgow rent strike of 1915. Briefly, rising interest rates, increases in the costs of repairs and maintenance and a wartime housing shortage led to rent rises being proposed by property owners in 1915. Because many men were away fighting in the war, households were essentially headed by women and so the action was seen as an attack on vulnerable women and children. There was a widespread rent strike within Glasgow headed by women such as Mary Barbour and their actions so alarmed the government that Lloyd George hastily introduced legislation to limit rent increases (Melling 1983). Barbour's role, interestingly, was rather belatedly recognised in March 2018 with the erection of a statue in her memory.

But, although the women's action was supported by the fledgling Independent Labour Party (ILP), a woman's role was still seen essentially as being a subservient one. For example, some of the ILP leaders such as John Maxton and John Wheatley voted and campaigned against the extension of public information and medical advice on contraception, which would have benefited many women at the time (McIvor 1996). Women had played a key role not just in 'keeping the home fires burning' during the war but also in the factories and war industries. Yet, speaking in 1918, Charles Robinson of the Motherwell Trades Council stated that the involvement of women in industry during the war had been 'demoralising', had had 'a depressing effect upon public morality' and that a woman's 'natural sphere is the home' (McIvor 1996: 188).

In fact, such views had already become outdated. The huge male death toll in the First World War meant that some women in the 1920s never married and so a generation of women emerged who worked to support themselves, as teachers or in the arts. Many women lived alone and some local authorities like Glasgow constructed homes for single women (Corporation of Glasgow 1948), while in Edinburgh, Viewpoint Housing Association was established specifically to house women. In industries such as agriculture and fishing, women had always been employed on farms or in occupations like fish gutting and processing (Smout [1986] 2010).

But it is clear that early in the twentieth century Scotland could be seen as a rather 'macho' nation, with women occupying a marginal role. In this chapter, we explore the ways in which the position changed, focusing on issues such as fertility and women's health, education, employment and the nature of both family and public life. We also reflect on attitudes to gender in twenty-first-century Scotland and ask if the 'macho' Scotsman is now dead or dying.

Changes in the position of women

Fertility, family and women's health

Perhaps the most significant – and liberating – development for women has been in regard to taking control of their fertility. Victorian families were large, partly because of a lack of contraception and partly because of high levels of infant mortality; many Victorian children were unlikely to survive infancy. But by 1900, the average family size fell to around six and the trend towards smaller families has continued. In the 2011 census, the average household size in Scotland was 2.19, slightly below the UK average of 2.3. While improvements in child health contributed to greater infant survival rates, there were also massive changes in access to contraception (particularly the pill) from the mid-1960s onwards, while abortion became legal in mainland UK in 1967 (Botting and Dunnell 2000).

There have therefore been a series of demographic changes that have affected the role of women within our society (National Records of Scotland 2018):

- First, women are having fewer children. The Scottish Registrar General identifies the general fertility rate (births per one thousand females aged between fifteen and forty-four) and this has fallen from 99.5 in 1962 to 51.3 in 2017. Another commonly used measure is the total fertility rate, which gives the average number of children women would expect to have across all their childbearing years. For the population to replace itself a total fertility rate of 2.1 is required, but in Scotland in 2017 the rate was 1.47 and the last time that Scotland met the replacement total fertility rate was in 1973. With smaller families, the demands of home and childcare on women are substantially reduced.
- Second, women are having children slightly later in life. The average age of mothers has risen from 27.4 in 1991 to 30.5 in 2017. So women are generally deferring childbearing until their thirties and this provides women with the opportunity to work and develop their careers before starting a family.
- The position is particularly marked within the professional classes. Analyses of births by age group, disaggregated by socio-economic data, shows that the age range when the greatest percentage of those in the higher managerial and professional group have children is between thirty and thirty-four. But for those in the routine and manual occupations, most births occur between ages twenty and twenty-four. So we may deduce that the ability to be in a higher status (and potentially higher paid) occupation leads to decisions to defer childbearing.
- In 2017 over half of births in Scotland (51.1 per cent) were to unmarried couples – although most births were actually registered by both parents, suggesting that most people are in stable relationships. But clearly fewer people feel the need to marry and so women (and men) seem to have chosen to retain a degree of independence. For those who do marry, the average age when this occurs is 34.2 for men and 32.5 for women, so marriage, like childbearing, is being deferred by people into their thirties.
- As levels of health within the population have improved, this has led to increased life expectancy. For those born around 1981, life expectancy was 69.1 for males and 75.3 for females, but for those born around 2015, this

has now increased to 77.1 for males and 81.2 for females. One result of an ageing society is an increase in pensioner households, many consisting of women living alone. In addition, the increased life expectancy for women has now led to an equalisation of retirement and pensionable ages between men and women across the UK. But the position does mean that women are now able to work longer if they choose to do so, or alternatively to enjoy a longer retirement.

- If we examine death rates, there are relatively few differences between men and women. The Scottish death rate is 10.7 deaths per 1,000 population. This is almost its lowest recorded level, but it is still higher than the UK average and higher than many other Western European countries. The leading cause of death in 2017 was heart disease, closely followed by dementia and Alzheimer's disease. More men than women died from heart disease and more women died from dementia and Alzheimer's, but the differences are not significant.

The overall demographic picture is one where women, by marrying later, having children later and having smaller families, are freeing themselves to play a greater role in the workforce. While the availability of childcare remains an issue for working parents, nevertheless it is clear that women are no longer confined to the domestic sphere. We discuss issues relating to female employment next.

Education

Education has long been regarded as one of the core institutions by which Scottish identity has been defined and has been associated 'with a common culture and various supposed qualities of the Scottish character such as individualism, social ambition and a respect for talent above birth' (Moore 2006). Crucial to this view of education was the notion of 'the lad o' pairts' or 'lad of parts', a boy who rose from humble origins to achieve great things, thanks to the benefits of a Scottish education. But the notion was always a masculine one and there was never an equivalent 'lass o' pairts' (Corr 1998). Indeed, Corr argues that this gender bias strikes at the heart of the egalitarian and democratic tradition of Scottish education.

But in the course of the nineteenth century, things did begin to change, partly as a result of compulsory school attendance after 1872 and standardised attainments in basic reading and writing for both sexes. There remained, however, gender differences within the curriculum with, for example, the introduction of compulsory needlework for girls in the 1860s (Moore 2006). Boys were often prohibited from attending such classes, even if they wanted to acquire these skills, for example if they intended to join a family tailoring business. Boys were instead encouraged to study woodwork and metalwork and it was the policy of the Scottish Education Department that boys and girls should be doing quite different practical courses. Women did gradually gain greater access to the academic subjects, including science that was not necessarily seen as a 'male' subject. Ultimately, the Sex Discrimination Act of 1975 and the introduction of a standard national curriculum in 1983 effectively aimed to remove gender disparities in the system (Croxford 2000).

In terms of the current position in Scottish schools, Breitenbach and Wasoff (2007) demonstrate that girls are more likely to stay on beyond the period of compulsory schooling and generally attain better results than boys. Indeed, surveys show that girls consistently outperform boys over a number of years, possibly because they could be considered to take their education more seriously. There still seems to be a gender bias in terms of subjects studied, however, with girls making up a majority of pupils in administration, art, biology, home economics and psychology, and boys dominating in economics, computing, design and physics (Scottish Government 2013c).

It is important also to consider the position of further and higher education in Scotland. The country has four ancient institutions and the country's approach to higher education has tended to be distinct from that of England. The emphasis was always on first principles and the broad, philosophical interpretation of knowledge and this generalist tradition contrasted with the specialism of the two English universities, Oxford and Cambridge. This approach characterised Scotland's intellectual life well into the nineteenth century (Davie [1961] 1999).

Women were able to attend classes at Anderson's Institution in Glasgow (part of what, in the 1960s, became the University of Strathclyde) as early as 1796 and in 1842 a single-sex Queens College opened in Glasgow. The Universities (Scotland) Act of 1889 allowed women to attend universities and all of the four ancient universities began offering degree-level examinations for women (Dick 2008). By the 1920s one-third of all students were women and by 1999 they formed a majority (Moore 2006). Women were particularly significant participants in the art world and in the late nineteenth century were increasingly prominent at the Glasgow School of Art (Burkhauser 2001).

Scottish Government data for 2009–11 showed that more women than men were going on to higher education (55 per cent compared to 45 per cent) with a similar proportion going on to further education colleges (Scottish Government 2013c). By 2017 the Scottish Funding Council identified the figures as being almost 59 per cent compared to 41 per cent respectively. As in schools, there is a gender difference in terms of subjects studied. Women are more likely to study medicine, arts and crafts, health care and social work, while engineering, technology and construction are more popular subjects for men. For those students who graduate, the percentage of graduates in positive destinations has generally been higher for women than men by around 5 per cent, although the gap is narrowing.

Employment

There have been considerable changes over the years in regard to the employment of women with a gradual shift away from the home and into the workplace. In the period from 1901–31, around 35 per cent of women were classed as economically active (McIvor 1996), with marital status being a key factor in whether or not women worked. It was rare for women to work after marriage and in 1911 only 5.3 per cent of the employed female labour force was married (Macdonald 2009). The significant number of working women in the 1920s and 1930s were generally single and this was in part a result of the death toll in the First World War and the lack of men for women to marry. Certainly women had worked during the war but there had been considerable opposition to this continuing, as we discussed in Chapter 5.

There were, however, some regional variations within Scotland. While the heavy industries of shipbuilding and locomotive building on Clydeside were the preserve of men, Dundee, on the other hand, was a city where the workforce was made up overwhelmingly of women as the jute mill owners fought off Indian competition by using low-paid female labour (Smout [1986] 2010). As early as 1901 some 31 per cent of the city's female population was employed in the textile mills, although this began to change after 1945 (Wright 2014). Edinburgh had significant numbers of women employed in administration and the service sector.

We have already referred to many of the factors that have affected women's participation in the workforce, including changes in fertility rates, smaller families and a decision to marry and have children later in life. Women entered the workforce in significant numbers during the Second World War, but many then returned to their homes, partly to have children (the post-war 'baby boom') and partly because they were encouraged to make way for men returning from the forces – although many women were unhappy to do so (Friedan 1963).

But in the longer term, there was a substantial growth in public service and health-related jobs during the 1950s, resulting from the establishment of the National Health Service (NHS) and the welfare state and many of these jobs were taken by women. A large proportion of the jobs were part-time and the proportion of women in part-time employment in Scotland rose from 5 per cent to 41 per cent between 1951 and 1981; in 1981, only 7 per cent of men worked part-time (McIvor 1996).

More recent data indicate that this trend has broadly continued. By 2017, there were over 170,000 more women in the Scottish labour market than in 2000. In 2017 the employment rate for females was 71 per cent and for men 78 per cent. This gap of 7 per cent had narrowed from 10 per cent in 2000 due to a faster rate of increase in female employment (Scottish Government 2018). But, as was the case in earlier decades, much of female employment was part-time. The overall unemployment rate in Scotland at the end of 2018 was 3.5 per cent, lower than the UK average. Female unemployment has tended to be slightly higher than that for men over a long period, and this has been attributed to men moving out of unemployment and inactivity into employment, while women moved out of inactivity into employment and unemployment.

There remain, however, barriers to women's participation in the workforce, as follows:

- First, many women have long been forced to juggle domestic and family responsibilities (Tilly and Scott 1987) and yet many employers are reluctant to provide flexible working arrangements that would assist mothers to enter or re-enter the workplace. The situation has been exacerbated by the growth in zero-hours contracts and the resultant unpredictability of working hours.
- Second, there remains a lack of affordable childcare. This issue has moved up the political agenda in Scotland and the Children and Young People (Scotland) Act 2014 extended the amount of free early education for three- and four-year-olds from 475 to 600 hours per year. But for younger children childcare is often unaffordable or unavailable (especially in rural areas or at certain times of the year). Citizens Advice Scotland (2014) points out that childcare is more expensive in Scotland – and the UK – than in many other European countries.

- Third, there remain significant pay gaps in terms of male and female earnings. The Scottish Government (2016a) identified this gap for full-time workers as 7.3 per cent, a figure that has remained fairly constant for at least six years. There has, however, been a long-term narrowing of the gap, which in 1997 stood at 18.4 per cent. The pay gap is almost non-existent in the public sector but is at its highest in the professional, financial and insurance sectors.
- There is also a significant occupational segregation with women continuing to be the majority of those working in health and social work (77 per cent) and education (75 per cent), while men dominate in construction (93 per cent), transport (76 per cent) and manufacturing (75 per cent). This means that, in certain industries, the absence of significant numbers of women can result in the operation of a 'glass ceiling', preventing women from gaining senior and managerial positions (Goodman *et al.* 2003).

We should note, however, that the gendered patterns of employment are broadly the same in Scotland as in other parts of the UK.

Family life

As we have already discussed, women were frequently regarded as the keepers of the domestic sphere and it was rare for women to go 'out' to work in the early twentieth century. But that is not to say that women did not work. Many worked on family farms, for example, and also had an important role in industries like fishing. There was also a considerable amount of home working and in the Highlands and Islands many women were weavers and knitters (Gordon 2006). Women were also often responsible for the family budget and the necessary task of making ends meet.

But there is little doubt that women took the lead role in housework, childcare and other forms of family caring – and often continue to do so. Housework, simply, is regarded as essentially 'women's work' (Brines 1994) and so women are often in the position of doing both paid and domestic work and having to juggle the two. In this respect, Scotland is probably no different from many other societies.

This view of women's role has been reflected in the design of many of our homes. Throughout the many government reports on housing design, the kitchen was always located at the rear of the house, for example, with women as the keepers of this domestic environment; the house became synonymous with the nuclear family unit. As more women entered paid employment, however, kitchens became smaller, although Munro and Madigan do not regard this as being to women's advantage:

> The design of the small fitted kitchen coincided with an increase in women's paid employment. Design lends credence to the confidence trick that implies that modern housework can be done 'at the flick of a switch', so that women can be expected to take on paid employment, without relinquishing any domestic commitments. Perhaps one of the key differences in women's and men's attitudes to housing is that for most women, the house remains a significant place of work. Most women still feel responsible for the tidiness and cleanliness of the house. (1989: 58)

Such an argument is supported by the work of Oakley (1974), who found that women spent an average of 77 hours per week on housework, while Bryson (2007) has argued that women do significantly more unpaid work than men, and that men have not matched women's increased time in employment with an equivalent contribution in the home. We explore the attitudes of Scots to women's role in more detail in the next section.

Women in public life

Individuals participate in public life in a number of ways, most obviously perhaps as political representatives or within government bodies that make public policy, but also in a range of public and voluntary sector organisations, which influence society in a number of different ways. We intend to focus on Scottish politics, on appointments to public sector bodies and also on the church that has traditionally played a key role within Scottish society.

Politics

Scottish women were heavily involved in a number of political campaigns, for example the Glasgow rent strike, to which we have referred (Melling 1983), and in the struggle for women's suffrage. The Edinburgh National Society for Women's Suffrage, founded in 1867, was one of the first in Britain (Innes and Rendall 2006). As women became more politically involved, various women's branches of the mainstream political parties were established, including the Women's Liberal Federation, the Scottish branch of the Primrose League and the first Scottish branch of the Women's Labour League, all in the late nineteenth and early twentieth centuries.

Following the first extension of the franchise to women in 1918, the first Scottish woman MP was the Duchess of Atholl, elected for Kinross and West Perthshire in 1923. She was described as an 'accidental trailblazer', as she had actually opposed women's suffrage, although she did have a record in public service (Innes and Rendall 2006). The first Scottish Labour MP was Jennie Lee, elected for North Lanark in 1929.

Women MPs were relatively few in number for many years, although the rise in support for the SNP from the late 1960s onwards led to the election of some high-profile and articulate women, such as Winnie Ewing and Margo MacDonald. The establishment of the Scottish Parliament in 1999 has, however, led to a significant increase in the number of women parliamentarians and in the 1999 elections 48 women were elected to Holyrood out of 129 Members of the Scottish Parliament (MSPs) (37.2 per cent). Although this percentage is a long way short of a gender balance, it nevertheless demonstrated that female representation could be significantly enhanced by gender quotas (in the case of the Labour Party) and later, in the case of the SNP, by the introduction of all-women shortlists in constituencies where the sitting member was standing down. In the Holyrood elections of 2016, however, the number of female MSPs elected was forty-five (34.9 per cent), identical to the position in the 2011 election. In the main, this was due to a strong performance by the Scottish Conservatives who, although led by a woman, elected only six female MSPs out of thirty-one.

In 2014 Scotland gained its first female first minister, Nicola Sturgeon, the leader of the SNP, and she immediately demonstrated a commitment to gender equality by announcing a cabinet with equal numbers of men and women; she continued this practice after her re-election as first minister in 2016. The current leader of the Scottish Conservatives is a woman, Ruth Davidson, and the Scottish Labour Party has had three female leaders during the period of devolution – Wendy Alexander, Johann Lamont and Kezia Dugdale.

In the context of the debate on equality, it is also of interest that Davidson, Dugdale and the co-convener of the Scottish Green Party – Patrick Harvie – are all gay. Scotland has, incidentally, a strong record in relation to lesbian, gay, bisexual and transgender (LGBT) rights. The country abolished 'Section 28' (which banned the teaching of homosexuality in schools) in 2000, three years before England and Wales, and in 2014 legislated for same-sex marriages in the Marriage and Civil Partnerships (Scotland) Act. In 2018, the Scottish Parliament passed the Historical Sexual Offences (Pardons and Disregards)

Act, a law that issued a formal pardon to men, living and dead, convicted of having consensual sex with other men before it was decriminalised.

While the Scottish Parliament has helped to increase female representation, the picture elsewhere was, for many years, less favourable. At the 2015 general election, the strong performance of the SNP in taking fifty-six out of Scotland's fifty-nine seats, led to twenty female MPs (34 per cent) being elected. But in the 2017 general election, the overall number fell to seventeen (29 per cent). As at Holyrood, this was the result of a strong Conservative performance; they elected thirteen MPs to Westminster but only one of whom was a woman. At the time of writing, just over 24 per cent of local councillors are women. This last figure represents a new high in women's representation in local government (Kenny and Mackay 2012) but may not necessarily be seen as a significant breakthrough.

In the 2019 European Parliamentary elections, Scotland elected three female MEPs out of six – Aileen McLeod (SNP), Sheila Ritchie (Liberal Democrat) and Nosheena Mobarik (Conservative). Of course, Brexit will mean that all will lose their seats.

Public bodies

Beyond party politics, women are also under-represented in public bodies. Such bodies have been required to produce equality schemes, but this does not appear to have had major impacts on the composition of the boards of such bodies. In 2011–12, a total of 33 per cent of applicants for public appointments in Scotland were female and 34 per cent of actual appointments were female (Scottish Government 2013c). More recent government statistics show that the proportion of female appointments reached 39 per cent in 2012–13, although the proportion of women who were board chairs was only 21 per cent (Scottish Government 2014b).

Hassan (2014) has commented on the fact that the pressure to increase women's participation in the Scottish Parliament has not filtered down to other public bodies. He draws attention in particular to the Scottish media and the frequent failure to use female presenters and commentators. Riddoch (2015) also draws attention to the absence of women from the boards of many public bodies, suggesting that this may change, not least as a result of the experience of the 2014 independence referendum, where groups like Women for Independence played such a high-profile role.

In 2018, the Scottish Government passed the Gender Representation on Public Boards (Scotland) Act, which aims to redress gender imbalances on the boards of public bodies. This would not, however, have any impact on the boards of private sector companies that are overwhelmingly male dominated.

Religion

We look at the role of women within the church in Scotland because the Church of Scotland in particular has played a key role in maintaining Scottish identity in the period after the Union of 1707. Religion has therefore been a significant part of Scottish life and it has sometimes been argued that more people still attend church services on a Sunday than football matches on a Saturday (Brown 2014).

But despite the core importance of religion in Scottish life, women have traditionally played a rather marginal role. In some respects, this may hark back to the Reformation itself and the very establishment of the Church of Scotland. Certainly John Knox tended to demonise women (Felch 1995), and was at the centre of a religious struggle with Mary Queen of Scots over the primacy of Presbyterianism versus Catholicism. In 1558, he published his famous *First Blast of the Trumpet Against the Monstrous Regiment of Women.*

Yet, although the Church of Scotland remained a very patriarchal organisation over the years, the majority of churchgoers were women and from 1888 women were ordained as deaconesses and allowed to preach. In 1969, the first woman minister was appointed and in 2004 the first female moderator of the General Assembly; there have now been four female moderators. So, at a time when the Church of England has only relatively recently permitted women to become bishops and when the Roman Catholic Church remains completely patriarchal, the Church of Scotland appears to have made some significant moves towards greater gender equality.

Attitudes to gender issues: the death of the 'macho' Scotsman?

As we have already noted, Scotland is often viewed as a somewhat 'macho' society and it has often been assumed that attitudes towards gender are more conservative in Scotland than elsewhere. Research suggests, however, that this position has been changing over the years. MacInnes (1998) first drew attention to these changes with his analysis of data on social attitudes across a number of European states and his findings can be summarised as follows:

- The notion that men should be regarded as the main 'breadwinner' of the family had almost entirely disappeared and Scotland was similar to the rest of Europe in this respect.
- Scots no longer believed in the ideal of the 'home-centred' female and did not believe that women's employment had adverse effects on the family.
- Scots, in common with those in other countries, still believed in marriage but also in divorce.

MacInnes (1998) concluded that Scots were not particularly conservative and, if anything, were slightly more egalitarian than other countries, at least in the sense that support for the idea of different roles for men and women was low. But attitudes to gender were broadly in line with other European countries. MacInnes does, however, add the caveat that these gender attitudes do not necessarily translate into changes in behaviour.

Differences in attitude and behaviour were discernible in terms of age and position in the life cycle, predominantly as a result of the social and economic changes affecting women more widely. Young Scottish men were still – to a certain extent – able to enjoy certain advantages and privileges over women, but nothing like the extent to which this had been true for earlier generations. So, 'the macho Scotsman, like his counterparts across Europe, is not yet a dying breed, but he is trapped in the quicksand of social and economic change' (MacInnes 1998: 121).

MacInnes subsequently revisited his research, using later data from the Scottish Social Attitudes Survey and found that, once again, Scottish gender attitudes were broadly in line with those elsewhere, and there was a commitment to gender equality. There had, however, been very limited change in individual behaviour. Only around one in twenty respondents disagreed with the idea that men should play a larger role in housework and childcare, but the reality fell short of this. So, although men and women in Scotland (and elsewhere in the UK) agree with the idea of gender equality, they often manage to avoid its implication in their everyday lives (MacInnes 2005: 111)

In another study, Tinklin *et al.* (2005) undertook a survey of almost two hundred young males and females in Scotland and explored attitudes to gender roles within work, the family and wider society. They found that young people held modern rather than traditional views of gender roles and there was a great deal of unanimity across the responses. Tinklin *et al.* believed that young people 'had really "got" the equal opportunities message', although their views were often tempered by the inequalities that they saw around them. Young women in particular were aware of how difficult it might be for them to successfully combine work and family roles.

The evidence would suggest that Scotland, like other Western countries, is adopting a more modern approach to gender roles, although inequalities in society nevertheless still remain.

Impact of devolution

While we have explored gender roles and attitudes to gender issues in Scotland, one of the difficulties in teasing out the specifically Scottish experience is the fact that the legislation affecting equal opportunities is reserved to Westminster. So the Scottish Parliament is able to have only limited impact in pursuing greater gender equality. Nevertheless, there are a number of areas where things have changed since devolution and we consider them here.

- First, and as we have already discussed above, there has been a conscious effort to increase levels of female representation in the Scottish Parliament. Prior to devolution, a range of campaigning groups including Engender, the Scottish Trades Union Congress (STUC) and the Woman's Claim of Right argued strongly for 50:50 representation and have continued to argue this case (Hassan 2014). The proportionality of the Scottish electoral system has also, arguably, increased women's chances of being elected (Stirbu 2011).
- Second, the Scotland Act 1998, which established the Scottish Parliament, required all proposed Scottish legislation to be 'equality proofed' and compliant with the European Convention on Human Rights. This 'equality proofing' has, in practice, not been a stand-alone process but continued throughout the passing of legislation. This has made the Parliamentary process at Holyrood different to that at Westminster but closer to many other European countries (Mackay and Bilton 2001).
- One of the earliest actions of the Scottish Government in 2000 was the repeal of Section 2A of the 1986 Local Government Act (Section 28 in England), which expressly prohibited the 'promotion' of homosexuality and was widely seen as an attack on gay men and women (Rahman 2004).

The repeal was often controversial and there was a 'Keep the Clause' campaign pursued by various individuals and church groups; the government minister responsible for piloting the legislation, Wendy Alexander, received a great deal of abuse. But the repeal was an important marker in the promotion of greater equality within Scotland. It was not repealed in the rest of the UK until 2003.

- The Scottish Parliament has made the tackling of domestic abuse a key priority. The origins for this perhaps lie with the Zero Tolerance Campaign that was established by Edinburgh Council's Women's Committee in 1992 (Mackay 1996) and there is research (McCarry 2010) that demonstrates that some young Scottish men still believe that a degree of violence towards women is acceptable. Shortly after the establishment of the Scottish Parliament, the then Scottish Executive set up a national strategy to tackle domestic abuse in 2003 (Scottish Executive 2003) and there have been a series of monitoring reports since then. A Domestic Abuse (Scotland) Act was passed in 2011, amending the law in relation to harassment as a form of abuse and extending provisions for legal aid.
- In common with the UK Parliament, the Scottish Parliament has legislated for civil partnerships and subsequently, same-sex marriages. The Marriage and Civil Partnership (Scotland) Act was passed in 2014. At the time of writing, the Scottish Government has signalled its intention to extend the availability of civil partnerships to all couples.
- There have been other pieces of specifically Scottish legislation that have benefited women. A good example is the introduction of free personal care for the elderly, first recommended by the Sutherland Report on Long-Term Care for Older People and enacted through the Community Care and Health (Scotland) Act of 2002 (Bowes and Bell 2007). The policy has aided women, partly as many older women lack the resources to pay for care themselves and partly because many informal carers are themselves women.

Despite the progress made in gender issues within the Scottish Parliament, equality remains reserved to Westminster and this will constrain the actions that the Scottish Parliament can take in this area. The Equality and Human Rights Commission operates across the UK, although there is a Scotland Committee and a Scottish Commissioner, Dr Lesley Sawers. This reflects the separate legislative system in Scotland and the need for variations in Commission research and guidance.

Conclusions

In summary, we can see clearly that historically Scotland has been a rather masculine country with women often playing marginalised roles and with few significant female historical figures. MacInnes (1998, 2005) has shown us clearly that the 'macho' Scotsman was for some time alive and well. But it is clear that things are changing.

We have shown how changes in women's fertility and health have led to significant demographic changes within the country and that in employment, education and public life the position of women has improved substantially. In some areas, this has been assisted by the process of devolution and the partial success of the Scottish Parliament in bringing more women into politics. The requirement for Parliament to 'equality-proof' its legislation has also led to issues of gender, ethnicity and other 'equality issues' gaining a greater prominence than might perhaps otherwise be the case.

Scotland, like many other Western countries, still has some way to go before greater gender equality can be achieved. Women are particularly under-represented in business and on both public and private sector boards, although there appears to be a commitment to address this issue in the near future.

Further reading

There are numerous books on the wider issues of gender – almost too many to mention. But two useful texts are Mary Evans and Carolyn Williams's *Gender: The Key Concepts* (2012) and Raewyn Connell's *Gender in World Perspective* (2009).

The best book on the gendered aspects of Scottish history is *Gender in Scottish History Since 1700* (2006), edited by Lynn Abrams *et al.* Esther Breitenbach's work is also highly relevant, for example, her report with Fran Wasoff for the Scottish Executive, *A Gender Audit of Statistics: Comparing the Position of Women and Men in Scotland* (2007), and her co-authored paper in *The Feminist Review*, 'Understanding Women in Scotland' (1998). In 2018, Edinburgh University Press published the comprehensive volume *The New Biographical Dictionary of Scottish Women*, edited by Elizabeth Ewan *et al.*

John MacInnes's papers on the 'macho' Scotsman are interesting and enjoyable reading. See 'The Myth of the Macho Scotsman: Attitudes to Gender, Work and the Family in the UK, Ireland and Europe' in *Scottish Affairs* (1998).

Importantly, the Scottish Government itself has published some useful reports on gender equality. See *Scottish Government Equality Outcomes: Gender: Evidence Review* (2013a), and *Women on Board: Quality Through Diversity* (2014b).

Chapter 7
'Ethnic' Scotland

Introduction

Scotland is often (and rightly) thought of as a country characterised by emigration and there is a significant Scottish diaspora, which we discuss in Chapter 10. But there is also a long history of immigration to Scotland, most notably by Irish families in the nineteenth century, but including large numbers of migrants from elsewhere in Europe and the Commonwealth. After the Second World War inward migration increased with significant movement from South Asia into the UK and in more recent times Glasgow has been a host city for large numbers of refugees and asylum seekers.

So the ethnic geography of the country has changed over the years and Scotland has become a more diverse and multicultural society. In this chapter, we begin by examining the 2011 census data to illustrate the various identities and ethnicities within the country. We then seek to explain how this pattern has evolved, by describing the various migrant groups who have made their home in Scotland, the changes that have taken place in recent years and we subsequently explore the concept of multiculturalism in Scotland, together with ongoing issues of racism and sectarianism.

Nationality and ethnicity in the 2011 census

Table 7.1 illustrates the population of Scotland, disaggregated by ethnic group. The first point to note is that the overall population of the country has increased. In part, this is due to natural increase, with births exceeding deaths, but the largest contributor to population growth has been increased inward migration; the Registrar General estimates that more people enter Scotland

Table 7.1 Ethnic groups in Scotland 2001 and 2011

Group	2001		2011		Change 2001–11 (000s)
	Number (000s)	%	Number (000s)	%	
White Scottish	4,459	86.1	4,446	84	−13
Other white British	374	7.4	417	7.9	+43
Irish	49	1.0	54	1.0	+5
Other white	78	1.5	167	3.2	+89
Mixed	13	0.3	20	0.4	+7
Pakistani	32	0.6	49	0.9	+18
Indian	15	0.3	33	0.6	+18
Chinese	16	0.3	34	0.6	+17
Other Asian	8	0.2	25	0.5	+17
Black (incl. African, Caribbean)	8	0.2	36	0.7	+28
Other	10	0.2	14	0.3	+4
Total	**5,062**	**100**	**5,295**	**100**	**+233**

Note: There are occasional rounding errors in the totals.
Source: National Records of Scotland (2013).

than leave it, resulting in a net increase due to migration in the year to mid-2018 of almost 21,000 (National Records of Scotland 2019).

There are three groups whose numbers have increased significantly between the censuses. The first is 'other white British' and this appears to represent a significant movement of people from elsewhere in the UK (particularly from England) moving to Scotland. Much of this will be labour migration, with individuals simply moving within the UK for job-related reasons or perhaps establishing businesses north of the border, while some people move to Scotland in later life, viewing the country as an attractive location in which to retire (Short and Stockdale 1999).

Indeed, English people are, strictly speaking, Scotland's largest minority – although they may not view themselves as such, not least because of England's dominant position within the UK as a whole and because such migration takes place within the overarching UK state. But there have been some instances of anti-English hostility in the past, for example where individuals are seen to have purchased holiday homes in rural areas at the expense of local people (Jedrej and Nuttall 1996; Watson 2003). Within the cities, the proportion of 'other white British' is highest in Edinburgh at 12 per cent.

The second, and most significant group in terms of increased migration is 'other white' and this may be explained almost entirely by movement from within the EU, and particularly from eastern Europe. Following the enlargement of the EU in 2004 to include many countries from the former Soviet bloc, there was significant migration of (initially mainly male) workers to Western European countries to seek work. The UK imposed few limits on migration from these 'accession' countries and in the first four years after enlargement, almost nine hundred thousand workers entered the UK. Poland, as the largest accession country, sent the largest number of workers and many moved to Scotland where they have been employed both within the public sector as drivers, care workers, teachers and health professionals and in the private sector in hospitality and catering, agriculture, manufacturing and food processing (Pollard *et al.* 2008). Although the numbers gradually tailed off and indeed many Poles later returned to their home country, significant numbers settled in the UK and have become integrated into the population as a whole (Sim *et al.* 2009). In Scotland in 2011 there were 61,000 Poles and they now represent a larger population grouping than the Irish. For some people, this significant in-migration was viewed as somehow threatening and there is no doubt that concerns about migration played a major part in the UK's decision to leave the EU in the 2016 referendum. Currently, EU nationals living in the UK can apply for 'settled status' to enable them to continue living in the UK after Brexit. It is not clear how regulations may change in the future.

The third grouping that has expanded is the 'black' group. In 2001, this was enumerated as a single group, but in 2011, distinctions were made between African and Caribbean groups, as well as those identifying as 'black British' or 'black Scottish'. In fact, the largest subgroup within the 'black' category was the African grouping, with 29,000 people. The growth here is almost entirely due to the large numbers of asylum seekers from African countries who have settled – mainly in greater Glasgow – and we discuss the experiences of asylum seekers and refugees later in this chapter.

But, while the 2011 census provides us with a snapshot of the various ethnic groups that make up Scotland today, it is increasingly out of date and cannot in any case give us the whole picture of a multinational and multicultural country that has evolved over centuries. We therefore move on to describe some of the historical patterns of migration and the groups who help to make up current Scottish society.

Patterns of immigration up to the 1930s

Undoubtedly the largest influx of migrants to Scotland occurred during the nineteenth century with the movement of Irish families following the potato famine. Some seasonal migration had taken place for many years with Irish workers seeking employment in agriculture, picking fruit and potatoes (MacRaild 2011), and this continued into the twentieth century. As migrant workers, they often lived in appalling conditions, a situation highlighted in 1937 when ten workers died in a fire in a farm bothy in Kirkintilloch (Holmes 2002), a tragedy that led to new legislation regarding the accommodation of agricultural workers.

Permanent migration resulted in around a quarter of a million Irish-born migrants living in Scotland by the 1850s, representing 7.2 per cent of the total population (Devine 1999). Irish migrants sought work and settled in the main industrial areas and were often employed to do work that Scots were less keen to do. The Irish were more likely to be employed in ironstone mining than coal mining, for example, as the former was a more arduous and unattractive job (Miles 1982). And in the textile industry, Irish people tended to gravitate towards Glasgow as the nineteenth-century centre for plain and cheaper cotton weaving, rather than to Paisley with its more skilled production, involving working with muslin, silk and thread.

Irish immigration to Scotland has often been associated with the Roman Catholic Church and issues of religious sectarianism (which we explore later in the chapter), but it is important to note that migrants to Scotland were from both Catholic and Protestant communities. Because migrant labour tended to be recruited by word of mouth, this led to some religious concentrations, for example in mining communities like Croy (Catholic) and Larkhall (Protestant). But Catholics sometimes found their employment opportunities blocked by blatant sectarianism. Belfast shipbuilders Harland and Wolff, for example, opened a yard at Govan on the Clyde in 1912, employing skilled Protestant workers. Their presence helped sharpen the Protestant identity of the local football club, Rangers, who did not sign their first Catholic player until 1989 (Bruce *et al.* 2004).

Most migrants from Ireland, however, were Roman Catholic and the Irish presence in Scotland may be seen in the growth in the numbers of Catholic churches (with Glasgow's St Andrew's cathedral being opened in 1816), with the establishment of Catholic schools and a strong voluntary sector including bodies like the St Vincent de Paul Society. Celtic Football Club was established in Glasgow's east end in 1887 partly to raise funds for the poor of the area and partly as a vehicle to bring together both Scottish and Irish communities in the city (Bruce *et al.* 2004).

The presence of two different Irish communities in Scotland has led to a continued problem of sectarianism, a somewhat ironic situation given that the 2011 census indicates that 37 per cent of Scots identified with no religion at all, and indeed all denominations have declining membership. But the Protestant Irish community in Scotland still marks the Battle of the Boyne in July of each year with Orange Lodge marches and there is ongoing rivalry on the football field between Rangers and Celtic, the two largest clubs. Such rivalry may sometimes be seen, in Freud's words, as the narcissism of minor differences, as there is now little measurable difference between the Protestant and Catholic populations in terms of participation in civic society or in educational attainment (Paterson and Iannelli 2006), although there is still some debate about employment experiences (Walls and Williams 2003; Battu 2005; Bruce *et al.* 2005). The influx of European football players means that the two large Glasgow clubs now employ players with a range of religious affiliations.

Sectarianism remains a problem, however (Devine 2000), and in 2002, the then First Minister Jack McConnell held a series of meetings with the main football clubs to try and confront it. The situation had been highlighted by the murder of a Celtic fan in Glasgow in 1995, which had led to the establishment of an anti-sectarian campaigning group, Nil by Mouth (Kelly 2003). The problem continued, however, and in 2012 the Scottish Parliament legislated against sectarian behaviour and threatening communications, following the sending of letter bombs to Neil Lennon, the then Celtic manager. Research from the Scottish Social Attitudes Survey confirms that most Scots believe that football rivalry is the main cause of sectarian tension (Hinchliffe *et al.* 2015).

In terms of identity, the majority of Irish migrants to Scotland appear to have been fully integrated into Scottish society and in 2011, those identifying as Irish comprised only 54,000 or 1 per cent of the total Scottish population. That is not to say, of course, that others do not have a strong awareness of an Irish background and some Scots-born footballers (for example Ray Houghton and Aiden McGeady) have opted to represent the Republic of Ireland rather than Scotland. But for the majority of those descended from Irish migrants, it would not appear to be the most significant element in their sense of identity.

Although on a much smaller scale to Irish migration, there was significant historical movement from several European countries into Scotland. One group of early migrants were the Italians, numbering around four thousand by 1901; as a result of chain migration, the wider Italian ethnic presence in Scotland was estimated as thirty thousand by the start of the twenty-first century (Macdonald 2009). Most Italian families moved from the Barga and Lucca areas of Tuscany and the majority were employed in the catering industry, many with their own businesses (Pieri 2005).

In contrast, Lithuanian immigrants in Scotland worked as waged labour and by 1914 there were around eight thousand Lithuanians in the industrial heartlands of Scotland. The largest concentrations were in Lanarkshire (Rodgers 1980) and they had developed shops, social clubs and their own newspaper. Numbers dwindled during the interwar years but there were a number of migrants displaced after the Second World War from Lithuania who settled in North Lanarkshire and numbers rose slightly (Millar 2005). There appears to be relatively little migration at present from Lithuania and so the community remains small. There is still, however, a Lithuanian social club, based in Bellshill.

There was a significant migration of Poles to Scotland during the Second World War, mostly soldiers fighting with the Allies. After the war, Poland became Communist controlled and many Poles opted to stay in Scotland, rather than return home. According to the 1951 census, there were 10,600 persons resident in Scotland but born in Poland and they became the basis for a Polish community, with the introduction of Polish masses at certain Roman Catholic churches and the establishment of Polish clubs (Ziarski-Kernberg 2005).

Finally, events in Europe in the interwar period led to an increase in Jewish migration to Scotland and by 1939, there were almost twenty thousand Jews in the country, of whom around fifteen thousand were in greater Glasgow (Collins 2008). Initially, there was a concentration in furniture and clothing manufacturing, but after 1945 the economic base of the community widened considerably. The population has declined markedly since the war, however, with little new inward migration and the 2011 census shows a Jewish population in the country of about six thousand (0.1 per cent). It has become increasingly suburbanised and concentrated in the East Renfrewshire suburbs to the south of Glasgow.

From elsewhere in the world, there had been some migration from South Asia in the nineteenth century, often reflecting trade and shipping routes. The East India Company had developed the jute trade in the 1830s, with jute being shipped from India to the power looms of Dundee (Audrey 2000). The Glasgow-based Anchor Line began sailing to Bombay and Calcutta (now Mumbai and Kolkata) following the opening of the Suez Canal and crews were often recruited in India, staying in Glasgow between voyages (McLellan 1956). This gradually translated into permanent settlement, although numbers were relatively small.

Glasgow and Clydeside had also been beneficiaries of the slave trade, particularly in the eighteenth century. Part of the city's wealth was based on tobacco imported from the plantations in Virginia, while Greenock was a major centre of sugar refining. Glasgow merchants sometimes kept slaves and so their presence in the city was not uncommon (Mullen 2009). The city's role in this trade with the Americas is commemorated in many street names such as Virginia Street and Jamaica Street, but is only now being more widely recognised as a shameful period in the city's history.

Much more recently, there was significant demand for industrial labour during the First World War and a number of steel plants in Lanarkshire recruited Asian workers, although not without trade union hostility as the newcomers were regarded as undercutting local wage levels (Dunlop and Miles 1990). Unsurprisingly, after the war, some individuals opted to become self-employed to avoid problems in the workplace, often becoming peddlers, hawkers and shopkeepers.

Another source of early Asian settlement was the university sector, with overseas students often moving to Scotland to study medicine. In 1883, the Edinburgh Indian Association was founded to meet the needs of Indian students and by the turn of the century had over two hundred members (Maan 1992).

So, although there had been considerable migration into Scotland before 1945, it had come from a relatively small number of areas, notably Ireland, a few European countries and South Asia. As a result, Scotland after the Second World War was overwhelmingly white. No specific data on ethnicity were collected in the 1951 census but 98.1 per cent of the Scottish population at that time was born in either the UK or the Irish Republic and this perhaps provides some indication of the absence of migrants from other parts of the world.

Post-war immigration

The most significant growth in the minority ethnic population within the UK came after the Second World War. In England, large numbers of West Indian families sailed to London on ships like the *Empire Windrush* (Phillips and Phillips 2009; Olusoga 2016) but in Scotland, most of the migrants were from Asia.

As well as reflecting previous trade links, it also reflected an expansion in the Scottish economy and severe labour shortages in some of the more unskilled occupations. South Asians filled many jobs that were relatively menial (Maan 1992), although some worked in the transport industry and Glasgow City Council had actively recruited in Punjab for individuals to work on the city's trams and buses as drivers and conductors (Edward 1993). In Dundee, a substantial number of Asian workers found employment in the city's jute mills. The newly established NHS also offered important opportunities for doctors and nurses recruited from overseas.

Miles (1982) has suggested that many minority ethnic workers found employment in declining industries and this subordinate position within the workforce helps to explain their sometimes marginalised position within society. There was also some evidence that younger people from the minority groups were finding it difficult to access appropriate employment. But, as was the case in the interwar period, many minority ethnic workers have moved into self-employment, often in the retailing and catering sectors and Audrey (2000) suggests that this indicates a population adopting a strategy of self-sufficiency and self-help, which will ultimately benefit their descendants. By the 2001 census, the proportion of Pakistanis who were self-employed was 32 per cent, more than three times the figure for white Scots (10 per cent).

The 2001 census highlighted a number of ways in which the Scottish black and minority ethnic (BME) population was disadvantaged:

- As well as experiencing difficulties in accessing some areas of employment, there were high levels of unemployment. At the time, 6 per cent of the total economically active population was unemployed but this rose to 36 per cent among the Pakistanis. Young Pakistanis in particular were likely to be unemployed.
- In housing terms, there was considerable overcrowding. This was a reflection of a larger household size within the BME groups. Around 12 per cent of white Scots were living in overcrowded conditions, as defined by the Scottish Registrar General's occupancy ratings. The figure rose to 31 per cent for both the Pakistanis and Bangladeshis.
- Partly perhaps because social rented housing was relatively small and often located in low-demand peripheral estates, most BME households had opted to live in the private sector in the inner city. These areas were usually well located for places of worship, specialist shops and minority ethnic

> voluntary organisations, but many of these houses (especially those rented from a private landlord) were in poor condition (Bowes *et al.* 1997). Home ownership rates were highest among the Pakistani and Indian communities (75 per cent and 71 per cent respectively) compared with a Scottish average of 67 per cent. It should be noted, however, that, within the private sector, there is now some movement away from inner cities and towards the suburbs (Houston 2010).

A major problem facing these 'visible' minorities has been racial harassment and there have been a number of studies of this. Some writers have highlighted a reluctance on the part of Scots to acknowledge that racism is a significant problem north of the border (Armstrong 1989) and a belief that it is more of a problem in places like London, where there are more significant numbers of visible minorities. Indeed, de Lima (2005) argues that racism in Scotland has actually been portrayed as an essentially English problem.

This view has, however, been challenged by Cant and Kelly (1995) and there is clear evidence of racist incidents within Scotland, ranging from the experiences of Asian council tenants in Glasgow (Bowes *et al.* 1990b) to 'everyday' racism in schools and places of employment (Hopkins 2004). More recently, since the events of 9/11 and following a rise in reported incidents of Muslim extremism, there appears to be increased evidence of Islamophobia (Bonino 2015). So racism is clearly an everyday experience for many people in Scotland, as it is for many living elsewhere in the UK.

But although it is clear that the BME population in Scotland has experienced discrimination and disadvantage, the population is generally regarded as settled and some inner-city areas like Govanhill in Glasgow have become noticeably more multicultural, with a range of organisations, shops and places of worship catering for the different ethnic groups (Audrey 2000). This early distribution of the BME population therefore reflects the prevailing social, economic and political conditions at the time, although cultural factors were also important (Phillips 1998). Phillips (1998) describes how the presence of established BME communities attracted other households with the same ethnic background, and so early patterns of settlement remained remarkably stable. Over time, there remained inequalities in housing and employment but there were some measurable spatial changes, with socio-economic advancement leading to the growth of a black middle class and moves by the BME population into the suburbs. These trends were identified in Glasgow by Bowes *et al.* (1990a), who noted that levels of segregation as measured by indices of dissimilarity had reduced. That said, Stillwell and Phillips (2006) suggest that, even where the BME population has suburbanised, there is still relatively little 'ethnic mixing' and this mirrors the position in many other British cities where there are issues of social segregation, housing and employment inequalities and harassment (Ratcliffe 2004). We will explore these issues further when we discuss integration and multiculturalism later in the chapter.

The most recent large-scale immigration has come from Eastern Europe following EU expansion in 2004, as we have already noted. Research for the Scottish Government by Rolfe and Metcalf (2009) concluded that the impact of such migrants had been generally beneficial in terms of their contribution to the country's economy, while they were not making significant demands on public services such as health, social care, education and housing. That said, many workers were living in poor quality accommodation, often unaware of their employment rights and poorly integrated into society.

At the time, there was no clear evidence regarding migrants' long-term intentions to stay in Scotland. Some broader UK-wide research, however, does seem to indicate that a proportion of the migrant population will remain in the UK (Spencer *et al.* 2007; Parutis 2014) and so one would expect the position to be similar north of the border. Certainly the large number of Polish people enumerated in Scotland in the 2011 census would appear to confirm this.

Refugees and asylum seekers

Until the 1990s, the UK had no domestic asylum legislation and most refugees arrived through organised programmes with their status already established. Examples include Vietnamese 'boat people' in the 1970s and in the 1990s refugees from Bosnia and Kosovo (Sales 2007), some of whom were settled in Scotland. But many of these dispersed groupings proved too small to be sustainable and there was rapid secondary migration, mainly to London (Robinson and Hale 1989).

Significant changes, however, were introduced in the 1999 Asylum and Immigration Act, which established the National Asylum Support System (NASS) and introduced compulsory dispersal for those needing accommodation, essentially to locations outside south-east England. The rationale was to 'spread the burden' and relieve pressures on the south-east, with housing availability being a key driver in the selection of dispersal locations. Much of this housing was low demand, however, and there was a strong association between dispersal locations and social deprivation (Hynes 2006).

By March 2003, a total of 92,685 asylum seekers were being supported by NASS (Gill and Crawley 2003); numbers later fell to 20,860 in 2013. In 2003, only 7.2 per cent of those accommodated by NASS were living in south-east England; most had been dispersed across the UK, with the largest single concentration (6,070) being in Glasgow. Indeed, the position of Glasgow is interesting. In the 2001 census, the proportion of the city's population with a BME background was only 5.5 per cent, compared to Birmingham (29.6 per cent) and Manchester (19.0 per cent). Yet the city contracted with NASS to provide 2,500 units of accommodation every year for five years and has consistently housed more asylum seekers than any other UK authority. Thus Glasgow illustrated the potential for new multicultural communities to become established in dispersal locations (Sim and Bowes 2007).

Additionally, the Home Office operates the Gateway Protection Programme of refugee settlement, which is a partnership between the UK Government and the United Nations High Commission for Refugees (UNHCR) and under this programme, a small number of Congolese refugees have been housed in North Lanarkshire (Sim 2015).

The countries from which most refugees currently come to the UK are Iran, Pakistan, Sri Lanka, Afghanistan, India, Bangladesh and Syria. Previously significant numbers of refugees have arrived from African countries such as the Democratic Republic of the Congo, Eritrea and Somalia. Detailed data are difficult to obtain but it appears that the nationality profile of refugees in Scotland mirrors that of the UK as a whole.

It is important to record here the complexity of the asylum and immigration regime in Scotland, because of the existence of devolved government. Legislation on asylum and immigration, as well as equality and human rights are matters for Westminster. But the agencies that deliver services to asylum seekers in Scotland, including housing, education, health and social services, are the responsibility of the Scottish Parliament and the Scottish Government. Refugee settlement and integration are also devolved matters, and the Scottish Government's Scottish Refugee Integration Forum (SRIF) (2003) has produced an action plan to guide policy implementation and delivery of support services in this area.

Indeed, the approach taken by the Scottish Government towards both asylum seekers and refugees has been somewhat different from that in other parts of the UK, where they have often been portrayed in a negative light.

For example, in an explicit attempt to 'counter the negative perceptions that many people hold' (Charlaff *et al.* 2004: 10), the Scottish Government (then the Scottish Executive) commissioned an audit of the skills, qualifications and aspirations of asylum seekers and refugees. This audit responded to the then First Minister Jack McConnell's comments in 2003 on Scotland's need for new immigrants and the approach is indicative of some tensions between control of borders through asylum and immigration policy (the preserve of the UK Home Office) and Scotland's need for a supplementary labour force (Wright 2004).

The Scottish Government has generally adopted a more positive attitude towards inward migration, partly for demographic reasons and partly because of a distaste for the 'dawn raids' that were carried out in order to deport asylum seekers who were believed to have overstayed. This has helped to create a climate, both social and political, in which immigrants may be valued. The Institute for Public Policy Research (IPPR) (2007), for example, has suggested that Scotland's more positive attitude is in stark contrast to that south of the border. It is possible that a focus on the opportunities presented by immigration, rather than on the difficulties, facilitates the integration process.

Audrey (2000) has argued that, in Glasgow and indeed in Scotland as a whole, multiculturalism has more prospect of success than in England, suggesting that the refugee population is more likely to become integrated within Scottish society. She points out that Scottish politics has not been racialised and right-wing parties like the British National Party are weak. There is therefore a fairly wide political consensus supporting the Scottish Government's policies of challenging racism and promoting integration, such as its 'One Scotland, Many Cultures' campaign, which demonstrates an awareness of the need to build a more multicultural Scottish society. Second, the Scottish dimension may also be important because Scots themselves may have multiple identities as both 'Scottish' and 'British' – or even 'not English'. Refugees likewise may find themselves able to negotiate multiple identities as part of the integration process.

The issue of refugee integration has become of greater importance, because of evidence that large numbers of refugee families who were dispersed to Glasgow by NASS are now choosing to remain in the city in the longer term. Charlaff *et al.*'s (2004) research suggested that 88 per cent of their respondents wished to remain in Scotland after they received refugee status, although it was unclear how realistic an aspiration this was. More recently, Netto (2011) found that just over two-thirds of her interviewees reported that they were 'very likely' to stay in Glasgow and she points to the 'connectedness to place' that many refugees felt after living in the city. Similarly, Mulvey (2013) found the majority of his research participants planning to stay in Glasgow, with those who planned to leave only doing so to obtain employment. As well as attachment to place, Mulvey suggests that a sense of gratitude towards the city for offering them accommodation and support had also encouraged people to stay.

The result of decisions by many refugees to settle permanently in Scotland is a changing ethnic geography (Sim 2015). In 2001, only 2 per cent of the Scottish population were from a BME group (102,000 people), but in 2011 this had risen to 4 per cent (211,000). While some of this change will result from natural increase, the bulk of the rise must be due to significant in-migration including both refugees and some international students. Within the BME population as a whole, there has been a change in the ethnicities represented. Between 2001 and 2011, for example, the Pakistanis – the largest settled minority group – increased in size from 0.6 per cent to 0.9 per cent of the overall population. But the group comprising black, African and Caribbean people increased in size from 0.2 per cent to 0.7 per cent. Given that significant numbers of refugees housed in Glasgow and Motherwell are of African origin, this must help to explain the change.

Indeed, Glasgow has begun slowly to approach the diversity of many English cities. In 2011 some 12 per cent of the city's population was of a BME background, a significant change from 5.5 per cent in 2001. Elsewhere in Scotland, both Edinburgh and Aberdeen recorded 8 per cent of their population being from BME groups, suggesting that they too are becoming more diverse. It is not possible yet to establish from the census the extent to which the changes in these cities are due to natural increase or to migration, but there is some evidence of onward migration of refugees within Scotland (Stewart 2012), essentially from Glasgow to other cities.

A multicultural society?

As the minority ethnic population of Scotland has grown, the country has perhaps become more multicultural and we should take a moment to try and define this term. Essentially, multiculturalism refers to a policy that has usually come about 'not so much by the emergence of a political movement but by a more fundamental movement of peoples. By immigration – specifically the immigration from outside Europe, of non-white peoples into predominantly white countries' (Modood 2007: 2). Some countries like the United States have never been at ease with multiculturalism and it was generally held that immigrants should enter a 'melting pot', whereby they would cast off their former ethnicities and identities, emerging as full American citizens (Yinger 1981). But the UK, as an imperial power, has generally adopted a different mindset, recognising that many people from former colonies may, in any case, have held British citizenship and – at least until the 1960s – would have had the right to move to the UK. They would not therefore be expected to abandon their own national identities as part of their move.

Multiculturalism refers to policies that recognise these different identities and cultural diversity and promote and institutionalise them. Such policies will include respect for different cultures, languages and faiths, freedom of expression for different groups within society and a recognition that the various cultures and beliefs that make up our society are all of equal value and validity (Mahamdallie 2011). In cities with extremely diverse populations, local and central government have developed a range of initiatives to accommodate this diversity (Livingstone 2011). But because the BME population of Scotland was, until the 2000s, comparatively small, multiculturalism rarely featured in policy debates. As we note above, however, after the establishment of the Scottish Parliament in 1999, and recognising the growing diversity of the population, the Scottish Government introduced an anti-racist campaign entitled 'One Scotland, Many Cultures' (Penrose and Howard 2008). There was also a recognition of the value to Scotland of increased immigration (Wright 2004), in contrast to the anti-immigrant political rhetoric that has emerged in some parts of the UK (McLaren and Johnson 2007). This different political rhetoric was very obvious during the EU referendum campaign in 2016, which resulted in very different voting patterns in Scotland and England.

Despite an apparent commitment to equality of opportunity, multiculturalism and diversity, however, it is still the case that there are numerous challenges for governments in London and in Edinburgh, in terms of achieving equality outcomes. The Scottish Government (2013a) published a review of the evidence on such outcomes in relation to BME groups, and their key findings were as follows:

- BME individuals are over-represented in both school-level and further and higher education, reflecting the younger age profile of the BME population. However, BME students tend to graduate with lower-class degrees than white students.

- As in previous decades, employment rates are lower for BME groups than for the white population, while self-employment rates are higher. This is a continuation of a long-standing feature of BME employment.
- People from BME groups are around twice as likely as white people to be in relative poverty. Partly this reflects a problem with low pay.
- BME people are under-represented in the social rented housing sector, but over-represented among the homeless. Overcrowding remains a problem for Pakistani, Bangladeshi and refugee families, reflecting the lack of appropriately sized accommodation in locations that are viewed as desirable and 'safe'.
- BME people participate less in sport than white people. There are relatively few black footballers in Scotland, compared to other countries, for example.
- Numbers of reported racist incidents have increased over time.[1]
- BME candidates have, however been successful in securing public appointments

One area where Scotland appears to have made significantly less progress than England is in the election of BME politicians. The first BME councillor in Scotland, Dr Jainti Saggar, was elected in Dundee in 1936 and served for eighteen years; but the following years saw few others elected in his wake. In the local elections of 2012 only 17 BME councillors were elected out of a Scottish total of 1,223 (Carrell 2012); in 2017 there were 15 BME councillors out of 1,227 (a total of 1.2 per cent and well below the proportion of BME people within the population as a whole. Most of those councillors elected were of Asian heritage and eight were in Glasgow.

At Parliamentary level, Mohammad Sarwar was elected as Labour MP for Glasgow Central in 1997 and retired in 2010, being succeeded by his son, Anas Sarwar. In 2015 Sarwar lost his seat but another BME candidate, Tasmina Ahmed-Sheikh, was elected as an SNP MP. In the 2017 general election, she lost her seat and there are now no Scottish BME MPs. In the Scottish Parliament, the first BME MSP was not elected until 2007 – Bashir Ahmad, for the SNP, who died in 2009. At the 2016 Holyrood elections, Humza Yousaf (SNP) and Anas Sarwar (Labour) were elected. Finally in the 2019 European elections, two minority ethnic MEPs were elected – Nosheena Mobarik (Conservative) and Louis Stedman-Bryce (Brexit Party). Both will lose their seats after the UK leaves the EU.

Despite the increased presence of BME people in our society, however, racial hostility remains a problem, as we have already discussed. We noted earlier that racism is not always acknowledged in Scotland and is sometimes seen as an 'English' problem. This rather schizophrenic view of minorities may be illustrated by attitudes towards asylum seekers. On the one hand, the arrival of large numbers of refugees and asylum seekers in Glasgow caused some concern and initially there was considerable hostility towards them. This culminated in the murder of Firsat Dag, a Turkish asylum seeker in 2001 and led to widespread (and very negative) publicity for the city (Coole 2002).

On the other hand, as refugee and asylum seeker households begin to put down roots and as children become settled in school, it becomes easier for local people to see them as having a contribution to make to the community. When asylum seekers are threatened with deportation, this has then allowed local people to campaign on their behalf and there are a number of voluntary groups who have fought against Home Office 'dawn raids', for example. Famously, a group of schoolgirls in the Drumchapel housing estate in Glasgow ran a high-profile campaign in 2005 to prevent some of their fellow classmates being deported. The 'Glasgow Girls' as they became known won the 'Scottish Campaign of the Year' award at the annual Scottish political awards ceremony and the National Theatre of Scotland presented a musical based on their work.

This shift in public attitudes has been identified by John Donaldson, then Head of Immigration Services at Glasgow City Council. He reported: 'There's been a sea-change in attitude in Glasgow. We used to get calls from Mr Angry saying "why are these people taking our houses?" Now we get phone calls saying "why is my neighbour being removed?" Now people see asylum seekers as very good neighbours and very much part of the community' (Forrest 2007: 22). Kay and Morrison (2013) emphasise the different policy stance taken by the Scottish Government in relation to refugees and in-migrants, in contrast to Westminster where they have often been demonised (Flynn 2013). Scotland may possibly now be seen as a more welcoming place in which to live.

Summary

In summary, we can see that Scotland has long been a country of immigration as well as emigration, albeit that historically migrants to the country originated from relatively few areas. The largest group of migrants came from Ireland while there were other migrants from elsewhere in the UK, from certain European countries and from parts of Asia. Although Scotland was a partner in the creation and administration of the British Empire, it never attracted large numbers of migrants from the full range of Commonwealth countries, in contrast to London and some of the larger English cities. As a result, it did not initially develop a multicultural tradition.

More recently, however, the increase in the numbers of people migrating from eastern Europe, coupled with the arrival of several thousand asylum seekers and refugees (primarily into Glasgow) has increased significantly the BME population.

Scottish society has therefore become noticeably more diverse and the ethnic geography of the country is changing. There is a view that Scotland has been a welcoming country to immigrants and, while there is some evidence of this (IPPR 2007), it is important that this is not overstated. The equality audit conducted by the Scottish Government (2013a) and to which we refer above, shows that BME people are still excluded from many parts of society and experience discrimination and racist incidents. That said, the success of BME individuals in securing public appointments, for example, suggests that some barriers at least are being broken down.

As well as racism, we have also referred to ongoing problems of sectarianism, associated with some religious tensions between the Protestant and Catholic communities. Although the evidence suggests that there is little difference between the two communities in regard to their inclusion and participation in Scottish society, bigotry still exists and the Scottish public tends in the main to associate this with football rivalries (Hinchliffe *et al.* 2015).

Significantly, the establishment of the Scottish Parliament in 1999 has enabled politicians and policymakers in Scotland to address many of these issues. Sectarianism has been an ongoing concern, leading to a number of debates and some legislation, while the integration of refugees is devolved to Holyrood. The Scottish Government's 'One Scotland, Many Cultures' campaign to which we have already referred (Penrose and Howard 2008) is a good example of a highly positive message being sent out by government to demonstrate that all members of society are valued equally. Indeed, during the independence referendum campaign in 2014, nationalist politicians argued strongly that they sought both an easing of immigration restrictions (to boost Scotland's economy) and to remain in the EU – in contrast to the anti-EU rhetoric emanating from parts of the Westminster establishment. In that sense, many politicians in Scotland see themselves as *inter*nationalist and politics has not, on the whole, become racialised as in some other parts of the UK.

One would not wish to overemphasise these issues. In many respects, Scotland is not so different from other parts of the UK and racism and sectarianism are still major problems. There does, however, seem to be a strong political will to address them.

Further reading

For statistics on minority ethnic groups, the census is the obvious source, which can be accessed at www.scotlandscensus.gov.uk/ethnicity-identity-language-and-religion. There are also lots of books on race and ethnicity across the UK, of which John Solomon's *Race and Racism in Britain* (2003) is a key text, although maybe a bit dated. See also Peter Fryer's *Staying Power: The History of Black People in Britain* (2018) and Tariq Modood's *Multiculturalism* (2007).

There are some interesting accounts of the experiences of minority ethnic groups in Scotland, for example, Bashir Maan's *Muslims in Scotland* (2014), Mary Edward's *Who Belongs to Glasgow? 200 Years of Migration* (2016) and Peter Hopkins's edited *Scotland's Muslims* (2019). There is also a new edited volume by Tom Devine and Angela McCarthy, entitled *New Scots: Scotland's Immigrant Communities Since 1945* (2018). A recent edited volume by Neil Davidson *et al.*, *No Problem Here: Racism in Scotland* (2018), challenges the positive image so often presented on Scotland and is a compelling read.

For information on refugees and asylum seekers in Scotland, the Scottish Refugee Council is probably the best source of information at www.scottishrefugeecouncil.org.uk. See, for example, Gareth Mulvey's 2013 report for the Council, *In Search of Normality: Refugee Integration in Scotland.*

We have also referred in this chapter to sectarianism in relation to Roman Catholic migrants, especially from Ireland. The best books are probably Tom Devine's edited volume, *Scotland's Shame? Bigotry and Sectarianism in Modern Scotland* (2000) and Steve Bruce *et al.*'s *Sectarianism in Scotland* (2004). Bruce and his colleagues have published a number of other papers, referenced in the Bibliography of this volume. See also the website of the organisation Nil by Mouth at https://nilbymouth.org, which campaigns against sectarianism.

Chapter 8
Political Scotland
Duncan McTavish

Introduction

Scotland and Scottish politics have long been influenced by its dual identities – Scottish and British. The subtle interplay of these has been a contextual background factor since 1707 and many aspects of Scottish history, from its participation in the British state and its empire through to the post-1945 growth of the welfare state and the political environment in the period up to and beyond devolution, cannot be considered seriously without the interplay of these dual identities. Consequently, convergence, co-existence and accommodation between Scotland and the UK run through some of the themes in this chapter. The chapter explores the current state of play of politics in Scotland through an analysis of politics at the local level, an outlining of some key players in the system and finally looks briefly at some aspects of politics beyond Scotland.

Politics at the local level

Scottish politics at the local level has shown a marked divergence to some other parts of the UK. There are obvious institutional and structural differences to England in particular. Where Scotland has a system of unitary authorities (thirty-two in number) each with a wide range of multifunctional responsibilities, ranging from pre-sixteen education provision to social work, roads, environmental regulation, leisure and recreation, child protection, etc., in England the landscape is very different with a multi-tiered environment (e.g. counties and districts) each with different responsibilities (in general, reduced over the last decade or so with the reduction of a role in education due to the growth of centrally funded academy and 'free' schools as well as other direct grant aided schools) and a small number of combined authorities. Wales has unitary authorities but smaller than those in Scotland and with fewer powers decentralised from Cardiff. Northern Ireland's local authorities generally have fewer powers than those in the rest of the UK. The electoral system that Scotland employs (single transferable voting) means that single-party control of councils is not the norm. Interestingly what is not much different in England or the devolved nations is the very high proportion of local government spend that comes from central government.

Since the early 2000s, the Scottish approach has been one based on place and the attempt to introduce and embed community planning, premised on local involvement and partnership. The Local Government in Scotland Act 2003 provided the initial statutory basis for community planning. It was introduced to enable public bodies to work together to deal with complex, long-term challenges that a single organisation could not deal with, for example inequalities in health, employability and levels of crime, as well as aspiring to involve local communities more in the decisions that affect people's lives. This was reinforced by the influential Christie Report, which recommended that major public service provision in Scotland should be based on prevention strategies (e.g. to counter longer-term spend in areas of health provision) and on community involvement in public service design and delivery (Christie 2011). Much public sector reform in Scotland has at least referenced Christie in its rationale. The Scottish Government and the Convention of Scottish Local Authorities (COSLA) published a joint Statement of Ambition in 2012 and since then have continued to promote community planning as central to effective public service reform. Community planning has subsequently been refreshed and embedded in the Scottish Government's Community Empowerment Act 2015, which introduced new statutory duties for community planning intended to give greater local locus in how services are run. This is much stronger than similar initiatives in England that, although led by local authorities, do not place statutory duties on other bodies – thereby likely to limit involvement of other major public sector players. In fact some international comparative research has indicated similar initiatives tend to focus on individual services rather than the place-based approaches used in Scotland (see Audit Scotland 2016), though this perhaps underplays the role of place-based initiatives in comparator countries, given that many local councils internationally have traditionally greater spend and power over service provision than is the case in either Scotland or the rest of the UK.[1]

Localisation and the power of place has had a presence in policy thinking in both Scotland and England (less so in Wales and Northern Ireland). This has favoured the development of community asset ownership on the premise that local people and communities should have control of assets to influence local decision-making and control of local issues and problems to much better effect than more distant government, be it local or central. In England the Quirk Review (Quirk 2007) recommended the transfer of public assets into community ownership, eventually leading to the creation of a specialised Asset Transfer Unit to facilitate the shift of assets from the public sector to community organisations, with additional specialised funding streams from sources such as the Big Lottery Fund supporting this. This appeared to gain some traction with the 2010 UK coalition government's support for David Cameron's 'Big Society'. This, however, lacked sustained credibility due to the thinking among many community and third-sector organisations (who after all were the expected delivery vehicles for the programme) who noted that this was occurring in a context of austerity and a desire to roll back the state per se rather than transfer state roles to communities (McTavish 2017). The 'Big Society' is now rarely referenced in policy debates, though some of the ideas of asset-led community development are being applied in areas of public health (see discussion later in this chapter).

Such policy initiatives have been more sustained in Scotland. Here, community land ownership has, in the last decade, been supported and promoted by the Scottish Government with legislative rights for Community Land Trusts to buy land, with a dedicated Land Fund providing community groups with funding for land purchase (Moore and McKee 2014); it is worth noting here that land ownership in Scotland is considerably more concentrated than the European norm. The first wave of community land ownership through buyout occurred in the 1990s in Assynt, Knoydart and the island of Eigg and this has increased to a total of 563,000 acres, much of it concentrated in the Western Isles (MacLeod 2017). Beyond the land ownership initiatives, the Scottish Government has given statutory backing to asset-based approaches. For example, an asset-based dimension with regard to health and well-being is specifically written into the statutory provision for the joint working of public bodies for national health outcomes (Scottish Government 2014a).[2]

The Community Empowerment Act 2015 makes a direct link between local communities and the possibility of community-based asset development (Scottish Government 2015). In addition, the Scottish Government's

'Strengthening Communities Programme' has a range of funding through a People and Community Fund, Aspiring Communities Fund and Community Choices Fund, totalling around £50 million in 2016–17 – small-scale but nonetheless a signal of commitment to the principle of asset-based community development.[3]

The mainstreaming of place, the potential for empowerment through localisation, appears as a defining feature of policy and politics at the local level in Scotland. This is a significant strand of thinking in Scottish local government. In contrast, English local government's concerns have been about the creation of combined authorities with some devolved responsibilities from central government mainly in the area of health – given some policy momentum by former Chancellor George Osborne's commitment to a 'northern powerhouse' – though momentum seems to have stalled with nine combined authorities in existence at the present time.[4] Many councils in England have been somewhat overwhelmed by central government fiscal restraint and therefore preoccupied with the challenges of meeting essential service delivery. In particular, the challenges of social care provision have led to councils lobbying central government and being given extra discretion on income raising through an additional council tax charge dedicated to social care budgets. Welsh concerns currently are about the size of councils, with proposals to reduce the number through merger; at the time of writing, no consensus between local councils and the Welsh Government has been reached. Devolved government in Northern Ireland is in abeyance with the suspension of Stormont.

Some key players in the system

Key players: parties and voters

Political parties are the key players in the system. This broad statement requires two caveats. First, the initial years of the Scottish Parliament with its Additional Member System brought a degree of proportionality never seen before in Scottish (or UK) politics. This saw some representation for smaller parties, the most notable of which was the Scottish Socialist Party; there was also representation from the Greens and a single MSP for the Senior Citizens' Party. Much of this minor-party representation has since diminished. The second caveat is that the Scottish Greens, though small in representation terms, increased their presence (from two to six MSPs between 2011 and

2016) with the party's rise in popularity (and increased party membership), largely attributed to their support for Scottish independence.

As will be seen below, support for the main parties has ebbed and flowed both at Westminster and Holyrood elections. Labour in large measure was responsible for delivering devolution, The SNP, though eventually supportive, was initially lukewarm, seeing this as a possible diversion from independence. Leadership within the Labour Party was provided by long-term supporters of some form of home rule, such as John Smith, Donald Dewar (later to become first minister) and Gordon Brown. There was, however, much indifference and even hostility within parts of the Labour Party nationally. Although Labour was by far the biggest party in the first devolved elections in 1999 and formed an administration with the Liberal Democrats, they gave the appearance of 'job done', with little in the way of vision for the devolved country's future. Jack McConnell as first minister was open to some mockery when his stated ambition for Holyrood was 'to do less but do it better'. Although Labour remained the largest party at Holyrood until 2007, its share of the popular vote in devolved elections steadily declined after the initial election in 1999 (Hassan and Shaw 2012). Labour has traditionally been a unified UK party, both in organisational terms (Labour staff in Scotland are employees of the UK party and party funding flows from the centre) and also in policy terms. This has been the case particularly after 1945, with the development of socio-economic programmes seen primarily on a UK basis, though recognising differences in Scotland's 'administrative devolution' articulated through the Scottish Office. Scotland, with its large number of Labour MPs and large Labour vote share from the 1960s right up to 2010, has always been of electoral importance to Labour and it is recognised in 2018 (by the current leadership) that a Labour majority at Westminster will be very difficult to achieve without some recovery in Scotland. The party has only seven Scottish MPs in 2018, compared with forty-one in 2010 and fifty-six when New Labour was first elected in 1997.

Labour has found it difficult to formulate a position that can simultaneously address its Scottish and UK challenges. With some notable exceptions, Labour's dominance of Scottish MPs at Westminster has been rather low-key and has contributed little heft to Labour thinking or policy development (see Cameron 2010), though Tom Johnston in the 1940s and 1950s, William Ross in the 1960s and John Smith and Gordon Brown in later decades are obvious exceptions. Loyalty to the UK party has often overridden a specific articulation of Scottish political demands when these arise, with commitments to devolution often seen as a defensive response to the rise of SNP voting among the traditional Labour support base. This was seen spectacularly during the 2014 independence referendum campaign. Labour in Scotland was clearly out of alignment with many of its traditional supporters when the party joined forces in 'Better Together' with the Conservatives to campaign for a 'No' vote; this misalignment carried over to the 2015 UK general election when Labour returned only one MP in Scotland, and the recovery since then has been very weak. The difficulty for Labour in Scotland is illustrated by the churn in Scottish Party leadership; there have been eight leaders since the first devolved election in 1999. It is unclear what the party's position is on another independence referendum, with the UK and Scottish Party leaders contradicting each other (Corbyn 'undecided, perhaps', Leonard 'no') within days in late September 2018. This difficulty, it should be noted, is not unknown for parties with a strong presence at state level and trying to reconcile this with substate or regional demands. For example, the left-of-centre Spanish Socialist Workers' Party (PSOE) in Spain, traditionally strong in Catalonia, suffered electorally there when the party backed down and reversed its initial support for a revised Statute of Autonomy in 2010 after the Constitutional Court rejected the revision.

As can be seen from Tables 8.1 to 8.3, there are both long-term and short-term trends in the post-devolution electoral fortunes of the main parties. The position of the Conservatives in Scotland is intriguing. Although originally opposed to devolution and the proportional electoral system, both of these have actually given a political presence to the Conservatives in Scotland. In 1997 the Conservatives had no Westminster seats from Scotland and, as recently as 2016, had only one. Until recently, the Conservatives won very few, if any, constituency seats at Holyrood, their representation composed of the proportional and regionally based additional member seats. In fact, the unpopularity of the party in Scotland saw a leading contender for the Scottish

Table 8.1 *Seats won (and % of total seats) at Holyrood elections*

	1999	2003	2007	2011	2016
Labour	56 (43.5%)	50 (39%)	46 (35.6%)	37 (28.6%)	24 (18.6%)
Conservative	18 (14%)	18 (14%)	17 (13.2%)	15 (11.7%)	31 (24%%)
Liberal Democrat	17 (13.2%)	17 (13.2%)	16 (12.4%)	5 (3.8%)	5 (3.8%)
SNP	35 (27%)	27 (22%)	47 (36.5%)	69 (53.6%)	63 (49%)
Greens	1 (0.8%)	7 (5.5%)	2 (1.5%)	2 (1.5%)	6 (4.6%)
Other	2 (1.5%)	8 (6.3%)	1 (0.8%)	1 (0.8%)	0

Table 8.2 Scottish seats won (and % of total seats) at UK general elections

	1997	2001	2005	2010	2015	2017
Labour	56 (77.8%)	56 (77.7%)	41 (69.5%)	41 (69.5%)	1 (1.7%)	7 (11.9%)
Conservative	0 (0%)	1 (1.4%)	1 (1.7%)	1 (1.7%)	1 (1.7%)	13 (22%)
Liberal Democrat	10 (13.9%)	10 (13.9%)	11 (18.6%)	11 (18.6%)	1 (1.7%)	4 (6.8%)
SNP	6 (8.3%)	5 (7%)	6 (10.2%)	6 (10.2%)	56 (95%)	35 (59.3%)

Table 8.3 Share of popular vote in 2015 and 2017 UK general elections in Scotland (and UK)

	2015	2017
Labour	24.3% (30.5%)	27.1% (40%)
Conservative	14.9% (36.8%)	28.6% (42.4%)
Liberal Democrat	7.5% (7.9%)	6.8% (7.4%)
SNP	49.9% (n/a)	36.9% (n/a)

leadership (Murdo Fraser) in 2011 attempt to create and brand a Scottish party, separate from the UK Conservatives – he was narrowly defeated by Ruth Davidson, who became leader of the party until 2019.

The Conservatives in Scotland have tended to be policy light. This is understandable, given the party's absence from key political debates in Scotland for most of the 1980s, 1990s and much of the opening decade of the twenty-first century. Ruth Davidson, during her leadership campaign, spoke of a 'line in the sand' indicating no more devolution from Westminster or increased powers were required by the Scottish Parliament;[5] this was modified to a limited extent over the EU Withdrawal Bill when debated at Holyrood on the issue of repatriation of powers from the EU to devolved legislatures. Some policy stances have smacked of political opportunism like the about-turn in 2018 (from support to opposition) on national primary school assessments. However, increased tax powers for Holyrood as a result of the Scotland Act 2016 has enabled the party to have a clearer position against any increased taxation. But what has given the party greatest traction is the ability to position itself as the party against independence and another independence referendum, gaining parliamentary support on this issue in some traditional areas of Conservative support in both Holyrood (2016) and Westminster (2017) elections. Although many of these areas had shown electoral support for the SNP prior to 2016–17, they were also areas that voted 'No' at the independence referendum in 2014.[6] A key challenge for the party in Scotland is that, unlike parts of England (as evidenced by the 2017 general election), there does not appear to be any electoral swing to the party in traditional working-class non-Conservative voting areas. This may be accounted for by differences in the political salience of Brexit as a political issue transgressing political party loyalties in both Scotland and England.

The SNP, as can be seen from Table 8.1, has achieved considerable visibility through the devolved parliament. The mix of constituency and regional list MSPs also gave this visibility a nationwide coverage. The party came to power in Holyrood in 2007 as a minority government and subsequently gained an overall majority in 2011 based on a perception of competent government addressing the concerns of importance to the electorate (Carman *et al.* 2014). The manifesto on which the party ran in 2011 gave a commitment to hold a referendum on Scottish independence and this took place in 2014. Since 2008 the SNP has been the leading party in Scotland, though only achieving this position at Westminster elections since 2015.

Nonetheless there are a series of dilemmas and challenges facing the SNP. First, Brexit has not yet led to a tipping point in Scotland in favour of independence. Opinion polls indicate some movement in favour of independence, but this is marginal. Furthermore, polling evidence indicates that up to one-third of SNP voters voted to leave the EU, so a pro-EU stance may not be an electoral advantage to the SNP. Second, the SNP's Sustainable Growth Commission (2018), chaired by Andrew Wilson, envisages some approaches to economic policy, including fiscal policy (specifically a reduction in fiscal deficit ratio) in an independent Scotland that may or may not enthuse people to support independence if this were the basis of an SNP/Scottish Government offer in a second referendum. Third, the SNP has been the party of government in Scotland for over a decade; parties of government generally lose support over time, though the SNP has shown resilience over this period.

In addition to the longer-term party alignment trends in Scotland, some other comments are worth noting. First, while it would be misleading to talk of a Conservative working-class voting base in England (the North–South electoral divide belies this), there is some evidence of age and cultural factors (e.g. 'metropolitan or global' versus 'traditional values, community or rural') as dimensions of political alignment, cross-cutting class as an electoral identifier (YouGov 2017). This had led to gains for Labour among younger voters and those in large cities and continued strong support for Conservatives in suburban and rural areas, but also some swings to the Conservatives in some working-class communities. Interestingly in Scotland, however, the surge in Conservative MPs in 2017 (from one to thirteen) was in areas of traditional Conservative support. Second, Labour in Scotland, though with a leader who is a Corbyn supporter, does not appear to have experienced a surge of new members or significant organisational support from Momentum. Third, there appears to be a growing conflation of the two political axes in Scotland (constitutional, yes or no to independence/left–right) with the 'No' support becoming more aligned with the political right and 'Yes' with the left. Finally, and a key question in Scottish politics – if, as yet, there is no independence bounce due to Brexit, what are the triggers for increased support for independence likely to be?

Key players: civic Scotland

Civic society can be described as the intervening layer between the state and the individual and comprises professional bodies, pressure or advocacy groups, voluntary organisations, church groups, trade unions and the like. Civic society has traditionally been very important in Scottish life. The Union of 1707 left in place separate and distinct Scottish legal, educational and religious arrangements relatively independent of the state. Over time these evolved in such a way that enabled the term 'autonomy' to be used for much of Scottish affairs. So despite being in a unified UK union, powerful elites emerged within a distinctive Scottish setting (Paterson 1994) and with an important role in the management of key aspects of political and social activity in Scotland. Furthermore, it was civic Scotland that in the nineteenth century preserved a sense of national distinctiveness. No less a figure than Robert Louis Stevenson encapsulated this and, in 1873, he wrote from Suffolk to his mother as follows:

> I cannot get over my astonishment – indeed it increases every day, at the hopeless gulph that there is between England and Scotland, and English and Scotch. Nothing is the same; and I feel as strange and outlandish here as I do in France or Germany. Everything by the wayside, in the houses, or about the people, strikes me with an unexpected unfamiliarity; I walk among surprises, for just when you think you have them, something wrong turns up. (Cited in Mehew 1997: 37–38)

In much more recent times, civic Scotland was a key driver in the campaign for a Scottish Parliament through the Scottish Constitutional Convention and later the Consultative Steering Group. In the initial years of the Scottish

Parliament, the Scottish Civic Forum was funded by the Scottish Executive to facilitate cross-party policy discussion, including civic society organisations (Lindsay 2006). More will be said later on the continuing influence of parts of civic society in Scotland. Yet it has also been asserted that civic society in Scotland is somewhat limiting, for while it includes many non-political and non-state bodies, there are large swathes of the country who are excluded (for example those disengaged from voting or civic activities more generally) and some issues not on the agenda for national debate and discourse (Hassan 2018). On the other hand, there could be an increasing role for local authorities to express community identities, thereby increasing social and civic capital as has been seen with the Islands (Scotland) Act 2018; similar potential may exist with the Community Empowerment Act 2015. It should also be remembered that political parties too are a representation of civic society, though the long-term trend in party membership weakens this. In parts of Europe, new types of party have emerged as civic society movements, for example Syriza in Greece and Podemos in Spain. There can also be new civic society mobilisation within existing political parties. In Scotland the SNP membership increased dramatically after the independence referendum and also increased after a recent (2018) staged walk out of SNP MPs from the House of Commons in protest over the time allocated in debate to Scotland's post-Brexit allocation of repatriated powers from Brussels. Membership stands, at the time of writing, at 120,000. Scottish Green membership increased four-fold to almost 9,000 in 2014. Labour's dramatic UK membership increase to over 500,000 from 2015 has not been matched by Scottish Labour. Scottish Conservative and Liberal Democrat membership is thought to be small, though both are rather coy regarding publication of membership numbers (see McTavish 2016).

Politics at the centre and tensions with centralisation

In some respects, Scottish politics can be thought of as relatively centralised in governance terms. This has been reinforced by something that the design of the proportional electoral system did not foresee: electoral and governmental dominance by one party. The representation system was intended to prevent this and instead lead to coalition building, consensus and compromise; indeed, coalition governments were the norm in the initial years of Holyrood. To be more specific, the aim was to prevent the SNP being the dominant party, given its key aim of secession from the UK. The last decade has turned this aim on its head.

Research has indicated that the Scottish Executive's power vis-à-vis that of the Scottish Parliament has been clear, even in the years before single-party control. While the 'Scottish policy style' (see Cairney 2009, 2011a, 2013) has been characterised as leaning towards partnership and collaboration, this has often meant central government acting in partnership with a range of partners including local government, professional and managerial interests in key sectors like health and education, with the Parliament's role not always to the forefront. This can be explained partly by history. Local government, NHS and third-sector organisations, for example, long predated the establishment of a devolved parliament, and therefore can present themselves as reservoirs of capacity and experience that can only be accreted over time by an elected legislature.

However, in some respects governance in Scotland has not always matched up to some of its initial ideals. For instance, the Constitutional Steering Group outlined that governance 'should embody and reflect the sharing of power between the people of Scotland, the legislators and the Scottish Executive'. Experience here has been mixed. Power sharing and the need to extend the reach by the Scottish Executive to the legislature was most obvious during the SNP's period of minority government between 2007 and 2011 and again since the 2016 election. These periods gave the Scottish Parliament a clear role in challenging and scrutinising government proposals. During the first two sessions under the Labour–Liberal Democrat coalition Parliament's role was more limited. From 2011 to 2016 there was an overall SNP majority in the legislature and this was a period characterised by executive dominance and no need to gain support from other parties at Holyrood. The Scottish Parliament's role was at times reduced when the well-disciplined SNP government utilised its majority of MSPs to full effect in the 2011 session. The operation of the committee system tends to magnify executive dominance: unlike Westminster, chairs are not elected by the Parliament and a reform of the committee system as a whole has been recommended by the independent McCormick Commission on Parliamentary Reform (2017). There are also capacity issues facing the committee system in undertaking legislative and executive scrutiny roles on behalf of Parliament. Given that there are twenty-five or so government ministers and with the three main opposition parties having a total of around thirty-five front benchers, there are only a limited number of remaining MSPs to fill committee seats. And with the extra powers devolved to Holyrood (and possibly more post-Brexit), even without independence, the committee system will come under strain without major redesign.

Despite the above comments regarding the centralisation of power by the executive vis-à-vis the legislature, the 'Scottish policy style' has been depicted as one that employs partnership and collaborative approaches. However, tensions can be seen between centred and decentred approaches to policy and politics. Four cases will illustrate some nuances here: policing; post-sixteen college education; professional consultation; and local government reform and local empowerment.

A unified police force, Police Scotland, was created in 2013. Previously, policing was organised through eight joint policing boards funded through local authorities with some council representation on each board's management. The creation of Police Scotland was justified on economic, efficiency and operational grounds. The main opposition parties were in support, though some Labour MSPs expressed misgivings. The Liberal Democrats were opposed as were some councils and seven of the eight chief constables of the existing forces who preferred a regional structure; only the chief constable of Strathclyde, Stephen House, was in support and he became Police Scotland's first chief constable. The initial years and tenures of the first two chief constables saw controversy through disputes between them and the Scottish Police Authority and over operational control of support staff, operational decisions over the use of 'stop and search' powers, in some instances the arming of police officers on routine duties, well-publicised control room failings, accusations of bullying and claims of dysfunctionality in the workings of the Scottish Police Authority. Although matters appear to have settled somewhat with the appointment a new chief constable – Ian Livingstone, a long-serving officer in the Scottish forces – and a new chair of the Scottish Police Authority (Susan Deacon a former Labour health minister at Holyrood), there does appear to be greater circumspection over further centralisation by the Scottish Government. The Smith Commission proposal for British Transport Police operations in Scotland to be devolved to Holyrood has been taken on board at Holyrood. However, initial plans to merge operations with Police Scotland have been put on hold for further consultation after opposition from rail unions, some MSPs and others, despite being passed by the Scottish Parliament.

A programme of college mergers was embarked upon between 2014 and 2016, reducing the number of colleges in Scotland to twenty-six, with management and direction organised in thirteen geographical hubs. Part of this programme included twenty-five colleges merging to create ten 'super colleges'. Such a merger programme, inevitably, was strongly centre driven (a process, interestingly, that was not attempted in the higher education sector) and has come in a period when overall funding to the college sector was reduced, in contrast to both school and higher education where budgets were protected. Yet even this top-down reform has left local flexibility especially in some rural areas but also in some urban settings where some colleges have continued to exist independently of the unified college structure but still within the regional hub setting (e.g. in Lanarkshire).

Reform in both health and education can be seen in the context of organisations with considerable measures of professional interest and control. Tensions are evident within education where government attempts to, among other things, empower and devolve some resources directly to head teachers in an attempt to reduce gaps in attainment levels. Opposition to the legislation from local authorities (in Scotland an important organisational and professional interest in school education) and from teaching unions has led to the legislation (the Education (Scotland) Bill) being dropped. Instead, some of the proposals are to be introduced without legislation but in agreement with local authorities.[7] A more nuanced picture is seen in health care and government's plans at the centre are often more congruent with professional interests in health care. The Scottish Government and the British Medical Association (BMA) agreed the first Scotland-only general practitioner (GP) contract in 2018 and it was welcomed with some enthusiasm by BMA Scotland.[8] The outgoing BMA Scottish Council Chair Peter Bennie (who was involved in negotiating the contract) made comments at the June 2018 BMA annual representative meeting in Brighton, perhaps resonating with some in the Scottish Government: 'We must aim for something better than the very low bar of simply being better than England'.[9] More generally, strategic decisions like the creation of large hub-based hospitals with concentrations of medical and support capacity, sometimes at the expense of more localised ward closures, have tended to be supported by medical professionals and their bodies in conjunction with government at the centre. This has been the case across different administrations at Holyrood. In fact, the pattern has often been (irrespective of party) centralisation of specialised activities driven by the government of the day with professional support; any local campaigning against this has been led by opposition parties or MSPs. This is the view of current Scottish Health Secretary Jeane Freeman MSP, previously a special adviser to Labour's First Minister Jack McConnell.[10] Local government reform and local empowerment present an interesting case of relationships and tensions between centre and locality. Although the strong central–local government partnership action has somewhat receded since the 2007 'Concordat' between the Scottish Government and councils reduced many central controls on council spending, there is still a considerable degree of partnership working embedded in central–local relations, as this chapter has indicated. The Community Empowerment Act 2015 may open up pathways to local control independent of central government, as witnessed through aspects of the Islands' legislation. However, some responses to the Local Governance Review launched by the Scottish Government and the COSLA may enhance central rather than local power. For instance, the Scottish Borders Council's innovative response to this review envisages the creation of a single-service delivery vehicle covering current local authority and NHS services. While such a proposal may make economic and operational sense, especially in an era of fiscal restraint, it would be likely to centralise even further many aspects of public services. It is not yet clear whether this proposal is an 'outlier' or will gain support elsewhere either locally or in central government (Scottish Borders Council 2018). Very little progress has been made to decentralise (or locally empower) the financing of local government. The Commission on Local Taxation set up by the Scottish Government and COSLA in 2015–16 concluded that reform was necessary (in the knowledge that the majority of local council finance came from the centre) and proposed options including a local income tax and a much more progressive property tax. In the event reform was modest involving some adjustment to council tax bandings. So as matters stand, the majority of council funding comes from central government, though the Scottish Greens only supported the SNP government's 2019 budget on the understanding that funding reform was strongly considered. As a result, the government is now consulting on giving local authorities the powers to introduce a Transient Visitor Levy (or Tourist Tax), and the Transport Bill, currently making its way through Parliament, will give local authorities the power to levy a local tax on workplace parking.

Scottish politics beyond Scotland

With the UK Government

Politics played outside and beyond Scotland is of vital importance in attempting to define and analyse political Scotland. Of prime importance is the relationship between Scottish and UK governments. The formal structure for this involves joint ministerial committees (JMCs) with the purpose of coordinating and developing understanding between devolved administrations and the UK Government, but except for on European matters, these have only met sporadically and erratically if at all.[11] Although in strict constitutional terms Westminster and the UK Government is sovereign, a recent report by the House of Commons Public Administration appears to recognise *de jure* and de facto realities:

> The UK Government's position is that the sovereignty of the Westminster Parliament is a constitutional fact. Yet the range and extent of areas where Parliament can legitimately exercise its power have been altered by the devolution settlements, which have introduced political considerations that has arguably qualified sovereignty within the UK. It is the exact nature of that qualification which is contested between the devolved administrations and the UK Government. It is, therefore, important that the government acknowledges the significance of devolution within the UK constitution and produces a 'Devolution Policy for the Union' which seeks to reconcile these fundamental differences. (House of Commons Public Administration and Constitutional Affairs Committee 2018: 3)

The report indicates that current arrangements are not fit for purpose and recommends that intergovernmental relations be regulated by statute – currently the JMCs are governed by a Memorandum of Understanding (established in 1999) between UK and devolved administrations. Whether this does occur as a result of leaving the EU or for any other reason remains to be seen, but experience would indicate scepticism, for these sentiments have been stated before. The parties to the Smith Commission recognised this increased complexity, calling for the urgent reform and scaling up of intergovernmental machinery, including a new Memorandum of Understanding, a stronger JMC, new bilateral forums to support cooperation between the Scottish and UK governments and 'much stronger and more transparent parliamentary scrutiny'. The interim report of the Devolution (Further Powers) Committee concluded that the current system of intergovernmental relations is 'not fit for purpose, the most significant challenge to be addressed in implementing the Smith Commission recommendations' (2015: 8).

Yet what is increasingly clear (and from a range of international comparisons too) is that where there are dual loyalties in pluri-national states a constant process of rebalancing between nations and central state is required.

Beyond the UK

Political Scotland's reach outwith the UK is of increasing significance, especially given that this can often be independent of British politics. An increasing range of issues are scaled beyond the nation state and this often creates space for stateless nations, substate entities or regions. For instance, some environmental issues can fall into this category and countries like Scotland can enter this space, as illustrated by Nicola Sturgeon's visit to sign an agreement with the Governor of California on actions to combat climate change in 2017. Less likely to result in a successful outcome is the Scottish Government's attempt to gain control over international migration into Scotland on the grounds of distinctive Scottish economic needs. Some aspects of economic policy in a globalised world can also create space for entities within the nation state. Scotland's efforts in attracting inward investment is an obvious case in point. Similarly, in 2018 the Scottish Government opened an office in Ottawa to foster Canadian–Scottish economic and other linkages. This follows on from a long-standing presence in Brussels (Scotland House). The logic of this initiative was clear since the UK's EU membership gave a range of legislative and policy competences to devolved Scotland (ranging from agriculture and fishing to aspects of training, labour market and social and economic development policy). Ironically, the UK's vote to leave the EU created space for Scottish Government action. Given Scotland's large majority vote to remain, the first minister immediately set upon a range of meetings with senior EU officials and politicians investing in a form of 'outside' membership of the EU's 'comitology', no doubt with a long-term view regarding a possible independent Scotland's application for EU membership. Cultural and intellectual linkages are ways in which political Scotland's reach can travel furth of Scotland – historically from the Scottish Enlightenment, to more contemporary cultural festivals with strong international heft, sometimes based on diasporic connections. Interestingly the Scottish Government's cabinet portfolio for culture includes external affairs.

Conclusion

In conclusion, there a number of issues relating to Scottish politics going forward that raise a series of questions. In the contemporary interplay of divergence or degrees of convergence and accommodation with the British system, are there a number of breaking points that may tip this balance dramatically?

These are the continued diminishing of the relevance of UK-based political parties in Scotland and the fracturing of multilevel governance between Scottish and UK governments, exacerbated by Brexit. One thing does seem clear. Irrespective of parties in power in Holyrood, Scottish politics will have a distinctive look to those at Westminster as has been the case since (and before) devolution). Nationalism as a force in Scotland is likely to continue, though a key feature of SNP governments has been their cautious approach to politics. This was evident in the 2011 election where, as well as promising an independence referendum, they had a strong focus on valence politics. This allowed people across Scotland, irrespective of their views on independence, to vote for the SNP as a potentially competent government.

In addition to the obvious question of a second independence referendum and whether this will actually lead to independence, there are a number of less high-profile questions concerning day-to-day politics. For instance, will the local empowerment legislation and the community land-ownership initiatives lead to a transformational change in the powers of local authorities and their communities (not necessarily the same thing)? Two comments are worth making. First, local government finance (as elsewhere in the UK) is largely dependent and therefore to an extent controlled by central government, though the Scottish Greens' support for the Scottish Government's budget has ensured some commitment to local government finance reform. Second, despite community asset ownership, land ownership in Scotland is highly concentrated by European standards and likely to remain so without a step change in policy.

Further reading

To consider some of the general concepts and ideas introduced here, and for a very sound introduction to the study of politics, a good text is *Politics* by Andrew Heywood (2019) now in its fifth edition. In terms of general texts on Scottish politics, two useful texts are Paul Cairney and Neil McGarvey's *Scottish Politics* (2013) and Duncan McTavish's edited volume *Politics in Scotland* (2016). Another, focusing particularly on politics since devolution, is Paul Cairney's *The Scottish Political System Since Devolution: From New Politics to the New Scottish Government* (2011b).

In terms of individual political parties, there are numerous books, such as Gerry Hassan's *The Scottish Labour Party: History, Institutions and Ideas* (2004) and a follow-up book, with Eric Shaw, *The Strange Death of Labour in Scotland* (2012). On the SNP is *The Scottish National Party: Transition to Power* by James Mitchell *et al.* (2011). Scottish Conservativism is covered in other works and we recommend *The Territorial Conservative Party: Devolution and Party Change in Scotland and Wales* by Alan Convery (2016).

A useful book on the 2014 independence referendum is *The Scottish Independence Referendum: Constitutional and Political Implications*, edited by Aileen McHarg *et al.* (2016).

Finally, information on voting behaviour can be found on websites such as YouGov at https://yougov.co.uk/topics/scotland/all or the excellent site www.britishelectionstudy.com, which includes a bibliography of publications that employ the data that can be found there.

Chapter 9

Elites in Scotland

David Torrance

Introduction

It was Henry Fairlie, a London-born journalist of Scottish descent, who first popularised the term 'the Establishment'. In a September 1955 column for the *Spectator*, he examined how the social circle around the Soviet spies Guy Burgess and Donald Maclean had moved to protect the men's families from press scrutiny.[1] Fairlie explained that he did not only mean the centres of official power – though they are certainly part of it – but rather the whole matrix of official and social relations within which power is exercised. The exercise of power in Britain (more specifically, in England) cannot be understood unless it is recognised that it is exercised socially (Fairlie 1955).[2]

We will come to Fairlie's parenthesised caveat later in this chapter, although it pointed towards a geographical dimension in the formation of elites within the UK, specifically Great Britain and Northern Ireland. In Wales, for example, irreverent reference is made to the 'Taffia' and in Scotland to the 'Scotia Nostra' and, within that, to the 'Gaelic mafia'. All three imply close Mafia-like ties, just without the gruesome violence.

Anthony Sampson acknowledged this with his reference to 'a ring of Establishments' (1962: 624), although some of those concerned with the Scottish 'ring' have been inclined to deny – or at least play down – its importance. Magnus Linklater and Robin Denniston's Sampsonesque account of power and influence in Scotland, *Anatomy of Scotland* (1992), observed that Scotland was 'a small country, and in finding out who runs it, we came, time and again, across some familiar figures'. They continued:

> It would, on the other hand, be very hard to talk about a Scottish 'establishment'. That small group of powerful men and women is more striking for the variety

> of their attitudes, and for their individuality, than for their common perceptions. In this they are markedly different from their counterparts in the south, where shared backgrounds, and, perhaps, proximity to the centre of government, forges a far clearer definition of what is meant by the ruling class. The Scottish top brass can be as intransigent as the average citizen, and at least as questioning about the status quo. (Linklater and Denniston 1992: xiv)

That those making this claim were products of independent schools (Eton and Westminster) as well as Oxbridge colleges is important,[3] although even those with a more modest curriculum vitae have been cynical about the idea of so-called 'village Scotland' possessing 'a tightly knit and supremely well-networked establishment or elite, where all the key players are on first-name terms' (Young 2002: 154). Rather, argued the veteran journalist Alf Young, there exist 'a whole series of smaller aspirant elites – in politics, business, the professions, the arts, academia, the media, the public realm, the social economy – that overlap to a greater or lesser extent but seldom coincide' (Young 2002: 155).

The Scottish aristocracy

Few, however, have denied the existence of a distinct – but at the same time UK-integrated – Scottish aristocracy. Long the target of polemics such as Tom Johnston's ironically titled *Our Scots Noble Families* ([1909] 1999), which argued that

> our Old Nobility is not noble, that its lands are stolen lands – stolen by either force or fraud; show people that the title-deeds are rapine, murder, massacre, cheating, or court harlotry; dissolve the halo of divinity that surrounds the hereditary title; let the people clearly understand that our present House of Lords is composed largely of descendants of successful pirates and rogues. ([1909] 1999: x)

At its apex is Her Majesty's household in Scotland, something described by George Rosie as the 'residue' of the ancient Scottish court. It has four 'households', heraldic or ceremonial, ecclesiastical (mainly ministers from the Church of Scotland, Scotland's 'national', or established, church), medical and finally the Royal Company of Archers, essentially the Queen's bodyguard north of the border and open to the 'right sorts of chap'.

Some positions within the royal Scottish household, such as Lord High Constable and the Master of the Household, are hereditary, while others are purely honorific, but every summer, to quote Roddy Martine, it 'serves and looks after the Queen when she resides in Scotland' (Martine 2002: 243). Many who serve in the household are Scottish peers, who until 1963 'elected' sixteen of their number to 'represent' Scotland in the House of Lords at a 'picturesque' ceremony at the Palace of Holyroodhouse (held concurrently with UK general elections). Following Lords reform in 1999, around nineteen of the remaining ninety-two 'hereditaries' in the Upper House are Scottish.

Scotland's premier peer is the Duke of Hamilton, whose younger brother, Lord James Douglas Hamilton, served as an MP and MSP in the House of Commons and Scottish Parliament, respectively. A third of the UK's twenty-four dukes are Scots, as are 25 per cent of its marquesses (numbering nine). There are fewer Scots earls and hardly any viscounts, though the Youngers of Leckie are prominent in the latter rank. The Duke of Buccleuch stands out in that he continues to maintain large estates in both Scotland and England.

Although not hereditary, knighthoods within the Order of the Thistle are in the personal gift of the Queen and therefore prestigious, the equivalent of the Order of the Garter in England. Restricted to sixteen at any one time, holders are generally drawn from the great and the good of Scotland, with an emphasis on business people and retired politicians. There are also four 'extra' knights and 'ladies' companions', all members of the Royal Family (the Duke of Edinburgh, Prince Charles, Princess Anne and Prince William). Every year, on the Sunday closest to St Andrew's Day, members of the Most Ancient and Most Noble Order of the Thistle process across Parliament Square and into the Thistle Chapel, where each is allowed to display a small armorial shield.

As in the rest of the UK, Scotland has an army of Lords Lieutenants, the Queen's local 'county' representatives, although 'county' is a very English term. Many Scottish aristocrats are also clan chiefs, which are not properly titled but nevertheless loom large in mythical portrayals of Scotland's elites. Martine (2002: 237) saw them as a 'prime example of how hereditary influence can survive when genuine authority and power is removed', the real clan system having been dismantled following the 1745 Jacobite uprising.

The Scottish aristocracy is inextricably bound up with land ownership in Scotland, something the campaigner and Scottish Green MSP Andy Wightman has charted in scrupulous detail. He has argued that while in other parts of Europe the pattern of land ownership has changed considerably over the past century, in Scotland it has remained more or less the same. Wightman quotes Sir John Sinclair's *First Statistical Account of Scotland*, which asserted that in 'no country in Europe are the rights of proprietors so well defined and so carefully protected' (Wightman 2002: 246). Frustratingly for activists such as himself, the timidity of land reform legislation has not matched plentiful rhetoric. Before devolution, it was widely believed the House of Lords would block anything too radical, as it had in the early twentieth century. Rather it has been restraint on the part of successive Scottish governments, perhaps influenced by Scottish Land and Estates, a sort of lobby group for private landowners.

Those on the political left in Scotland, therefore, have often struggled to square the circle between radicalism and monarchism. In a 2011 interview, for example, former First Minister and SNP leader Alex Salmond said the Queen did not define a class structure as in England. 'I'm not saying Scotland is a classless society,' he argued, 'but I still think inequalities in Scotland are not generally linked to the monarchy' (Macintyre 2011: n.p.).

Tom Johnston ([1909] 1999) went from the scourge of aristocrats to their friend, while Nicola Sturgeon, Salmond's successor as first minister, abandoned her youthful republicanism on assuming office in November 2014. The Princess Royal, Princess Anne, has a particularly high profile in Scotland, largely on account of her patronage of the Scottish rugby union, although her daughter Zara was also married at Edinburgh's Canongate Kirk.

Business and finance

The Earl of Airlie represents the point at which the Scottish aristocracy overlaps with Scotland's business elite. He was related to the Queen through his brother, the late Sir Angus Ogilvy (a businessman), who was married to Princess Alexandra of Kent. Virginia, the Countess of Airlie, was also a Lady to the Bedchamber. Airlie resigned from the merchant banking firm Schroders in 1984 to become Lord Chamberlain, in which position he planned Princess Diana's funeral in 1997. Merchant banking also forms the basis of Edinburgh's financial elite, clustered around Charlotte Square, the graceful Georgian New Town square that also includes the official residences of the first minister and the moderator of the General Assembly of the Church of Scotland.

Today, Scotland's business community extends beyond Edinburgh's New Town, reaching up Lothian Road to the Standard Life company headquarters and beyond the city limits to the Royal Bank of Scotland (RBS) headquarters at Gogarburn to the west. Glasgow has its own financial services sector (including the Clydesdale Bank), while the mighty Aberdeen Asset

Management ensures the central belt does not get all the action. The Scottish banking sector has long been one of the most important pillars of the Scottish Establishment, although for a long time this was accompanied by the usual mythology about the sector being more egalitarian and socially conscious than its equivalent in the south-east of England.

The well-charted financial hubris that culminated in the bailing out of RBS in 2008 was traumatic enough to put paid to that. Significantly, former First Minister Alex Salmond emerged from that world, having worked as an economist (and de facto public relations (PR) man) for the more modest Royal Bank of Scotland during the 1980s. Nevertheless, that experience did much to shape Salmond's particular brand of neo-liberal, business-friendly 'social democratic' ideology, although aspects of it are common across the political spectrum in Scotland.

Scotland's business elite is also an international one, with 42 per cent of chief executive officers (CEOs) and chairs of the top one hundred companies based in Scotland having attended a school outside the UK and 31 per cent having graduated from a non-UK university. Similarly, 47 per cent of those in the FTSE 350 (again based in Scotland) attended a school outside the UK (SMCPC 2014, 2015). But then before the Great Financial Crash, Scottish companies like RBS and Scottish Power had transformed themselves into truly global players, contributing a high-profile Scottish element to an already powerful international financial community. Cairn Energy chairman Bill Gammell, for example, was, in 2001, not only a close friend of then US President George W. Bush, but also of the then Prime Minister Tony Blair, having shared rooms with him at Fettes.

These had replaced Scotland's old industrial elites, mainly focused on shipbuilding and other heavy industries on Scotland's West Coast, boardrooms replacing dockyards in the latter half of the twentieth century. A key moment had been RBS's takeover of NatWest in 2000, which propelled Fred Goodwin (later – and then formerly – Sir Fred) to financial fame as chief executive. The Bank of Scotland also merged with Halifax to form the Edinburgh headquartered HBOS. Meanwhile, entrepreneurs such as Sir Brian Souter (a frequent donor to the SNP), Sir Tom Hunter and John Boyle amassed significant fortunes in transport, sportswear and property.

In April 2007, Sir Tom was reported by the *Sunday Times* 'Rich List' to be Scotland's first home-grown billionaire, although he was overtaken as Scotland's richest man later that year by Jim McColl (another SNP donor) of the Glasgow engineering firm Clyde Blowers. Sir Ian Wood – one of

Scotland's sixteen Knights of the Thistle – also rose to prominence as an Aberdeen-based oilman.

Edinburgh and Glasgow are home to a myriad of organisations that formerly represented Scotland's business elites. Although the Scottish Council (Development and Industry) (SCDI) still exists, it is not the force it once was, while the STUC is also a shadow of its former self, now largely reliant on the Scottish Government for funding. The Confederation of British Industry (CBI) in Scotland used to enjoy a friendly, corporatist relationship with the STUC, but during the 2012–14 Scottish independence referendum aligned itself rather too closely with the 'Better Together' 'No' campaign, even at one point registering itself as an official campaigner. It took a while for it to rebuild relations with the still-dominant SNP after a majority 'No' vote.

After taking office in 2007, the newly elected First Minister Alex Salmond established a Lyndon Johnson-style Council of Economic Advisers, of which Jim McColl is a member. In 2008, Sir Angus Grossart was also put in charge of the Scottish Futures Trust, intended as an alternative to the discredited public–private partnerships of the Blair era. Sir Angus features prominently in accounts of the Scottish Establishment. The (short-lived) newspaper for Scotland's business elite, *Business a.m.*, depicted Grossart as a large pink octopus with his tentacles spreading across the page, a reference to his numerous board positions with banks, businesses, the media and Rangers Football Club.

Grossart is a product of Glasgow Academy, Glasgow University and the Faculty of Advocates (where he devilled for the future Lord Chancellor Lord Mackay of Clashfern), and he set up Noble Grossart with Sir Iain Noble (a nephew of the former Scottish Secretary Michael Noble) in 1969, which almost half a century later continues to make investments and advise businesses on strategy. Although one would take Sir Angus for a conservative supporter of the Union, he has straddled Scotland's political divide with aplomb. 'My party is the Grossart party,' he told a newspaper in referendum year, 2014. 'Our only affiliate is the dinner party. We may issue our manifesto on the day after the vote' (Dey 2014).[4]

Scotland has a reputation for entrepreneurial prowess rather at odds with its economic might, which even in the late nineteenth century was structurally weak (Anderson 2018). Many sought their fortunes elsewhere. Alexander Geddes, for example, made his money in the United States, returning to Scotland to build Blairmore House near Huntly in Aberdeenshire. His son, Ian Donald Cameron, was born there in 1932, later becoming a stockbroker. In 1966, he fathered David Cameron, who in 2010 would become the UK prime minister. And while he (David Cameron) would never experience Blairmore, he regularly enjoyed the delights of his Astor in-laws' estate on the Isle of Jura.

As well as old business elites, there is evidence of newer communities in Scotland. In her contribution to Gerry Hassan and Chris Warhurst's *The Anatomy of New Scotland* in 2002, Elinor Kelly has wondered if Asians in Scotland amounted to the formation of a new 'elite' (Kelly 2002: 295). Ethnic minorities are generally missing from Scotland's corridors of power (though Mohammad and Anas Sarwar, a former MP and sitting MSP respectively, are notable exceptions),[5] but there are around a dozen Asian millionaires in Scotland, among which the Sarwar's family firm, United Wholesalers, is prominent. Wealth in Scotland is, however, relative, and while some of the UK's most expensive addresses are situated in Edinburgh, Aberdeen and St Andrews, the number of higher rate taxpayers north of the border is limited. Any Scottish finance secretary hoping to tax the rich until the pips squeak would not hear – or yield – very much.[6]

The 'Edinburgh' elite/professions

If that constituted a new Scottish elite, then it was far removed from the three old professional elites explicitly protected, and perhaps nourished, by the Anglo-Scottish Union of 1707. Although that Treaty wound up the old Parliament of Scotland, it granted institutional autonomy when it came to matters spiritual (the Church of Scotland), educational and legal (a distinct system of Scots law).

All three initially shared the cramped surroundings of Edinburgh's Old Town, 'the Kirk' on the Mound and the University of Edinburgh at Old College, not far from where Parliament Hall was swallowed up by the Faculty of Advocates and law courts. Over time, this spawned a significant body of legal professionals, many of whom lived and worked in the 'Square Mile' (in Edinburgh's New Town) and populated the Faculty, Scottish Bench and, in London, two 'Law Lords', later Justices of the Supreme Court.

Legal elites

For a long time, law mingled with politics, with the Lord Advocate – the Attorney General-like chief prosecutor – practically running Scotland during the nineteenth century, while to this day many leading Scottish politicians have backgrounds in law. Scotland's legal elite is paradoxical in generally being

Unionist (that is, pro-Union) but also nationalist, with a belief in the superiority of Scots (over English) law and the need to protect it from Anglicising influences, something the legal academic (and SNP politician) Andrew Dewar Gibb once called 'legal nationalism'.

The current first minister of Scotland, Nicola Sturgeon, was a solicitor, as were many of her colleagues between 1999 and today, including ministers Roseanna Cunningham and Kenny MacAskill and the MSP Duncan Hamilton, later an advocate and party adviser. The inaugural first minister of Scotland, Donald Dewar, his Liberal Democrat deputy Jim Wallace and the Scottish Parliament's first presiding officer, Sir David Steel, were all lawyers, as was the first leader of the Scottish Conservative Party, the late David McLetchie, and his successor, Annabel Goldie.

Writing in 2002, Andrew Cubie believed the Faculty of Advocates to be 'one of the most respected and prestigious parts of the Scottish Establishment, based in stunning premises by Parliament House in Edinburgh' (Cubie 2002: 96). It has a dean, vice dean, treasurer, clerk and a keeper of its library (the dean is elected and usually becomes a High Court judge). Of the body of advocates, a certain proportion are QCs, or Queen's Counsel. A year's 'devilling' is unpaid, which favours a certain demographic. Cubie said his colleagues in the 1960s were 'from a very narrow base of background and schooling', while an 'unrepresentativeness in relation to wider society' remained (Cubie 2002: 94, 99).

The *Elitist Britain* report found that 71 per cent of senior judges in England and Wales had attended private schools and 75 per cent had attended either Oxford or Cambridge University. *Elitist Scotland* found the senior judiciary in Scotland to be 'somewhat less unrepresentative', with fourteen out of its thirty-one judges educated in the UK (45 per cent) having been so privately – meaning senior Scottish judges were eight times more likely to have attended an independent school than the wider population – and four (11 per cent) educated at Oxbridge (SMCPC 2014, 2015).

The church elite

Scotland's ecclesiastical elite, although much diminished, remains a visible presence in Edinburgh, with the Kirk's General Assembly housed in an imposing building on the Mound, a short walk from St Giles' Cathedral. Nearby is the Free Church of Scotland and its college, while not far from that is St John's, home to the Scottish Episcopal Church, still the spiritual home to many of Edinburgh's great and the good. The Archbishop of Edinburgh and St Andrews, a senior figure in the Catholic Church in Scotland, also has a residence in one of the Scottish capital's smarter suburbs.

Strikingly, many senior figures in Scottish politics have been sons (and daughters) 'of the Manse', meaning they grew up with fathers who were Kirk ministers. These include the aforementioned Sir David Steel, leader of the UK Liberal Party in the 1970s and 1980s, Gordon Brown, prime minister between 2007 and 2010, as well as Douglas Alexander, an MP and Labour minister, and his sister Wendy, an MSP, Scottish minister and briefly leader of the Scottish Labour Party. Although generally from modest backgrounds in financial terms, products of the Manse tend to have a conceit of themselves as outsiders.

The Church of Scotland committed itself to devolution for Scotland in 1948, campaigning heavily in the late 1980s and 1990s, this political activity a substitute – as with the STUC – for its declining authority in the moral sphere. It was fitting, therefore, that for several years the Scottish Parliament convened at the Kirk's General Assembly hall (just as the Northern Ireland Parliament had gathered in Belfast's Union Theological College for more than a decade). At the same time, devolution weakened Scotland's religious elite, for prior to 1999 there had been much talk of the annual General Assembly acting as a surrogate Scots Parliament, its ministers representing every part of Scotland and preoccupied with matters social and educational as well as religious.

The educational elite

We have already discussed aspects of Scottish education in Chapter 5, and it is in the educational arena where mythology collides perhaps most strongly with reality in a Scottish context. As with Scots law, the 'Scottish education system' has long prided itself on its supposed superiority to that in England, although there is little empirical evidence for this claim. Writing in 1992, the journalist Peter Jones also maintained that education in Scotland possessed a 'different ethos', while alluding to its 'relatively small independent fee-paying schools sector' (1992: 98). This belief extends well beyond Scotland, with London-based journalist Jonathan Freedland claiming in 2014 that 'Scotland has only a few private schools' (2014: n.p.).

In 2018, Scotland had seventy-four independent schools, with a particular concentration in Edinburgh, where nearly a quarter of the city's secondary pupils attend 'public' schools. They in turn feed into the 'holy trinity' of Scotland's professional elites and even Jones acknowledged a disproportionate influence, these schools being 'responsible for educating much of Scotland's elite' (1992: 105). In 2018, the total number of pupils at independent schools was 29,475, or 4.1 per cent of the school-age population (Scottish Council of Independent Schools 2018).

If Scotland has an equivalent of Eton it is Fettes in Edinburgh, which has produced both a Chancellor of the Exchequer (Selwyn Lloyd) and a prime minister (Tony Blair), while generations of the same families, usually lawyers, have been educated at eminent institutions such as the Edinburgh Academy (usually referred to as 'the Academy'). The Scottish capital does not have a monopoly on independent schools, with Robert Gordon in Aberdeen (of which the Cabinet Minister Michael Gove is a product) and Hutcheson's in Glasgow.

Gordonstoun in the north-east of Scotland, meanwhile, educated Prince Charles, while his son, Prince William, studied History of Art at St Andrews. While many of the Scottish aristocrats discussed at the beginning of this chapter tend to be educated in England, those who were not attended schools such as Gordonstoun, Fettes, Loretto (on the outskirts of Edinburgh) and Trinity College, Glenalmond. It is also important to note that privilege is not confined to independent schools, as the Social Mobility and Child Poverty Commission (SMCPC) observed, 'many of those who attend state schools are from highly advantaged social backgrounds' (SMCPC 2015: 3).

The proportion of privately educated MSPs is fewer than in the House of Commons, although the predominance of Glasgow University graduates makes it something akin to a Scottish Oxbridge, with fully a quarter having studied there in one capacity or another, slightly greater than the 24 per cent of MPs who studied at Oxford or Cambridge (Leask 2014). The SMCPC thought it 'remarkable' that 47 per cent of MSPs – and 46 per cent of Scottish MPs – had attended one of Scotland's four ancient universities (St Andrews, Aberdeen, Glasgow and Edinburgh). By contrast, it also found that fewer than one in seven students (13 per cent) at the four ancient universities in Scotland came from working-class backgrounds (SMCPC 2015).

If Scottish politicians have been educated privately, they tend not to mention it. Nevertheless, following the 2016 Holyrood election, Members of the Scottish Parliament are five times more likely than the average Scot to have been privately educated; 20 per cent, up from 17 per cent in the 2011–16 Parliament. The increase was mainly down to the increase in Scottish

Conservative representation, thirteen of the thirty-one Tory MSPs being independently educated,[7] although five of Scottish Labour's twenty-one MSPs were too, including party leader Richard Leonard and former deputy leader Anas Sarwar (Leask 2016). That 20 per cent compared with 33 per cent of Westminster MPs (from the across the UK) being educated privately.

In spite of the fact that almost one in four of those deemed by the SMCPC to constitute the 'Scottish elite' attended private schools – more than four times the proportion of the Scottish population as a whole (SMCPC 2015), discussion of the educational elite produced by Scotland's independent schools has previously tended to be absent from political debate, curious given the nation's view of itself as 'radical' and left wing. However, the Scottish Parliament is currently (July 2019) considering the Non-Domestic Rates Bill, which will remove private schools' exemption from paying rates. Their charitable status has also been questioned. A rare acknowledgement of this elite came from Alex Bell, an Old Fettesian and sometime policy adviser to the SNP and the Scottish Government. In his book, *The People We Can Be*, he judged that 'private schools weaken the public system and feed a network of privilege that can last well into adult life' (Bell 2014).

Bell also alluded to something that has received more attention, the uneven nature of university admissions. 'Free' higher education – or rather the absence of tuition fees – is regularly depicted as a 'core part of Scotland's educational tradition' (Scottish Government 2013b: 198), although that tradition is more mythical than real. 'In Scotland,' concluded Elizabeth Weedon, 'the assumption that the absence of tuition fees would automatically produce an egalitarian higher education system has been undermined by systematic data analysis'. Students from lower socio-economic backgrounds, by contrast, were 'more likely to attend colleges, which have experienced a significant reduction in funding over recent years' (Weedon 2015: 107–108). There has been much media commentary – as well as opposition attacks – on free tuition in higher education acting as a 'middle-class subsidy'.

Politics and government

Scotland's educational elite naturally overlaps with its political elite. For a while, there was even a tradition under which the retiring permanent under-secretary at the old Scottish Office (the UK Government department that existed from 1885 to 1999) became principal of Glasgow University. Both (the late) Sir William Kerr Fraser and Sir Muir Russell followed this path, having previously frequented Edinburgh's New Club, perhaps the most prominent example of the 'clubland' Linklater and Denniston considered 'alien to the Scottish character' in 1992 (Linklater and Denniston 1992: xiv). 'Russell is not merely a pillar of the Scottish Establishment,' judged Kenneth Roy, 'he is the Scottish Establishment personified. When Jericho falls – or its twenty-first-century equivalent, Garnethill – this is the man who will still be standing after the last trumpet has sounded' (2018: n.p.).

The Civil Service in Scotland, although as much part of the Home Civil Service as any Whitehall department, is a microcosm of subtle differences between Scottish and English elites. While the *Elitist Britain?* report found that 55 per cent of UK permanent secretaries attended private schools and 57 per cent Oxbridge, by contrast none of the last three permanent secretaries of the Scottish Government were educated privately and only one attended Oxbridge. At the same time, nearly nine out of ten of Scotland's top civil servants went to either one of the four ancient Scottish universities, Oxbridge or a Russell Group university. St Andrew's House, therefore, is not some sort of egalitarian paradise.

The days of knighted mandarins lunching at the New Club, however, seem distant, although the political Establishment today takes different, once unthinkable forms. While for decades the Scottish Labour and Conservative parties competed for primacy as Scotland's political rulers (Labour most successfully in local government), since 2007 the SNP has, 'incredibly' in the view of *Guardian* columnist Martin Kettle, become 'Scotland's establishment party' (Kettle 2016: n.p.). Not only was the SNP not averse to political dynasties (such as the Ewings), but this new SNP elite has even inherited some of the more negative features of the old Scottish Labour elite, chiefly infighting in Lanarkshire local government.

This is what the commentator Iain Macwhirter once dubbed the 'Lanarkshire Mafia', a 'hard school of politics that made people like John Reid, Helen Liddell and one Jack McConnell', who dominated Scottish politics – in Scotland and at Westminster – in the 1990s and 2000s (2002: 29). The *Sun* newspaper even speculated that Henry McLeish, forced to resign as first minister in 2001, fell not through corruption but because he 'wasn't a Catholic, wasn't a Protestant and hadn't gone to Glasgow University and wasn't a member of the Lanarkshire Mafia' (Macwhirter 2002: 29); this a reference to the more ecumenical Glasgow University 'set' that had produced politicians such as John Smith, Donald Dewar, Sir Menzies Campbell and Sir Neil MacCormick a generation or two earlier.

The 'Establishment', of course, constantly renews itself, even finding room for those opposed to the British state, although at least part of the SNP's appeal lay in continuing to depict itself as anti-establishment outsiders, even after more than a decade in devolved government. Simultaneously it toned down its republicanism and reached an accommodation with Scotland's business and educational elites, thereby vindicating Tom Nairn's (1968) categorisation of Scottish nationalism as 'bourgeois'. Several nationalists, like Sean Connery and George Reid accepted knighthoods, though party policy has always disdained peerages.

This has created tensions within Scotland's pro-independence movement, which assumed an ostentatiously anti-establishment tenor, particularly during the 2012–14 independence referendum campaign. More recently, after the SNP commissioned a 'Sustainable Growth Commission' on the economic case for independence, the former Labour MP and MSP Dennis Canavan, who had chaired the 'Yes Scotland' campaign, accused the SNP of having only consulted the 'Scottish Establishment' rather than, for example, Scotland's trade unions (Hutcheon 2018). And while Michael Gray acknowledged that the existence of what he called 'a conservative establishment' in Scotland was not the fault of the SNP, as a 'party now claiming to represent a mass movement for popular change' it therefore had 'a responsibility to confront the unearned elitism in Scottish society' (Gray 2015: n.p.).

Policy and media elites

The author of the SNP's 'Growth Commission' report was Andrew Wilson, a former SNP MSP, banker and lobbyist who arguably sat at the apex of Scotland's political, business and media elite in 2018. His firm, Charlotte Street Partners (CSP), drew fire from left-wing supporters of independence, concerned that the SNP was repeating (what they saw as) the mistakes of New Labour.

In the late 1990s, the fledgling Scottish Parliament had been rocked by 'Lobbygate', a now obscure row involving Kevin Reid (son of the then Scottish Secretary John Reid), who fell victim to an *Observer* sting operation revealing apparently privileged access to Scottish ministers. Although there was no conclusive evidence that ministers or their aides had acted improperly, it led to a Standards Committee inquiry and talk of creating a formal register of lobbyists. Lobbying certainly increased post-devolution, its elite interconnections analysed by Philip Schlesinger, David Miller and William Dinan in their 2001 book *Open Scotland?*

Charlotte Street Partners had been founded with help from the ubiquitous Sir Angus Grossart, while it attracted an ecumenical range of talent from politics and the media, not only Wilson, but Kevin Pringle (a long-standing aide of Alex Salmond), Malcolm Robertson (son of former Defence Secretary George Robertson) and others with useful connections.[8] All of them moved easily between the media, politics, business and policymaking.

Another alumni of CSP was Chris Deerin, a newspaper columnist who left to work in academia before taking charge of Reform Scotland, one of the country's few long-standing think tanks, its (limited) competition including the David Hume Institute and the respected Fraser of Allander Institute at the University of Strathclyde. As with CSP, think tanks often intersect with members of the Scottish media, which like other Scottish elites has experienced decline in the first two decades of the twenty-first century.

'As far as I'm concerned,' said Tom Nairn of two elite groups, 'Scotland will be reborn the day the last minister is strangled with the last copy of the *Sunday Post*' (1968: n.p.). By that reckoning, Scotland must be closer to rebirth than it was in the late 1960s when Nairn wrote those words, although DC Thomson, publisher of the *Sunday Post*, was doing rather better than the Kirk half a century later, even if it – like most other newspapers in the developed world – has experienced a steep decline in circulation.

'The Scots like their newspapers,' observed Linklater in 1992, 'and they like them to be Scottish' (Linklater and Denniston 1992: 126). Then, Scotland prided itself on having a higher proportion of newspaper readers than in England, although that was no longer true a quarter century later. At its height, the *Scotsman* had been Scotland's *Times*-like newspaper of record, while by 2018 the well-resourced Scottish edition of *The Times* fulfilled that role.

As with the UK media, the demographic of the industry was not representative. One former editor of the *Herald* (formerly the *Glasgow Herald*) was Mark Douglas-Home, Old Etonian and nephew of a former prime minister; his wife, Collette, a *Scottish Daily Mail* columnist. *Elitist Scotland* found that while almost a third of those at the top of the Scottish media were privately educated (29 per cent) – a proportion more than five times higher than for the Scottish population – this was much less than in the UK as a whole (SMCPC 2015).

Working-class voices were rare, though the award-winning writer and journalist Darren McGarvey (aka the rapper Loki) broke through with his book *Poverty Safari: Understanding the Anger of Britain's Underclass* (McGarvey 2017). As in other areas, some in Scotland's media elite maintain a view of themselves as outsiders. Arnold Kemp, a long-standing editor of the *Glasgow Herald*, once told Magnus Linklater (then editor of the *Scotsman*), that they were 'outwith the Scottish Establishment – which is exactly how it should be' (2012: 4).

In the 1990s, Wark Clements – a television production company formed by husband and wife team Kirsty Wark and Alan Clements – arguably represented a broadcasting elite. Wark was close to leading Labour politicians – Donald Dewar appointed her to a panel tasked with choosing an architect for the new Scottish Parliament, while a holiday with Jack McConnell (first minister from 2001 to 2007) provoked much media comment at the time. Wark and Clements were known for hosting influential dinner parties at their home in Glasgow's West End. The popular novelist Alexander McCall Smith, meanwhile, captured Edinburgh's New Town elite in his 'Scotland Street' series of novels, while the annual Edinburgh International Festival has long been a fixture of the Scottish Establishment calendar.

Linklater had made reference to the 'Gaelic Mafia' in his 1992 book, something that had 'emerged on the tide of revivalism and growing self-confidence in the indigenous language and culture of the Highlands' (Linklater and Denniston 1992: 226). Unlike the real mafia, however, this one enjoyed generous public funding via Comataidh Craolaidh Gaidhlig (CCG, Gaelic Broadcasting Committee), which was critical to the growth of independent Gaelic production companies.

CCG formed part of what Rosie called Scotland's 'very own quangocracy' (2002: 126), which survived even a Henry McLeish-era 'cull'. The *Scottish Review*, a popular online magazine founded by veteran journalist Kenneth Roy, devoted much attention to Jeane Freeman, later Scotland's health secretary but at one point a professional quangocrat. During Alex Salmond's term as first minister, the Scottish Government also enjoyed close links with the Scottish Council of Voluntary Organisations (SCVO). Martin Sime, a former chief executive, took a six-month round-the-world sabbatical in 2008–09 funded by a £8,900 government grant, which led to accusations of too close a relationship with the Scottish Government (Sime was a university contemporary of Alex Salmond's).

The SCVO had long been the lynchpin of what is called 'civic Scotland', another Scottish elite closely associated with the campaign for devolution in the 1980s and 1990s and, later, for independence. Not all, of course, rejected the constitutional status quo. Professor Jim Gallagher, an academic and former civil servant, was a prominent example of a pro-Union member of the Scottish Establishment. Although social organisations like the Tuesday Club, Ramsay Garden seminars (once hosted by a former press secretary to the Queen) and, most exclusively, the Speculative Society were all ecumenical, they tended to have a Unionist tenor. As Nicoll remarked of the latter, the Scottish Establishment is 'so small that its members all know each other and, a little tragically, want to hang out together, often in breeches' (2003: n.p.).[9]

Conclusion: the gap between rhetoric and reality

Lindsay Paterson *et al.* concluded that people in Scotland 'are more likely to think of themselves as working class despite their class of origin and own social class' (2001: 109). Upwardly mobile Scots who have joined the professional middle class tend to cling on to their former class identity, thereby strengthening what David McCrone (2017) called Scotland's 'myth' of egalitarianism, a myth being a story (or stories) people tell about themselves in order to explain themselves to the world as well as express a set of values or an identity.

This myth is regularly reinforced by politicians in Scotland. Nicola Sturgeon, for example, regularly deploys the term 'meritocracy' (as does Theresa May), apparently having missed the point that it was intended by the sociologist Michael Young as a warning rather than an aspiration. By most standard measurements, social mobility in Scotland is little different to that in England, despite the prevalence of such myths.

As the journalist Roddy Martine wrote of Scottish elites:

> They meet at their clubs – the New Club in Edinburgh, the Western in Glasgow, the Honourable Company of Edinburgh Golfers at Muirfield in East Lothian and the Royal and Ancient Golf Club of St Andrews. They go racing together at Ayr and Kelso, and to point-to-points in Fife and Berwickshire. They entertain each other in their homes. They have law degrees and chartered accountancy qualifications; they sit on the boards of each other's companies; they are involved with managing other people's money globally. Their children go to the same schools and marry one another, and their wives organise charity events. They are religious, but not sectarian. (2001: n.p.)

If there is a difference, it is one of degree rather than substance. As the *Elitist Scotland* report concluded, while what it classified as the 'top' of Scottish society was 'significantly unrepresentative' of the Scottish population, it was 'less so than the top of British society' (SMCPC 2015).

As the chair of the SMCPC, the former Labour Cabinet Minister Alan Milburn suggested in a speech in Edinburgh shortly after the independence referendum that it was 'hard to avoid Sir John Major's conclusion that there remains a closed shop at the top of British society. Nor is Scotland exempt from such elitism' (2014: n.p.). For a long time, and especially since 2007, the constitutional focus of Scottish politics had served to obscure the old cleavages of class and privilege.

Further reading

There are lots of textbooks that deal with issues of class and elites. A useful introduction is provided by Mike Savage's *Social Class in the 21st Century* (2015), while a recent Marxist analysis is provided by Charles Umney in *Class Matters* (2018).

In seeking to address the power of elites, politicians in Scotland have long proclaimed their ambitions to make the country fairer and less unequal. There is an interesting analysis of this in Michael Keating's edited book *A Wealthier, Fairer Scotland* (2017), in which contributors assess the abilities of Scotland to meet these ambitions.

Perhaps the two most useful books on Scottish elites are both edited collections – Gerry Hassan and Chris Warhurst's *The Anatomy of New Scotland: Power, Influence and Change* (2002) and Magnus Linklater and Robin Denniston's *Anatomy of Scotland: How Scotland Works* (1992).

In terms of political elites, Lindsay Paterson *et al.*'s *New Scotland, New Politics?* (2001) is a critical look at the country, post-devolution. And, given the importance of education in creating elites, we would suggest Sheila Riddell *et al.*'s book *Higher Education in Scotland and the UK: Diverging or Converging Systems?* (2015), which contains chapters exploring this topic.

Finally, the report *Elitist Scotland?* published by the SMCPC in 2015 is an important read.

Chapter 10
Scotland abroad

Introduction

Although much of this book is concerned with aspects of Scottish politics and Scottish society within Scotland itself, we must also have regard to the important and sizeable Scottish communities elsewhere. Scotland is a country that has experienced large-scale emigration for centuries and there now exists a substantial diaspora population outside the country. We explore the Scottish diaspora in England in Chapter 11, where individuals and families have moved from Scotland but remained within the UK. In this chapter we look at the Scots who have emigrated and who live elsewhere in the world.

Estimates of the size of the Scottish diaspora vary widely and nobody really knows how many people across the world claim Scottish ancestry. Politicians Kenny MacAskill and Henry McLeish (2007) have suggested that estimates range from 40 to 80 million, compared to a 'home' population actually residing in Scotland of 5.25 million. The Scottish Diaspora Forum, part of the country's 2009 Year of Homecoming, referred in its online publicity to a diaspora of 'more than thirty million'. Rutherford (2009), seeking to devise a diaspora typology for the Scottish Government, divided the diaspora into those who had been born in Scotland and who now lived outside Scotland (1.3 million) and those living elsewhere who claimed Scottish ancestry (16.9 million). He also suggested that there were a further 40 million who claimed an affinity with the country, without perhaps having a direct personal or family connection. Regardless of how accurate these figures may or may not be, the numbers are huge, relative to the Scottish homeland population.

Although the diaspora may be found in all parts of the world, the largest groupings are acknowledged to be in North America and Australasia. Data from the 2010 US census, for example, show that 5.5 million people in the United States claimed Scottish ancestry, making the Scots the eighth largest ancestral grouping. In Australia in 2006 some 1.5 million people claimed Scottish ancestry – over 7 per cent of the total (Prentis 2008) – while in New Zealand, the 2013 census identified almost 26,000 residents born in Scotland and a further 14,000 or so who claimed a Scottish ethnic identity (Te Ara 2017).

For many years, North America was viewed as perhaps the obvious emigrant destination by many Scots. From the eighteenth century onwards, Scots were settling in significant numbers in the Carolinas (Dobson 1994) and many were also finding work in New England. Within Canada, there had been Scottish settlement through the eighteenth century, but it was the voyage of the ship *Hector* from Wester Ross to Nova Scotia in 1773, with two hundred Highlanders on board, which initiated large-scale Scottish settlement on the east coast of Canada (Harper 2003).

Emigration was helped by the nineteenth-century establishment of shipping companies, often with Scottish support. The Cunard company was founded in 1840 with the backing of Glaswegians George Burns and David MacIver and in 1856 both the Allan Line and the Anchor Line began operating between Glasgow and New York. By the 1880s, the Donaldson Line was sailing to Portland, Maine and to Baltimore (Aspinwall, 1985).

Perhaps the huge significance of Scottish – and particularly Highland – emigration to North America is best illustrated by an entry in James Boswell's journal from his 1773 tour to the Hebrides with Dr Samuel Johnson:

> In the evening the company danced as usual. We performed, with much activity, a dance which, I suppose, the emigration from Skye has occasioned. They call it *America*. Each of the couples, after the common involutions and evolutions, successively whirls round in a circle, till all are in motion; and the dance seems intended to show how emigration catches, till a whole neighbourhood is set afloat. (Cited in Hunter 1994: 39)

This journal entry has become widely used in describing emigration from Scotland. The Gaelic rock band Runrig, based in Skye, had great popular success with their song 'A Dance Called America' and James Hunter used it as the title for his 1994 book on Scottish emigration to North America.

It should be clear already that the nature of the diaspora varies. There are those who were born and brought up in Scotland and who have migrated as adults, often for employment reasons. While clearly a part of the diaspora, such individuals are first-generation migrants, whose migration may not be permanent and who may return or retire to the homeland at some point. There are Scots in Europe, for example, many of whom are Scots born and who have taken advantage of UK membership of the EU to work elsewhere. But in countries like America and Australia those who claim Scottish ancestry may be the second-, third- and fourth-generation diaspora, often claiming a hyphenated and 'symbolic' identity (Gans 1979).

Gans believed that immigrants become integrated in a process culminating in their absorption into the larger culture. Thus, first-generation immigrants are essentially assimilated into the host society but often, in the third or fourth generation there is a renewed interest in ethnic origins. This may not necessarily involve participation in ethnic cultures and organisations. Rather, individuals are 'more concerned with … the *feeling* of being Jewish, or Italian, or Polish, and with finding ways of feeling and expressing that identity in suitable ways' (Gans 1979: 7, emphasis added). He did not believe that these 'feelings' could be considered a serious return to or revival of a previous ethnicity.

Types of diaspora

The term 'diaspora' is of Greek origin and refers to a sowing or scattering of seed. The Greeks themselves used it to refer simply to migration, although later it came to be associated with forced resettlement, particularly the dispersal of the Jews from Palestine (Adamson 2008). But in recent years, the term 'diaspora' has been used ever more loosely to cover a range of emigrant groups, many of whom have been largely assimilated into their host societies.

Albeit that 'diaspora' is therefore a slippery concept, various writers have done their best to identify and define different forms of diaspora. Cohen (2008), for example, identifies five types, as follows:

- *Victim* diasporas include forced migration – from early times to more recent refugee groups. The Jews and Armenians would be the classic examples but so too would be a large proportion of the Irish. Some Scots emigrants could be classified as a 'victim' diaspora, forced from the homeland for economic or political reasons. Perhaps the most significant series of events relate to the Highland Clearances, where thousands of Highlanders were forcibly removed from their crofts and smallholdings by landowners in the eighteenth and nineteenth centuries. Additionally, some left of their own accord, either because they feared forced clearance or because it was becoming increasingly difficult to farm relatively poor land (Devine 1994; Richards

1999, 2000). Other examples of forced exile relate to political events such as the conflicts involving the Covenanters in the seventeenth century, or the Jacobite risings of 1715, 1719 and 1745 (Pittock 1998), after which defeated Jacobites fled or were expelled to the colonies.

- *Labour* diasporas include indentured workers, guest workers and the like. Examples would include Indians, Turks and Chinese labourers. We would suggest that most Scots emigrants would not fit in this group.
- More important from the Scots' point of view was the *trade* diaspora, whereby individuals have moved to work in trade, business and the professions. Within the United States, for example, there were emigrant Scots farmers in Carolina, miners in Appalachia and weavers and textile workers in New England (Calder 2006). Some Scots established significant business enterprises in the countries to which they migrated. American examples include: Andrew Carnegie from Dunfermline, who made his fortune in the steel industry before becoming a leading benefactor; Alexander Graham Bell from Edinburgh, the inventor of the telephone and founder of the Bell Telephone Company; and David Dunbar Buick from Arbroath, who established the Buick Motor Company. Elsewhere, the rise of Hong Kong as an international centre of trade and wealth owes much to the activities of William Jardine from Dumfriesshire and James Matheson from Sutherland, who established the Jardine Matheson company there.
- A fourth group is the *imperial* diaspora, of which the British are possibly the best example, with many individuals moving across the globe to defend and administer the empire. Scots formed a disproportionately large part of the British Army throughout this period, although they had a lesser role as far as colonial administration was concerned (Fry, 2001).
- A fifth and final group is the *hybrid* or *deterritorialised* diaspora, where there may not be a specific homeland with which to connect. Examples include diasporas that are defined by their religion rather than by a territory, or cross-national groups like the Roma. This does not apply to the Scots who retain a homeland with which the diaspora can connect.

In commenting on thinking on diasporas, Butler (2001) has added an additional distinguishing feature, namely the existence of a diaspora over at least two generations. She argues that a single-generation diaspora may only be in temporary exile and that true diasporas should be multigenerational.

This idea of a multigenerational diaspora is important in the case of the Scots, as it is clear that many members of the Scottish diaspora have retained a strong sense of identity in their new homelands and many retain a connection with Scotland itself. We will return to this later.

What is interesting about Scottish emigration is the fact that it occurred at a time when the country itself was industrialising. The countries that, in the words of Devine 'consistently topped the league tables as the source of proportionately most emigrants' (2011: 87) were Ireland, Norway and Scotland. Elsewhere in Europe, countries like Greece and Italy also sent huge numbers of emigrants overseas, particularly to the United States. But, with the exception of Scotland, these countries had essentially agrarian economies. In contrast, the expanding industries of central Scotland were providing a destination for migrants from Ireland and the Scottish Highlands at the same time as many Scots were emigrating. The explanation for this may lie in the low wage economy of central Scotland and the lack of opportunity for social mobility, which would lead to continued emigration. By the 1920s, the population of the country actually fell, by over forty thousand (Devine 2011).

To a large extent, emigration was actually encouraged. The British Government passed the Empire Settlement Act in 1922 that provided for financial assistance for potential emigrants and, by the next year, some organised emigration schemes were under way, particularly from the Highlands and Islands. Migration was, of course, selective and when emigrant ships like the *Marloch* and *Metagama* sailed from the Hebrides, they took many of the islands' younger and more economically active people with them (Wilkie 2001). Although such schemes were partially stopped by the Second World War, there was a renewed enthusiasm for emigration from the later 1940s onwards. GI brides headed for America, while many Commonwealth countries promoting the attractions of a 'new life' overseas. Assisted passages were available, of which perhaps the best known was the 'Ten Pound Poms' scheme launched in 1947 by Australia's new Ministry of Immigration. Aspiring adult migrants only had to pay £10 for a one-way trip (Harper 2012). Schemes such as these were attractive to emigrants from England as well, but large-scale English emigration began to tail off by the 1970s, whereas it continued in Scotland until the 2000s (Devine 2011). By 2011, however, immigration exceeded emigration and Scotland's population subsequently rose to its highest recorded level of 5,438,000 in 2017 (National Records of Scotland 2019).

Perhaps the most significant change in relation to Scottish emigration came after the UK's entry to the EU in 1973. There had long been a Scottish presence in many north European countries stemming from trade links that went back many centuries – and well before the 1707 Union with England

(Devine 2011). There was also a strong intellectual connection, with significant numbers of Scots studying at European universities, particularly in France and the Netherlands. And there were also significant military alliances with some Scots mercenaries fighting in Europe (Harper 2003). The most important alliance was the 'Auld Alliance' between Scotland and France, first signed in 1295. But these diasporas were not permanent and Scots settlers would have become integrated within their host societies, usually through marriage. After 1973, however, the EU began to attract Scots workers, not least following the discovery of North Sea oil. The associated investment by European companies like Shell and Elf led to movement of workers between the north-east of Scotland and Europe, while there was an increasing Scottish presence in Brussels itself (Mitchell 1995). A new Scottish diaspora therefore began to emerge – although at the time of writing, it is likely that this will be affected by the UK's departure from the EU.

Estimates of the current numbers of Scots living in Europe are difficult to obtain. Sriskandarajah and Drew (2006) show that there were 1.66 million UK citizens living within the EU but outside the UK. Assuming that the Scottish proportion was similar to their proportion within the UK, then we may estimate that there were around 150,000 Scots living within the EU, a figure generally agreed by Carr and Cavanagh (2009).

A continuing sense of identity

Butler's (2001) argument that diasporas should be multigenerational reflects the fact that many expatriate Scots have continued to feel a strong sense of Scottish identity. For many years, in the United States for example, it had been assumed that immigrants would go through the 'melting pot' (Yinger 1981), becoming assimilated into being American citizens with an essentially American identity (Schlesinger 1991). But in fact, research by Glazer and Moynihan (1963) and Novak (1971) show that many immigrants continued to have an awareness of their historical identity and to be members of a recognisable ethnic or national group. An increasing number of third- and fourth-generation immigrants began to explore their ancestries and family histories and to assert a hyphenated identity as Italian-Americans, Scottish-Americans and so on. The strength of these identities has led social scientists to rethink models of ethnicity that are rooted in assumptions about the inevitability of assimilation. New ideas about ethnicity have therefore stressed the fluid and dynamic nature of ethnic identification, resulting in a model 'that emphasises the socially 'constructed' aspects of ethnicity, that is, the ways in which ethnic boundaries, identities and cultures are negotiated, defined and produced through social interaction inside and outside ethnic communities' (Nagel 1994: 1001). If we continue with our focus on America, then we can see that hyphenated Americans were *choosing* to retain their ethnicity, rather than being assimilated into an undifferentiated American society. It echoes Waters's comment about a 'particular American need to be "from somewhere"' (1990: 150). Individuals appear to have increasingly embraced a kind of symbolic ethnicity (Gans 1979) that, in some cases, reflects one's ancestral inheritance but may also reflect personal choice. Such choices also change throughout an individual's lifetime. Some aspects of one's identity may be fixed, such as gender, skin colour and so on, but other aspects including a person's affiliation to a given group will shift over time. Although Scottish identity has never apparently been as popular a 'choice' within America as, for example, an Irish identity, it does appear that it is gaining in popularity, perhaps assisted by events such as Tartan Day, established in 1998 as a vehicle for American Scots to celebrate their heritage (Hague 2002), and by a growth in the numbers of Scottish heritage organisations and Highland Games. Hague (2001) established that the number of Highland Games and Scottish festivals within the United States increased from around 75 in the mid-1980s to 205 by 2000. He suggested that, as well as the growing interest in genealogy and heritage throughout this period, the release of the film *Braveheart* in 1995 also spurred the growth of Scottish heritage organisations. In addition, US military bodies and a number of states have all registered their own official tartans. On the other side of the globe, Sullivan (2009) in her study of the Royal Caledonian Society of Melbourne, drew attention not only to the relatively small numbers of members actually born in Scotland, but also to the growing contingent of members who had apparently no immediate relationship with Scotland 'beyond their own decision to identify personally with the diasporic acts of their often-distant Scottish ancestors'.

There is, of course, a reverse position of Scots working within the diaspora who choose *not* to be part of diaspora organisations, perhaps because they see them as backward-looking and a hindrance to their desire to become fully part of their new host society. Sim (2011a) interviewed some individuals in America who were native-born Scots who felt that organisations such as the New York Tartan Army, which facilitated the following of the Scottish national football team, were more appropriate bodies to belong to than the more traditional diaspora societies, which were thought to promote a rather sentimental and 'shortbread tin' image of Scotland.

Thus the sense of identity within diaspora societies is extraordinarily complex. Within the Scottish homeland itself, this sense of identity may be important on particular national occasions but is not something about which Scots have to think too hard. As Kiely *et al.* have suggested, 'in their everyday interactions, people's national identity is often seen to be of little immediate relevance' (2001: 34). Thus for much of the time an individual's national identity is a part of their sense of self that can become naturalised and absorbed into his or her mundane and banal everyday practices.

As Billig has pointed out, our identities are constantly reinforced by the national symbols we see all around us, including flags, banknotes, coins and newspapers – the 'continual "flagging" or reminding of nationhood' (1995: 6). Thus Scots living in Scotland can incorporate, adopt and maintain a national identity without having to try too hard. The most subtle comments, accents, references to a shared past and all sorts of casual and formal interactions can locate and cement individuals into the web of identifiers and markers that associate them with a particular identity. As Edensor notes, 'National identity is, then, partly sustained through the circulation of representations of spectacular and mundane cultural elements … the gestures and habits, and examples of tradition and modernity which are held in common by large numbers of people' (2002: 139). Thus a national identity can become something that is mundane, taken for granted and perhaps not thought about too deeply. For Scots living in Scotland, one does not have to try too hard to be Scottish on a daily basis; one simply *is* Scottish. But for members of the Scottish diaspora, it is of course not possible to take one's Scottish identity for granted in this way and so there has to be a much greater effort expended in maintaining that identity. This process may be assisted by membership of diaspora organisations, events like Tartan Day and spectacles such as Highland Games and cultural displays. Participating in these events and activities may involve a great deal of effort, time, contacts and money and so, unsurprisingly, they have tended to become the preserve of the middle classes and essentially a leisure-time pursuit. This has led Novak (1971) to describe those who take part as the 'Saturday ethnics'.

Many diaspora identities are primarily historical in outlook and so they tend to focus on history, heritage and genealogy. Sarup (1996) has suggested that identities are fabricated, that is, they are both invented and constructed. Thus, 'the past figures importantly in people's self-representations because it is through recollections of the past that people represent themselves to themselves' (Sarup 1996: 40).

Historical representations, of course, are themselves often inventions. One writer who specialised in debunking historical myths was Hugh Trevor-Roper. He wrote extensively about Scotland, arguing that: 'In Scotland, it seems to me, myth has played a far more important part in history than it has in England. Indeed, I believe that the whole history of Scotland has been coloured by myth; and that myth, in Scotland, is never driven out by reality, or by reason, but lingers on until another myth has been discovered, or elaborated, to replace it' (Trevor-Roper, 2008: xx). Trevor-Roper (2008) probably overstates his case but the point is nevertheless well made. That is, that one should not dismiss the constructions of Scotland or Scottishness held by members of the diaspora as being somehow inauthentic. Such constructions of identity should be understood in the context within which they emerge and the ways in which they are used. There are, for example, 'Scottish traditions' that have developed within the diaspora but that would not be widely recognised within Scotland itself. These include Tartan Day itself, the Scottish-American 'Kirkin' o' the Tartan', involving the blessing of tartans, and the format of Scottish-American Highland Games with their clan tents and clan parades. These traditions may be Scottish diaspora 'traditions' rather than homeland ones but they have a resonance for all that and contribute to a continuing sense of identity.

As expatriate communities increasingly renew their interest in their culture, their history and their homelands, it is precisely the 'indistinct memory' of the homeland that is attractive. This allows diasporas to mythologise and romanticise the homeland, so that their knowledge of it becomes more imagined than real. In relation to the Scottish diaspora, for example, Roberts writes about the characteristics of Highland Games in America: 'This isn't Scotland, of course: Scotland isn't so self-consciously *Scottish* … This is, in fact, Jefferson County, Florida. The food is more barbeque than haggis and half the guys in kilts also wear Florida State T-shirts. But they've come to celebrate a place – or at least the idea of a place – most of them have never seen' (1999: 24). But while some commentators might dismiss such romanticised Scottishness, Ray (2001) is critical of those who claim that symbolic ethnicity lacks 'reality'; she argues that this would deny the 'deep emotional investment people make in voluntary or reclaimed identities'. For the individuals concerned, such identities are not symbolic but primordial or 'voices in the blood' (Ray 2001: 13).

Connecting with the homeland

This rediscovery of a historical identity has led many members of the Scottish diaspora to seek to reconnect with the Scottish homeland and indeed, much of the literature on diasporas focuses on homeland relationships. Sometimes there is a political dimension to this relationship, for example the activities of the Irish Northern Aid Committee (Noraid) in America, which has raised financial support for the nationalist movement in Northern Ireland (Wilson 1995). But the Scottish diaspora appears to have much less interest in politics and seeks a primarily ancestral connection, often based on a somewhat romanticised view of the homeland. Thus for Butler, 'diasporan representations of the homeland are part of the project of constructing diasporan identity, rather than homeland actuality' (2001: 5). This echoes Handlin (1973), who suggests that the upheavals and hardships involved in migration cause many migrants to look back fondly to their previous life, even though they may know it is a past that is already changing and to which they can no longer belong. Dezell, for example, writes of the Irish-Americans heading 'home' to Ireland, crossing the country in tour buses, 'longing for an illusory place' (2002: 206).

Within homelands themselves, attitudes to diasporas have also undergone significant change. In Ireland, for example, the then President Mary Robinson, in an address to the Houses of the Oireachtas in 1995 argued strongly that Ireland should cherish its diaspora. She referred to the huge numbers of Irish people living across the world and suggested that Ireland needed to respond to desires for dialogue, interaction and practical links involving trade and business. The diaspora therefore can be seen as a significant potential resource and in recent years the Irish Government has developed a new diaspora policy (Irish Department of Foreign Affairs and Trade 2015), involving the appointment of a minister with responsibility for diaspora affairs, a global Irish hub and newsletter that provide information for the diaspora and a fund to support media coverage of diaspora issues. While emphasising the importance of business connections, the policy also emphasises the ancestral connection, going so far as to make available a certificate of Irish heritage for anyone of Irish ancestry not born on the island of Ireland.

Brinkerhoff (2009) highlights the ways in which homeland governments can provide an 'enabling' environment with which diasporas can engage. She notes that diasporas can contribute to homeland economies (through remittances, investment or skills transfer), they can contribute politically and they can contribute in other ways. One of the most significant recent developments has been diaspora tourism, assisted by the growth of the Internet and cheaper air travel. Timothy (2011) and Basu (2007) refer to those tourists revisiting their homelands to undertake genealogical research or to visit sites of personal meaning. Some homelands operate 'homecoming' events such as the Scottish Year of Homecoming in 2009 (Sim and Leith 2013), the 2013 Gathering in Ireland and the Birthright Israel and Israel Experience programmes for Jewish youth from across the globe (Timothy 2011).

The development of diaspora tourism reflects the fact that, over several generations, diasporas may still wish to visit the home of their ancestors, without necessarily having a desire to move back themselves. Thus a 'homing desire' may be seen as something quite separate from a desire for a homeland (Brah 1996). Indeed, some diasporas may become relatively deterritorialised and cease to have a meaningful relationship with the homeland at all. Adamson (2008) suggests a 'constructivist' approach to diasporas that treats them as 'imagined communities' (Anderson 1983) transcending national boundaries. So a diaspora becomes a global community beyond any single state in which they may be a minority, perhaps a means of asserting a national or religious identity on a transnational basis; thus one may speak of a 'Muslim diaspora' that is not linked to any particular territory. Brubaker similarly refers to 'identity' as crossing state boundaries, such that diasporas should not be thought of necessarily as bounded entities but rather, 'it may be more fruitful, and certainly more precise, to speak of diasporic stances, projects, claims, idioms, practices and so on' (2005: 13). In this way, membership of a diaspora may be seen as highly flexible.

The Scottish Government and the diaspora

This discussion about the ongoing relationship between diasporas and homelands leads us to consider the specific relationship that Scotland has with those Scots – and their descendants – who live abroad, and here we must explore an alternative way of classifying diasporas.

From 2007 onwards, the SNP-led Scottish Government has continued the work of its predecessors, seeking to build on the ties of the diaspora, envisaging members as a potentially significant economic resource for Scotland and Scottish products throughout the world. The Scottish Government commissioned several reports discussing, defining and considering the nature of its relationship with the diaspora. Rutherford (2009) identified eight areas of possible value that the diaspora represented to the Scottish Government, namely investment, transfers, trade, tourism, knowledge transfer, international influence, immigration and circular migration. He also sought to disaggregate the diaspora into different groups. These included:

- the *lived* diaspora, consisting of individuals born in Scotland or who had lived and worked or studied in Scotland and who had subsequently migrated from it;
- the *ancestral* diaspora, consisting of those who can trace their heritage and familial roots to Scotland and that might include individuals with a Scottish connection over several generations; and
- the *affinity* diaspora, which consists of those who feel a connection to Scotland, who may be active through cultural or extended family groups, or who may simply be attracted to the heritage or culture of the country (Hesse (2011a) has shown that many Europeans are attracted to a Scottish culture as somehow appearing 'noble', although they may have no other direct Scottish connection).

Links between the Scottish diaspora and the homeland have been facilitated by the political changes within Scotland itself. The ability for direct communication, following the establishment of the Scottish Government in 1999, has allowed Scotland to begin to follow in the footsteps of countries like Ireland in reaching out to their diasporas. Although international relations are, strictly speaking, reserved to Westminster, Scottish governments have actively sought to create a broader international profile and engagement with the diaspora is a core element in this, albeit with a specific slant towards North America. In 2000, the then First Minister Henry McLeish attended Tartan Day celebrations in New York, as did his successor Jack McConnell. The related policy focus was on the development of 'an international network of Scottish influencers that can assist Scottish economic success' throughout the world (Scottish Executive 2001: 2) and this led to the establishment of the GlobalScot network. Essentially, this exists to build an international network of individuals with business and entrepreneurial skills who can contribute to the Scottish economy and to develop synergies between the growing confidence of Scotland and the involvement and return of the diaspora (MacRae and Wight 2011).

The SNP-led Scottish Government, seeking to build on diaspora ties, published its *Diaspora Engagement Plan* in 2010. This outlined for the first time the Scottish Government's 'ambitions for harnessing the power of Scotland's diaspora' (Scottish Government 2010: 1–2). The diaspora was seen as a potential 'resource', which could 'contribute to the government's core purpose of increasing sustainable economic growth for Scotland'. The three ways in which this could be achieved were identified as bringing the diaspora to Scotland to 'live, learn, visit, work and return'; promoting Scotland to the diaspora itself; and to 'manage' the reputation Scotland had with the diaspora, as 'an independent-minded and responsible nation' (Scottish Government 2010: 1–2).

Perhaps because of the primary focus on economic growth, the plan was targeted particularly at the *lived* diaspora – those who had been born or who had lived in Scotland and then emigrated – and the *reverse* diaspora, namely immigrants to Scotland. Interestingly, and in contrast to other countries that are developing a more cultural and tourism focus in their diaspora strategies, Scotland's plan paid only limited attention to the *ancestral* diaspora, although this is undoubtedly its largest element. It may be that the contribution of the ancestral diaspora has been insufficiently recognised and the plan does highlight this as an unfinished task (Scottish Government 2010: 2). It sees it as a priority to 'work with VisitScotland, the national tourist agency, to develop a delivery plan to improve connections and service delivery around ancestral tourism opportunities and build connections with Affinity and Ancestral Diaspora groups' (Scottish Government 2010: 2). Subsequently, VisitScotland have established an Ancestral Tourism Welcome Scheme, and of course, major initiatives like the Years of Homecoming in 2009 and 2014 have been targeted directly at ancestral Scots.

Another area where there has been significant development has been in relation to genealogical research. The enthusiasm for such research within diaspora communities is beyond doubt, but now across Scotland – and Britain as a whole – there has been a significant growth in interest in genealogical research, in 'roots' and in family histories. There are now several magazines, books and Internet sites available to help individuals trace their ancestors, and records of births, marriages and deaths are increasingly available online for wide use. A particularly popular television programme in the UK from 2004 onwards has been the BBC's *Who Do You Think You Are?* in which celebrities are assisted in researching their family trees. An American version was launched in March 2010. In a collaboration between the General Register Office for Scotland, the National Archives of Scotland and the Court of the Lord Lyon, there is now a website entitled 'Scotland's People',[1] on which have been loaded certificates of births, marriages and deaths, census records, parish registers and copies of wills and testaments. Such websites and publications serve to enhance and simplify the search for one's roots and, indeed, Birtwistle (2005) suggests that Scotland has led the way in the development of 'genealogical tourism'.

The varying strength of the diaspora

We have discussed the nature of diasporas and described Cohen's (2008) classification of them as being victim, trade, labour or imperial in nature. We have sought to place the Scottish diaspora within this classification. We have further explored the Scottish diaspora in terms of its ancestral, lived or affinity nature (Rutherford 2009). But it is clear that there are many different Scottish diasporas across the globe and we would suggest that the longevity of these individual diasporas, the strength of a continuing sense of identity and the ongoing relationship with the homeland is dependent on their geographical location. We would therefore suggest a further way in which the Scottish diaspora(s) may be classified.

In Chapter 11, we look specifically at those Scots who live in England and they may be regarded as the *near* diaspora. They occupy a rather unusual position, being outside their homeland but remaining within the same state, which is the UK. Over time, many individuals will therefore have increasingly felt 'British', but it was important for them, as Colley (1994) points out, to be Scottish as well. Scottish organisations have played an important role in helping to maintain their sense of identity, to a large extent holding the diaspora together. But many of these societies are in a severe decline, as evidenced by the work of Sim (2011b) in Merseyside and McCarthy (2007) in Hull. Partly, this is due to a reduction in migration from Scotland to England, partly also to an apparent lack of interest in their Scottish ancestry among the second and third generations of Scottish migrant families (Leith and Sim 2012). A third reason would appear to be the close proximity of the Scottish homeland itself. Scots living in England can travel back to Scotland within a matter of hours to visit friends and family and to experience Scottish activities, so they may feel that they have little need of diaspora organisations to help them to maintain a Scottish identity. Certainly, the Scottish diaspora consciousness seems to be relatively weak within England.

As we have noted there is a significant Scottish presence in European countries and there are also a significant number of Scottish organisations. This particular diaspora, which we might regard as a *middle* diaspora, is generally a *lived* one, consisting of many people who were born and/or brought up in Scotland and who have moved within the EU to work. The diaspora has established a number of Scottish societies in recent years but, interestingly, these have attracted many non-Scots to join, as individuals seem to be attracted by Scottish culture and Scottish activities (Hesse 2011a). The sense of identity within this diaspora seems to be strong, not least because many of its members are native Scots, and as with the diaspora in England, travel to the homeland is relatively easy. In the longer term, however, the Scottish diaspora in Europe may lose its identity, as it is located in non-English speaking countries. The children of Scots may grow up speaking another language, may marry non-Scots and assimilate into their host society. So the survival of the diaspora will depend on its being refreshed by newer migrants from the homeland.

The *far* diaspora comprises those Scots families who live overseas – in North America, in Australasia and in other parts of the world. While these groups do contain native Scots, it is an essentially *ancestral* diaspora, which has survived over a number of generations. As we have noted above, there is a strong sense of identity, a strong interest in family history and genealogy and a significant range of Scottish organisations and Scottish activities. But travel to the homeland is more difficult, even in these days of cheaper air travel, and so the view of the homeland held by this diaspora may be a rather romanticised one as many individuals have never been able to experience Scotland at first hand.

These different diasporas all have a sense of a Scottish identity and all retain, to some degree, a connection to the homeland, but the strength of the connection appears to vary with distance from it. In the words of Mark Twain, 'distance lends enchantment to the view' (1869: 138). Thus we have divergent visions of Scottishness in various parts of the world, all fuelled by stories unique to their own settings, albeit strongly influenced by a romantic and mythic interpretation.

Conclusions

The varied nature of the Scottish diaspora reflects different motivations for emigration, different destinations and different histories within the societies to which they move. We may wish to reflect on the impact that the diaspora had (and continues to have) around the world. By the act of emigrating Scots were, it was believed, continuing a long-held tradition of 'maintaining and extending' the Scottish aspects of empire, spreading Scottish-based Presbyterian ideas, educational styles and further enhancing commercial networks around the world (Devine 2011). Wherever the Scottish diaspora went, it took myriad ideas and practices, some among the best of history, such as the ideas of the Scottish Enlightenment, some among the worst, such as slavery. We would not argue, as Herman (2002) does, that the Scots were responsible for 'inventing' the modern world, but this consideration of the diaspora should acknowledge the positive (as well as the negative) contributions that Scots have made in numerous societies throughout the world. The connections that exist today, and the esteem in which Scots and Scotland are held in different countries, may help to fuel the positive attachment that many individuals, even those lacking any familial connection, have to Scottish culture and history.

We can, therefore, move to identify some themes emerging from this chapter. First, there exists among the diaspora a mythic and romantic vision of Scotland. Such a vision may once have been heavily influenced by earlier Hollywood visions such as '*Brigadoon*, *Whisky Galore*, and *Local Hero*' (Edensor 1997: 139), but they have been somewhat displaced by the more modern, and less fanciful, gritty explorations of Scottishness such as *Braveheart* and *Rob Roy*, with their depictions of bravery, masculinity, independence and action – not to mention the modern urban challenges depicted in *Trainspotting* and *Sweet Sixteen*.

Second, we must acknowledge the importance of history, culture and ancestry, and the diaspora have a strong sense of worship of these. It is the cultural background of Scotland and Scots that calls to the bulk of the contemporary diaspora, albeit a culture that may well have never existed in the form that the diaspora perceive it. Yet these misperceptions should not invalidate the nature of the diaspora vision, let alone diaspora Scottishness itself. Even within the Scottish homeland, there is no one single perception of what Scotland is or what it should be. As Sullivan (2014) notes, it is important that the homeland and the Scots who inhabit Scotland respect the identity of the diaspora as much as the diaspora respect them. It is this mutual respect that will help perpetuate and preserve the strength and size of the Scottish diaspora.

There can be little doubt that since devolution and the creation of a Scottish government and as a result of the increased activity of that government on the world stage, Scotland and its diaspora have come to know each other better. While events such as Tartan Day are inventions of the diaspora, the Years of Homecoming in 2009 and 2014 were very much home-grown, and a call from home for the diaspora to come and see what Scotland is all about. The act of returning home has a huge symbolism that only those who have been members of the diaspora can truly appreciate. The modern Scottish diaspora may have differing ideas of what Scotland is and what being Scottish is about, but they know where it is. More links have been forged with the diaspora since the millennium and the process continues.

Further reading

There are a number of books on the Scottish diaspora. Historical texts include Tom Devine's *To the Ends of the Earth: Scotland's Global Diaspora, 1750–2010* (2011), Marjory Harper's *Scotland No More? The Scots Who Left Scotland in the Twentieth Century* (2012), her subsequent book *Testimonies of Transition: Voices from the Scottish Diaspora* (2018) and James Hunter's *A Dance Called America: The Scottish Highlands, the United States and Canada* (1994).

There are studies of individual diasporas, such as Duncan Sim's *American Scots: The Scottish Diaspora and the USA* (2011a), Malcolm Prentis's *The Scots in Australia* (2008) and Jenni Calder's *Scots in Canada* (2003).

Paul Basu's book *Highland Homecomings: Genealogy and Heritage Tourism in the Scottish Diaspora* (2007) is a good account of diaspora Scots returning 'home'.

There are also some important Scottish Government reports on diaspora policy including Carr and Cavanagh's *Scotland's Diaspora and Overseas-Born Population* (2009) and Rutherford's *Engaging with the Scottish Diaspora: Rationale, Benefits and Challenges* (2009).

An interesting project that considers, celebrates and involves the Scottish diaspora itself can be found at www.scottishdiasporatapestry.org and the project tapestry continues to tour regularly.

Finally, Murray Leith and Duncan Sim's edited book, *The Modern Scottish Diaspora: Contemporary Debates and Perspectives* (2014) includes chapters on a range of diaspora issues as it seeks to bring diaspora studies into the contemporary social science realm.

Chapter 11
Scotland in England

Introduction

The previous chapter discussed, in some depth, the contemporary nature of the term diaspora and provided a consideration of the differing typologies that can be applied to such groups, in order to make sense of their origins, composition, activity and reasons for existence within differing polities. As we noted, the Scottish diaspora around the world is quite varied in terms of its origin and locale, as well as its driving motivation and level of organised activity. In our analysis, we divided the Scottish diaspora into simple geographical groups; the *far*, the *middle* and the *near*. Having considered the *far* diaspora in some detail in Chapter 10, we now turn to a *near* Scottish diaspora – in fact the nearest to Scotland, namely the Scots in England.

As this chapter will show, a Scottish person living in England is an individual in perhaps a somewhat anomalous sociopolitical position. While such individuals hold the same citizenship and state identity as the vast majority within their resident nation and state (England and the UK), they do not however hold the same nationality. Thus, while they are, in obvious legal and political respects, non-immigrants, they are nonetheless transnational migrants, being Scottish and living in another country – England. This clearly separates them from their fellow citizens, that vast majority with whom they share a common citizenship. Yet, despite such an interestingly anomalous position, contemporary academic considerations of the Scots in England remain rather limited. It is clear that the Scottish diaspora has been subject to extensive analysis, from the historical (see, for example, Fry 2001; Devine 2003, 2011), to the literary (Macdonald 2012) and linguistic perspectives (Newton 2015). Likewise, the far Scottish diaspora has also been investigated; from America

(Sim 2011a) to Australia (Prentis 2008). Yet the nearer of the Scottish diaspora has been far less analysed. Some recent studies have been undertaken of the Scots and Scottish culture in Europe (Hesse 2011a, 2011b; Sim and Leith 2014; Leith and Sim 2016), but there has been only limited analysis of the Scots in England. McCrone and Bechhofer carried out some work from a sociological perspective (see their 2012 work for instance) and there are a number of recent historically focused works (for example, Burnett 2007; McCarthy 2007; Sim 2011b), but few approaching the subject from a sociopolitical perspective. However, certain recent analysis has been undertaken (Leith and Sim 2012; Mycock 2014) and some interesting considerations, in light of recent constitutional changes, have been made. We will consider these within this chapter.

Roots of the Scots in England

We have previously noted that the growth of the British Empire, in which Scots played a significant part (Fry 2001; Devine 2003, 2011), was one of the main drivers behind Scottish emigration. This emigration was to a wide range of destinations and it was numerically significant (if one considers the contemporary population size of Scotland itself). The opportunities presented by the Anglo–Scottish Union, and then the resultant empire, were clear not only to the elites and the petty nobility of Scotland, but also to the many members of an emergent middle class, as well as those working class with limited prospects at home. This was especially the case during periods of significant social and industrial change in the eighteenth and nineteenth centuries. However, there can be little doubt that the movement of peoples from Scotland to the wider world, and especially to England, had begun long before the formal Treaty of Union in 1707. As Devine, in his sweeping historical consideration of the diaspora states, '[F]rom the thirteenth century to the present, Scots have been leaving their homeland in significant numbers. Throughout the last seven centuries movement to England has been a constant feature' (2011: xiv). Indeed, Samuel Johnson famously, and not kindly, noted that 'the noblest prospect which a Scotchman ever sees is the high road that leads him to England' (cited in Mack 2006: 53). There can be little doubt that this was a well-trodden road, irrespective of how the prospect was viewed. Interestingly though, this pattern was somewhat reversed in the later twentieth century, with many English-born residents heading north, particularly into the Highlands and Islands of Scotland, perhaps in search of a better quality of life (Jones *et al.* 1984).

Such movement encompassed a broad swathe of social classes, from the lowest cattle drover driving his herd to Carlisle or beyond, to Scotch Corner in North Yorkshire, to the individual of the highest social standing. Nor were these migrants always to return. In 1603, James VI of Scotland, already proclaimed as James I in England, left Edinburgh, heading south to his new capital city of London. As history has shown, he was certainly not the first Scot to head to London, but he was the first Scot to sit on the English throne. This action, the Union of the Crowns, was the first step towards what would result in the formal political union of 1707 that would create the UK. Famously, James left his Scottish subjects with a promise that he would return regularly; every three years. He spectacularly failed to keep this promise, however, returning to Scotland only once, fourteen years later, and then never again (Croft 2003). Thus he represents one of the most famous historical examples of the near Scottish diaspora, undertaking what has been noted as a common action for a Scot in England: heading south, with the 'myth' of return (McCrone 2017), however unlikely such an action will ever be.

Our work is not, however, a history text, nor an analysis of the reasons for Scottish migration to England or beyond. Yet the relationship with England, the social, political and economic union that is the UK, continues to be a mainstay of contemporary discussion within Scottish politics and society, as recent events such as the independence referendum of 2014, the elections to Westminster in 2015 and 2017 (and the elections to Holyrood in 2016) clearly illustrate. The Scottish political debate in the first and second decades of the twenty-first century have been heavily focused on and about the nature of Scotland's relationship with the rest of the UK – what has been dubbed the 'constitutional question'. Nor is this likely to change in the short term. With the continued success of the SNP in terms of political and electoral performance from 2007 onwards, the issues of potential Scottish independence and continued devolution within the framework of the UK remain at the forefront of any contemporary sociopolitical discussion (see Chapter 8 for further discussion on this). Thus, the nature of the Scottish homeland's relationship with its nearest diaspora in England is of considerable importance. Any change to Scotland's relationship with the rest of the UK will greatly impact on the relationship with that aspect of the contemporary diaspora. Therefore, we will consider the recent patterns of Scottish migration to England, before moving to a consideration of the state and nature of the current Scottish diaspora in England, the lack of voice for that diaspora (in terms of Scotland and Scotland's relationship within the UK), contemporary English attitudes towards Scotland and then conclude with a consideration of the implications of the ongoing relationship between the two nations for this nearest diaspora.

Patterns of Scottish migration in England

As Table 11.1 clearly illustrates, there has been a continual and ongoing Scottish presence in most major cities across England for much of the past two centuries. However, this has not always been as large as might have been thought. In 1851 Scots made up less than 1 per cent of the total population of England, and there was considerable concentration of the Scottish diaspora in specific urban areas, such as Liverpool and Newcastle. Obviously, the actual numerical size of the diaspora would increase over the next few decades, but this would tend to be in line with the increasing population of England as a whole, so the percentage of Scots remained fairly static, or even declined.

Whatever the numbers, a distinct historical pattern of Scottish migration can be discerned from Table 11.1. The idea that London is the centre of attraction for a Scot heading south is not necessarily borne out by the data available. The maritime and heavy industries of the northern English cities offered significant employment opportunities to migrant Scots, while the commercial and financial businesses of London may also have done so, but in lesser numbers overall. Clearly, the traditional heavy industries of Scotland generated individuals able to work in those areas, throughout the UK. Liverpool undoubtedly saw a significant inflow of Scottish migrants, with a peak in the late 1800s. Likewise, Newcastle attracted large numbers, actually surpassing Liverpool throughout this period, with a high figure of 6.9 per cent of the population being Scots born in 1871. Obviously, being the city closest to the Scottish border, Newcastle, while witnessing a decline from historical highs, maintained its status as the city with the highest population of Scots-born residents throughout the next century and a half. Of course, many Scots may well feel at home in Northumbria, which, while an English county, has significantly similar cultural elements (such as haggis, kilts and bagpipes that would appeal to a Scottish émigré – who often find themselves more drawn to such things outwith Scotland, than Scots who remain in Scotland). This perhaps explains why Newcastle remains, even today, most significant as a 'home-from-home' for Scots, with a statistically higher percentage of its population Scottish born than any other English city – well ahead of its closest rival Leeds and almost double the percentage of London Scots.

Table 11.1 Scots born in selected English cities 1851–2011[*]

Year	Liverpool		Newcastle		Manchester		Leeds		Birmingham		London	
	No. of Scots	% of Pop.	No. of Scots	% of Pop.	No. of Scots	% of Pop.	No. of Scots	% of Pop.	No. of Scots	% of Pop.	No. of Scots	% of Pop.
1851	9,242	3.6	5,745	6.5	3,209	1.4	1,268	0.7	1,100	0.5	29,668	1.3
1861	17,870	4.0	4,981	4.6	7,971	1.7	1,402	0.7	1,432	0.5	35,733	1.3
1871	20,394	4.1	8,906	6.9	7,176	2.0	2,198	0.8	1,545	0.4	41,029	1.3
1881	20,434	3.7	8,732	6.0	6,089	1.8	2,654	0.9	1,667	0.4	49,554	1.3
1891	15,276	2.9	11,085	5.9	7,599	1.5	3,347	0.9	2,007	0.4	53,390	1.3
1901	16,998	2.5	12,031	5.7	7,515	1.4	3,911	0.9	2,335	0.4	56,605	1.2
1911	14,275	1.9	11,990	4.5	9,065	1.3	3,678	0.8	2,184	0.4	50,938	1.1
1921	12,301	1.5	10,278	3.7	8,239	1.1	3,873	0.8	4,809	0.5	49,881	1.1
1931	10,340	1.2	8,780	3.1	8,473	1.1	4,315	0.9	5,670	0.6	54,673	1.2
1941	No census											
1951	8,192	1.0	7,443	2.5	9,018	1.3	6,338	1.2	13,005	1.2	62,980	1.9
1961	6,700	0.9	6,096	2.3	8,756	1.3	6,813	1.3	13.139	1.2	59,704	1.9
1971	5,350	0.9	4,840	2.2	9,155	1.7	8,085	1.6	11,960	1.2	129,680	1.7
1981	3,951	0.8	5,672	2.1	7,571	1.7	11,193	1.6	11,422	1.1	109,901	1.7
1991	3,277	0.7	5,571	2.1	6,864	1.7	9,955	1.5	9,793	1.0	109,265	1.7
2001	3,376	0.8	6,249	2.4	6,938	1.8	11,813	1.6	8,453	0,9	108,680	1.5
2011	3,196	0.7	5,698	2.0	6,545	1.3	10,281	1.4	6,855	0.6	89,527	1.1

* All cities have undergone boundary changes during the period covered, however it is unlikely that these will have had significant impact on the proportion of Scots in each city.

Other northern cities, such as Manchester and Leeds, had a more balanced number of Scots for much of the late 1800s through to the early part of the twentieth century. Interestingly, both cities witnessed a slight surge in the middle and latter part of the twentieth century, while Newcastle and Liverpool decline slightly during the same period. Birmingham saw a similar pattern, with Scottish migration peaking there in 1951–71, while it peaked in Manchester and Leeds in 1971–2001. This would reflect changes in employment opportunities and associated industrial decline both within Scotland itself (in encouraging emigration) and within the English cities that were their destinations. In exploring governmental regional development policy, Jones argues that economic structural problems in central Scotland were 'the basis of appreciable net out-migration to the rest of Britain' (1986: 159). So, Scottish migration into England was strongly driven by economic factors during the mid- to late twentieth century, and the changing targets of that migration, away from Newcastle and towards Manchester, Leeds and Birmingham, illustrate the nature of changing employment opportunities. It is clear therefore, that much of the Scottish migration into England during this period was driven by employment – and this remains the case today. In interviews conducted among Scots in England, the premise for the initial move was often economic or opportunity based (Leith and Sim 2012).

There are some specific and interesting cases that clearly illustrate how Scottish migration to England is so often due to employment-related opportunities and the town of Corby is perhaps the best-known example of this. In 1932, the iron and steel company Stewarts and Lloyds sought to develop iron ore deposits in Northamptonshire in the English East Midlands and recruited its labour force for the new site directly from their existing plants in Lanarkshire. Almost overnight Corby was transformed from a small English rural village to a 'new' town, but very much a Scottish one (Pocock 1960). Migration to Corby from Scotland remained steady during much of the late twentieth century but would decline as the iron and steel industry itself declined. According to the 2001 census, there were 10,063 Scottish-born in the Corby urban area, or 18.9 per cent of the local population. By 2011, there were 7,765 Scots born, equalling 12.7 per cent of the populace. The 'pull' factor to encourage inward migration to Corby is clearly no longer there and the Scottish population is no longer being renewed by incoming migrants. There are still a number of Scottish associations in the town and elements of a Scottish identity, however (Harper 2013). There is a locally organised and held Highland Games, and the local superstore still sells more Irn Bru (*the* national Scottish soft drink) than any other store in England (Bagshawe 2010). Thus we can see the contemporary pattern of Scottish migration to England reflected in this specific example. As with the rest of England, initially driven by industrial change and supported by ongoing employment opportunities, the relative size of the Scottish diaspora in Corby has begun to reduce in recent years; with a clear 6 per cent decline in the first decade of this century alone. Nonetheless, Scots still numbered one in eight of the local populace and Corby would emerge as a talking point during the discussions on potential Scottish independence and further devolution in 2013–14, illustrating the ongoing influence of the English-based Scottish diaspora.

London, the capital city to which James I/VI eagerly moved and where he largely remained, despite his promises to Scotland, has always been a magnet for all individuals across the regions and nations of the UK. Yet, while it has a fair representation of Scots, with over a hundred thousand from the 1980s through to the first decade of the twenty-first century (roughly 2 per cent of the entire population of Scotland during that same period of time), this number has declined in recent years to less than ninety thousand. There was a high point of the Scottish presence in London at 1.9 per cent in 1951 – clearly an influence of the Second World War and immediate post-war movement. Armitage (2005) considers this era to be one of the greatest periods of Scottish out-migration, but it is also one of the least researched. The Scottish myths of migration often focus on movement during the eighteenth and nineteenth centuries, to America, Australia and the wider British Empire, but the continual movement of Scots into England during the twentieth century rarely seems to feature within such discussions.

Yet, the decline from historical highs, in terms of overall percentage of the wider population, is as clear for London Scots as it is for those living in Corby or other cities and towns. In fact, this element of decline of Scottish-born residents, and Scottish individuals, can be witnessed across all the records considered here. Almost every city listed, Newcastle included, is at an historic low for Scottish-born residents, although Leeds remains an interesting outlier in that regard. Clearly, the former drivers of migration, heavy industry or specific employment opportunities, have lessened and, furthermore, with the increasing provision of facilities such as roads, electrification, rural broadband and other state-provided supports in wider rural Scotland, the push factors have also clearly decreased.

The state and nature of the contemporary Scottish diaspora in England

As we have clearly illustrated, there has been a continuous stream of migrants from Scotland to England over the past few centuries. The 2011 UK census reports that in the year before the census, 94,064 people moved into England from other parts of the UK, while at the same time, 41,319 people moved into Scotland from other parts of the UK (ONS 2015). While it is impossible to ascertain how many of those people moving into England were Scottish per se, it is clear that there is an ongoing level of migration within the UK and considerable movement between the constituent nations and regions. In the 2011 census, there were 708,872 Scots-born individuals resident in England, amounting to 1.3 per cent of the total population. This again represents a decline in recent overall numbers but is still a significant proportion of Scottish-born residents within the UK as a whole. In 2011 the Scottish population stood at 5,295,000 (National Records of Scotland 2016), which included 4,411,884 Scottish-born individuals or 83.3 per cent of the Scottish resident population. Therefore, Scottish-born individuals living in England represent 16 per cent of the Scottish-born population living in Scotland.

This figure would seem to suggest that while the economic attractions of England have become less obvious – or at least less enticing, given the decline of the traditional industrial base and manufacturing economy – nevertheless they remain important. Given the increasing housing shortage and lack of traditional industry-based employment England may well be becoming a less obvious destination for Scottish migrants, but it remains significant. Despite this ongoing migration, however, there are no clear visible groupings or particularly Scottish enclaves within England. Cities such as London – or Newcastle for that matter – lack any specific 'little Scotlands' and there is only a limited range of 'Scottish' clubs. Indeed, in comparison with North America, for example, there appears to be a general paucity of diaspora associations outside of specific 'Scottish' towns such as Corby. In their analysis, Leith and Sim (2012) clearly noted that despite the presence of one million plus Scottish-born/ancestral Scots in England there was only limited ongoing diaspora activity and very few connections between the widely dispersed populations. The local diaspora associations that did exist and did hold events on a regular basis were located in a few towns and cities (such as Liverpool) and these were in clear decline (Sim 2011b), with the number of participants and members reducing every year. Research has shown that Scottish associations and diaspora activity in cities with smaller Scottish populations such as Hull are also in significant decline (McCarthy 2007) and this suggests that the Scots in England have chosen not to retain these aspects of their national identity. Instead, over time, they appear to be absorbed into the host population, eventually becoming wholly 'English'.

In his recent analysis of the Scots in England, which he labelled an 'invisible ethnicity', Mycock, drawing on existing research, has identified what he called 'three significant and interconnected factors that have retarded its formation and recognition in either the host or home nation' (2014: 105). The first of these refers directly to the anomalous nature of the diaspora itself, which we identified at the beginning of this chapter. Mycock states that there is a clear lack of any contemporary drive to create diaspora organisations due to the lack of any significant problems Scots have in terms of being part of the wider British state and related sociopolitical culture. It is, relatively speaking, easy for Scots to be part of the wider 'British' sense of belonging, or at least it has been in the past. Recent political devolution and subsequent movement of power to the Scottish Parliament from Westminster may possibly have an impact on that sense of identity and ability to integrate smoothly. Mycock also states the romanticised nature of Scottishness, often prevalent among more distant diaspora groups, is not present in the English-based diaspora. Drawing on the work of Sim and McIntosh (2007), Mycock notes that the proximity to Scotland and the ready access to media and other information sources ensures a 'realistic comprehension of Scottish current affairs and society' (2014: 106). This agrees with the findings of Leith and Sim (2012). The road home to Scotland may lie just outside the front door, and the A1 and M6 make it easy to be in Scotland in a matter of hours.

The second factor identified by Mycock is that the Scots, as residents in England, are part of the 'host society' and have full citizenship, access and legal rights on an equal footing. While there may well be elements of *Scotophobia* (which we discuss below) in England, Mycock considers these to be normal aspects of English 'myopia or arrogance'. As part of the UK, Scottish people come under the civic, multi-ethnic British components of society and thus, simply put, fit in, for the most part.

His third 'influential factor' relates to Scotland and Scottish official attitudes. He points out that there is a lack of formal recognition of the Scottish diaspora in England by Scotland itself. He argues that, while understood, the act of migration by individual Scots and Scottish families is not always positively perceived, or framed, within Scotland. He states that the need to stem the 'brain drain', or even general migration from Scotland, has been a political issue across the Scottish party spectrum for many years. But historical views concerning migration, as well as the current need to maintain Scotland's population, have often focused on a more victim-based mentality, echoing events ranging from the defeat of the Jacobite cause or the Highland Clearances (Mycock 2014) to more recent deindustrialisation of the country under the Thatcher government.

This analysis, and the wider recent (albeit limited) research surrounding the Scottish population of England, allows us to draw some conclusions about the current state of Scotland *in* England. As we can witness through the census data, and as commented on by several researchers, the Scottish population in England has experienced a recent decline, suggesting a reduction in internal state migration southwards. Furthermore, those diaspora associations and activities that have existed in England over the past few decades have also begun to decline. In addition, and perhaps most importantly of all (and clearly related to the previous point), research has shown that succeeding diaspora generations – the children of Scottish emigrants who would be regarded as an *ancestral* diaspora – tend to adopt an English national identity. While it is true that some do acknowledge their ancestry and hence the Scottish identity that is available to them, the vast majority appear not to (Leith and Sim 2012). Mycock (2014) argues that this means that, to future generations, Scottishness is either 'less attractive' or it fails to provide the sociopolitical capital that would encourage the embracing of this identity.

Therefore, while there has been and continues to be a steady stream of Scottish migrants to England, it is clear that subsequent generations of those migrants are absorbed into the wider community and become part of the majority English-British cultural group. Also, the stream of migrants seems to be in decline, and this may reflect the changing socio-economic and perhaps even the changing sociopolitical climate within the wider UK.

The lack of voice for Scotland's nearest contemporary diaspora

One key aspect of the relationship that Mycock (2014) identified above, and that is highly significant in light of the contemporary political scene *in* Scotland is what he labels the 'absent voice' of the English-based Scottish diaspora. As his analysis indicates, and as recent events even more so clearly illustrate, the majority of the referenda held in the UK (a relatively recent phenomenon for Scottish and British politics) have not been UK-wide. In fact, since 1973, only three of the twelve referenda have been open to all voters across the UK – including the most recent one held in 2016 on whether the UK should leave the EU. The other nine have all been held on a national (or, in Northern Ireland, regional) basis. Thus, the 2014 referendum on whether Scotland should remain part of the UK, one that would clearly affect the sociopolitical basis of belonging for every individual within the near Scottish diaspora in England, did not allow the roughly 700,000–800,000 members of that diaspora to cast a vote. The 2014 Scottish independence referendum franchise was predicated on residency – and the election register for the Scottish Parliament was employed to allow those participants to vote. Thus, approximately 500,000 English, 20,000 Welsh, 36,000 Northern Irish and roughly 500,000 other individuals from EU and Commonwealth countries resident in Scotland were eligible to vote. This caused 'some heated political and public debate' (Mycock 2014: 110) around the issue. The town of Corby figured in such media discussion – with local politicians voicing their displeasure at being excluded and stating that individuals who would be welcome to a Scottish passport should be allowed a vote (BBC 2012). At the local Highland Games held in July 2014, a mock referendum, employing the wording of the ballot to be held in Scotland, saw 72 per cent of around six hundred participants vote 'No' (Silk 2014).

It is important to note that the regular norm in international matters is for citizens resident in other places to vote in their home country affairs. Thus, US citizens can register to vote in their home state irrespective of where in the world they live and many countries allow their foreign-based voters to partake in presidential or legislative elections or national plebiscites. Given how scattered the Scottish diaspora is across the world, however, it would have been an extraordinarily difficult task in 2014 to enrol all such individuals and enable them to vote. Both the Scottish and Westminster governments therefore opted to use residency as the criterion for voting eligibility.

It is clear though that recent government decisions, both at a Scottish and UK level, have not been kind to the English-based Scottish diaspora. Unable to vote on issues impacting directly on the sociopolitical relationship between their nation and their state, in either 1979, 1997 or 2014, English-based Scots have been bystanders to decisions that could well have made them strangers in a strange land or, at least technically, foreign nationals in a land in which their children have become fully integrated and firmly

English. But the position is already shifting. As the UK prepares to leave the EU and with the possibility of Scottish independence still on the political agenda, what might be the future for Scots living in England? Might Scots come to be viewed as 'foreigners'? Or is it that the situation has already begun to change? Devolution has clearly had an impact upon how Scotland is perceived by the English, and future changes in the relationship between Scotland and England could clearly have a further and perhaps a less positive impact.

While the relationship between Scotland and England has long been one of partnership, albeit an unequal and imbalanced one, and the flow of peoples between the two nations easy and continuous (although again, rather lopsided), what does the future hold? There already existed a somewhat anti-Scottish sentiment in parts of the media (Seenan 2005) and wider English society and recent constitutional decisions have clearly impacted on this situation.

Contemporary English attitudes towards Scotland: an increased 'Scotophobia'?

After the referendum of 2016, when the UK voted to leave the EU (an event popularly known as 'Brexit'), there was a notable increase in the number of xenophobic, language and related criminal acts, including the murder of Europeans resident in the UK (BBC 2016a, 2016b). One report noted a slightly longer-term trend beyond and prior to Brexit, with the Runnymede Trust stating that 'figures show that race hate crimes recorded by the police have increased by 15 per cent in England and Wales compared to 2013/14 (42,930 cases in 2014/15). Over the same period, religious hate crime increased by 43 per cent (3,254 cases in 2014/15)' (Runnymede Trust 2016: n.p.). While such figures are in themselves troubling, they represent a facet of any society experiencing inward migration from other areas – especially areas where individuals have different cultures, customs, religious practices and language. Indeed, this is not a new issue within the UK. For many years, minorities, whether they be defined by their colour, race, ethnicity, religious affiliation or language, have suffered varying levels of discrimination. The Scots, however, while subject to some forms of abuse in England, have been able, at the middle to higher levels of society certainly, to fully engage in, and gain from, the Union. Even at the working-class level there is little doubt that Scots have been able to benefit economically from moving south and seeking employment throughout the long period of Union between the two nations. However, while Scots have shared a monarch with England for over four hundred years, and with the wider UK a government for over three hundred, they have, during these centuries and despite achieving success at a variety of levels, often faced varying degrees of hostility either from individuals or within the media.

Yet we must remember that while subject to some abuse, and challenge, the Scots have, at the same time been able to gain access to the core of the economic system (it was, after all, a Scotsman who founded the Bank of England) and the political system. Significant numbers of Scots have been members of the Cabinet and several have occupied the highest offices in the land, up to and including being the prime minister. The twenty-first century opened with the first two prime ministers being Scottish born and while one of them was raised in England, the other was firmly a 'home-grown' Scot. It may be, however, that following devolution, it is much less likely that a Scots-born individual will, in future, become the UK prime minister. The first decades of the devolution century witnessed some negative comments about the influence of Scots in UK affairs – yet such complaints are not new.

The first Scottish-born prime minister of the UK was John Stuart, third Earl of Bute, and Devine reports that while he held his office for only a short time, the attacks on him 'and on Scots in general' were 'relentless', due to the increasing number of Scots holding UK state offices and the suspicion that 'Lord Bute was favouring his own kind' (2011: 10). This attitude and behaviour was reflected almost 250 years later, with accusations by a leading political media figure that a small coterie of Scottish politicians, a 'Scottish Raj', were making all the important decisions at the heart of British government (*Sunday Times* 2005). Disparaging comments about Scotland are regular aspects of political input from some media figures.[1] Just as the Earl of Bute was satirised in print in his day, the Scottish influence on contemporary UK politics was lampooned and personified by the vulgar, foul-mouthed personage of 'Malcolm Tucker', a fictional spin doctor to a fictional prime minister in the popular BBC comedy, *The Thick of It*. Of course, there is no doubt that as many Scots laughed as loudly as other UK nationalities did at this satire.

The ongoing relationship between the two nations

We have continually referred to the changing Scottish/UK sociopolitical landscape of the late twentieth and early twenty-first century. There can be no doubt that, while we have not witnessed the emergence of a distinctly 'new' politics in Scotland, the presence of a Scottish Parliament and the decisions made by Scotland for Scotland (or 'Scottish solutions for Scottish problems'

(Leith and Sim 2012)) have led to some ripples in the relationship between Scotland and England. While the sociopolitical relationship has been created and continued by the elites within both nations, the attitudes of the masses are clearly important. As we discussed in Chapter 3, the Scots have long held a strong and distinct sense of identity. Many have long shared that identity with Britishness, while others have insisted on the fact they are not British but Scottish. In fact, as the twenty-first century has progressed, the number of Scots who have felt Scottish rather than British has increased, with the number of individuals cleaving to both identities reducing. However, the situation in England has been rather different. For perhaps a variety of reasons, the English have not always clearly differentiated between their national and state identities. As Curtice and Heath have pointed out, England has long shared statehood with four other national identities and they suggest that the English have never seemed unhappy with this state of affairs (2000). Of course, as the significantly largest partner in population terms, England has always been dominant. Also, this comment was made when devolution was quite literally in its infancy and there had never been a UK legislature other than Westminster, and hence no rival to London-based legislative decision-making.

Throughout the period of Union, England had long held a dual identity (Heath and Kellas 1998) and, for the majority of English-based residents, being English and British was a synonymous state of being. That is not to say that some English people did not, as the Scots have long done, differentiate themselves and see themselves as English rather than British. However, this was a small percentage of the population – in fact in 1997, only 7 per cent of respondents to a mass survey declared themselves English and not British (British Election Study 1997). This was, of course, the same year that devolution was decided upon by the people of Scotland, Wales and London. Since then, there have been evident changes, in both how people in England view Scotland and the idea of devolution and in how English people view themselves – it may well be that there is a correlation between these views.

For instance, only two years later in 1999 the proportion of individuals who responded that they were English and not British had risen 10 per cent to 17 per cent (Curtice and Heath 2000). The authors of this study reported that this clear example of people in England becoming more aware of their English identity was 'in response to the introduction of devolution in the rest of the UK' (Curtice and Heath 2000: 172) and that the presence of 'little Englanders' who wanted to shut out the outside world was 'alive and well'. The very same study was specifically asked about Scottish devolution. In 1997 only 6 per cent of respondents in England felt that Scotland should be independent from the UK and the EU, and 8 per cent from the UK, but not Europe. A minority, but clear plurality, 38 per cent thought that Scotland should have its own parliament with some taxation powers and 17 per cent thought it should have a parliament with no taxation powers. However, 23 per cent of those in England thought that Scotland should not have an elected parliament at all. Clearly, a sizeable minority of 23 per cent did not want Scotland to be devolved and 14 per cent thought it should be independent.

In a similar study carried out a decade later in 2007, there had been remarkably limited change in both English attitudes towards devolution and Scotland and to English identity. Although 19 per cent now identified themselves as 'English, not British' this was only a 2 per cent increase over two years. However, there had been a decrease in the number of English people who felt 'both English and British' and this had fallen from 45 per cent in 1997 to 31 per cent in 2007 (Curtice 2009). In analysing the data, Curtice noted, however, that 'for the most part there is an overwhelming preference to maintain the Union' and that 'there seems to be little reason to think that the experience of devolution elsewhere in the UK has given rise to sufficient resentment' (Curtice 2009: 7). Indeed, 36 per cent wanted Scotland to have a parliament with taxation powers and 12 per cent with a parliament alone, while 19 per cent wanted Scotland to be independent and only 18 per cent thought it should not have a parliament.

At the same time, the changing relationship between Scotland and the rest of the UK did have an impact upon how Scotland was viewed by England in fiscal matters. While continuing to support the Union, attitudes in England on government spending in Scotland were split. In 2007 some 38 per cent felt that Scotland had 'pretty much its fair share' of public spending, 32 per cent felt it was 'much more' or little more' than Scotland's fair share and 75 per cent either agreed or strongly agreed that Scotland should pay for its services out of taxes raised in Scotland. Nonetheless, while money matters were clearly an issue to England, ten years of devolution had seen little shift and no real growth of resentment. However, those ten years had seen the governments of both the UK and of Scotland in broad agreement, with respectively a Labour and Labour–Liberal Democrat coalition in charge. In 2007, the SNP became the ruling party of Scotland, and thus presented a clear divide between the two governing elites.

By 2011, after four years of SNP government in Scotland and a year of Conservative–Liberal Democrat coalition government in Westminster, a shift in English attitudes was evident. In 1997, 55 per cent had wished Scotland to remain part of the UK, but by 2011 this had shifted to a minority view – with only 44 per cent supporting Scotland's continued part in the Union. At the same time, support for Scotland leaving the UK had risen to 26 per cent. It was stated that there were some signs of an English backlash (Curtice and Ormston 2012) and this is clearly evident in financial areas. In 2011, attitudes in England towards Scotland's share of public spending had clearly shifted, with 44 per cent feeling Scotland got too much and only 30 per cent saying it got its fair share; 23 per cent were unsure (Curtice and Ormston 2012). Furthermore, 65 per cent in England felt that Scottish MPs should not be allowed to vote on English matters – the West Lothian question had firmly come home to roost. What is clear is that after a little over a decade of devolution, there was 'evidence of growing discontent … that may now be beginning to be accompanied by some erosion of previous support for the Union' (Curtice and Ormston 2012: 130).

In 2007, when asked (in England only) if England would be financially better off, worse off or about the same if Scotland should become independent, 61 per cent said there would no difference and only 13 per cent thought England would be better off. By 2017, only 28 per cent thought there would be no difference and 33 per cent thought England would be better off. There has been a clear change in attitudes towards Scotland in England and in attitudes towards the relationship between the two nations.

Concluding thoughts

The continued presence of a large number of Scots-born individuals in England points to the positive nature of the relationship between the two nations, which exist, alongside their other neighbours, within the same state. Since 1707, the movement has been one of fellow citizens, if also one of different nationalities. At the same time, it is clear that the Scots have felt welcome and able to move freely within the UK and we have illustrated how they have become fully integrated, with their descendants usually becoming integral members of the majority population within one generation. However, there has always been some level of friction between the two peoples, with cultural, social, economic and political differences all playing their part. The relationship has been generally peaceful and long-standing, with mostly benign attitudes at reign. There can be little doubt, however, that there has been significant sociopolitical change in the last two decades and that this has impacted upon the relationship between Scotland and England. How this will play out in the future is uncertain, but with clearly stated differences between the two nations in terms of electoral party support, membership of the EU and attitudes towards the UK Union also in flux, Scotland's future relationship with England and the position of the Scots in England will clearly be subject to ongoing change.

Further reading

Our previous chapter suggested further reading for diaspora studies in general. As for this chapter, there is no one book on the Scottish diaspora in England but there is coverage within other books on the diaspora such as Tom Devine's *To the Ends of the Earth: Scotland's Global Diaspora* (2011).

There are a number of useful academic papers, including Marjory Harper's '"Come to Corby": A Scottish Steel Town in the Heart of England' in *Immigrants and Minorities* (2013), Duncan Sim's 'The Scottish Community and Scottish Organisations on Merseyside: Development and Decline of a Diaspora' in *Journal of Scottish Historical Studies* (2011), Angela McCarthy's 'The Scots' Society of St Andrew, Hull, 1910–2001: Immigrant, Ethnic and Transnational Association' in *Immigrants and Minorities* (2007) and Murray Leith and Duncan Sim's 'Second Generation Identities: The Scottish Diaspora in England' in *Sociological Research Online* (2012) or their 'The Scots in England: A Different Kind of Diaspora?' in *National Identities* (2019).

See also Andrew Mycock's very interesting chapter, 'Invisible and Inaudible? England's Scottish Diaspora and the Politics of the Union' in Leith and Sim's edited volume *The Modern Scottish Diaspora* (2014).

Finally, David McCrone and Frank Bechhofer look at the issue of returning migrants in their chapter 'Coming Home: Return Migrants in Twenty-First-Century Scotland' in Mario Varricchio's edited collection *Back to Caledonia* (2012).

Chapter 12
Art and culture in Scotland

Introduction

Cultural identity is important to any nation, perhaps doubly so to a stateless nation such as Scotland, as culture can help to preserve the nation's distinctiveness. Macdonald (2009), for example, highlights how Scotland, both as a part of the UK and of the British Empire and as a nation in its own right, could be seen as both central and marginal to the major cultural forces of the age. She notes how cultural images have emerged indigenously, while at the same time the country's culture also reflects a popular imagery ascribed to it by others. She sees Scottish culture therefore as a 'vibrant cacophony of competing voices' (Macdonald 2009: 289).

As we will explore later in this chapter, culture has been placed at the heart of government policy in the years since devolution. The then First Minister Jack McConnell made a St Andrew's Day speech in 2003 in which he referred to culture as being at the core of government and crucial to help shape Scotland's future and national identity (Bonnar 2014). The present SNP government minister for culture, Fiona Hyslop, has similarly argued the intrinsic value of culture to the nation, championing it as an 'intrinsic and public good'. This has been in sharp contrast to her former Westminster counterpart, Maria Miller MP, who argued that culture could only be valued in terms of its economic impact (Archer 2014; Behr and Brennan 2014).

Because cultural policy is devolved, it occupies a larger percentage of the Scottish Government's remit than it does in the UK as a whole. Scotland's relatively small size also means that those involved in the cultural and creative industries are more connected with each other and with the government. Their importance may be seen by the fact that they contribute annually almost

£3 billion to the Scottish economy and employ more than 63,000 people (Archer 2014).

In this chapter, we explore various aspects of Scottish culture, including literature, language, music, theatre, film and art, and we also look at the Scottish Government's cultural policies and how they are contributing to the nation's sense of well-being, as well as its sense of identity.

Literature

It is not, of course, possible in a short chapter to discuss in detail Scotland's literary history and this is covered much more extensively elsewhere (for example Crawford 2007). For many, the country's earliest popular literature is focused on the poems of Robert Burns in the late eighteenth century and the Waverley novels of Sir Walter Scott in the early nineteenth. Both were writing at a time when Scotland was already part of the UK yet both wrote from a very distinctive Scottish standpoint. Burns's poems were written primarily in the Scots language and Scott's novels often deal with aspects of Scottish history, for example the Jacobite risings, with which the British state would not have been comfortable. Yet Scott managed to be relatively ambivalent in his novels, treating Scottish history in a rather nostalgic way and presenting the rebels as heroes of a culture that had actually vanished (Gardiner 2005).

During the mid-nineteenth century, however, Gardiner (2005) suggests that there was a 'deafening silence' in Scottish literature with writers such as Thomas Carlyle being very Anglocentric. Only with Robert Louis Stevenson was there something of a revival, although many of his stories, such as *Kidnapped* and its sequel *Catriona*, followed Scott in embracing a rather romanticised Scottish history. The late nineteenth century was also the period of the 'kailyard', which we have discussed in more detail in Chapter 4. Writers such as J. M. Barrie and Ian McLaren described a small-town Scotland, peopled by local 'worthies', far removed from the urbanised existence experienced by most Scots at the time and far removed from the hardships of real rural life.

One of Stevenson's most famous works, *The Strange Case of Dr Jekyll and Mr Hyde*, published in 1886 can, in Gardiner's (2005) view, be read as illustrating the identity split between Scottishness and Britishness. The split is also evident in the work of John Buchan (1875–1940), who was proudly both British and Scottish. His novels, like *The Thirty-Nine Steps* and *Prester John* may have had a Scottish setting but had a strong British imperial plot. Buchan himself may be seen as part of the British Establishment, of course, being Governor General of Canada for the last five years of his life.

A significant shift in Scottish literature came during the interwar period, often referred to as the 'Scottish Renaissance'. The poet Christopher Murray Grieve, writing in the Scots language under the name of Hugh McDiarmid, published *A Drunk Man Looks at the Thistle* in 1926, an epic poem that explored a range of issues around Scotland and its sense of identity. Neil Gunn, from Caithness, wrote a wide range of powerful novels set in the Highlands, exploring the rural farming and fishing experiences, his most famous being *The Silver Darlings*. Gunn had a strong sense of a modern Scotland evolving through the time he was writing, while retaining an interest in the country's past. These, he believed, underpinned the country's sense of itself (Crawford 2007). Other writers of this period included Compton Mackenzie and R. B. Cunninghame Graham and all four became involved in nationalist politics, helping to found the National Party of Scotland in 1928, which became the modern SNP in 1934.

On the east side of the country, Lewis Grassic Gibbon's novels, most famously the trilogy begun by *Sunset Song* (published in 1932) and collected in *A Scots Quair*, portrayed a harsh rural experience far removed from the cosiness of the 'kailyard school'. *Sunset Song* has regularly been voted as the country's favourite novel and it has been adapted both for television and cinema.

These interwar authors helped to shift the focus of Scottish writers' activities back to Scotland and McDiarmid in particular, by choosing to write in the Scots language, was making a particularly political point. His actions made it easier for authors who came after him to use colloquial Scots in their work, without feeling the need to pander to wider audiences who might struggle with some of the dialect. Recent examples include the poets Tom Leonard and Liz Lochhead and writers such as Irvine Welsh, Alasdair Gray and James Kelman. Kelman is interesting as an author who refuses to compromise in his writing. In 1994, when his novel *How Late It Was, How Late* won the Booker Prize, one of the judges Rabbi Julia Neuberger resigned, complaining that she found the novel 'in broad Glaswegian dialect ... was too much, too inaccessible' (McGlynn 2002: 50).

What is significant here is, first, the greater confidence among modern Scottish writers to write about Scottish issues using local language and dialect. This perhaps reflects the greater confidence that many Scots have in their national identity. Second, there is a strong connection between Scottish writing and nationalist, or at least pro-devolution politics. Crawford notes the parallels between the nature of modern Scottish literature and the recovery of a Parliament in Edinburgh:

> While its approach is through imaginative reshaping, selection and honing, this literature is often quickened by substantial problems in society. These difficulties are far from uniquely Scottish but writers have often looked to markedly Scottish forms of local language – in vocabulary, allusion or structure – in order to articulate them. Though the word is a slippery one, a 'democratic' urge within Scottish writing has grown in strength, going beyond the boundaries of conventional politics, and beyond Scotland itself'. (2007: 660)

Language

It is appropriate at this juncture to move on to a more detailed consideration of language and to the different voices of Scotland. As the numbers of writers choosing to use the Scots language and dialects has increased, so too has interest in the country's language(s). Kay (1986), for example, has described in some detail the different dialects across the country and the variations in syntax and grammar that accompany them. He notes that there is now a much greater acceptance of dialect in schools and places of employment and a greater willingness perhaps to reject the anglicised 'received pronunciation' with which we are so familiar on the BBC.

The tension between speaking colloquially and speaking 'properly' was perfectly captured by the Glasgow poet Tom Leonard:

> This is thi
> six a clock
> news thi
> man said n
> thi reason
> a talk wia
> BBC accent
> iz coz yi
> widny wahnt
> mi ti talk
> aboot thi
> trooth wia
> voice lik
> wanna you
> scruff. (1984: 88)

The poem is spelt phonetically to highlight the poet's criticism of a perceived 'correct' way to speak. He mocks the BBC newsreader for presuming that, if the news was read in a Glasgow accent, then somehow it would appear less trustworthy.

Poets like Edwin Morgan and Liz Lochhead, like Leonard, have also used the Glasgow dialect. Interestingly, and perhaps a sign of a recognition of the value of dialect, both Morgan and Lochhead have served a period as Scotland's 'Makar' or national poet, the Scottish equivalent of being appointed Poet Laureate. The current Makar, Jackie Kay, also writes in Scots as well as English and has identified 'glaikit' (stupid) as her favourite word. She has described Scots as a 'great cauldron full of riches' and her poem 'Old Tongue' (Kay 2005) laments the fact that those who move away from Scotland lose their Scottish words in the process.

It is important at this point, however, to note that Scotland does, of course, have another indigenous language and one that is also undergoing a revival, namely Gaelic. At the 2011 census, a total of 87,100 people had some Gaelic language skills, either in terms of speaking, reading or understanding the language. This represented 1.7 per cent of the population and was a slight fall from 2001. However, there was an increase of 8.6 per cent in the numbers of Gaelic speakers under the age of twenty-five, reflecting perhaps a growing interest in Gaelic and the introduction in various parts of the country of Gaelic-medium education (see Chapter 5). In 2015–16, there were 5,200 children in Gaelic-medium nurseries, primary and secondary schools (Scottish Government 2017a).

Gaelic has long had a literature of its own, of course, particularly in poetry and song (Thomson 1992), but it has perhaps not been widely read across Scotland. In recent years, however, poets like Raasay-based Sorley MacLean (1911–96) have received significant attention and some of his poems like 'Hallaig', about the Highland Clearances, have been partly set to music.

Gaelic music and song have long been celebrated at the annual Mòd, established in 1891 by An Comunn Gàidhealach, the Gaelic arts and cultural organisation. But more recently, Gaelic has been used in popular music by bands such as Runrig and Capercaillie and solo singers like Julie Fowlis; their performances and songwriting have demonstrated that Gaelic can be used to deal with and sing about current (often political) issues. The Celtic Connections music festival in Glasgow every January features a wide range of Gaelic musicians.

The position has been aided by the Gaelic Language Act of 2005 that placed on a statutory footing Bòrd na Gàidhlig, whose role is to promote the language, and the Bòrd now has the powers to prepare a national Gaelic Language Plan (Scottish Government 2017a). Public bodies, such as local authorities, may also be required to prepare such plans. At the same time, the BBC established a Gaelic language channel, BBC Alba, in 2008 and from 2011 this became available on Freeview, allowing it to be accessed by the whole country. The most recent available figures suggest that BBC Alba attracts around seven hundred thousand viewers per week (BBC 2015), remarkable given that most of these viewers will have to make use of subtitles. Oliver (2005) suggests that this indicates a shift within Gaelic from traditional to modern, from Gemeinschaft to Gesellschaft, so that Gaelic is not solely restricted to a remote corner of the Highlands and Islands (a 'Gàidhealtachd') but now essentially belongs to all of Scottish society.

Music

Discussions about the Mòd lead us perhaps on to a broader consideration of Scottish music, where there are several strands to consider. First of all, there is a strong tradition of folksong in Scotland, dating back centuries; some of these songs were captured by Robert Burns, although Burns himself was of course a prolific songwriter. Similarly, Sir Walter Scott sought to capture and record the rich tradition of Border ballads, publishing his *Minstrelsy of the Scottish Border* in 1802–3. Elsewhere in Scotland, there was a substantial musical heritage in bagpipe music, the tradition of Highland and Island fiddlers and the 'bothy ballads' of rural Aberdeenshire and the north-east.

In the early twentieth century, however, Scotland was perhaps best known for its music hall tradition, exemplified by the worldwide success of Harry Lauder, and the more local success of people like Tommy Lorne, Harry Gordon and Will Fyffe, the last named noted for his theme song, 'I Belong to Glasgow'. There is no doubt that Lauder's success was a reflection of his time (Maloney 2010) and music hall frequently dealt in stereotypes, but history has not judged him kindly. Hugh McDiarmid hated the way that Lauder had portrayed his homeland and, more recently, he has been criticised for what Nairn (1977) has described as 'sub-cultural Scotchery'. Hence, for many: 'Lauder epitomises ... the kitsch vulgarity of tartanry and the sentimental couthiness of the Kailyard. He is the archetypal Uncle Tam, capering shamefully, kilt, tam o'shanter, waggly walking-stick and all ... the minstrel progenitor of a pervasive shortbread and calendar caricature of Scotland' (Goldie 2000: 10). The Scottish music hall tradition continued well into the post-war era, not least with television shows such as *The White Heather Club*, hosted by entertainer Andy Stewart, but it now survives essentially only in annual pantomimes.

Significantly, the period after the Second World War saw a revival in the Scottish folksong tradition, aided by the establishment of a School of Scottish Studies at Edinburgh University (Munro 1991). The writer and poet Hamish Henderson (2004) played a hugely important role in this by travelling across Scotland interviewing farmers, shepherds and travelling people and attending ceilidhs and musical events all over the country and recording poems, songs and stories. His work gradually paved the way for a more widespread revival in folk music and acted as a bridge between the Scottish Renaissance of the 1930s and contemporary culture (Finlay 1998). In the subsequent decades, a number of folk groups emerged such as the Joe Gordon Folk Four, Robin Hall and Jimmie Macgregor and the Corries. By the start of the twenty-first century, there were a number of significant solo artists like Karine Polwart and Sheena Wellington, bands such as Skerryvore and Skippinish and even the bagpipes had entered popular music with the success of the Red Hot Chilli Pipers. Many of these artists have played at the annual Celtic Connections music festival in Glasgow, which has acted as an important showcase for Scottish folk music (and international music with Scottish connections).

Orchestral music and dance has also been increasingly important in Scotland. The BBC's Scottish Symphony Orchestra was established in 1925 but the post-war period saw the founding of the Scottish National Orchestra in 1950 (a development from an older Scottish Orchestra and given the 'Royal' prefix in 1977), Scottish Opera in 1962, Scottish Theatre Ballet (later simply 'Scottish Ballet') in 1969, the Scottish Chamber Orchestra in 1974 and the contemporary Scottish Dance Theatre in 1986. Following on the heels of the Edinburgh International Festival, founded in 1947 and that we discuss below, it demonstrated a significant flowering of Scottish culture. It has enabled Pittock (2008) to suggest that Scotland has developed a significant cultural autonomy, quite distinct from the rest of the UK.

Nor should one forget the contribution of Scotland to modern popular music, from soloists like Lulu and Annie Lennox, through the Average White Band and Simple Minds, to Orange Juice, Deacon Blue, Texas and Travis. Some bands have openly flaunted their Scottishness, such as the Bay City

Rollers with their use of tartan, and the Proclaimers with their refusal to 'tone down' their distinctive Fife accents (Macdonald 2009).

Many of these musicians have also been openly nationalist in their politics and it is significant that one of the most active groups in the 'Yes' campaign during the 2014 independence referendum was the National Collective, made up of artists, writers and musicians from across Scotland. Non-party political in nature, they saw independence as a way of stimulating further cultural development in the country.

Stage and screen

As with music, Scotland has a long theatrical tradition, although the country had no playwrights of the calibre of Shakespeare and lacked royal patronage after the Union of the Crowns in 1603. Nevertheless, early dramas exist, such as Allan Ramsay's *The Gentle Shepherd* (1725), John Hume's *Douglas* (1756) and, perhaps most importantly, Sir David Lyndsay's *Satire of the Three Estates*, dating from 1552. Largely forgotten for almost four hundred years, Lyndsay's play was revived at the second Edinburgh Festival in 1948, where its staging was seen as something of a triumph (Harvie 2003).

The establishment of the Edinburgh Festival itself in 1947 came about as a kind of 'post-war rallying point' for the arts and to contribute to their revival. It also helped to revive Edinburgh itself after the war. It had a European significance, not least because many of the other major European arts festivals such as Munich, Salzburg and Bayreuth, were not able to reopen until the 1950s (Harvie 2003). The festival had, and continues to have, a dual role, in bringing international culture to Scotland and to present Scottish culture to the world.

Since its foundation, the core International Festival has spawned a number of other accompanying 'festivals'. Some such as the Film Festival and the Festival Fringe also date from 1947, while others such as the Military Tattoo (1950) and the Book Festival (1983) came later. Research by Biggar Economics (2014) suggested that Edinburgh's cultural venues (including hosting the Festivals) supported five thousand full-time equivalent (FTE) jobs and contributed £194 million to the Scottish economy. It also helped to sustain a theatre infrastructure in Scotland by working with other companies and artists. Updated research by BOP Consulting (2016) suggested that the contribution to the Scottish economy had risen to £313 million and approximately 5,600 FTE jobs were supported.

Indeed, there have been important developments in theatre elsewhere in Scotland. The Citizens' Theatre in Glasgow was established in 1943 by the playwright James Bridie (Bannister 1955), eventually becoming a leading theatre venue after 1969 with the appointment of Giles Havergal as director (Macdonald 2009). There were similar developments in Edinburgh (the Traverse Theatre in 1963) and in Dundee, a permanent repertory company established in 1999.

The increased sense of a Scottish identity that stimulated developments in music and literature was also seen in the theatre, from the 1970s onwards. Possibly the most influential company was 7:84, established in 1971 by the playwright John McGrath, his wife Elizabeth MacLennan and brother-in-law David MacLennan. By 1973 it was touring Scotland with *The Cheviot, the Stag and the Black, Black Oil*, a significant and hugely popular piece of agitprop theatre about landownership, the Highland Clearances and the exploitation of rural communities. David MacLennan subsequently founded a second similar company, Wildcat Theatre productions, in 1978. Both companies were enormously influential in bringing political debate into the theatre and raising awareness of aspects of Scottish history and identity (DiCenzo 1996; Stevenson 2002).

Perhaps the most significant recent development has been the establishment of a National Theatre of Scotland (NTS) in 2003, another reflection of an enhanced Scottish consciousness (Leach 2007). In sharp contrast to the English National Theatre in London, the NTS does not have a building of its own, although it has headquarters and rehearsal space in Glasgow. It operates as a 'theatre without walls', commissioning plays from existing theatres, companies and playwrights and taking its productions across Scotland. Within a very short time, the NTS had proved itself with the production of a stunningly successful *Black Watch*, exploring the regiment's history. As well as touring Scotland, the play has been presented in England, Ireland, Australia, New Zealand and the United States.

But, although Scottish theatre appears healthy, the same is not entirely true for Scottish film and, at the time of writing, there is still ongoing debate concerning the need to establish a sizeable film studio in the country. Nor has Scotland necessarily been well served by its portrayal on-screen in a range of Hollywood films over the years.

We have already referred, in Chapter 4, to the tartanry of such films as *Brigadoon*. Many of the earlier films about Scotland stressed a rather romanticised, tartan version of Scotland, as in films like *Bonnie Prince Charlie*

(1948), starring David Niven, *Whisky Galore* (1949) and *Kidnapped* (1971), starring Michael Caine (Butt 2010). Even later films by some Scottish directors like Bill Forsyth were not immune to a somewhat whimsical, almost 'kailyard' treatment of Scotland, a prime example being *Local Hero* (1983) (Edensor 2002). To be fair, there have also been a range of more recent films that have been grittier and in some respects, perhaps more realistic in their portrayal of Scottish urban life, including *Shallow Grave* (1994), *Small Faces* (1996) and *Ratcatcher* (1999), as well as film adaptations of novels such as *Trainspotting* (1996), its sequel in 2017 and *Young Adam* (2003), all starring Ewan McGregor.

The film that perhaps best epitomises Scotland's somewhat ambiguous relationship to its history and to its portrayal is *Braveheart*, about the Scottish hero William Wallace, directed by and starring Mel Gibson, and released in 1995 (Edensor 2002). The film has been criticised by historians for its serious factual inaccuracies with Ewen suggesting that the film 'almost totally sacrifices historical accuracy for epic adventure' (1995: 1220). There have also been criticisms of the use of tartan and face paint, not to mention the fact that the Battle of Stirling Bridge, the scene of Wallace's greatest triumph, appears to take place with no bridge visible on the screen. And yet, the film was hugely successful, winning five Oscars, including Best Picture.

Within Scotland itself, the film struck a particular chord, perhaps because of the timing of its release. It emerged at a time when John Major's Conservative government was approaching its end and when it was becoming clear that legislation to establish the new Scottish Parliament would soon be enacted – as it was two years later. As a result, the film was embraced by nationalist politicians as well as the wider public and Edensor (1997) describes how there was a request to show the film to the Scottish international football team to induce patriotic feeling and spur the team to victory. Perhaps the secret of *Braveheart*'s success was the fact that it showed Scotland in a positive light as well as depicting a famous victory, and so was relatively free of the kailyard whimsy that so often characterised previous films about Scotland. Scots seemed willing therefore to forgive it its faults.

On the small screen, Scotland's portrayal has reflected that of Hollywood. In the 1950s and 1960s, Scotland was seen on television in the tartanry of *The White Heather Cub*, as well as in cosy dramas like *Dr Finlay's Casebook*. Scottish Television's 'soap', *Take the High Road*, was a classic example of kailyardism (Gardiner 2005). But there was a shift from the 1970s onwards with a number of significant BBC television dramas such as *Sunset Song*, *Tutti Frutti* and *Your Cheatin' Heart*, as well as the introduction in 2002 of a BBC Scotland 'soap'

River City; set on Clydeside, it could perhaps be seen as a kind of Scottish *EastEnders* – certainly grittier and more urban in its approach than many Scottish television programmes that had gone before.

For many in Scotland, however, the problem with Scottish broadcasting is the fact that in many respects it is not really 'Scottish'. The BBC did not open a television studio in Scotland until 1955 and there were initially very limited Scottish contributions to the UK schedules. Thus: 'BBC Scotland did as well as could be expected as a regional outpost of a nationwide corporation, but, like all Scottish arms of nationalised industries, it lacked sufficient independence and funds to truly meet the needs of the home market' (Macdonald 2009: 340–341). In the years since devolution, dissatisfaction with the position has grown and the BBC has faced increased criticism for being too London dominated. In 2008, the Scottish Government appointed a Scottish Broadcasting Commission to examine broadcasting in Scotland and in their final report, *Platform for Success*, they recommended a new framework for broadcasting, including a new Scottish digital network. Criticisms of the BBC's approach to Scottish news came to a head during the independence referendum when it was viewed in some quarters as being too supportive of the 'status quo' and of giving insufficient coverage to the 'Yes' campaign. There were a number of demonstrations by political activists outside the BBC's Scottish headquarters.

Their complaints did appear to have a degree of substance, given that a research study carried out the previous year by the BBC Trust itself discovered that fewer than half of Scots believed that the BBC accurately reflected their lives (Miller 2013). In 2015, the Corporation's Audience Council for Scotland urged a less 'anglified' perspective and argued for BBC Scotland to be given greater authority and resources to commission its own programmes (BBC Trust 2015). This may be seen against the background of the BBC's charter renewal process. In its submission to the UK Government as part of this process, the Scottish Government (2016b) claimed that the income from licence fees in Scotland was £323 million but expenditure by the BBC in Scotland was only £190.5 million. The BBC has now attempted to address the issue by launching a dedicated BBC Scotland channel in early 2019, broadcasting between 7 pm and midnight. As well as Scottish news and sport, there are opportunities for new comedy and drama, although a large proportion of programmes are repeats (BBC 2018); detailed viewing figures are not yet available. In addition, there are of course many programmes made elsewhere in the UK that are watched by a Scottish audience and so the situation is not clear-cut, but the debate does reflect a growing dissatisfaction with the present position and it will be interesting to monitor the success or otherwise of the new BBC Scotland channel.

Commercial television in Scotland is represented by Scottish Television (STV), which has held the franchise since 1957. In 1997, it took over Grampian Television, which had been based in Aberdeen and provided services to the north of the country. In *Scotsport*, which broadcast from 1957 to 2008, the channel had what was reputed to be the longest-running television sports programme in the world and its crime series *Taggart* was also characterised by longevity, being shown across the UK from 1983 to 2010. At the time of writing, when most commercial companies use a single 'ITV' brand, Scottish Television retains an 'STV' branding in its broadcasts, perhaps to emphasise Scottish distinctiveness.

Art and architecture

The earliest examples of Scottish art are the carvings and illuminated manuscripts that we associate with Pictish stones and early Christianity. But Scotland suffered, first from the Reformation whose Calvinists frowned on much medieval church art and this resulted in the loss of a lot of early stained glass and paintings. Second, the Union of the Crowns led to a loss of royal patronage and so it was not perhaps until the eighteenth century that a more recent distinctive Scottish art began to appear.

Painters from that period, such as Allan Ramsay, Henry Raeburn and David Wilkie, were essentially portrait painters, often commissioned to record members of the Scottish aristocracy. Some of them did paint landscapes but it was not until the nineteenth century that a significant body of Scottish landscape art appeared. Individuals such as Alexander Nasmyth, John Knox and Horatio McCulloch were significant figures but perhaps the best known (albeit born in England) was Sir Edwin Landseer, a recipient of the patronage of Queen Victoria. His paintings of romantic Scottish landscapes and of majestic animals in *Stag at Bay* and *Monarch of the Glen* captured the Victorian imagination (Ormond 2005).

From the late nineteenth century developments in Scottish art are associated with the Glasgow School, a loose group reflecting the growing importance of the city as a cultural centre. The Glasgow School of Art had been established in 1853 but its present home is the famous building designed by the artist and architect Charles Rennie Mackintosh in 1897. Mackintosh himself, his wife

Margaret MacDonald, her sister Frances and her husband Herbert Macnair became known as 'the Four' or the 'Glasgow Four' and were hugely significant in the development of art nouveau, the Celtic revival and the Arts and Crafts Movement. Another group of artists operating in the city at the same time were known as the 'Glasgow Boys', including James Guthrie, Joseph Crawhall, George Henry and E. A. Walton (Billcliffe 1988).

Elsewhere in Scotland, and slightly later, the 'Scottish Colourists' comprised John Fergusson, Francis Cadell, Samuel Peploe and Leslie Hunter. All four knew each other, spent time in France and exhibited in the years after the First World War (Long 1999).

In more recent times, there have been a number of significant Scottish painters, including John Bellany (1942–2013), whose work focused mainly on the east-coast fishing villages, and a number of Glasgow-born or trained artists including Peter Howson, Ken Currie and Adrian Wiszniewski. The most financially successful Scottish painter is probably Jack Vettriano from Fife; his prints sell well but he has received little critical acclaim (Lyall 2006).

Current artistic developments in Scotland have been in the direction of art installations rather than painting, however. In the mid-1980s the Glasgow School of Art established a new sculpture and environmental art programme and this has encouraged a new group of artists with only a limited interest in traditional painting. The success of the programme may be measured by the significant number of Glasgow-trained artists who have won or been finalists for the prestigious Turner Prize (Lowndes 2010).

While there are therefore a significant number of Scottish artists and Scotland has contributed much to the art world, there is perhaps no clear view as to whether this can be regarded as 'Scottish' art or whether there is a distinctive 'Scottish' style. And the remit of the country's national galleries has been to acquire the best of both Scottish and international art; thus, like many other national collections, it reflects 'the internationalism and indeed interculturalism of art' (Hamilton and Scullion 2003). Nevertheless, as they point out, some questions have been raised about acquisition policies that appear to prioritise expensive European paintings, sometimes to the exclusion of Scottish artists.

We have already referred to the architecture of Charles Rennie Mackintosh but there was, of course, a Scottish tradition of architecture dating back to the medieval period. Buildings dating from this time were almost exclusively castles or fortified houses or church buildings. Scottish domestic architecture, however, tends to date essentially from the eighteenth century and the work of architects like the Adam brothers in shaping cities like Edinburgh. Their work on Edinburgh New Town in the classical style was, together with the city's reputation as a centre for the Enlightenment, responsible for the city becoming known as the 'Athens of the North'.

Domestic architecture in Scotland was often done in a vernacular or local style, using local materials. In Glasgow, early nineteenth-century building was carried out in yellow sandstone, quarried locally; when that ran out, red sandstone was imported from Ayrshire. In Aberdeen, the local granite quarries provided the building material that gave the city its distinctive character.

Many nineteenth-century buildings in Scotland were of a Gothic style, as was the case elsewhere in Victorian Britain. But this style was often combined with what is often referred to as 'Scots baronial', the use of turrets, mock battlements and stepped gables harking back to Scottish medieval castles. Major nineteenth-century buildings such as Stirling's Wallace Monument, constructed between 1859 and 1869, exemplify this style. Indeed, even architects such as Mackintosh, who pioneered art nouveau design, incorporated elements of Scots baronial into his most famous buildings such as the Glasgow School of Art. Another exponent of the style was Robert Lorimer in buildings such as the Scottish National War Memorial at Edinburgh Castle, which opened in 1927 (Glendinning *et al.* 1996).

More recent twentieth- and twenty-first-century Scottish architecture has not perhaps differed significantly from architecture elsewhere and architects have embraced the use of new materials and building techniques. Many of the country's most significant public buildings have in fact been designed by non-Scots, including Glasgow's Burrell Gallery by Barry Gasson from England, the Riverside Museum by the Iraqi Zaha Hadid and the Scottish Parliament itself, designed by the Catalan Enric Miralles.

Cultural policy

For many years, there was no distinctive Scottish cultural policy and it was generally aligned with policy elsewhere in the UK, particularly in the area of museums and galleries (Orr 2008). Although there was a flourishing cultural scene in Scottish theatre and other parts of the arts, funding was ultimately controlled by the Arts Council of Great Britain, established in 1967. The Scottish Arts Council was not set up as a separate body until 1994.

'Culture' gained a more significant profile from the late 1980s onwards, partly as a result of the selection of Glasgow as the 1990 European Capital of

Culture. The city had already begun to regenerate itself as a 'post-industrial city', with the arts as a key component, and had adopted the slogan 'Glasgow's Miles Better'. It had already won the right to host the National Garden Festival in 1988 and had opened the Burrell Gallery in 1983 (Garcia 2004). Although there were criticisms of the Glasgow event as being elitist and ignoring the city's working-class communities (Mooney 2004), the year of the City of Culture had a transformative effect.

A key legacy was a major change in the city's image from a tired negative stereotype to being a place for shopping, business, conferences and major cultural events, so the event may be seen as a classic example of civic boosterism. There was also an expansion in local community arts and a lasting built legacy in the construction of the Glasgow Royal Concert Hall (Garcia 2004). There is no doubt that there was a major focus on the economic legacy of the event but 'in Glasgow, as in most cities aspiring to host a major event, the key objective was to improve the international profile of the city and accelerate inward investment, which the city public agencies claim was fully achieved' (Garcia 2004: 108).

Indeed, the use of cultural events to regenerate cities has been keenly pursued in recent years. Both Aberdeen and Dundee competed for the title of UK City of Culture 2017, losing out to Hull. More recently, Paisley and Perth competed for the 2021 title, losing to Coventry.

Although there was some administrative devolution of Scottish cultural policy in the years before political devolution, there is no doubt that the establishment of the Scottish Parliament in 1999 allowed for a Scottish-specific cultural policy to be developed. The new Scottish administration sought to shape the country's cultural policy, and a public consultation began that year. In 2000, the then Scottish Executive published its initial report, entitled *Creating Our Future: Minding Our Past* (Scottish Executive 2000), which suggested that Scottish culture would include a substantial nod to the country's past heritage.

There appeared to be a broad agreement within the cultural communities that the then cultural agency infrastructure was ineffective and uncoordinated, that Scottish culture should be integrated within the country's education system and that the international image of culture needed to banish the 'tartan and shortbread' image (Bonnar 2014). The strategy was moved forward by the then First Minister Jack McConnell in 2003 and moves were made to create a new public body to fund the creative industries with the publication of a draft Culture (Scotland) Bill. This body, to be called Creative Scotland, was to be formed from a merger of the Scottish Arts Council and Scottish Screen. In the event, there was considerable debate about the way a future Creative Scotland would function, debate that continued after its establishment, and the new agency was not finally set up until 2010 (Stevenson 2014). Central government has also funded important initiatives such as a National Audit of Museums and Galleries, which identified the importance of locally held items to the National Collection and led to a Museums Recognition Scheme (Orr 2008).

Although the evolution of a cultural strategy has not perhaps been a smooth one, Bonnar (2014) believes that this simply reflects the rather turbulent political journey of the country as a whole during the early years of devolution. She suggests that now 'the political and public confidence built up over 14 years of devolution has resulted in an increasingly clear expression of what culture means for Scotland and where that differs from that articulated by Westminster politicians' (Bonnar 2014: 145).

Conclusions

We have already explored the importance of culture for nations and the ways in which participation in arts and culture may encourage active citizenship. In Scotland, culture is particularly important as a means of promoting the country's identity and distinguishing it from a wider UK cultural agenda. Everitt (2001) notes the weight placed on the identity-forming function of culture by the devolved governments of both Scotland and Wales.

As we have noted earlier, Scottish politicians have tended to emphasise the significance of culture per se, rather than focusing on its narrow economic potential. The early Scottish administrations pushed the notion of cultural rights for all and, although this is a very subjective notion and one for which it is difficult to legislate, cultural 'entitlement' is an important concept (Orr 2008). Maxwell quotes the respected cultural critic Joyce McMillan who has suggested that the arts have the power to 'transform Scotland's view of itself – to reframe the nation not as a problematic provincial backwater but as a powerhouse of twenty-first-century creativity, generating work that is recognised on a global level for its ability to articulate the human condition' (2012: 140). She goes on to argue that the achievements of the Scottish arts scene are due in large measure to the contributions of public policy and the financial support the arts receive from the Scottish Government (McMillan 2010).

The late Stephen Maxwell was an important nationalist thinker and argued that independence was essential for the country to prosper – artistically as in other walks of life. He believed that Scottish art and culture would inevitably become a great deal more international in its outlook and gain greater international recognition. But it may be that devolution has already had a huge impact in this regard. He quotes the writer Edwin Muir's view, expressed in the 1930s, that Scotland was neither a nation nor a province and had a blank, rather than a 'centre' in the middle of it. Maxwell suggests that the blank at the centre of Scottish life 'has begun to fill up with a deal more writing, acting, arguing, singing and dancing, painting and exhibition-making and general craic about Scotland and its place in a turbulent world than any respectable hiatus could be expected to accommodate' (2012: 150–151).

This is similar to the position advanced by Orr (2008). Noting that Scottish cultural policy has changed significantly since devolution, she highlights in particular its greater visibility, with culture being intrinsically valued at every level. This reflects the view of successive Scottish governments, of whatever political hue, that culture is a basic human right, part of national identity and part of the country's ongoing view of itself.

Further reading

There are some interesting texts on cultural policy generally, such as Michael Gardiner's *Modern Scottish Culture, Edinburgh* (2005), while Tim Edensor explores the links between culture and identity in *National Identity, Popular Culture and Everyday Life* (2002). See also Cairns Craig's *The Wealth of the Nation: Scotland, Culture and Independence* (2018). There are some useful chapters on the use of tartanry in the creative and cultural industries in Ian Brown's edited volume *From Tartan to Tartanry: Scottish Culture, History and Myth* (2010a).

In terms of specific areas of the arts, we would suggest Robert Crawford's *Scotland's Books: The Penguin History of Scottish Literature* (2007), and the 2014 special issue on Scottish cultural policy in *Cultural Trends* (Volume 23.3). As far as broadcasting and the arts are concerned, some of the publications by the BBC are useful. See, for example, www.bbc.co.uk/bbctrust/who_we_are/audience_councils/scotland, while the journal *Scottish Affairs* published a special edition in 2018 (Volume 27.1), on the national media, specifically the press.

For a useful exploration of the position of Gaelic within modern Scotland, see *Gaelic in Contemporary Scotland*, edited by MacLeod and Smith-Christmas (2018).

The impact of massive cultural events like the Edinburgh Festival are covered in Jen Harvie's paper 'Cultural Effects of the Edinburgh International Festival: Elitism, Identities, Industries' in *Contemporary Theatre Review* (2003) and the 2014 consultancy report by Biggar Economics, *Edinburgh's Cultural Venues Impact 2013/14*, is interesting.

Finally, for a discussion of government policy on culture and the arts, see the Scottish Government's 2000 report on *Creating Our Future, Minding Our Past: Scotland's National Cultural Strategy*. There is also a useful analysis entitled 'Instrumental or Intrinsic? Cultural Policy in Scotland Since Devolution' by Joanne Orr in *Cultural Trends* (2008).

Chapter 13
Scotland, tourism and heritage

Introduction

This chapter explores the relationship between Scotland's heritage and its large and significant tourist industry. We will discuss how tourism has developed in Scotland, how the country 'sells' itself, the relevance of the imagery associated with Scotland (tartan and the like) and the various elements that make up the tourist industry. The chapter builds on some of the topics we have already discussed elsewhere, such as Scotland's imagery (Chapter 4), diaspora and what might be termed 'roots' tourism (Chapter 10) and aspects of the country's cultural heritage (Chapter 12).

Heritage and tourism are vital to the Scottish economy. According to VisitScotland, the national tourist body, visitor expenditure in Scotland in 2017 was just under £11.3 billion, made up of expenditure from overnight visitors of £5.3 billion and expenditure by day visitors of £6 billion (VisitScotland 2018). The growth in spend from 2016 had been a significant 17 per cent and this was attributed to a favourable exchange rate, events surrounding the Year of History, Heritage and Archaeology in 2017 and the ongoing popularity of what they called 'set-jetting' – or visiting the film locations of television dramas such as the historical time-travel series *Outlander* by the American writer Diana Gabaldon. The direct tourism spending generated a further £11 billion of economic activity in the wider Scottish supply chain and contributed around £6 billion of Scottish GDP. This represented about 4.5 per cent of total Scottish GDP. Employment in the tourism-related industries sector in Scotland was around 217,000, accounting for around 8.5 per cent of employment in Scotland. The sector will continue to grow and the Scottish Government has produced strategies for the sector. These are discussed later in this chapter.

Tourism in Scotland has a long history and those who have visited the country have come for a range of different reasons and with different expectations. Butler (1985) has suggested that there have been five periods in the country's tourism development. First, the years before 1745 was the age of the explorer, when the country was rarely visited and transport was difficult. Second was the period following the battle of Culloden, from 1746 to around 1810, when the first tourists began to appear and travellers such as Boswell and Johnson made their way around the Hebrides. Third was the period from 1810 to 1865, which Butler referred to as 'romance, red deer and royalty', when Queen Victoria's purchase of the Balmoral estate in Aberdeenshire encouraged others to seek out Scotland for holidays (often for the hunting, shooting and fishing). Fourth was the period of the railways and hotel development from 1865 to 1914, when transport to and within Scotland was revolutionised. Fifth, in the twentieth century, the advent of the motor car effectively made all of Scotland accessible and visitable.

We begin by describing some of these developments to gain a picture of how tourism has grown over the years.

The early Scottish tourists

Scotland had become a tourist destination of sorts from the end of the seventeenth century and Martin Martin's *Description of the Western Islands* was published in 1695, bringing to public notice a then relatively unknown part of the country (Martin 1695). His book aroused the interest of Samuel Johnson and James Boswell who famously undertook a tour of the Hebrides in the 1770s. The Highlands and Islands were, at that time, viewed warily, partly because they were thought to be fairly uncivilised, and partly because this was only thirty years after the Jacobite Rising of 1745 and these areas had been particularly supportive of the Jacobite cause. Boswell's account of the trip gives us a flavour of their thoughts:

> Dr Johnson had for many years given me hopes that we should go together, and visit the Hebrides. Martin's account of those islands had impressed us with a notion that we might there contemplate a system of life almost totally different from what we had been accustomed to see; and, to find simplicity and wildness, and all the circumstances of remote time or place, so near to our native great island, was an object within the reach of reasonable curiosity … We reckoned there would be some inconveniencies and hardships, and perhaps a little danger; but these we were persuaded were magnified in the imagination of every body. (Chapman 1930: 167)

Johnson himself was interested in the people he met and fascinated by what he thought of as a rather primitive society. He was less interested in the scenery, which he often found desolate and barren. Similarly, Dorothy Wordsworth, touring Scotland in 1803, while finding Scottish nature being perfect for a visit, nevertheless remarked on the wilderness and desolation that she saw (Bhandari 2014). However, it was the scenery that seemed to attract the tourists and travellers who followed them. They were fascinated by the isolation and remoteness and liked the sense of exploration and discovery.

Getting to many parts of Scotland at that time was a challenge in itself. During the first half of the eighteenth century, there had been some significant road building for military purposes, as a means of moving troops into the Highlands to suppress any uprisings. General George Wade was initially responsible for their construction and this role was later taken on by William Caulfield (Salmond 1934). At the beginning of the nineteenth century, road building for more peaceful purposes was undertaken by Thomas Telford, who also undertook major bridge and canal building. Telford's Caledonian Canal along the Great Glen from Fort William to Inverness was opened in 1822, while the Crinan Canal across Kintyre, built by John Rennie, was opened in 1801.

The Highlands and Islands were really opened up to tourism by the development of the steamship. Henry Bell's *Comet*, the world's first paddle steamer, had been built at Port Glasgow on the Clyde in 1812 and within a relatively few years, steamer sailings were being advertised around the Firth of Clyde and to places such as Inveraray and Oban (Durie 2003). New steamship companies developed such as J. and G. Burns, David Hutcheson and, famously, David MacBrayne, still extant as part of Caledonian MacBrayne or Calmac, the current provider of ferry services on the west coast of Scotland.

The coming of the railways revolutionised tourism in rural Scotland. The Highland Railway was completed to Inverness in 1863 and by 1874 had reached Wick and Thurso in the far north. Various branches followed, most importantly the Dingwall and Skye railway that reached Kyle of Lochalsh in 1897. Further south, the railway reached Oban in 1880, Fort William in 1894 and Mallaig in 1901 (Nock 1950; Durie 2003). As well as the important economic benefits the railways brought, particularly for activities like the fish trade, they facilitated steamer connections and, by providing restaurant and observation coaches, made rail travel a tourist experience in itself.

The Scottish Highlands finally gained the royal seal of approval as a holiday destination when Queen Victoria purchased the Balmoral estate in 1852. This in turn led other members of the wealthy elite to purchase land and property in Scotland (Wightman *et al.* 2002) and led to the development of tourism for sports such as stalking, shooting and fishing.

Nineteenth-century travellers were enthralled by the wild and picturesque scenery of the Highlands, their enthusiasm whetted by a range of painters, writers and composers. In the late 1820s, Felix Mendelssohn had sailed to Staffa and was inspired by the sight of Fingal's Cave to write his Hebrides overture, premiered in 1832. There were also a number of Victorian painters who specialised in painting Highland scenery, perhaps the best known being Sir Edwin Landseer, a favourite of Queen Victoria as discussed in Chapter 12. His *Monarch of the Glen* of 1851 is a widely recognised and iconic painting (Ormond 2005). Other painters of that era were Horatio McCulloch during the 1850s and 1860s, who specialised in mountain scenery in areas such as Glencoe, and William McTaggart, famous in the 1860s to 1890s for his seascapes.

Perhaps the writer who had the greatest influence on the nascent tourist industry was, of course, Sir Walter Scott. His historical novels and romances, such as *Rob Roy*, boosted tourism in and around Loch Katrine in the Trossachs; it is little surprise that the steamship currently sailing on the loch is named after him. Scott in fact wrote about many areas of Scotland, including Edinburgh where he lived for part of his life and his homeland in the Borders, so his influence on tourism extended widely as visitors sought out the locations in his novels.

Railway and steamer developments were not just influential in the Highlands and Islands. On the Firth of Clyde, the railways carried passengers from Glasgow and the central belt to piers at Largs, Wemyss Bay, Fairlie, Ardrossan and many other places where they could catch steamers to a range of Clyde Coast resorts and islands. Island towns like Rothesay and Millport became synonymous with Glasgow holidays as families took the opportunity to go 'doon the watter' (Armstrong and Williams 2005).

The late nineteenth century was also a period of widespread hotel construction, to cater for the increased number of travellers. The railway companies themselves built some hotels, at Gleneagles, Turnberry, Kyle of Lochalsh and elsewhere and new hotels transformed emerging tourist towns such as Oban (Durie 2003). There was also a significant development in spa towns as Victorians 'took the waters' in Peebles, Crieff, Dunblane and Strathpeffer and large 'hydropathic' hotels were built (Durie *et al.* 2006a).

In the early twentieth century, those with access to a motor car were able to travel widely across Scotland but car ownership was extremely limited. In the

1920s and 1930s, the spread of tourism and the increased numbers of people taking holidays was, of course, linked to the gradual introduction of paid holidays for working-class families. During the 1920s, some people used their weekends to venture into the countryside, cycling, rambling and youth hostelling; the Scottish Youth Hostels Association, for example, was established in 1931. But the development of local 'fairs' holidays, and campaigns by the trade union movement culminating in the 1938 Holidays with Pay Act led to a substantial growth in summer tourist traffic – albeit cut short by the Second World War (Brown 1996).

After the war, bodies such as the Automobile Association, Royal Automobile Club and petrol companies like Shell produced a range of maps and guidebooks for the motorist as more and more families acquired a car (Gold and Gold 1995). Coach companies also developed, offering tours of Scotland in competition with the railways (Seaton 1998). So by the 1960s, tourism in Scotland was an important industry and contributing significantly to the country's economy.

But while tourism was clearly hugely important to Scotland, what exactly were tourists seeking when they visited? And what image of Scotland were they presented with, in order to encourage them to come? We have already described the imagery associated with Scotland and the role played by writers like Sir Walter Scott in popularising tartan (in Chapter 4). We move on here therefore to explore the use of such imagery in relation to tourism and how the country is marketed.

How is Scotland marketed?

Imagery is hugely important in the marketing of Scotland and sometimes there is a tendency to fall back on stereotypes. For example, the British Tourist Authority used familiar imagery to market Scotland in 1994:

> Scotland conjures up images of dramatic mountains, shimmering lochs, tartans, bagpipes and fine malt whisky. Scotland is all of this and more besides … it is a land rich in romantic baronial castles, Highland Games and the historic towns and cities. Explore the beautiful Highlands, the wooded glens, meandering salmon rivers and traditional fishing villages. (1994: 34)

One might have expected that some of this stereotypical imagery might have been toned down over the years, but at the time of writing, part of the website of VisitScotland, the national tourist agency, contains a section, entitled

'What makes Scotland Unique?' It goes on: 'Is it our love of whisky, kilts and ceilidhs? The monster at the bottom of our loch, or the prickly plant we use as our national symbol? We give you a quick round-up of the 7 things we think make us special – from our love of dancing and our bright blue and white flag to our bagpipes, kilts and tug o' war'.[1] Presumably, for those in the business of tourism promotion, the continued use of such imagery is important in bringing visitors to Scotland.

Some years ago, Gold and Gold (1995) undertook research into the content of the marketing material being produced by what was then the Scottish Tourist Board. In a rather tongue-in-cheek analysis of the glossy photographs that were used in the publications, Gold and Gold suggested that there were eight different types of clichéd shot that were almost always used. Part of their analysis is worth reproducing here:

- Photographs of hills and distant mountains, invariably in warm summer colouring. Although there may be mists or striking cloud effects, the scenery usually seems accessible to the casual hillwalker … the terrain is inviting, never menacing.
- Two walkers, one male and one female, admiring a sunlit panorama of mountain and glen … The male stands slightly in front of his companion and points authoritatively at an item of interest in the far distance. She gazes appreciatively in the appropriate direction. Some thistles in full bloom are an optional extra.
- A solitary kilted piper … stands on the brow of a hill, knee-deep in purple heather or a thick textured grass. A light breeze … is clearly not strong enough to disrupt proceedings.
- A building (normally a highland castle or white-walled thatched croft house) situated by the lochside. A rowing boat is usually moored at the water's edge to give foreground interest.
- Deserted Hebridean shore pictures.
- Golfers on a coastal links course … Tartan trousers or tartan fabrics on a golf bag are a common additional referent.
- A 'fishing' picture, either a solitary angler … or the brightly painted prows of fishing boats.
- The profile of Edinburgh's Castle and Old Town … Unwanted detail, such as the roofs of Waverley railway station is normally filtered out by choice of lens, camera angle or careful foreground screening. (1995: 5–6)

Many of us will smile on reading this as such stereotypes are quite familiar to us. Nevertheless, they continue to be an important way in which Scotland is marketed to the outside world.

What therefore is Scotland actually 'selling' to the outside world? 'Scotland the brand' is essentially historical and the emphasis on history and genealogy may be seen to contribute to a rather stereotyped view of the country, a Scotland that does not and perhaps never did exist. But that appears to be what many visitors expect and so, in managing these expectations, the country is using an iconography that is essentially backward-looking. Scotland's heritage is economically valuable and iconic images such as tartan, whisky and shortbread may be highly successful tools of a marketing strategy linked to that heritage, even though they are frequently 'Highland' images that do not reflect the 'Lowland' experience of most Scots. But even where alternative imagery is used, it is often backward-looking. Thus in Shetland, two homecoming events for returning Shetlanders (named 'Hamefarins') in 1960 and 1985 unashamedly used Norse rather than Highland imagery. Visitors therefore encountered men crowned by 'Viking' helmets and armed with battleaxes (Callahan 1998). Interestingly, Northlink, which is the ferry company currently sailing between Orkney, Shetland and the mainland, has adopted this Norse imagery on its ships.

Such events may, therefore, be seen in many ways as 'staged authenticity'. Chhabra *et al.*, in their study of Highland Games in America, distinguish between Games in Scotland that are broadly authentic in that they are composed of traditional activities (albeit adapted over the years) and American Games that are 'staged authenticity since they are reconstructed in the memory of a Scottish Highland past' (2003: 706). The Gathering at Holyrood Park in Edinburgh during the 2009 Year of Homecoming probably owed more to the American than the Scottish tradition, not least in that there was a significant presence of clan tents, to allow visitors to explore their genealogy and clan affiliations.

In their influential book *Scotland – the Brand* McCrone *et al.* (1995) agree that much of what passes for Scottish 'heritage' is fabricated. They argue further that 'it has a negative psychological effect on Scots by confining them to stereotypes of themselves which are judged to have adverse political consequences … The judgement is that just as sporting images of Scotland generate "ninety-minute nationalists", so the heritage and tourist industries have created music-hall Scots and shortbread-tin images of Scotland' (McCrone *et al.* 1995: 182).

Although McCrone and his colleagues were writing over twenty years ago, much of their analysis has a resonance today. Nevertheless, there have been significant changes within the country's tourist industry and so we move on to discuss the various forms that the industry takes and the different types of tourism that Scotland is generating.

Types of tourism

Tourism is a complex phenomenon that, as MacLellan and Smith (1998) point out, only really attracted academic attention in the later twentieth century. They suggest that tourist trips cover a wide range of activities and of motivating factors. Some of these are associated with exploring Scotland's heritage while others may involve family visits, conference trips and visits of personal meaning.

Heritage tourism

Heritage tourism has developed substantially over the years and was perceptively studied by Robert Hewison in his book *The Heritage Industry* (1987). His central thesis was that, as the UK has declined economically with traditional industries closing and older housing demolished, we become ever more concerned to preserve them, or at least some vestiges of them. Hence, his exploration of Wigan Pier, once a symbol for George Orwell (1937) of the ugliness and working-class poverty wrought by the Industrial Revolution in the north of England, but now a 'heritage' centre where visitors can explore exhibitions entitled 'The Way We Were' and where museum assistants wear clogs to ensure authenticity.

Our concern to preserve the past is, of course, long standing. The Victorians were keen to create a 'heritage' and in Scotland, a number of important bodies were established to curate the nation's past. In 1851, the National Museum of Antiquities was established in Edinburgh, followed by the Royal Scottish Museum in 1854, the National Gallery in 1859 and the Scottish National Portrait Gallery in 1889 (McCrone *et al.* 1995). To record and safeguard the country's ancient monuments and historical sites, the Royal Commission on Ancient and Historical Monuments was created in 1908. In 2015, it merged with Historic Scotland, a government agency that existed to promote the country's built heritage, into a single body called Historic Environment Scotland.

What has been striking in Hewison's view, is that 'heritage' as we now understand it, no longer simply covers castles and ancient monuments but events and artefacts that are relatively recent. Thus, 'the past is getting closer' (Hewison

1987: 83). Within Scotland, we can see a range of museums that cover what might be termed 'social history' such as the People's Palace in Glasgow, Summerlee Museum of Industrial Life in Coatbridge, the Scottish Mining Museum in Newtongrange, the Tenement House in Glasgow, heritage railway and transport centres such as Bo'ness in West Lothian and crofting museums in the Highlands. As well as helping younger visitors to understand the recent past, they allow older ones to indulge in a bit of nostalgia and many of the museums have 'hands-on' participative events and displays. Even the country's older castles and abbeys have got in on the act with battle re-enactments and the like.

There has been a significant increase in the numbers of museums within Scotland. The Scottish Government's strategy for the museum sector (Museums Galleries Scotland 2012) identified 340 museums and galleries in Scotland, caring for more than 12 million objects. At one level, this was extraordinarily impressive with almost every geographic community in the country either hosting a museum or having access to one, but they ranged from large national museums with collections of international significance to small local museums, often underfunded and kept alive through the efforts of volunteers. Nevertheless, the sector was estimated to contribute £662 million to the economy and employed over 3,800 people. The strategy aimed to improve the sustainability of collections, not least through identifying new sources of income, strengthening the connections with local communities, increasing the potential of the workforce and moving into more global markets.

Part of the challenge for museums of course is to reflect what the strategy refers to as 'the nuances of our culture'. This is illustrated in McLean and Cooke's (2003) exploration of the Museum of Scotland in Edinburgh. At one level, the museum needs to record the nation's history, even if some of this includes rather tired tartan mythology; at the same time, it needs to reflect the more contemporary Scotland with which visitors are able to identify. Museum visitors were aware of the tensions that this created. There are tensions too within social history museums. Carnegie's (2006) study of the People's Palace in Glasgow suggested that, while some staff and curators were keen to 'push against the boundaries' by developing displays and exploring the life experiences of communities, some of their audiences were believed to feel threatened by this and sought to protect community memories. Inevitably therefore, museums become a compromise in how we examine, explore and interpret the past.

There is no doubt that Scotland's built heritage, whether it be ancient castles or more recent residential and industrial buildings are hugely significant in the country's tourist industry. The government's tourism strategy (discussed later) highlights heritage tourism and 2017 was designated by VisitScotland as the Year of History, Heritage and Archaeology. Preparation for this event was led by a Heritage Tourism Group, who produced a strategy entitled 'People Make Heritage 2020'.[2] The group divided heritage into three pillars, namely 'built heritage', which included famous buildings, monuments, castles and World Heritage Sites; 'cultural heritage', which included museums and gardens and also performing arts, sport, literature and food and drink; and 'contemporary culture', which included music, films and festivals.

We can identify much of Scotland's heritage within these categories. For many tourists, the attraction is the country's more ancient history, the romance of clans and castles, for others, more recent social history. The performing arts and festivals are a major pull for tourists (Prentice and Andersen 2003) and we have discussed the importance of events such as the Edinburgh International Festival in Chapter 12. The country's food and drink industries are also hugely important (Hughes 1995), with whisky contributing £3.8 billion to Scottish exports in 2015 (Scottish Government 2017b) and the development of 'whisky trails' to encourage tourists to visit a range of distilleries, for example in Speyside, have been a major success.

So heritage tourism has many facets and is a key element in Scotland's economy. Heritage attractions act as places to showcase the nation's distinctiveness, its identity and its culture (Bhandari 2014) and they are a major element in the selling of 'Scotland the brand'.

Countryside tourism

An important element of heritage tourism involves the country's natural heritage and this is linked closely to Scotland, the brand and the imagery associated with it. An image of misty mountains, lochs and glens may be a somewhat romanticised picture of the country, but it appears to exercise a strong pull for those who wish to visit and take advantage of the countryside. Scotland's landscapes encompass a huge array of habitats from mountains, lochs, forests, moors, coastline and islands. As a result, the country is home to a wide range of wildlife (Curtin 2013). But, of course, this landscape is not a 'wilderness' by accident, although it may sometimes be marketed as Europe's last great wilderness (Habron 1998). The comparative emptiness of many of these rural areas, particularly in the Highlands, is the result of the clearance of villages and people by their landlords in the eighteenth and nineteenth centuries.

Nevertheless, the existence of such 'wild' areas means that Scotland has 36 country parks and 3 regional parks, 94 forests, 15 country estates, 47 national nature reserves (NNRs), 67 local nature reserves (LNRs), 120 Scottish Wildlife Trust (SWT) reserves and 40 reserves belonging to the Royal Society for the Protection of Birds (Curtin 2013). Interestingly, although the country is the birthplace of John Muir, the founder of the National Parks movement in America, Scotland itself had no National Parks until 2000. The Ramsay Committee had recommended their establishment in Scotland at the same time as they were being set up in England and Wales (Moir 1991) but no action was taken. In the event, one of the first acts of the new Scottish Parliament was to pass legislation establishing National Parks in Loch Lomond and the Trossachs and in the Cairngorms in 2002–03. Interestingly, and in contrast to parks south of the border, one of the aims of National Parks in Scotland is to promote sustainable economic and social development of the area's communities, a recognition that the interest of those who live in the parks should be protected.

The other significant development in the Scottish countryside has been the creation of a number of long-distance walking trails. These were relatively common from the 1920s onwards in other countries but did not make their appearance in the UK until the 1960s. In Scotland, the first trail was the West Highland Way, from Milngavie near Glasgow to Fort William, opened in 1980 (Morrow 2005). Since then a substantial network has been developed including the Southern Uplands Way, the Speyside Way, the Great Glen Way and so on. Research into users of the trails has shown that they enjoy a positive experience, because of the strong relationship that walkers forge with their surroundings and the sense of achievement they attain from completing a multi-day, challenging walk (den Breejen 2007).

Other outdoor pursuits enjoyed in Scotland include, of course, mountaineering and hillwalking and a particular 'sport' is the climbing or 'bagging' of Munros – mountains over three thousand feet in height. There are numerous locations for other outdoor and adventure sports from sailing and other water sports (canoeing, kayaking, white water rafting, etc.) to mountain biking and golf. We discuss this in more detail in Chapter 14.

Roots tourism

Roots tourism is a version of heritage tourism that has become increasingly significant within Scotland and has involved individuals with an ancestral connection to Scotland seeking their 'roots' – the places where their ancestors originated. It has been aided by the growth of the Internet and the availability of affordable air travel and researchers such as Timothy (2011) and Basu (2007) refer to those tourists revisiting their homelands to undertake genealogical research or to visit sites of personal meaning. Within Scotland, such tourism – generally from within the Scottish diaspora – has been encouraged by 'homecoming' events such as the International Clan Gatherings in 1951 and 1977, the Scottish Years of Homecoming in 2009 and 2014 (Sim and Leith 2013) and local initiatives such as gatherings of individual clans (Basu 2005) or, in the case of the Clan MacLeod, a regular 'clan parliament' to discuss clan affairs (Grant 1959; Hunter 2005).

Research suggests that diaspora tourists are essentially motivated by nostalgia and by an interest in exploring their heritage. Huang *et al.* (2011) refer to them as being 'in-between' domestic and international tourists in that while they may be 'foreigners' in their countries of origin, they nevertheless share the same cultural background and connection to the destination as domestic tourists do. Basu (2004) notes how diaspora tourists themselves often use words such as 'homecoming', 'quest' and 'pilgrimage' to describe their journey back to Scotland and so these journeys take on an almost spiritual aspect.

The growth in diaspora tourism has become particularly important within the United States, reflecting what Waters (1990) referred to as the American need to be 'from somewhere'. Gans (1979) has referred to white people searching for a 'symbolic ethnicity', while Novak (1971) uses the term 'Saturday ethnics' – the phrase reminds us that those who explore their heritage tend to be those who have the wealth and the leisure time to do so, often at weekends.

Certainly the diaspora tourists who travel to Scotland seem to be older and more affluent, whose children have left home; they have the resources to make the journey back to the 'homeland' and to visit sites that are meaningful to their history (Basu 2004). They appear to visit their share of castles, museums and other attractions, but Newland and Taylor (2010) point out that they are more likely than most international tourists to have or to make connections with the local economy, partly because they may stay with relatives, and to visit places other than the better known tourist attractions; diaspora tourism is also much less seasonal.

A key element in roots or diaspora tourism is genealogical research and the tracing of ancestors. Such research has been assisted by Internet sites on to which have been loaded birth, marriage, death and census records, as well as parish registers, wills and testaments.[3] Indeed, Fowler (2003) and Birtwistle (2005) suggest that Scotland has led in the development of 'genealogical tourism'.

Guided tourism

Guided tourism is a phenomenon that has grown in recent years. For many years, coach companies provided tours of Scotland and shipping companies operated a number of cruises around the Hebrides, either day trips from ports such as Oban or longer cruises to far-flung islands such as St Kilda (Bray 1986; Durie 2003). Within the last twenty years or so, however, the market appears to have undergone significant changes.

First, the cruising industry is now global (Brida and Zapata 2010) and Scotland has become a calling point on European and North Atlantic cruises. Ports such as Greenock and Leith have developed deep-water facilities to cater for cruise liners, and smaller towns with deep-water facilities such as Invergordon in the north of Scotland have also been able to benefit. Although cruise passengers can disembark at Greenock, Leith or elsewhere and have a short guided trip to local places of interest, these tours and timings are strictly controlled.

Second, there has been a huge growth in guided tours by bus and coach – but often at the younger end of the market. While the larger forty-seater coaches continue to tour Scotland, there are now a significant number of operators of small sixteen-seater minibuses that offer guided tours on a more informal and personalised basis. The largest operator in Scotland is Rabbie's, founded in 1993 and that now has over forty coaches, over a hundred employees, bases in Edinburgh, Glasgow and Inverness and a turnover of £8.5 million. Many of these companies target younger backpackers who are looking for shorter, more informal – but still guided – tours of Scotland. The tour guides themselves are important interpreters and mediators of Scotland's history for those who participate in these tours (Bhandari 2014).

For those who prefer to drive themselves around Scotland, the tourist industry is also making significant attempts to 'steer' drivers into the less travelled areas of Scotland. Perhaps the most high-profile example of this is the North Coast 500, increasingly becoming referred to as 'Scotland's Route 66'. The route begins and ends in Inverness, but the five hundred miles of the title consists of the road north to John o' Groats, along the northern coast of Scotland and down the west coast to Kyle of Lochalsh, with a return to

Inverness. This northern part of the country was seen as being underdeveloped for tourism and the North Coast 500 idea was developed by the North Highland Initiative, a non-profit consortium set up to help the economy in this area. This concept of developing themed touring routes or self-drive trails has become more common in countries such as Australia and the United States and it is interesting that it is now happening in Scotland. Such themed touring routes can encourage tourism development, provide a more satisfactory tourism experience and maximise economic benefits to local businesses (Hardy 2003).

The walking trails that have been developed in Scotland and that we have discussed above are also a form of guided tourism, as visitors are directed on to specific waymarked routes rather than being encouraged into the more remote and wilder parts of the country. In part this is because the pressures created by visitors are more easily managed if limited to specific areas.

Business/conference tourism

Business/conference tourism is increasingly important to Scotland and was estimated by VisitScotland to be worth approximately £800 million to the Scottish economy and this represented around 18 per cent of total tourist expenditure in the country. There are large international conference venues in the big cities, although many of the business meetings and conferences take place in smaller venues such as hotels. The government's strategy for tourism identifies business tourism as a key opportunity for growth. An industry-led group called Business Tourism for Scotland works with the government to oversee the strategic opportunities.

This section has provided a flavour of the different elements within the Scottish tourist industry, much of it linked to the country's built and natural heritage. The Scottish Government is keen to identify opportunities to expand and develop the industry, building on these different elements and so we now turn to examine current government policy.

Scottish Government policy

Current Scottish Government policy is based on a strategy entitled 'Tourism Scotland 2020', originally developed in 2012 (Scottish Tourism Alliance 2012). It identified four areas of strength, namely nature, heritage and related activities; business tourism; visits to towns and cities; and visits to events and festivals. The report acknowledged that there were some failings in the tourist experience including variable quality of accommodation, travel and eating out and variable Internet and mobile phone coverage. The report also argued for the country to act more collectively in promoting tourism, reflecting Dewar's (2011) briefing to the Scottish Parliament that listed a myriad of different bodies, all with a role in promoting or supporting tourism and heritage.

The government's strategy continues to focus on the four key elements noted above, but sees it as a priority to improve what it calls the 'customer journey'. The market for tourism was seen as being a mix of traditional market sources (the rest of the UK, Europe, North America and Australasia) and 'emerging' markets in India, China, Russia and Brazil.

A review of the strategy in 2017 (Scottish Tourism Alliance 2017) noted much progress, while focusing additionally on the importance of supporting leadership within the industry, encouraging investment and supporting digital capabilities. Interestingly and reflecting newer markets, there had been a focus on attracting Chinese visitors to Scotland.

Much of the review document focuses on the promotion of tourist activities, on attracting business tourism and conferences and tourism associated with significant events and festivals. Although heritage tourism remains crucial, and visitors are encouraged to explore ancestral links and undertake genealogical research, there is very little focus on the tartanry that has characterised so much of Scotland's previous marketing efforts. And yet, we know that tartan, bagpipes and Highland Games are the things that are so attractive to many overseas visitors, so there is a tension between trying to move the visitor experience into newer areas without sacrificing the things that have been associated in the past with Scotland the brand. Indeed, many American visitors are disappointed at the lack of focus on tartan, and Hume (2010) relates how one of his American respondents suggested that he should travel to the United States to see how Highland heritage was protected, as Scotland itself was failing to do so. This provides a classic illustration of how the myths and reality of the Scottish visitor experience so often collide.

Conclusions

This chapter has demonstrated that tourism is a vital element in the Scottish economy. Tourists have been coming to Scotland since the seventeenth century, but numbers have grown, especially in the late twentieth and early twenty-first centuries, as we have become more mobile and many people have more leisure time and more disposable income.

For the early visitors like Martin Martin, Samuel Johnson and James Boswell, a journey to some parts of Scotland was very much a hazardous trip into the unknown. But now, tourist numbers – especially in the Highlands and Islands – are such that they themselves are creating problems and hazards and the tourist pressures are beginning to damage the local infrastructure and ecology. New developments to try and 'guide' tourists, such as long-distance paths and motor trails like the North Coast 500, which we have discussed, may help to manage the tourist influx. But this in turn may focus the pressures on areas that are struggling to cope, ranging from cities like Edinburgh to parts of the Highlands. As a result, at the time of writing, the Scottish Parliament is debating giving local authorities the right to charge a 'tourist tax' (see COSLA 2018). By charging overnight visitors a small amount, as is the case in many other countries, additional income may be generated that can then be invested in improved visitor facilities.

In some respects then, Scotland may have become a victim of its own success. Over the years, the country has sold a brand focused very much on heritage – the built heritage of castles and ancient monuments, the natural heritage of mountains and lochs and the cultural heritage of clans and tartans. The branding has clearly been successful but Scotland now needs to manage the resultant impact.

But what is the future of this 'heritage brand' and the tourist industry it has spawned? The tourist agency VisitScotland itself believes that visitors are increasingly seeking 'experiences' rather than 'products', with an emphasis on the experience of road trips, adventure holidays, wild camping and the like, rather than simply visiting a location. This would seem to suggest that Scotland should not necessarily continue to rely on its traditional heritage branding and indeed, VisitScotland (2016) point out the potential of newer forms of tourism such as book tours and festivals. In Edinburgh, for example, fans of Ian Rankin's crime novels featuring Inspector Rebus can tour 'Rebus's Edinburgh', while there are now significant numbers of book festivals and Wigtown became Scotland's 'book town' in 1998 (Seaton 1999).

Yeoman *et al.* (2009) agree that the focus has shifted somewhat towards activity holidays, although culture-based holidays have also grown in importance, particularly among older people. They point out the changing demography of tourist visitors, with larger numbers of active retired people ('empty nesters') from within the post-war 'baby boomer' generation, many of whom are relatively affluent. Those seeking activity holidays are more likely to be younger – and possibly less affluent – people who have become a sizeable 'backpacker' tourist market, interested in walking, camping and similar activities (Hindle *et al.* 2015).

Tourists are therefore wanting new and different experiences, and these change all the time. Just as Victorian tourists visited the Trossachs because they had read Sir Walter Scott's novels, so today's tourists will seek to visit Glenfinnan Viaduct near Fort William (where J. K. Rowling's Harry Potter novels have been filmed), or Rosslyn Chapel near Edinburgh (a setting in Dan Brown's *Da Vinci Code*) or Glencoe, where the James Bond movie *Skyfall* was filmed.

Heritage continues to be important, however, even if tourists are seeking new ways to experience it. As Morgan *et al.* (2002) have pointed out, today's tourists are not asking 'what can we do on holiday?' but 'who can we be on holiday?' They may be looking for escapism, culture and discovery, and history and heritage will continue to have a role if marketed in the right way. As Durie *et al.* point out:

> Destinations without any myths and legends have no interesting stories to tell their tourists. A destination without a past is bland, having no birthdays or anniversaries to celebrate. Destinations without history have no culture or character to bring tourists to their shores. Therefore, it is history that gives a destination a colourful past in which a sense of place is created. (2006: 43–44)

Further reading

There are a number of accounts of the development of Scottish tourism and its prospects, such as Alastair Durie's *Scotland for the Holidays: Tourism in Scotland, 1780–1939* (2003) and Rory MacLellan and Ronnie Smith's edited *Tourism in Scotland* (1998). As regards the close connection between tourism and heritage, we would recommend as a general text, Dallen Timothy's *Cultural Heritage and Tourism: An Introduction* (2011) and, in relation to Scotland in particular, Kalyan Bhandari's *Tourism and National Identity: Heritage and Nationhood in Scotland* (2014).

Of course, the way in which Scotland brands itself has a major impact on its tourism industries and a classic text is *Scotland – the Brand: the Making of Scottish Heritage* by David McCrone *et al.* (1995). Also highly recommended is *Imagining Scotland: Tradition, Representation and Promotion in Scottish Tourism Since 1750*, by John and Margaret Gold (1995).

Scotland has seen a number of homecomings by its diaspora in recent years and has led the way in 'genealogical' or 'ancestral' tourism. The work of Paul Basu is important here, for example his *Highland Homecomings: Genealogy and Heritage Tourism in the Scottish Diaspora* (2007). See also Moira Birtwistle's chapter 'Genealogical Tourism: The Scottish

Market Opportunities' in Marina Novelli's *Niche Tourism: Contemporary Issues, Trends and Cases* (2005) and S. Fowler's paper 'Ancestral Tourism' in *Insights* (2003).

Finally, it is important to look at Scottish Government policy on tourism, which can be accessed at www.gov.scot/policies/tourism-and-events. There is a useful briefing report by Jim Dewar entitled *Tourism in Scotland*, published in 2011 by the Scottish Parliament Information Centre (SPICe). Publications by the Scottish Tourism Alliance are also useful, such as *Tourism Scotland 2020: The Future of Our Industry in Our Hands* (2012), together with their annual policy reviews.

Chapter 14
Scotland and sport

Introduction

Around fifty years ago, the relationship between individuals and sport tended to be limited to participation, spectating or consuming reports of sporting events in the media. As Houlihan notes, 'there were few professional athletes and even fewer professional administrators; the symbiotic relationship between the television companies and sport was only just emerging; and the rampant commercialisation of sport, especially football, was still some years away' (2008: 1). He notes how sport was not necessarily viewed by government as a matter of public policy concern.

Clearly, the picture is very different today. Sport has become professional and commercialised, governing bodies have expanded and there are a number of dedicated sports channels on television and radio. Sport has also become an important area of study within universities. Social scientists study sport and its abilities to enhance social capital, reduce social exclusion and contribute to urban regeneration. Academics and professionals in the field of health study sport's role in improving fitness and reducing obesity. Government too has taken an increasing interest in sport because of the contribution it can make to society's health and well-being; sport is therefore viewed as a useful instrument for achieving non-sport objectives (Houlihan 2008).

In this chapter, we explore sport in Scotland in three ways. First, we will examine how sport is a key element within Scottish society – in other words, sport is 'something important that we do'. Second, we will explore how sport – and in particular the fielding of Scottish sports teams – has assisted in strengthening the sense of Scottish identity. In this respect, sport is perhaps 'who we are'. And finally, we will look at the relationship between sport and the images that others have of Scotland and how Scotland and Scottish sport is regarded externally. Sport is therefore 'what others think of us'.

Sport and Scottish society

Many writers have argued that sport is an important element in strengthening and expanding civil society. In 1995, the then Secretary General to the Council of Europe, Daniel Tarschys, stated: 'The hidden face of sport is also the tens of thousands of enthusiasts who find, in their football, rowing, athletics, and rock climbing clubs, a place for meeting and exchange, but above all the training ground for community life' (Maguire *et al.* 2002: 109). His words remain relevant in that participation in sport may lead to taking on responsibilities, following rules, accepting one another, cooperating and working together, looking for consensus and developing a team spirit. So sport is key to the development of social capital and the promotion of social inclusion.

The concept of social capital developed by Coleman (1988) has now been widely accepted. Originally Coleman's interest was in society's capacity for educational achievement, but it is now applied much more widely and Harris (1998), for example, has argued that it applies strongly to sport and leisure activities. If we are concerned that social inclusion and social capital are related to a broader participation in wider society, then sport has a role to play (Jarvie 2003).

Jarvie (2003) argues that sport may be a significant vehicle for civic pride and this can strengthen local communities. He explores the role of local football teams in Scotland to show how successful performance on the field can provide a 'lift' to the communities in which they are based. Thus, cup-winning teams such as Aberdeen (Scottish Cup in 1983), Motherwell (in 1991), Kilmarnock (in 1997) and Raith Rovers (Scottish League Cup in 1995) have followed their victories with parades in their home-town streets and they have often been given the freedom of their respective towns and cities. Their sporting achievements have been applauded because their success has been shared 'by both the local community and local politicians, who use sport to reinforce notions of civic pride, social memory and loyalty to a town or area' (Jarvie 2003: 145). Sporting success may be particularly important in relatively small towns like Motherwell or Kilmarnock, compared with Glasgow where the successes – both national and international – of large clubs like Rangers and Celtic are perhaps more taken for granted. Hague and Mercer's (1998) study of Raith Rovers football club is an important illustration of how memories create an awareness of and a feeling of belonging to a particular location. Their work suggests that Raith Rovers are a reference that triggers wider memories of the town and people of Kirkcaldy.

For Scotland's two largest clubs of Rangers and Celtic, pride and memory are rather more complex as the clubs have historically been linked to wider religious identities (Protestant in the case of Rangers, Roman Catholic for Celtic), reflecting their history and the circumstances of their foundation (Bradley 2006). Although the clubs have subscribed to initiatives to reduce sectarian tensions, and historical practices such as the absence of any Catholic player being signed by Rangers have long since been abandoned, there remain issues of sectarianism (as we discussed in Chapter 7).

Sport in Scotland is also interwoven with the country's economic and political history. Many of football's iconic figures – particularly managers like Bill Shankly, Matt Busby, Jock Stein and Alex Ferguson – have their roots in industrial areas and they 'came to represent aspects of the Scottish character and legitimised a pride in a particular working-class image of Scottish identity' (Boyle 2000: 22). In many mining areas, success on the football field represented a way of avoiding going 'down the pits', one of the best examples being Bill Shankly from Glenbuck in Ayrshire. The village in fact no longer even exists, but its erstwhile football team, the Glenbuck Cherrypickers, produced a significant number of professional footballers (Powley and Gillan 2015).

The links with local communities have, however, weakened over time. Perhaps until the 1960s, most people were employed relatively locally and few commuted any significant distance to work. It was also common for individuals to work on Saturday mornings. The result was that Saturday afternoons were spent watching the local team in action. In more recent times, families have become increasingly mobile and have greater leisure time and so it has become relatively common for football supporters to travel longer distances to watch the bigger teams (such as Rangers and Celtic). Attendances at the smaller teams in lower divisions have therefore dwindled. The pattern has been replicated elsewhere, so that in England, for example, the larger teams (such as Manchester United, Liverpool, Arsenal and Chelsea) are increasingly attracting support from across the country and becoming 'global' brands (Edensor and Millington 2008). There remains a great reservoir of civic pride invested in these smaller teams, however, which has ensured that although Scotland has a population of only 5.3 million, it supports forty-two professional football teams in four divisions. As Morrow (2006) has argued, this position may not be sustainable in the longer term and some clubs are professional in name only, but nevertheless they survive.

The significance of football in any discussion of Scottish sport may be illustrated by the high proportion of the population that attends games regularly. Analysis of attendances across Europe shows that in only four countries is the proportion of the population attending games over 3 per cent. These are the Faroe Islands, Iceland, Cyprus and Scotland. Actual attendances are, of course, much greater in countries like England and Germany but the *proportions* attending are smaller.[1]

One of the significant developments in recent years has been the emergence of a strong Scottish women's football team in the 1970s and they came under the aegis of the Scottish Football Association in 1998. By 2014, they had reached nineteenth place in the Fédération Internationale de Football Association (FIFA) world rankings and achieved a play-off place in their qualification group for the 2015 FIFA Women's World Cup. As at July 2019, they were in twentieth place and had actually qualified for the 2019 Women's World Cup in France – although they failed to progress beyond the early stages. The growing involvement of women in football is mirrored by an increase in the numbers of women (and families) attending the men's game as spectators. This trend has been encouraged by the introduction of seating at all top-tier football stadia, following government legislation arising from the Hillsborough stadium disaster in 1989.

In terms of ethnicity, however, football in Scotland remains predominantly white. Ibrox Stadium (the ground of Glasgow Rangers) has hosted the final of the UK Asian Football Championships (in 2013) and Celtic were hosts in 2018; there is a thriving Asian football scene in the city. At international level, Andrew Watson (1856–1921) is widely considered to be the world's first black person to play association football for his country, representing Scotland three times between 1881 and 1882. But the numbers of BME players who have played for the national team remains tiny. Nigel Quashie was capped fourteen times between 2004 and 2006, Chris Iwelumo (born in Coatbridge) four times (2008–10) and Ikechi Anya (born in Glasgow but playing in England) is a current Scottish internationalist, having won twenty-nine caps.

Although we have so far focused on football, we must not ignore the wide range of other sports played in Scotland. Rugby union is played widely across the country with a system of national and regional leagues and, as in football, Scotland has its own national team, distinct from the other 'home nations'. It is perhaps viewed as a less working-class game than football (Green *et al.*

2005), partly perhaps because it is widely played within the independent schools sector and partly perhaps because the national rugby stadium is at Murrayfield in Edinburgh, whereas football's spiritual home is Hampden Park in the more working-class city of Glasgow.

Because Scotland has its own national team, rugby has been an important marker of national identity (Maguire and Tuck 1998). Scotland participates in the Six Nations Championship (the four home nations plus France and Italy) and the annual fixture between Scotland and England, where the teams compete for the Calcutta Cup, is one where national loyalties are very much in evidence.

Golf is a sport that Scotland has given to the world. Its origins are somewhat unclear but it is mentioned in Scottish legislation in the fifteenth century. St Andrews is the world home of golf with the Royal and Ancient Golf Club the sport's supreme authority. The sport is played widely within Scotland and, while there are a number of wealthy private clubs, there is a wide network of publicly accessible municipal courses available for people to play on. Even in St Andrews, local people have access to the 'show' courses. St Andrews is an important tourist destination as the home of golf and the sport is used extensively in tourist marketing (Butler 2005).

Other sports that are distinctive within Scotland include shinty, played essentially within the Highlands and closely related to hurling in Ireland. Like other sports, it too has had a role in defining national identity and historically was linked to radical Highland politics (Reid 1998). Another Scottish sport is curling, developed in Scotland in the sixteenth century and that has been exported to a number of other countries such as Canada. It is played across Scotland and probably achieved its highest profile in recent years when an all-Scottish team led by Rhona Martin won the gold medal at the 2002 Winter Olympics in Salt Lake City (Reid 2010).

As might be expected in a country with large rural and mountainous areas, outdoor pursuits have also become increasingly significant, perhaps reflecting increased leisure time and greater individual mobility allowing access to the countryside. The growth in popularity of rambling, cycling and youth hostelling came in the interwar period, in part as an escape from the pressures of work and of urban living. In England, it manifested itself in events such as the mass trespass of Kinder Scout in the Peak District in 1932, during which five ramblers were arrested; the event was commemorated by the singer Ewan MacColl in his song 'The Manchester Rambler' (Hey 2011). It led indirectly to the establishment of the Ramblers Association, the growth of the newly established Youth Hostels Association and, after the Second World War, the creation of a system of National Parks, including the Peak District.

In Scotland, the Scottish Youth Hostels Association was founded in 1931 and there was a similar expansion of rambling, cycling and hillwalking. Lorimer (1997) points out that the formation of a hostelling association in Scotland separate from England and Wales was an early indication of a growing awareness of Scottish identity, while the movement in Scotland was also quite politicised in campaigning against large landowners and seeking to ensure full access to the Scottish mountains.

By the late twentieth century, there had been a huge expansion of facilities for walkers and climbers, with the creation of long-distance footpaths such as the West Highland Way, Southern Uplands Way and the Speyside Way. Meanwhile, television shows such as Muriel Gray's *The Munro Show* encouraging climbers to 'bag' Munros (mountains over three thousand feet) and to try and climb them all. As we have noted in Chapter 13, the pressures that these developments brought to the Scottish countryside were managed in the most pressured areas by the creation of Scotland's first National Parks in Loch Lomond and the Trossachs and in the Cairngorms in 2002–03. The necessary legislation was among the first Acts passed by the newly established Scottish Parliament. National Parks had actually been recommended for Scotland by the Ramsay Committee in 1945, following the Second World War, but unlike in England and Wales, they were never introduced.

Subsequently, the ancient tradition of the right to universal access to the land in Scotland was codified into Scots law by the Land Reform (Scotland) Act 2003. It specifically established a right to be on land for recreational and educational purposes and a right to cross land; the legislation was accompanied by the publication of a Scottish Outdoor Access Code. Further land reform legislation was enacted by the Scottish Parliament in the Land Reform (Scotland) Act 2016, to which we referred in Chapter 4.

While most sports enjoy widespread support and participation, we should not forget that Scotland provides for significant 'elite' sports, such as hunting and shooting. Extensive areas within the Scottish Highlands are used as sporting estates, some of them foreign-owned and dating from the nineteenth century when Queen Victoria's enjoyment of Balmoral encouraged other members of the wealthy elite to purchase land and property in Scotland (Wightman *et al.* 2002). While hunting is sometimes derided as being the preserve of the rich, nevertheless the sporting estates contribute to the country's economy and they support over seven thousand full-time equivalent jobs. As

Wightman *et al.* (2002) argue, there is a need for more research into how recreational sports can be developed and promoted for the benefit of the country as a whole.

Finally, it is important to acknowledge the importance of sport as a tool for regenerating our society, particularly certain parts of our towns and cities. New sports stadia, for example, have important community uses, mainly for sporting activities but they may also contain function rooms for meetings, conferences and the like and hence they attract business. The power of sport to regenerate whole communities was perhaps seen most recently in 2014, when Glasgow hosted the Commonwealth Games. At one level, the Commonwealth Games are important to Scotland because they represent an opportunity for the country to represent itself, rather than being subsumed into 'Team GB' as happens with the Olympic Games. But, as well as being used as a symbol of national identity, the 2014 Commonwealth Games were used as a means to transform the somewhat rundown East End of Glasgow (Matheson 2010). A number of major sporting facilities were built within the East End, including a National Indoor Sports arena and the Sir Chris Hoy Velodrome; the Tollcross swimming pool was upgraded as part of the process. The Athletes Village that was constructed in the city's Dalmarnock district has subsequently been used for housing, some private and some rented. Similar regeneration, of course, took place in London, as part of the city's hosting of the 2012 Olympics (Poynter 2009).

Such regeneration is not without controversy. There was some opposition within Glasgow, for example, to the demolition of older housing to make way for the Athletes Village amid claims of the area being 'socially cleansed' (Porter 2009) and one family held out against the demolitions for some time. There can be little question, however, that the new housing is superior to that which it replaced and much of it is socially rented.

Sport and Scottish national identity

We have already touched on the role of sport in helping to define Scottish national identity. When Scots sit in stadia like Murrayfield or Hampden Park, willing the national team to succeed, they are essentially part of what Benedict Anderson (1983) would refer to as an 'imagined community'. They are part of a 'community' of passionate supporters, albeit that they may know few other people present and the sense of community may only last for the period of the game in question. But such flag-waving events are hugely important in heightening national feelings and emotions. As Bradley states:

> It is this fervent passion and the interaction of the historical memory, national symbolism and human emotion, evoked in the context of competition with 'the other' (however temporary), that is likely to raise political or nationalist emotions with the possibility of translation into more substantial political expression, especially if the social trajectory and conditions are appropriate. (2002: 185)

Sport has been hugely significant in the development of national identity across the globe. Throughout the 1970s for example, Julius Nyerere, president of Tanzania, often remarked that sport helped bridge the gap between national and global recognition and this was important for the emerging African nations (Jarvie and Thornton 2012). During the apartheid era in South Africa, sport became highly politicised and many nations refused to compete against all-white South African teams. A key element of the African National Congress's campaign against apartheid was their argument that 'one cannot play normal sport in an abnormal society'. After the collapse of apartheid and the election of Nelson Mandela as president, he was able to argue that sport was part of the glue that held the new nation together (Jarvie and Thornton 2012). This was demonstrated most effectively in 1995, when South Africa won the Rugby World Cup, with a predominantly white team but with black support; the event was subsequently dramatised in the 2009 film *Invictus*, starring Morgan Freeman and Matt Damon. In 2010, South Africa successfully staged the FIFA Football World Cup, the first African nation to do so.

Closer to home, sport has been important in assisting the international recognition of the east European nations that have emerged from the break-up of the Soviet Union, Yugoslavia and Czechoslovakia and of consolidating their national identity. The international football organisation FIFA has therefore admitted a number of new members in recent years. To illustrate the point with a Scottish connection, in July 2007, Glasgow Rangers played (and beat) the Montenegrin champions Zeta Golubovci FC. The game was significant, not for the result, but for being the first time that a team from Montenegro had been able to compete in the European Champions League, following the country's independence from Serbia.

So sport, and perhaps football in particular, is highly significant in an international context. For historical reasons, all the four 'home nations' (Scotland, England, Wales and Northern Ireland) have been represented independently in international football, a privilege that is jealously guarded by the Scottish Football Association. Nor indeed is there a single UK team in sports such as rugby or cricket. Sport is an important part of civil society, alongside the church, the law and education, in which Scotland has developed a distinct identity while remaining within the UK. Sport became an obvious way in which Scots could assert their identity. Henry Drucker stated that 'football in Scottish life is much more than a sport. It's really an arena in which Scotland and Scots can assert themselves and play a role in international affairs' (cited in Forsyth 1990: 178). Football commentator Stuart Cosgrove suggests that 'Scotland has spent a century and more craving for football to relieve the dilemma of nationalism' (1991: 143), sport in his view becoming a substitute for nationalist politics.

The connection between Scottish sport and Scottish politics has been highlighted in a number of ways. In 1978, Scotland travelled to the football World Cup in Argentina and were widely expected to do well. In fact, they failed to progress beyond the first round and suffered the ignominy of having a player sent home after failing a drugs test. The blow to national pride and self-confidence has been regarded by some political commentators as contributing to the somewhat half-hearted support for devolution in the 1979 referendum. The low 'Yes' vote that year led to devolution being abandoned for another eighteen years (Jarvie 1993).

Some nationalist politicians have themselves expressed frustration at the failure of Scottish football supporters to translate their seemingly 'nationalist' fervour into votes for Scottish nationalist candidates at the ballot box. Following the 1992 general election in which he lost his seat, Jim Sillars, the prominent SNP politician, stated: 'The great problem is that Scotland has too many ninety-minute patriots whose nationalist outpourings are expressed only at major sporting events' (cited in Jarvie and Walker 1994: 5). Sillars's 'ninety minute patriots' phrase is one that has become well used in subsequent years and links to the concept of sport as a 'substitute' for nationalist politics in modern Scotland (Jarvie and Walker 1994).

Sillars's comments have, to a considerable extent, been overtaken by events, notably the 2014 independence referendum and the electoral successes of the SNP, both of which have demonstrated that serious political debate can indeed take place outside the sporting arena.

One aspect of Scottish sport that has not perhaps changed, however, and one crucial to Scotland's sense of identity is the use of 'othering', in which England is the 'other', against which support for Scottish teams is measured.

This is noticeable at events such as football and rugby matches, where Scotland supporters increasingly wear the kilt and use face paint to distinguish themselves from their English rivals. In the past, however, football's 'Tartan Army' was not always viewed in a positive light. They were often viewed with suspicion in England, a view seemingly justified by various incidents of drunkenness and the destruction of the Wembley turf and goalposts after an England versus Scotland game in 1977.

But the Tartan Army has reinvented itself as a group of friendly and fun-loving supporters, simply pleased to follow the national team and to be present at international competitions. It is no accident that the adoption of a more positive image has come about at a time when English football fans have been castigated for their poor behaviour. As Giulianotti explains:

> Externally, at matches overseas, a vital part of the Tartan Army's social repertoire involves establishing their national identity through a differentiation from England and 'Englishness'. By presenting themselves as 'anti-English', the Scots play upon the international stereotype that 'English fans are hooligans, hence the Scottish fans are also 'anti-hooligan' … The Tartan Army have become adept at winning over local media, posing for photographs or giving interviews that thank them for their hospitality, etc. The Scottish press have tended to mark out their national identity, vis-à-vis English-based competitors, by contrasting the friendliness of their compatriots (Scots fans) with the hooliganism of others (the English). (1999: 36–37)

Although we have focused on football as a vehicle for Scottish identity, the same issues are present in the more middle-class game of rugby. Jarvie and Walker (1994) suggest that the adoption by the rather conservative Scottish rugby union of 'Flower of Scotland' as the national anthem to be played at Murrayfield was significant. They quote the *Guardian* report on the 1991 Calcutta Cup match between Scotland and England:

> The message of Murrayfield this weekend was bigger than scrummaging techniques and line-out skills. It seemed etched in emotion on the faces of the players as they sang Flower of Scotland. It boiled constantly around the arena. Sometimes events happening send a clearer signal than a thousand pieces of newspaper. Murrayfield was a message of Scottish identity and nationhood. (*Guardian* 28 October 1991, cited in Jarvie and Walker 1994: 5)

Oddly, England persists at many sporting occasions in using 'God Save the Queen' as its anthem, although, as the anthem for the whole UK, it would seem inappropriate to do so. There has been debate in both academic and political circles as to whether it is perhaps time for England to have a national sporting anthem of its own (Hunter 2003). Indeed, it was only when the European football championships were held in England in 1996 that fans began extensively to use the St George's flag to show support, rather than the (inappropriate) Union Jack.

There are in fact relatively few sports where a UK-wide team competes. One of these is tennis, where the most successful 'British' player in recent years has been Andy Murray, a Scot. Prior to injury, Murray reached the world number one position, he has won Wimbledon and led the British Davis Cup team to victory. Yet there has been much debate as to whether he is a successful British or Scottish player. The man himself stated in 2006, however, that 'he would support whoever England is playing' in the 2006 World Cup and at the time of the referendum in 2014, he tweeted a comment supporting Scottish independence. This led some English newspapers to ask if the 'British' public would ever love Andy Murray again (Dickson 2014).

The major sporting event where a UK team participates is the Olympic Games. Perhaps because the 2012 Games were held in London, it was suggested by both the British Olympic Committee and by senior politicians at the time that it would be appropriate for a UK-wide football team to take part. This was poorly received outside England and the Football Associations of Scotland, Wales and Northern Ireland refused to cooperate. They viewed the creation of a UK-wide team as a threat to their independent existence (McRury and Poynter 2010; Ewen 2012), despite receiving assurances from FIFA to the contrary. In the event, a 'British' team did indeed participate but it was almost exclusively English (with a handful of Welsh players). Possibly as a result of the controversy, no British team competed at the Rio Olympics in 2016.

Scottish sport: the view from elsewhere

Looked at from a Scottish perspective, sport appears to be an important element within Scottish society and a key element in the country's sense of identity. But Scotland's position within the wider sporting world seems at times to be much less clear. Thus, while football is a sport that is seen from within the country to be part of daily life, Scotland is not necessarily seen by outsiders as a significant footballing nation. At the same time, some elite field sports that attract fewer participants appear to be part of the country's imagery – part of

'Scotland the brand' (McCrone *et al.* 1995). In this section, we begin to explore how Scottish sport is viewed from outside Scotland – how others see us, as it were.

Although football and rugby are hugely important within Scotland itself, it seems unlikely that tourists without a connection to Scotland would make a special journey to watch the national teams. In football, for example, Scotland is ranked forty-fifth in the FIFA world rankings (July 2019) and last qualified for a major international competition in 1998. The external view of Scotland as a sporting destination is therefore generally related to other activities, notably field sports, mountaineering and, of course, golf.

An important part of the imagery associated with Scotland is the Highland Games, an image frequently used in tourist marketing. Their significance is often local and there are large numbers of small towns and villages across the country that host Highland Games and similar gatherings, primarily during the summer. For many Scots, particularly in the larger cities and in the central belt, they are of much lesser importance. Although some forms of sporting contests had taken place across the Highlands for many years, the first 'modern' Highland Games appear to have taken place at Braemar in 1817 and they spread across the country from the 1820s onwards (Brewster *et al.* 2009). They began to attract the support of royalty with Queen Victoria making her first appearance at the Braemar Gathering in 1848; the Gathering has continued to have royal patronage to the present day.

For a long time, the different Highland Games were organised in a fairly informal way, varying by locality, but in 1946 the Scottish Games Association was formed as the overseeing body. At present, there are around a hundred Highland Games taking place across Scotland every year, with many more taking place within the Scottish diaspora, particularly in the United States. Brewster *et al.* (2009) highlight the importance of Highland Games, first as powerful community-based events, but also in their potential role in harnessing tourism spending throughout the country. They therefore play an important role in the image that is marketed by Scotland across the globe.

Royalty has, as we have already seen, played a significant part in popularising and publicising field sports within Scotland and the country is viewed as an important destination for tourists keen on deerstalking, fishing and the like. The Victorian painter Edwin Landseer enjoyed royal patronage and created a number of images of stags, most famously in his work *Monarch of the Glen*. He was also used by Queen Victoria to paint scenes of royalty shooting them. For his painting entitled *Royal Sports on Hill and Loch* the Queen made her wishes very clear:

> It is to be thus: I stepping out of the boat at loch Muich, Albert in his Highland Dress assisting me out, and I am looking at a Stag which he is supposed to have just killed. Bertie is on the deer pony with McDonald (whom Landseer much admires) standing behind, with rifles and plaids on shoulders. In the water, holding the boat, are several of the men in their kilts – salmon are also lying on the ground. The picture is intended to represent me meeting Albert, who has been stalking, whilst I have been fishing, and the whole is quite constant with the truth. (Cited in Jarvie and Reid 1999: 33)

Queen Victoria's desire to record a scene in this particular way may make us smile. But we should not underestimate the impact that the Queen and the Royal Family had (and perhaps continue to have) in popularising the Highlands as an area for sport. The areas were seen as remote and barbaric in the early nineteenth century, but royalty and better communications opened up the Highlands to sporting tourists. Field sports therefore became a significant element in the marketing of Scotland to overseas visitors (Seaton 1998).

The Highlands have also contributed to images of Scotland as a destination for mountaineers and hillwalkers. We have already referred to the growth in the numbers of 'Munro baggers' coming to Scotland. McCrone *et al.* (1995) explore the ways in which marketing materials use pictures of majestic and rugged mountain scenery to attract outsiders to visit. Investment in areas like the Cairngorms in terms of hostel accommodation for hillwalkers, the publication of extensive climbing guides and the like have all helped to promote this particular image of Scotland as a place for outdoor sports.

Golf is a sport with its world headquarters in Scotland – at St Andrews – and the country is viewed, particularly from places like North America as a 'must' for golfers to visit. Golf is used extensively in marketing strategies and Gold and Gold have analysed the rather clichéd ways in which the sport is portrayed in tourist brochures. They note the widespread use of pictures of 'golfers on a coastal links course. Driving off from a tee adjacent to the ocean, they stare intently into the distance to watch the flight of a ball driven impeccably by one of their number. Tartan trousers or tartan fabrics on a golf bag are a common additional referent' (1995: 6).

While the tone of their analysis is perhaps rather 'tongue-in-cheek', there is no mistaking the importance of the sport to the country's economy. To illustrate this, we might refer to the considerable investment made by the current American President Donald Trump in Scottish golf. Trump's mother was Scottish and so he saw it as appropriate for him to invest in his ancestral 'homeland'. In 2010, he began work on the development of a new golf course at Balmedie, north of Aberdeen and four years later, he purchased the internationally known course at Turnberry in Ayrshire. The text that is used in his online marketing of the Balmedie course is interesting:

> I am both proud and excited to share with you my most recent addition to the Trump golf portfolio, in the Home of Golf, Scotland.
>
> I have been actively looking for links land in Europe for the past few years, and of course my preference was Scotland over any other country because I am half Scottish. My Mother, Mary MacLeod, is from Stornoway on the Isle of Lewis. She grew up in a simple croft until she landed in Manhattan at the age of 20 and her first language was Gaelic.
>
> When I saw this piece of land I was overwhelmed by the imposing dunes and rugged Aberdeenshire coastline. I knew that this was the perfect site for Trump International, Scotland. I have never seen such an unspoiled and dramatic seaside landscape and the location makes it perfect for our development. Our site is close to two of the world's most famous courses and is just 15 minutes by car from Aberdeen Airport.[2]

The description of the coastline, the dunes and the reference to Scotland as 'the home of golf' all contribute to the image of the country being a prime destination for golfers. Trump's language is perhaps rather flowery and tends to romanticise Scotland – but this is perhaps not unusual for a member of the Scottish diaspora.

It does, however, illustrate the external view of Scottish sport, which is often rather romantic and backward-looking. Tourist marketing of Highland Games and field sports is symptomatic of a 'hills and glens' imagery of Scotland, while the marketing of golf is often restricted to the more picturesque championship courses. Indeed, the image and the marketing of Scotland for sport are very selective. The country may be seen as the home of golf, but other sports are not marketed in anything like the same way nor have such an international profile.

That said, the country is still viewed externally as one very capable of hosting major international events. We have already referred to the regeneration of east Glasgow resulting from the 2014 Commonwealth Games. In fact, these were the third Games held in Scotland, Edinburgh having hosted them in 1970 and 1986. The award of the 1970 Commonwealth Games to the city led to the construction of Meadowbank stadium as an important part of the city's sporting infrastructure. The 1986 Commonwealth Games were less successful and suffered a financial loss; this resulted from the boycotting of the event by a number of countries because of the UK's support for the apartheid regime in South Africa (Downes 2002).

Scotland has, naturally, hosted major golf championships. The British Open has been held on a large number of courses across the country, including St Andrews, Muirfield, Troon, Turnberry and Carnoustie. In 2014, the country hosted the Ryder Cup for only the second time, the event being held at Gleneagles.

Although football is perhaps the dominant sport within Scotland itself, the country has never hosted a major football finals tournament, although Scotland and the Republic of Ireland submitted a joint bid to host the 2008 Union of European Football Associations (UEFA) European football championships. Glasgow's Hampden Park football stadium has, however, hosted the final of the UEFA Champions League in 1960, 1976 and 2002, as well as the UEFA Cup Final in 2007.

Conclusions

As is the case with many other relatively small countries, sport plays a significant part within Scottish society. It also plays a crucial part in maintaining the country's national identity. As a 'stateless nation', Scotland is not a member in its own right of the United Nations or the EU, but it is an independent member of the international football organisations UEFA and FIFA and has the right to field its own national team. In other sports too, such as rugby and cricket, Scotland field its own team and is not part of a wider 'British' representation. Therefore sport has helped to define the country, especially perhaps against the English 'other' and this has maintained an element of distinctiveness and independence from an all-consuming UK identity.

Scotland's sporting successes, however, have been variable. There have been notable individual successes, such as Andy Murray in tennis, but in team sports such as football, rugby and cricket Scotland has not fared so well in recent years. The country last qualified for a major football championship in 1998 and in the Rugby World Cup Scotland has only once reached the semi-finals – in 1991. Yet, small countries can and do achieve success. At the time of writing (July 2019), Belgium is joint top of the FIFA world football rankings, despite having a population of only eleven million, so it is clearly possible for a relatively small country to achieve major success.

In the case of Scotland, sustained success in team sports would perhaps allow the importance of sport at home to be matched by recognition abroad.

Further reading

There are a number of books concerning sport and wider society, such as Barrie Houlihan's *Sport and Society: A Student Introduction* (2008) and *Sport Worlds: A Sociological Perspective* by Joseph Maguire *et al.* (2002).

Sport plays a significant role in the creation and maintenance of a national identity and there is important reading in Grant Jarvie and Graham Walker's *Scottish Sport in the Making of the Nation: Ninety Minute Patriots?* (1994), Grant Jarvie's *Sport, Culture and Society: An Introduction* (2012) and a paper by Grant Jarvie *et al.*, 'Promoting Scotland, Diplomacy and Influence Through Sport' in *Scottish Affairs* (2017). See also John Hunter's paper, 'Flying the Flag: Identities, the Nation and Sport' in *Identities* (2003) and Gary Armstrong and Richard Giulianotti's edited *Football Cultures and Identities* (1999).

As might perhaps be expected, there is a wealth of writing on Scottish football, including Raymond Boyle's 'What Football Means to Scotland (Or What "fitba" Tells Us About Scotland!)' in *Critical Quarterly* (2000), Joe Bradley's 'The Patriot Game: Football's Famous "Tartan Army" ' in *International Review for the Sociology of Sport* (2002) and Stephen Morrow's 'Scottish Football: It's a Funny Old Business' in *Journal of Sports Economics* (2006).

Irene Reid has written about more minor sports such as shinty in *Sports Historian* (1998) and curling in *Sport in Society* (2010). For those with an interest in Highland Games, they should consult David Webster's *World History of Highland Games* (2011).

Chapter 15
Conclusion: Contemporary Scotland

Introduction

In our introduction, we sketched a picture of Scotland and Scottish society in which we sought to illustrate the nature of change that had produced this Scotland of the early twenty-first century. A Scotland that in the past few decades had undergone significant social, economic and most of all political change. We spoke of the huge shift in living conditions, of the nature of employment, of the social positioning of Scottish society from a very conservative to a more progressive form and of the underpinning movement of how the people of Scotland view themselves and their relationships with others. We also considered, as a thread throughout, the wider political changes that, after three hundred years of a singular legislative entity – the UK state – Scotland had gained a devolved legislature and the ability to write its own laws, set its own taxes and thus highlight its own, distinct and particular, social and political preferences and agenda. We then began to colour in the wider picture of Scotland, by stepping into the main themes of our work and providing distinct chapters analysing those themes.

What we can witness from our discussion is much of what we would expect, given the changes that have taken place – especially as a result of devolution. With a legislature and a resultant executive (given the parliamentary nature of Scotland's system) focused solely on the nation and with limited constitutional abilities to go beyond that focus, Scotland has witnessed many new laws and socio-economic-political initiatives as a result. There can be little doubt that many of these would not have occurred had Scotland not voted for devolution in 1997. Subsequently, Scotland has been something of an experimenter within the UK. It has undertaken significant social changes through legislation – whether that be as simple as making all prescriptions free of charge, or the more complicated matter of diverging income tax levels from the wider UK (by introducing both slightly higher and lower rates).

Scotland has thus been a legislative trail blazer, passing legislation that has then been taken up by other UK nations/regions, such as the Welsh Assembly, or passed into English law at Westminster. The most obvious example of this is the 2005 smoking ban, which showed that it was both possible and would be accepted by the vast majority of the population. Bans in Wales, Northern Ireland and England followed quickly. At the same time England has not undertaken all measures adopted by Scotland, one of the most publicly obvious being the continuation of tuition fees at English universities. While such acts are legislative in nature, they serve as examples of the ongoing sociopolitical changes between England and Scotland that have taken place over the last two decades. As we point out in Chapter 11 specifically, this will no doubt have an impact upon the relationship between the nations and the residents of each, but the implications of such are not clear at this point.

Nevertheless, proclamations of success and change that could be attached to devolution in Scotland must be tempered in some respects. While there can be no doubt that devolution has very much become the settled nature of Scottish politics and society, it has failed to meet some of the high expectations that initial advocates and watchers proclaimed. Early texts on the subject of devolution spoke of 'a new politics' or the emergence of a system in which control would be shared among Scottish society and not just a replication of 'Westminster-lite' politics.

However, what we have witnessed seems to be somewhat of just such replication, albeit with a slight twist. Any hopes that an adversarial political system would be left behind in Westminster and not exported into Scotland have been dashed (although the validity of such hopes was surely suspect, given the nature of politics itself). The strong presence of minority parties has not been replicated across the last decade of Scottish politics and no true 'multi-party' system has emerged – although a dominant party system has. Furthermore, as Duncan McTavish points out in Chapter 8, there seems to be a growing conflation between the traditional political axis of left and right, to those of more constitutional power for Scotland (left = yes, right = no). What is clear is that the constitutional question, first in relation to Scotland's place in the UK and then to the UK's place/role in the EU, has certainly become the driving force behind many voters' decisions.

Furthermore, Scottish society remains, in many ways, as unbalanced and challenged as ever. The myth of egalitarianism, which the Scots have always liked to invoke through the phrase 'we are all Jock Tamson's Bairns', remains a myth with little firm foundation in fact or evidence. It can certainly not be used to distinguish Scotland from England or the wider UK. As David Torrance points out, this is a myth regularly employed by politicians in Scotland (see Chapter 9) but social mobility in both nations remains one of a degree of perception rather than any firm reality.

We, the people in Scotland, may wish to see ourselves as more egalitarian, more working class, more accepting and more open and we certainly often do so while contrasting ourselves to our neighbours to the south, the English. Certainly, debates during the run up to the independence referendum in 2014 and the EU referendum in 2016 often saw Scotland being portrayed as more internationalist in outlook and not as anti-immigrant as other parts of the UK. However, whether the issue be one of gender, race or ethnicity, the evidence challenges modern Scotland to understand that while change has certainly taken place, challenges remain. Elements of Scottish society clearly maintain less-positive attitudes towards gender parity and racial and anti-immigrant rhetoric and action can be found across Scotland. However, we must stress that the evidence points to clearly positive changes and movement and it seems that as a nation Scotland is moving towards a more balanced and equal social position for women and minorities.

What can be clearly seen in our discussion are clear threads that run through our presentation and analysis of the modern state of the nation of Scotland. Our work, from our first chapters on history and identity, through to our chapters considering the arts and sport, has highlighted certain trends – trends that continue to be of importance to the Scotland of today as much as they did to the Scotland over the preceding centuries. Among these are the relationship with England and the associated idea of Britishness, the battles between elites for the direction of the future Scotland and the importance of myths and legends versus material facts. We can witness these facts today, whether the subject be the need to address 'potential shortcomings' in the Scottish educational system (see Chapter 5) or Scotland's relationship within the UK and the EU. We will now consider these trends.

Continuing important trends

Relationship with England

Long before it would become a formal part of the UK, that is the UK state, Scotland had a long and involved relationship with England. The nature of Scotland was heavily influenced at key points by the physical and political geography of the British Isles that means Scotland shares its only land border with England. Even while sometimes struggling with that relationship, Scotland has always maintained a sense of nationhood and identity. Since its establishment as an independent kingdom, and even with its subsequent royal and then political marriage into the UK, Scotland has done so as an entity operating on what it saw and clearly evinced as its own terms. As discussed earlier, narratives placing Scotland in some sort of colonial relationship vis-à-vis the UK are recent additions to the rhetorical debates. However, whether the partnership nature of that relationship has always been fully recognised by England remains questionable and whether it can survive the wider current constitutional debates is a key contemporary issue.

The Scottish Government, formed by the SNP, has the stated goal of independence for Scotland and thus its continued and continual emphasis on that goal should surprise no one. Furthermore, the Scottish Government also continues to seek to ensure clarity of Scottish identity, culture and activity within the contemporary UK. We have discussed that significant government activity focuses on the identity-forming function of culture, which is illustrated by the distinct cultural agenda within Scotland. At the same time, Scotland has a distinct set of myths and images that drive the nature of Scottish identity. Modern Scotland seems quite happy to embrace elements of these myths, without them directly challenging the symbiotic sense of identity many Scots hold with Britishness. What is clear is that in 2014, a majority of voters in Scotland clearly stated that they wished to remain part of the UK, with a result of 55.3 per cent to 44.7 per cent. The turnout for this vote was 84.59 per cent of registered voters in Scotland. This represented 3,623,344 votes cast in what must stand as one of the largest statements at a ballot box among democracies in recent times. At the same time, the pro-independence minority vote was higher than many had predicted when the Scottish Government's consultation paper was published in early 2010.

Elite activity and the battle for the future of Scotland

Whatever the result in 2014, however, the debate among the political elites has not ceased and that brings us to our second trend, that of elite manoeuvrings for the control of the future and a choice on the social, economic and political direction of Scotland, be that within or without the wider UK. This debate not only clearly continues unabated, but is one that has very much emerged and been greatly emphasised during the past decades at a level not seen since perhaps those following the formation of the Union itself. Since the late 1960s, there have been political battles first to establish a distinct Scottish legislature, which after an initial defeat regrouped and resulted in the devolved Scottish Parliament, established in 1999. Then, just over a decade later, Scotland would enter a period of activity revolving around that one question answered in 2014 – should Scotland be an independent country and an independent state in its own right, after being part of the UK since 1707? As noted above, the answer was clearly 'No' from voters, but rarely is anything in politics final. In fact, it has been strongly argued by the SNP, who it must be remembered have been the ruling party of the Scottish Government for the last decade and more, that the UK-wide vote to leave the EU has resulted in the very 'significant or material change' that the last SNP general election manifesto stated would be cause to reopen negotiations for a second referendum debate on Scotland's status within the UK. Obviously, this is not the position shared by the UK Government, formed by the Conservative party, who would be required to agree to such a vote taking place. The authority to hold the 2014 referendum was granted to the Scottish Government by the UK Government, as required by the Scotland Act 1998. Although this was done through a formal legislative process, it was publicly agreed by the Edinburgh Agreement, signed in October 2012 by then Scottish First Minister Alex Salmond and UK Prime Minister David Cameron. Theresa May, The UK prime minister in 2018, and her successor in 2019, Boris Johnson, have both publicly stated they will not make another such agreement.

Noticeably, what makes these elite-driven events involving Scotland's place in the UK, and the wider UK's place in Europe, distinct from those that formed the first Union in 1707 is the involvement of the masses in the decision-making process. There can be no doubt that the decisions of 1979, 1997, 2014 and 2016 all involved the voters of Scotland (and in 2016 the whole UK) and thus the mass voice was present within the debate. Yet, the influence of the mass voice is limited at times, and Scotland's voice is only one within the larger body of the UK; the Scottish mass decision in 2016 was very much diluted in that regard. Furthermore, as our discussion on identity in Chapter 3 illustrated, the masses can often differ from the elite in terms of what they consider Scotland and Scottishness to be. The battle for the future of Scotland takes place at a level that many Scottish residents do not engage with. At the last Scottish Parliament election turnout was up 5 per cent, at an average of

55 per cent, but this remains well below the level of the 2015 and 2017 UK general elections and the 2014 independence referendum.

Whatever the result of the elections, this book has been written as the UK is poised to leave the EU. Scotland voted overwhelmingly to remain but will be leaving as part of the UK. Therefore, it is clear that the political and constitutional battle lines remain and the issue of Scotland's future statehood status remains an ongoing subject. We will return to the discussion around the EU below.

Myths and legends

Scotland, as a conception, an image and an idea, is not singular and certainly there does not exist an accepted idea of what Scotland is or should be. Just as individuals have multilayered identities and just as our national identity is so often interconnected and complex (although we so often reduce it to a sense of 'us' and 'them' in Scotland, as do other nationalities), so imagery, national culture and values are multiform. This issue of Scotland connects Scots throughout the world. Just as we have examined the Scottish diaspora as much as the resident Scottish population, we can certainly demonstrate that all share this notion of differing ideas of who and what Scotland is. We illustrated in Chapter 10 that the Scottish diaspora often have perceptions of Scottishness that are somewhat at odds with those held by modern residents of Scotland. Yet clearly they feel a connection to Scotland and just as much a strong sense of Scottishness as the majority that reside within the national borders.

Any discussion of national identity must clearly recognise that the foundation myths of that national identity are often subject to personal preferences and whims, even while founded in history and factual events. While many may disagree on the actual resultant outcomes of the Battle of Bannockburn in 1314, it has come to be perceived as the milestone for the establishment of Scottish independence in the fourteenth century. The importance of such myths becomes evident. Likewise, who and what constitutes a Scot in the modern era is clearly a matter for discussion with a clear divergence of thought on the issue – and an even more clear divergence between the elites and masses within Scotland. Nevertheless, what our analysis and consideration of contemporary Scottishness illustrates so evidently is that national identity in Scotland remains a very deeply felt, strongly held sense of belonging.

Yet, Scottish national identity is often closely intertwined with a clear sense of Britishness for many Scottish residents today. There is also the added element of being European – an identity that has now taken on a clear and firm sense of political belonging, one that may serve to challenge the relationship between Scottishness and Britishness. What we also illustrated was that the masses place clear boundaries around this sense of identity – boundaries that are not fully in agreement or indicative of those expressed by elites across the Scottish political spectrum. These issues were echoed in later chapters, such as our discussion on images of Scotland and Scotland abroad and specifically in England. Thus, it is clear that national identity, Scottishness, remains dear to those who identify with Scotland, that national identity is not a singular, but a multiform, complex and intertwined sense of individuality held by a collection of people who draw upon their myths, legends, culture and history to make a connection to the greater whole – Scotland.

Whither Scotland and Brexit?

It would be impossible to end a discussion on Scotland, and on the future of Scotland, in early 2019 without closing on the issue of Brexit. As we face the potential for further significant change in and for Scotland, the importance of history, identity and culture as aspects of the current debates on that future should not be underestimated. We have already noted that while a debate is ongoing in Scotland about its place and role within the UK, the UK has also reconsidered its role within the EU. Much of the imagery, rhetoric and symbology of the debate around Brexit has invoked history, such as oft-flammable rhetoric involving the Second World War and emphases on freedom and independence, some of which invokes 1066 or the Magna Carta. Of course, the last two events took place long before Scotland and England joined together in Union, and their invocation within the debate can be both amusing and annoying to Scots as a result. The proclaimer 'except in Scotland' should perhaps be employed more widely within political debating circles than it currently is. Furthermore, given Scotland's overwhelming support to remain, the issue of the EU presents an interesting case for all the mainstream Scottish political parties and the SNP in particular. Every major Scottish political party leader was in favour of the UK remaining within the EU and all campaigned for the remain vote to succeed. Subsequently, both Labour and Conservative party leaders in Scotland have struggled with the stance of their party versus the stance of the wider UK party. This has left the SNP, and the more peripheral Liberal Democrats, as the only parties able to maintain an ideologically coherent narrative on the issue.

Yet, this is not as clear an issue for the SNP as it would at first seem. When the UK sought to join the European Economic Community (EEC) in 1975 the SNP leadership was vehemently opposed to membership, arguing that it represented a challenge to Scotland's 'very existence' and it was an elite and undemocratic organisation. Even today, a significant number of supporters of Scottish independence oppose membership of the EU, albeit they constitute a minority. While the other major parties all suffer defections and resignations from the party whip in Westminster, SNP MPs may present a united front on the issue, but it remains a dividing issue for many within the party too.

Yet it is clear that the end result of Brexit will include the entire UK and will not allow Scotland any divergent relationship with Europe that will differentiate it from England. Given the position of the Scottish Government, and the preference of the majority of Scottish voters, this is likely to place further strain on the constitutional relationship and current format of the UK. As our discussion on Scottish history clearly establishes, Scotland's relationship with England, be it social, economic or political, stretches back long before 1707. Yet it is that formal Union of 1707 that remains pivotal to the discussion on the relationship around and involving Scotland and England, and the wider UK. Such a difference of opinion between two nations on any key political issue, let alone a constitutional one such as Brexit, is clearly problematic. While it is always difficult for social scientists of any stripe to prognosticate, it is very easy to say that we have not witnessed the end of the discussion on Scotland's constitutional position within the UK and the likelihood of another referendum on Scottish independence remains significant. Whatever the future of Scotland will be, we can safely say that will be.

Notes

3 Scotland's identity

1 All respondents within the data analysed within this chapter are adults living in Scotland at the time of the survey.

7 'Ethnic' Scotland

1 Note that since this report was written, race crimes have shown a downward trend.

8 Political Scotland

1 It should be noted that partnership delivery and community planning on a significant scale are very difficult both in conception and implementation. Audit Scotland reports in 2014 and 2016 indicated that significant achievements had been made but that the ambitious aims had not yet been achieved. International research points in the same direction, noting that many changes are often incremental rather than transformational (e.g. see OECD 2011).

2 The contrast with England is of interest. There, policy concern over asset-based community development is largely articulated through health-related matters. The influential Marmot Review (2010) indicated that to reduce health inequalities in England improvement in social and community capital was required. Subsequently, Public Health England has been a strong advocate of community-centred approaches for health and well-being (e.g. Public Health England 2015). However, there is no statutory basis but there is guidance on the importance of community engagement as a strategy for health improvement; there is specific mention of such in the NHS England Five-Year Forward Review and guidance to clinical commissioning groups. Many of the local government initiatives in England on asset-based development are health focused, though this is an under-researched area.

3 https://beta.gov.scot/policies/community-empowerment/empowering-communities-fund (accessed 3 October 2018).

4 www.local.gov.uk/topics/devolution/combined-authorities (accessed 3 October 2018).

5 www.bbc.co.uk/news/uk-scotland-scotland-politics-21938594 (accessed 8 October 2018).
6 The seats won by the Conservatives in Scotland in 2017 were: West Aberdeenshire and Kincardine; Gordon; Banff and Buchan; Ochil and South Perthshire; Ayr, Carrick and Cumnock; Angus; Dumfries and Galloway; Stirling; Berwickshire, Roxburgh and Selkirk; East Renfrewshire; Dumfriesshire, Clydesdale and Tweeddale; Moray; and Aberdeen South.
7 www.bbc.co.uk/news/uk-scotland-scotland-politics-44616793 (accessed 9 October 2018).
8 www.bma.org.uk/news/2018/january/scotland-proceeds-with-separate-gp-contract (accessed 9 October 2018).
9 www.bma.org.uk/connecting-doctors/b/work/posts/beating-england-isn-t-enough (accessed 9 October 2018).
10 www.holyrood.com/articles/inside-politics/exclusive-interview-jeane-freeman-her-nursing-heritage-and-priorities-nhs (accessed 30 September 2018).
11 www.instituteforgovernment.org.uk/explainers/brexit-devolution-joint-ministerial-committee (accessed 10 October 2018).

9 Elites in Scotland

1 It was A. J. P. Taylor who first used the phrase 'the Establishment' in a 1953 *New Statesman* essay.
2 Writing in 2001, the journalist Roddy Martine made a similar point, observing that the Scottish Establishment's 'power base' was 'the most formidable force of all. It is social' (2001: n.p.).
3 Veronica Linklater, married to one of the book's authors, was later ennobled as Baroness Linklater of Butterstone, joining her first cousin, Viscount Thurso, in the House of Lords. Both were grandchildren of Sir Archibald Sinclair, one-time Scottish secretary and leader of the UK Liberal Party.
4 Sir Angus caused controversy in late 2017 by inviting former Trump strategist Steve Bannon to address a gathering of 'Scotland International' and again in 2018 by personally accepting a Pushkin Award from Russian President Vladimir Putin.
5 After leaving the House of Commons in 2010, Mohammad Sarwar returned to his native Pakistan to pursue a political career there, serving as Governor of Punjab (twice) and a senator.
6 That said, in late 2018 the Scottish Fiscal Commission predicted that the number of Scots paying the top rate of income tax would rise by almost 50 per cent over the next five years, with rising earnings 'sucking' more people into the additional rate band (Scottish Fiscal Commission 2018).
7 An interesting phenomenon in the 2016 Holyrood election was a return of what used to be termed 'knights of the shire' to the Scottish Conservative benches, newly elected MSPs like Donald Cameron (of Lochiel), Sir Edward Mountain (fourth baronet) and Alexander Burnett (a descendent of Tsar Nicholas I), succeeding outgoing members such as Sir Jamie McGrigor (sixth baronet) and Sir Alex Fergusson (newly knighted but related to others).
8 Malcolm Robertson is married to Jane Smith, a daughter of the late Labour Party leader and Scots lawyer John Smith. Another of his daughters, Sarah Smith, became a

high-profile BBC network broadcaster, while his widow, Baroness Smith, is a member of the House of Lords.

9 During debates over Skye Bridge tolls in the 1990s, 'Robbie the Pict' highlighted the fact that members of the Speculative Society headed up the bridge company (Sir Iain Noble) and led the Scottish Office department responsible for its private finance (James Douglas-Hamilton), while twelve of the fourteen judges who presided over related hearings were also 'Spec' members.

10 Scotland abroad

1 www.scotlandspeople.gov.uk (accessed 2 December 2019).

11 Scotland in England

1 www.youtube.com/watch?v=fo_eoW1DJaU (accessed 4 December 2019).

13 Scotland, tourism and heritage

1 www.visitscotland.com/about/uniquely-scottish (accessed 2 December 2019).

2 https://scottishtourismalliance.co.uk/wp-content/uploads/2019/03/People-Make-Heritage-Heritage-Tourism-2020-Strategy.pdf (accessed 2 December 2019).

3 Such as www.scotlandspeople.gov.uk (accessed 2 December 2019).

14 Scotland and sport

1 www.sportingintelligence.com/2012/04/02/revealed-the-most-dedicated-football-nations-the-faroes-iceland-cyprus-scotland-and-england-020403 (accessed 2 December 2019).

2 www.trumpgolfscotland.com/files/Recruitment%20Day%20Pack%20(2).pdf (accessed 2 December 2019).

Bibliography

Abrams, L., Gordon, E., Simonton, D. and Yeo, E. J. (eds) (2006), *Gender in Scottish history since 1700*, Edinburgh: Edinburgh University Press.

Adamson, F. (2008), 'Constructing the diaspora: diaspora identity politics and transnational social movements', http://citation.allacademic.com/meta/p_mla_apa_research_citation/2/5/1/1/7/pages251176/p251176-1.php (accessed 2 December 2019).

Aiton, A. (2019), *Labour market update February 2019*, Edinburgh: Scottish Parliament Information Centre.

Allan, G. (2015), 'Forecasts of the Scottish economy', *Fraser of Allander Institute Economic Commentary* 38.3, pp. 30–40.

Anderson, B. (1983), *Imagined communities: reflections on the origin and spread of nationalism*, London: Verso.

Anderson, M. (2018), *Scotland's populations from the 1850s to today*, Oxford: Oxford University Press.

Anderson, R. (1985), 'In search of the "lad of parts": the mythical history of Scottish education', *History Workshop Journal* 19.1, pp. 82–104.

Archer, J. (2014), 'Unlocking potential, embracing ambition', *Cultural Trends* 23.3, pp. 193–196.

Armitage, D. (2005), 'The Scottish diaspora', in J. Wormald (ed.), *Scotland: a history*, Oxford: Oxford University Press, pp. 272–303.

Armstrong, B. (1989), *A people without prejudice? The experience of racism in Scotland*, London: Runnymede Trust.

Armstrong, G. and Giulianotti, R. (eds) (1999), Football cultures and identities, London: Macmillan.

Armstrong, J. A. (1982), *Nations before nationalism*, Chapel Hill: University of North Carolina Press.

Armstrong, J. A. and Williams, D. M. (2005), 'The steamboat and popular tourism', *Journal of Transport History* 26.1, pp. 61–77.

Ashcroft, B. (2015), 'The Scottish economy: outlook and appraisal', *Fraser of Allander Institute Economic Commentary* 38.3, pp. 3–29.

Aspinwall, B. (1985), 'The Scots in the United States', in Cage, R. A. (ed.), *The Scots abroad: labour, capital, enterprise 1750–1914*, London: Croom Helm, pp. 80–110.

Audit Scotland (2016), *Community planning: an update*, www.audit-scotland.gov.uk/uploads/docs/report/2016/nr_160303_community_planning.pdf (accessed 2 October 2018).

Bibliography

Audrey, S. (2000), *Multiculturalism in practice: Irish, Jewish, Italian and Pakistani migration to Scotland*, Aldershot: Ashgate.

Bagshawe, L. (2010). 'Parliamentary debates', *Parliamentary Debates (Hansard). House of Commons*, col. 525–527, 10 June, www.publications.parliament.uk/pa/cm201011/cmhansrd/cm100610/debtext/100610-0014.htm#10061031001092 (accessed 2 December 2019).

Bannister, W. (1955), *James Bridie and his theatre*, London: Rockliff.

Barker, A. and Stockdale, A. (2008), 'Out of the wilderness? Achieving sustainable development within Scottish national parks', *Journal of Environmental Management* 88.1, pp. 181–193.

Basu, P. (2004), 'Route metaphors of "roots-tourism" in the Scottish highland diaspora', in Coleman, S. and Eade, J. (eds), *Reframing pilgrimage: cultures in motion*, London: Routledge, pp. 150–174.

Basu, P. (2005), 'Macpherson country: genealogical identities, spatial histories and the Scottish diasporic clanscape', *Cultural Geographies* 12, pp. 123–150.

Basu, P. (2007), *Highland homecomings: genealogy and heritage tourism in the Scottish diaspora*, London: Routledge.

Battu, H. (2005), *Is there an earnings penalty to being Catholic in Scotland?* Stirling: University of Stirling.

BBC (2012), 'Scottish independence: Corby "should have vote"', www.bbc.co.uk/news/uk-england-northamptonshire-20122435 (accessed 4 December 2019).

BBC (2015), *BBC Scotland management review 2014/15*, London: BBC.

BBC (2016a), 'Brexit watch: at-a-glance day-by-day summer briefing', www.bbc.co.uk/news/uk-politics-36881718 (accessed 2 December 2019).

BBC (2016b), 'Harlow murder inquiry: concerns remain over alleged "hate crime"', www.bbc.co.uk/news/uk-england-essex-37327581 (accessed 2 December 2019).

BBC (2018), 'February 2019 date for new BBC Scotland television channel', www.bbc.co.uk/news/uk-scotland-44126219 (accessed 2 December 2019).

BBC Trust (2015), www.bbc.co.uk/bbctrust/who_we_are/audience_councils/scotland (accessed 2 December 2019).

Bechhofer, F. and McCrone, D. (2009), *National identity, nationalism and constitutional change*, London: Palgrave Macmillan.

Behr, A. and Brennan, M. (2014), 'The place of popular music in Scotland's cultural policy', *Cultural Trends* 23.3, pp. 169–177.

Bell, A. (2014), *The people we can be: or how to be £500 better off, build a fairer society and a better planet*, Edinburgh: Luath.

Bhandari, K. (2014), *Tourism and national identity: heritage and nationhood in Scotland*, Bristol: Channel View.

Biggar Economics (2014), *Edinburgh's cultural venues impact 2013/14*, Roslin: Biggar Economics.

Billcliffe, R. (1988), *The Glasgow Boys: the Glasgow School of Painting 1875–1895*, London: John Murray.

Billig, M. (1995), *Banal nationalism*, London: Sage.

Birtwistle, M. (2005), 'Genealogy tourism: the Scottish market opportunities', in Novelli, M. (ed.), *Niche tourism: contemporary issues, trends and cases*, Oxford: Elsevier, pp. 59–72.

Black, G., Smith, R. C., Kheria, S. and Porter, G. (2015), 'Scotland the brand: marketing the myth', *Scottish Affairs* 24.1, pp. 47–77.

Bloomer, K. (2015), 'Scottish education: what needs to be done?', Reform Scotland, https://reformscotland.com/2015/09/scottish-education-what-needs-to-be-done-keir-bloomer (accessed 2 December 2019).

Bodlore-Penlaez, M. (2012), *Atlas of stateless nations in Europe*, Talybont: Y Lolfa.

Bonino, S. (2015), 'Scottiah Muslims through a decade of change: wounded by the stigma, healed by Islam, rescued by Scotland', *Scottish Affairs* 24.1, pp. 78–105.

Bonnar, A. (2014), 'What does culture mean to you? The practice and process of consultation on cultural policy in Scotland since devolution', *Cultural Trends* 23.3, pp. 136–147.

BOP Consulting (2016), *Edinburgh festivals 2015 impact study*, London: BOP.

Botting, B. and Dunnell, K. (2000), 'Trends in fertility and contraception in the last quarter of the 20th century', *Population Trends* 100, pp. 32–39.

Bowes, A. and Bell, D. (2007), 'Free personal care for older people in Scotland: issues and implications', *Social Policy and Society* 6.3, pp. 435–445.

Bowes, A., Dar, N. and Sim, D. (1997), 'Tenure preference and housing strategy: an exploration of Pakistani experiences', *Housing Studies* 12.1, pp. 63–84.

Bowes, A., McCluskey, J. and Sim, D. (1990a), 'The changing nature of Glasgow's ethnic-minority community', *Scottish Geographical Magazine* 106.2, pp. 99–107.

Bowes, A., McCluskey, J. and Sim, D. (1990b), 'Racism and harassment of Asians in Glasgow', *Ethnic and Racial Studies* 13.1, pp. 71–91.

Bowie, K. (2008), 'Popular resistance, religion and the union of 1707', in Devine, T. M. (ed.), Scotland and the Union 1707-2007, Edinburgh: Edinburgh University Press, pp. 39–53.

Bowman, M. (1995), 'Cardiac Celts: images of the Celts in contemporary British paganism', in Harvey, G. and Hardman, C. (eds), *Paganism today*, London: Thorsons, pp. 242–251.

Boyle, M. (1997), 'Civic boosterism in the politics of local economic development: "institutional positions" and "strategic orientations" in the consumption of hallmark events', *Environment and Planning A* 29.11, pp. 1975–1997.

Boyle, R. (2000), 'What football means to Scotland (or what "fitba" tells us about Scotland!)', *Critical Quarterly* 42.4, pp. 21–29.

Brah, A. (1996), *Cartographies of diaspora: contesting identities*, London: Routledge.

Bradley, J. M. (2002), 'The patriot game: football's famous "Tartan Army"', *International Review for the Sociology of Sport* 37.2, pp. 177–197.

Bradley, J. M. (2006), 'Sport and the contestation of ethnic identity: football and Irishness in Scotland', *Journal of Ethnic and Migration Studies* 32.7, pp. 1189–1208.

Bray, E. (1986), *The discovery of the Hebrides*, Glasgow: Collins.

Breitenbach, E., Brown, A. and Myers, F. (1998), 'Understanding women in Scotland', *Feminist Review* 58, pp. 44–65.

Breitenbach, E. and Wasoff, F. (2007), *A gender audit of statistics: comparing the position of women and men in Scotland*, Edinburgh: Scottish Executive Social Research.

Brewster, M., Connell, J. and Page, S. (2009), 'The Scottish Highland Games: evolution, development and role as a community event', *Current Issues in Tourism* 12.3, pp. 271–293.

Brida, J. G. and Zapata, S. (2010), 'Cruise tourism: economic, socio-cultural and environmental impacts', *International Journal of Leisure and Tourism Marketing* 1.3, pp. 205–226.

Brines, J. (1994), 'Economic dependency, gender, and the division of labor at home', *American Journal of Sociology* 100.3, pp. 652–688.

Brinkerhoff, J. (2009), 'Creating an enabling environment for diasporas' participation in homeland development', *International Migration* 50.1, pp. 75–95.

British Election Study (1997), www.britishelectionstudy.com (accessed 2 December 2019).

British Tourist Authority (1994), *The lands of Britain: your vacation planner*, London: BTA.

Brivati, B. (2002), 'Gordon Brown', in Jefferys, K. (ed.), *Labour forces: from Ernest Bevin to Gordon Brown*, London: I. B. Tauris, pp. 237–250.

Broun, D. (1994), 'The origins of Scottish identity', in Bjorn, C., Grant, A. and Stringer, K. J. (eds), *Nations, nationalism and patriotism in the European past*, Copenhagen Academic Press, pp. 35–55.

Broun, D. (2007), Scottish *independence and the idea* of Britain from the Picts to Alexander III, Edinburgh: Edinburgh University Press.

Broun, D. (2015), 'Britain and the beginning of Scotland', *Journal of the British Academy* 3, pp. 107–137.

Brown, C. G. (1996), 'Popular culture and the continuing struggle for rational recreation', in Devine, T. and Finlay, R. (eds), *Scotland in the twentieth century*, Edinburgh: Edinburgh University Press, pp. 210–229.

Brown, G. (2014), *My Scotland, our Britain: a future worth sharing*, London: Simon & Schuster.

Brown, I. (2010a), *From tartan to tartanry: Scottish culture, history and myth*, Edinburgh: Edinburgh University Press.

Brown, I. (2010b), 'Tartan, tartanry and hybridity', in Brown, I. (ed.), *From tartan to tartanry: Scottish culture, history and myth*, Edinburgh: Edinburgh University Press, pp. 1–12.

Brubaker, R. (2005), 'The "diaspora" diaspora', *Ethnic and Racial Studies*, 28.1, pp. 1–19.

Bruce, S., Glendinning, T., Paterson, I. and Rosie, M. (2004), *Sectarianism in Scotland*, Edinburgh: Edinburgh University Press.

Bruce, S., Glendinning, T., Paterson, I. and Rosie, M. (2005), 'Religious discrimination in Scotland: fact or myth?', *Ethnic and Racial Studies* 28.1, pp. 151–168.

Bryce, T. G. K., Humes, W. M., Gillies, D. and Kennedy, A. (eds) (2018), Scottish education (5th ed.), Edinburgh: Edinburgh University Press.

Bryden, J. and Geisler, C. (2007). 'Community-based land reform: lessons from Scotland', *Land Use Policy* 24.1, pp. 24–34.

Bryson, V. (2007), *Gender and the politics of time: feminist theory and contemporary debates*, Bristol: Polity.

Burkhauser, J. (2001), *Glasgow girls: women in art and design 1880–1920*, Edinburgh: Canongate.

Burnett, J. A. (2007), 'Hail brither Scots o' coaly Tyne: networking and identity among Scottish migrants in the north-east of England, ca. 1860–2000', Immigrants and Minorities 25.1, pp. 1–21.

Butler, K. D. (2001), 'Defining diaspora, refining a discourse', *Diaspora* 10.2, pp. 189–219.

Butler, R. W. (1985), 'Evolution of tourism in the Scottish Highlands', *Annals of Tourism Research* 12.3, pp. 371–391.

Butler, R. W. (2005), 'The influence of sport on destination development: the case of golf at St Andrews, Scotland', in Higham, J. (ed.), *Sport tourism destinations: issues, opportunities and analysis*, Oxford: Elsevier, pp. 274–282.

Butler, R. W. (2007), 'The history and development of royal tourism in Scotland: Balmoral the ultimate holiday home', in Long, P. and Palmer, N. J. (eds), *Royal tourism: excursions around monarchy*, Clevedon: Channel View, pp. 51–61.

Butt, R. (2010), 'Looking at tartan in film: history, identity and spectacle', in Brown, I. (ed.), *From tartan to tartanry: Scottish culture, history and myth*, Edinburgh: Edinburgh University Press, pp. 1166–1179.

Cairney, P. (2009), 'The "British policy style" and mental health: beyond the headlines', *Journal of Social Policy* 38.4, pp. 671–688.

Bibliography

Cairney, P. (2011a), 'The new British policy style: from a British to a Scottish political tradition?', *Political Studies Review* 9.2, pp. 208–220.

Cairney, P. (2011b), *The Scottish political system since devolution: from new politics to the new Scottish government*, Exeter: Academic Imprints.

Cairney, P. (2013), 'Territorial policy communities and the Scottish policy style: the case of compulsory education', *Scottish Affairs* 82.1, pp 73–97.

Cairney, P. and McGarvey, N. (2013), *Scottish politics* (2nd ed.), London: Palgrave Macmillan.

Calder, J. (2003), *Scots in Canada*, Edinburgh: Luath.

Calder, J. (2006), *Scots in the USA*, Edinburgh: Luath.

Callahan, R. (1998), 'Ethnic politics and tourism: A British case study', *Annals of Tourism Research* 25.4, pp. 818–836.

Cameron, E. (2010), *Impaled upon the thistle: Scotland since 1880*, Edinburgh: Edinburgh University Press.

Cant, B. and Kelly, E. (1995), 'Why is there a need for racial equality activity in Scotland?', *Scottish Affairs* 12, pp. 9–26.

Carman, C., Johns, R. and Mitchell, J. (2014), *More Scottish than British: the 2011 Scottish Parliament election*, London: Palgrave.

Carnegie, E. (2006), '"It wasn't all bad": representations of working-class cultures within social history museums and their impacts on audiences', *Museum and Society* 4.2, pp. 69–83.

Carr, J. and Cavanagh L. (2009), *Scotland's diaspora and overseas-born population*, Edinburgh: Scottish Government, www.scotland.gov.uk/Resource/Doc/285746/0087034.pdf (accessed 2 December 2019).

Carrell, S. (2012), 'Racial equality in Scottish councils: less male, less stale but still very pale', *Guardian*, www.theguardian.com/uk/scotland-blog/2012/may/18/scottish-councils-still-pale (accessed 2 December 2019).

Cavanagh, L., Eirich, F. and McLaren, J. (2008), *Fresh talent working in Scotland scheme: an evidence review*, Edinburgh: Scottish Government Social Research.

Chapman, M. (1992), *The Celts: the construction of a myth*, London: Macmillan.

Chapman, R. W. (ed.) (1930), *Johnson's journey to the western islands of Scotland and Boswell's journal of a tour to the Hebrides with Samuel Johnson*, London: Oxford University Press.

Charlaff, L., Ibrani, K., Lowe, M., Marsden, R. and Turnay, L. (2004), *Refugees and asylum seekers in Scotland: a skills and aspirations audit*, Edinburgh: Scottish Executive.

Checkland, S. G. (1981), *The upas tree: Glasgow 1875–1975*, Glasgow: University of Glasgow Press.

Chhabra, D., Healy, R. and Sills, E. (2003), 'Staged authenticity and heritage tourism', *Annals of Tourism Research* 30.3, pp. 702–719.

Christie, C. (2011), *Commission on the future delivery of public services*, Edinburgh. APS Group.

Citizens Advice Scotland (2014), *Working at the edge: childcare*, www.cas.org.uk/publications/working-edge-childcare (accessed 2 December 2019).

Cohen, R. (2008), *Global diasporas: an introduction* (2nd ed.), London: Routledge.

Coleman, J. (1988), 'Social capital in the creation of human capital', *American Journal of Sociology* 94, pp. 95–119.

Colley, L. (1994), *Britons: forging the nation 1707–1837*, New Haven, CT and London, Yale University Press.

Collins, K. E. (2008), *Scotland's Jews: a guide to the history and community of the Jews in Scotland*, Glasgow: Scottish Council of Jewish Communities.

Connell, R. (2009), *Gender in world perspective*, Cambridge: Polity.

Convention of Scottish Local Authorities (COSLA) (2018), *Transient visitor tax*, Edinburgh: COSLA, www.cosla.gov.uk/sites/default/files/private/coslatransient visitortax.pdf (accessed 2 December 2019).

Convery A. (2016), *The territorial Conservative Party: devolution and party change in Scotland and Wales*, Manchester: Manchester University Press.

Cook, R. (1999), 'The home-ly kailyard nation: nineteenth-century narratives of the Highland and the myth of Merrie Auld Scotland', *ELH* 66.4, pp. 1053–1073.

Cooke, S. and McLean, F. (2002), 'Our common inheritance? Narratives of self and other in the national museum of Scotland', in Harvey, D., Jones, R., McInroy, N. and Milligan, C. (eds), *Celtic geographies: old culture, new times*, Abingdon: Routledge, pp. 109–122.

Coole, C. (2002), 'A warm welcome? Scottish and UK media reporting of an asylum-seeker murder', *Media, Culture and Society* 24, pp. 839–852.

Corporation of Glasgow (1948), *Review of operations 1919–1947*, Glasgow: Glasgow Corporation Housing Department.

Corr, H. (1998), 'Where is the lass o' pairts?: gender, identity and education in nineteenth century Scotland', in Broun, D., Finlay, R. and Lynch, M. (eds), *Image and identity: the making and re-making of Scotland through the ages*, Edinburgh: John Donald, pp. 220–228.

Cosgrove, S. (1991), *Hampden Babylon: sex and scandal in Scottish football*, Edinburgh: Canongate.

Cowan, E. (2008), *'For freedom alone': the Declaration of Arbroath 1320*, Edinburgh: Birlinn.

Craig, C. (1996), *Out of history: narrative paradigms in Scottish and British culture*, Edinburgh: Polygon.

Craig, C. (2018), The wealth of the nation: Scotland, culture and independence, Edinburgh: Edinburgh University Press.

Crane, T. C., Hamilton, J. A. and Wilson, L. E. (2004), 'Scottish dress, ethnicity and self-identity', *Journal of Fashion Marketing and Management* 8.1, pp. 66–83.

Crawford, R. (2007), *Scotland's books: the Penguin history of Scottish literature*, London: Penguin.

Croft, Pauline (2003), *King James*. Basingstoke and New York: Palgrave Macmillan.

Croxford, L. (2000), 'Gender and national curriculum', in Salisbury, J. and Riddell, S. (eds), *Gender, policy and educational change: shifting agendas in the UK and Europe*, London: Routledge, pp. 115–133.

Cubie, A. (2002), 'The legal profession', in Hassan, G. and Warhurst, C. (eds), *The anatomy of new Scotland: power, influence and change*, Edinburgh: Mainstream, pp. 94–102.

Curtice, J. (2009), 'Is there an English backlash? Reactions to devolution', in Park, A., Curtice, J., Thomson, K., Phillips, M. and Clery, E. (eds), British social attitudes: the 25th report (25th ed.), London: NatCen Social Research.

Curtice, J. and Heath, A. (2000), 'Is the English Lion about to roar? National identity after devolution', in Jowell, R., Curtice, J., Park, A., Thomson, K., Jarvis, L., Bromley, C. and Stratford, N. (eds), *British social attitudes: the 17th report*, London: Sage, pp. 155–174.

Curtice, J. and Ormston, R. (2012), 'The state of the union: public opinion and the Scottish question', in Park, A., Clery, E., Curtice, J., Phillips, M. and Utting, D. (eds), *British social attitudes: the 29th report*, London, NatCen Social Research, pp. 116–137.

Curtin, S. (2013), 'Lessons from Scotland: British wildlife tourism demand, product development and destination management', *Journal of Destination Marketing and Management* 2, pp. 196–211.

Damer, S. (1990), *Glasgow: going for a song*, London: Lawrence & Wishart.

Davidson, N. (2000), *The origins of Scottish nationhood*, London: Pluto.

Davidson, N., Liinpää, M., McBride, M. and Virdee, S. (eds) (2018), *No problem here: racism in Scotland*, Edinburgh: Luath.

Davie, G. [1961] (1999), *The democratic intellect: Scotland and her universities in the nineteenth century*, Edinburgh: Edinburgh University Press.

Davies, N. (1996), *Europe: a history*, London: Pimlico.

Davies, N. (2012), *Vanished kingdoms: the history of half-forgotten Europe*, Harmondsworth: Penguin.

de Lima, P. (2005), 'An inclusive Scotland? The Scottish Executive and racial equality', in Mooney, G. and Scott, G. (eds), *Exploring social policy in the 'new' Scotland*, Bristol: Policy Press, pp. 135–157.

den Breejen, L. (2007), 'The experiences of long-distance walking: a case study of the West Highland Way in Scotland', *Tourism Management* 28.6, pp. 1417–1427.

Denholm, A. (2016), 'College student numbers plummet to lowest level on record', *Herald*, 14 January, www.heraldscotland.com/news/14205104.College_student_numbers_plummet_to_lowest_level_on_record (accessed 2 December 2019).

Denholm, J. and Macleod, D. (2002), 'Educating the Scots: the renewal of the democratic intellect', in Hassan, G. and Warhurst, C. (eds), *Anatomy of the new Scotland*, Edinburgh: Mainstream, pp. 114–123.

Devine, T. (1994), *Clanship to crofters' war: the social transformation of the Scottish Highlands*, Manchester: Manchester University Press.

Devine, T. (1999), *The Scottish nation 1700–2000*, London: Allen Lane.

Devine, T. (ed.) (2000), *Scotland's shame? Bigotry and sectarianism in modern Scotland*, Edinburgh: Mainstream.

Devine, T. (2003), *Scotland's Empire 1600–1815*, London: Allen Lane.

Devine, T. (2008), *Scotland and the Union 1707–2007*, Edinburgh: Edinburgh University Press.

Devine, T. (2011), *To the ends of the earth: Scotland's global diaspora, 1750–2010*, London: Allen Lane.

Devine, T. (2012), *The Scottish nation: a modern history*, London: Penguin.

Devine, T. (2018), *The Scottish Clearances: a history of the dispossessed*, London: Allen Lane.

Devine, T., Lee, C. and Peden, G. (eds) (2005), *The transformation of Scotland: the economy since* 1700, Edinburgh: Edinburgh University Press.

Devine, T. and McCarthy, A. (eds) (2018), *New Scots: Scotland's immigrant communities since* 1945, Edinburgh: Edinburgh University Press.

Devolution (Further Powers) Committee (2015), *Changing relationships: parliamentary scrutiny of intergovernmental relations, 8th report (Session 4)*, Edinburgh: Scottish Parliament.

Dewar, J. (2011), *Tourism in Scotland*, SPICe Briefing 11/35, Edinburgh: Scottish Parliament Information Centre.

Dey, I. (2014), 'Scotland's wily puppet master, still pulling all the right strings', *The Times*, 2 March.

Dezell, M. (2002), *Irish America: coming into clover*, New York: Anchor.

DiCenzo, M. (1996), *The politics of alternative theatre in Britain, 1968–1990: the case of 7:84 Scotland*, Cambridge: Cambridge University Press.

Dick, D. (2008), 'Women in Scottish education from 1850', *History Scotland* 8.2, pp. 42–46.

Dickson, M. (2014), 'Will the British public ever love Andy Murray again after expressing his support for Scottish independence?', *Daily Mail*, 19 September, www.dailymail.co.uk/sport/tennis/article-2761653/Will-British-public-love-Andy-Murray-expressing-support-Scottish-independence.html (accessed 2 December 2019).

Di Domenico, C. and Di Domenico, M. (2007), 'Heritage and urban renewal in Dundee: learning from the past when planning for the future of a post-industrial city', *Journal of Retail and Leisure Property* 6, pp. 327–339.

Dobson, D. (1994), *Scottish emigration to colonial America, 1607–1785*, Athens: University of Georgia Press.

Downes, A. D. (2002), 'Sport and international diplomacy: the case of the commonwealth Caribbean and the anti-apartheid campaign, 1959–1992', *Sports Historian* 22.2, pp. 23–45.

Dunlop, A. and Miles, R. (1990), 'Recovering the history of Asian migration to Scotland', *Immigrants and Minorities* 9.2, pp. 145–167.

Durie, A. J. (2003), *Scotland for the holidays: tourism in Scotland, 1780–1939*, Edinburgh: Tuckwell Press.

Durie, A. J., Bradley, J. and Dupree, M. (2006a), *Water is best: the hydros and health tourism in Scotland, 1840–1940*, Edinburgh: John Donald.

Durie, A. J., Yeoamn, I. and McMahon-Beattie, U. (2006b), 'How the history of Scotland creates a sense of place', *Place Branding* 2.1, pp. 43–52.

Edensor, T. (1997), 'Reading *Braveheart*: representing and contesting Scottish identity', *Scottish Affairs* 21, pp. 135–158.

Edensor, T. (2002), *National identity, popular culture and everyday life*, Oxford: Berg.

Edensor, T. and Millington, S. (2008), '"This is our city": branding football and local embeddedness', *Global Networks* 8.2, pp. 172–193.

Edward, M. (1993), *Who belongs to Glasgow? 200 years of migration*, Glasgow: Glasgow City Libraries.

Edwards, O. D. (1989), *A claim of right for Scotland*, Edinburgh: Polygon.

Evans, M. and Williams, C. H. (eds) (2012), *Gender: the key concepts*, London: Routledge.

Everitt, A. (2001), 'Culture and citizenship', *Political Quarterly* 72.s1, pp. 64–73.

Ewan, E., Pipes, R., Rendal, J. and Reynolds, S. (eds) (2018), *The new biographical dictionary of Scottish women*, Edinburgh: Edinburgh University Press.

Ewen, E. (1995), 'Braveheart', *American Historical Review* 100.4, pp. 1219–1221.

Ewen, N. (2012), 'Team GB or no Team GB, that is the question: Olympic football and the post-war crisis of Britishness', *Sport in History* 32.2, pp. 302–324.

Ewing, W. and Russell, M. (2004), *Stop the world: the autobiography of Winnie Ewing*, Edinburgh: Birlinn.

Faiers, J. (2008), *Tartan*, Oxford: Berg.

Fairlie, H. (1955), 'Political commentary', *The Spectator*, 23 September.

Felch, S. M. (1995), 'The rhetoric of biblical authority: John Knox and the question of women', *Sixteenth Century Journal* 26.4, pp. 805–822.

Ferguson, T. and Cunnison, J. (1956), *In their early twenties: a study of Glasgow youth*, Oxford: Oxford University Press.

Finlay, A. (1998), 'Hamish Henderson and the modem folksong revival', *Studies in Scottish Literature* 30.1, http://scholarcommons.sc.edu/ssl/vol30/iss1/24 (accessed 2 December 2019).

Finlay, I., Sheridan, M., McKay, J. and Nudzor, H. (2010), 'Young people on the margins: in need of more choices and more chances in twenty-first century Scotland', *British Educational Research Journal* 36.5, pp. 851–867.

Finlay, R. (2011), 'National identity, union and empire c.1850–c.1970', in Mackenzie, J. M. and Devine, T. M. (eds), *Scotland and the British Empire*, Oxford: Oxford University Press, pp. 280–317.

Firn, J. R. (1975), 'External control and regional development: the case of Scotland', *Environment and Planning A* 7.4, pp. 393–414.

Flynn, A. (2013), '"Bongo Bongo" and reconfiguring the "other"', *Anthropology Today* 29.5, pp. 1–2.
Forrest, A. (2007), 'Asylum: the new dawn', *Sunday Herald,* 7 October, p. 22.
Forsyth, R. (1990), *The only game: the Scots and world football*, Edinburgh: John Donald.
Foster, J. (1989), 'Nationality, social change and class: transformation of national identity in Scotland', in McCrone, D., Kendrick, S. and Straw, P. (eds), *The making of Scotland: nation, culture and social change*, Edinburgh: Edinburgh University Press, pp. 31–52.
Foster, J. and Woolfson, C. (1986), *The politics of the UCS work-in: class alliance and the right to work*, London: Lawrence & Wishart.
Fowler, S. (2003), 'Ancestral tourism', *Insights*, March, pp. D31–D36.
Fraser, D. (2002), ['Personal reflection'], in Devine, T. and Logue, P. (eds), *Being Scottish*, Edinburgh: Polygon, pp. 77–79.
Freedland, J. (2014), 'An independent Scotland?', *New York Review of Books* 61.5, 20 March.
Friedan, B. (1963), *The feminine mystique*, New York: Norton.
Fry, M. (2001), *The Scottish empire*, Edinburgh: Birlinn.
Fryer, P. (2018), *Staying power: the history of black people in Britain*, London: Pluto Press.
Gans, H. (1979), 'Symbolic ethnicity: the future of ethnic groups and cultures in America', *Ethnic and Racial Studies* 2.1, pp. 1–20.
Garcia, B. (2004), 'Urban regeneration, arts programming and major events: Glasgow 1990, Sydney 2000 and Barcelona 2004', *International Journal of Cultural Policy* 10.1, pp. 103–118.
Gardiner, M. (2005), *Modern Scottish culture*, Edinburgh: Edinburgh University Press
Gellner, E. (1972), *Thought and change*, London: Weidenfeld & Nicolson.
Gellner, E. (1983), *Nations and nationalism*, Ithaca, NY: Cornell University Press.
Gibb, A. (1989), 'Policy and politics in Scottish housing since 1945', in Rodger, R. (ed.), *Scottish housing in the twentieth century*, Leicester: Leicester University Press, pp. 155–183.
Gill, M. and Crawley, H. (2003), *Asylum in the UK*, London: Institute for Public Policy Research.
Gillespie, G. (2016), *State of the economy*, Edinburgh: Scottish Government Office of Chief Economic Adviser.
Giulianotti, R. (1999), 'Hooligans and carnival fans: football supporter cultures', in Armstrong, G. and Giulianotti, R. (eds), *Football cultures and identities*, London: Macmillan, pp. 29–40.
Giulianotti, R. (2005), 'The sociability of sport: Scotland football supporters as interpreted through the sociology of Georg Simmel', *International Review for the Sociology of Sport* 40.3, pp. 289–306.
Glazer, N. and Moynihan, D. P. (1963), *Beyond the melting pot: the Negroes, Puerto Ricans, Jews, Italians and Irish of New York City*, Cambridge, MA: MIT Press.
Glendinning, M., MacInnes, R. and MacKechnie, A. (1996), *A history of Scottish architecture, from the Renaissance to the present day*, Edinburgh: Edinburgh University Press.
Gold, J. and Gold, M. (1995), *Imagining Scotland: tradition, representation and promotion in Scottish tourism since 1750*, Aldershot: Scolar.
Gold, J. and Gold, M. (2002), 'Understanding narratives of nationhood: film-makers and Culloden', *Journal of Geography* 101, pp. 261–270.
Goldie, D. (2000), '"Will ye stop yer tickling, Jock?": modern and postmodern Scottish comedy', *Critical Quarterly* 42.4, pp. 7–18.
Goodman, J. S., Fields, D. L. and Blum, T. C. (2003), 'Cracks in the glass ceiling: in what kinds of organizations do women make it to the top?', *Group and Organization Management* 28.4, pp. 475–501.

Gordon, E. (2006), 'The family', in Abrams, L., Gordon, E., Simonton, D. and Yeo, E. (eds), *Gender in Scottish history since 1700*, Edinburgh: Edinburgh University Press, pp. 235–267.

Grant, I. F. (1959), *The MacLeods: the history of a clan, 1200–1956*, London: Faber & Faber.

Gray, M. (2015), 'SNP must tackle the Scottish establishment … not just that of Westminster', *The National*, 13 October.

Green, K., Smith, A. and Roberts, K. (2005), 'Social class, young people, sport and physical education', in Green, K. and Hardman, K. (eds), *Physical education: essential issues*, London: Sage, pp. 180–196.

Guthrie, D. (1946), 'Leiden and Edinburgh: a medical partnership', *British Medical Bulletin* 4, p. 218.

Habron, D. (1998), 'Visual perception of wild land in Scotland', *Landscape and Urban Planning* 42.1, pp. 45–56.

Hague, E. (2001), 'Haggis and heritage: representing Scotland in the United States', in Horne, J. (ed.), *Leisure cultures, consumption and commodification*, Brighton: Leisure Studies Association Publication 74, pp. 107–129.

Hague, E. (2002), 'National Tartan Day: rewriting history in the United States', *Scottish Affairs* 38, pp. 94–124.

Hague, E. and Mercer, J. (1998), 'Geographical memory and urban identity in Scotland', *Geography* 83.2, pp. 105–116.

Hague, E. and Sebesta, E. H. (2008), 'Neo-confederacy, culture and ethnicity: a white Anglo-Saxon Southern people', in Hague, E., Sebesta, E. H. and Beirich, H. (eds), *Neo-confederacy: a critical introduction*, Austin TX: University of Texas Press, pp. 97–130.

Hamilton, C. and Scullion, A. (2003), 'Flagship or flagging? The post-devolution role of Scotland's "national" companies', *Scottish Affairs* 42, pp. 98–114.

Handlin, O. (1973), *The uprooted: the epic story of the great migrations that made the American people*, Boston: Little, Brown.

Hanham, H. (1969), *Scottish nationalism*, London: Faber & Faber.

Hardy, A. (2003), 'An investigation into the key factors necessary for the development of iconic touring routes', *Journal of Vacation Marketing* 9.4, pp. 314–330.

Harper, M. (2003), *Adventurers and exiles: the great Scottish exodus*, London: Profile.

Harper, M. (2012), *Scotland no more? The Scots who left Scotland in the twentieth century*, Edinburgh: Luath.

Harper, M. (2013), '"Come to Corby": a Scottish steel town in the heart of England', *Immigrants and Minorities* 31.1, pp. 27–47.

Harper, M. (2018), *Testimonies of transition: voices from the Scottish diaspora*, Edinburgh: Luath.

Harris, J. (1998), 'Civil society, physical activity and the involvement of sport sociologists in the preparation of physical activity professionals', *Sociology of Sport* 15.2, pp. 138–153.

Harvie, C. (1993), *No gods and precious few heroes: Scotland since 1914*, Edinburgh: Edinburgh University Press.

Harvie, C. (2002), *Scotland: a short history*, Oxford: Oxford University Press.

Harvie, C. and Jones, P. (2000), *The road to home rule: images of Scotland's cause*, Edinburgh: Polygon.

Harvie, J. (2003), 'Cultural effects of the Edinburgh International Festival: elitism, identities, industries', *Contemporary Theatre Review* 13.4, pp. 12–26.

Hassan, G. (2004), *The Scottish Labour Party: history, institutions and ideas*, Edinburgh: Edinburgh University Press.

Hassan, G. (2014), *Independence of the Scottish mind: elite narratives, public spaces and the making of a modern nation*, London: Palgrave.

Hassan, G. (2018), 'Civil society, the rise and fall of civil Scotland and contextualising media', *Scottish Affairs*, 27.1, pp 36–44.

Hassan, G. and Shaw, E. (2012), *The strange death of Labour Scotland*, Edinburgh: Edinburgh University Press.

Hassan, G. and Warhurst, C. (eds) (2002), *The anatomy of new Scotland: power, influence and change*, Edinburgh: Mainstream.

Heath, A., and Kellas, J. (1998), 'Nationalism and constitutional questions', *Scottish Affairs* [Special Issue], pp. 110–127.

Hechter, M. (1975), *Internal colonialism: the Celtic fringe in British national development*, London: Transaction.

Henderson, A. (2007), *Hierarchies of belonging: national identity and political culture in Scotland and Quebec*, Montreal and Kingston: McGill–Queens University Press.

Henderson, H. (2004), *Alias MacAlias: writings on songs, folk and literature*, Edinburgh: Polygon.

Herman, A. (2002), *The Scottish Enlightenment: the Scots' invention of the modern world*, London: Fourth Estate.

Hesse, D. (2011a), 'Roots and hearts: Homecoming Scotland 2009 and the Scots of Europe', *Scottish Affairs* 77, pp. 90–109.

Hesse, D. (2011b), 'Scots for a day: the Highland Games of mainland Europe', *History Scotland* 11, pp. 24–30.

Hewison, R. (1987), *The heritage industry: Britain in a climate of decline*, London: Methuen.

Hey, D. (2011), 'Kinder Scout and the legend of the mass trespass', *Agricultural History Review* 59.2, pp. 199–216.

Heywood, A (2019), *Politics* (5th ed.), London: Palgrave.

Hinchliffe, S., Marcinkiewicz, A., Curtice, J. and Ormston, R. (2015), *Scottish social attitudes survey 2014: public attitudes to sectarianism in Scotland*, Edinburgh: Scottish Government Social Research.

Hindle, N., Martin, A. and Nash, R. (2015), 'Tourism development and the backpacker market in Highland Scotland', *Tourism and Hospitality Research* 15.3, pp. 178–192.

Hobsbawm, E. (1990), *Nations and nationalism since 1780*, Cambridge: Cambridge University Press.

Hobsbawm, E. and Ranger, T. (eds) (1983), *The invention of tradition*, Cambridge: Cambridge University Press.

Hollywood, E., Brown, R., Danson, M. and McQuaid, R. (2007), 'Demographic and labour market change: the dynamics of older workers in the Scottish labour market', *Scottish Geographical Journal* 123.4, pp. 242–256.

Holmes, H. (2002), 'Remembering their history: memories of Irish migratory agricultural workers in Scotland', *Human Affairs* 2, pp. 139–152.

Hopkins, N., Reicher, S., Harrison, K, Cassidy, C., Bull, R. and Levine, M. (2007), 'Helping to improve the group stereotype: on the strategic dimension of prosocial behavior', *Personality and Social Psychology Bulletin* 33.6, pp. 776–788.

Hopkins, P. (2004), 'Everyday racism in Scotland: a case study of East Pollokshields', *Scottish Affairs* 49, pp. 88–103.

Hopkins, P. (ed.) (2019), *Scotland's Muslims*, Edinburgh: Edinburgh University Press.

Houlihan, B. (2008), *Sport and society: a student introduction*, London: Sage.

House of Commons Public Administration and Constitutional Affairs Committee (2018), Devolution and exiting the EU: reconciling differences and building strong relationships, eighth report of session 2017–19 *HC 1485*. Edinburgh: House of Commons Public Administration and Constitutional Affairs Committee.

Houston, D. (2010), 'Changing ethnic segregation and housing disadvantage in Dundee', *Scottish Geographical Journal* 126.4, pp. 285–298.

Huang, W.-J., Haller, W. J. and Ramshaw, G. P. (2011), 'The journey "home": an exploratory analysis of second-generation immigrants' homeland travel', http://scholarworks.umass.edu/cgi/viewcontent.cgi?article=1281&context=gradconf_hospitality (accessed 4 July 2017).

Hughes, G. (1995), 'Authenticity in tourism', *Annals of Tourism Research* 22.4, pp. 781–803.

Hume, I. M. (2010), 'Tartanry into tartan: heritage, tourism and material culture', in Brown, I. (ed.), *From tartan to tartanry: Scottish culture, history and myth*, Edinburgh: Edinburgh University Press, pp. 82–92.

Hunter, J. S. (1994), *A dance called America: the Scottish Highlands, the United States and Canada*, Edinburgh: Mainstream.

Hunter, J. S. (2003), 'Flying the flag: identities, the nation and sport', *Identities* 10.4, pp. 409–425.

Hunter, J. S. (2005), *Scottish exodus: travels among a worldwide clan*, Edinburgh: Mainstream.

Hunter, J. S. (2012), *From the low tide of the sea to the highest mountain tops: community ownership of land in the Highlands and Islands of Scotland*, Lewis: Islands Book Trust.

Hutcheon, P. (2018), 'Former yes Scotland chair: SNP Growth Commission relied on "Scottish establishment" for report', *Herald on Sunday*, 3 June.

Hutchison, I. (2001), *Scottish politics in the twentieth century*, London: Palgrave.

Hynes, P. (2006), *The compulsory dispersal of asylum seekers and processes of social exclusion in England*, London: Middlesex University and ESRC.

Ichijo, A. (2004), *Scottish nationalism and the idea of Europe*, London: Routledge.

Innes, S. and Rendall, J. (2006), 'Women, gender and politics', in Abrams, L., Gordon, E., Simonton, D. and Yeo, E. (eds.), Gender in Scottish history since 1700, Edinburgh: Edinburgh University Press, pp. 43–83.

Institute for Public Policy Research (2007), *The reception and integration of new migrant communities*, London: IPPR.

Irish Department of Foreign Affairs and Trade (2015), *Global Irish: Ireland's diaspora policy*, Dublin: Irish Department of Foreign Affairs and Trade.

Jack, I. (1987), *Before the oil ran out: Britain 1977–87*, London: Secker & Warburg.

Jarvie, G. (1993), 'Sport, nationalism and cultural identity', in Allison, L. (ed.), *The changing politics of sport*, Manchester: Manchester University Press, pp. 58–83.

Jarvie, G. (2003), 'Communitarianism, sport and social capital', *International Review for the Sociology of Sport* 38.2, pp. 139–153.

Jarvie, G. (2012), *Sport, culture and society: an introduction*, London: Routledge.

Jarvie, G., Murray, S. and Macdonald, S. (2017), 'Promoting Scotland, diplomacy and influence through sport', Scottish Affairs 26.1, pp. 1–22.

Jarvie, G. and Reid, I. A. (1999), 'Scottish sport, nationalist politics and culture', *Culture, Sport, Society* 2.2, pp. 22–43.

Jarvie, G. and Thornton, J. (2012), *Sport, culture and society: an introduction*, London: Routledge.

Jarvie, G. and Walker, G. (1994), *Scottish sport in the making of the nation: ninety minute patriots?* Leicester: Leicester University Press.

Jedrej, C. and Nuttall, M. (1996), *White settlers: the impact of rural repopulation in Scotland*, Luxembourg: Harwood.

Jeffery, C. (2008), 'Where stands the Union now? Scottish–English relations after devolution', in Devine, T. (ed.), *Scotland and the Union 1707–2007*, Edinburgh: Edinburgh University Press, pp. 195–209.

Johnston, T. [1909] (1999), *Our Scots noble families*, Glendaruel: Argyll.

Jones, H. (1986), 'Evolution of Scottish migration patterns: a social relations of production approach', *Scottish Geographical Magazine*, 102.3, pp. 151–164.

Jones, H., Ford, N., Caird, J. and Berry, W. (1984), 'Counter-urbanisation in social context: long distance migration to the Highlands and Islands of Scotland', *Professional Geographer*, 36, pp. 437–444.

Jones, P. (1992), 'Education', in Linklater, M. and Denniston, R. (eds), *Anatomy of Scotland: how Scotland works*, Edinburgh: Chambers, pp. 97–125.

Kay, B. (1986), *Scots: the mither tongue*, Edinburgh: Mainstream.

Kay, J. (2005), 'The old tongue', in Kay, J., *Life mask*, Hexham: Bloodaxe, p. 50.

Kay, R. and Morrison, A. (2013), *Evidencing the social and cultural benefits and costs of migration in Scotland*, Edinburgh: COSLA.

Keating, M. (1988), *The city that refused to die: Glasgow – the politics of urban regeneration*, Aberdeen: Aberdeen University Press.

Keating, M. (2001), *Nations against the state: the new politics of nationalism in Quebec, Catalonia and Scotland* (2nd ed.), London: Palgrave.

Keating, M. (2010), *The government of Scotland: public policy making after devolution*, Edinburgh: Edinburgh University Press.

Keating, M. (ed.) (2017), *A wealthier, fairer Scotland*, Edinburgh: Edinburgh University Press.

Kedourie, E. (1960), *Nationalism*, London: Hutchinson.

Kellas, J. (1973), *The Scottish political system*, Cambridge: Cambridge University Press.

Kelly, E. (2002), 'Asians in Scotland: the formation of an elite', in Hassan, G. and Warhurst, C. (eds), *The anatomy of new Scotland: power, influence and change*, Edinburgh: Mainstream, pp. 295–305.

Kelly, E. (2003), 'Challenging sectarianism in Scotland: the prism of racism', *Scottish Affairs* 42, pp. 32–56.

Kemp, J. (2012), 'Introduction', in Kemp, J. (ed.), *Confusion to our enemies: selected journalism of Arnold Kemp (1939-2002)*, Castle Douglas: Neil Wilson, pp. 1–10.

Kenny, M. and Mackay, F. (2012), 'Less male, pale and stale? Women and the 2012 Scottish local government elections', *Scottish Affairs* 80, pp. 20–32.

Kerevan, G. (1981), 'Arguments within Scottish Marxism', *Bulletin of Scottish Politics* 1.2, pp. 118–119.

Kerr, R. and Robinson, S. (2016), 'Gentlemen, players and remoralisation of banking: solution or diversion', in Dorn, N. (ed.), *Controlling capital: public and private regulation of financial markets*, Abingdon: Routledge, pp. 126–138.

Kettle, M. (2016), 'What now for Nicola Sturgeon and the rebels who became the Scottish establishment?', *The Guardian*, 29 April.

Kiely, R., Bechhofer, F., Stewart, R. and McCrone, D. (2001), 'The markers and rules of Scottish national identity', *Sociological Review* 49.1, pp. 33–55.

Land Reform Review Group (2014), *The land of Scotland and the common good*, Edinburgh: Scottish Government.

Leach, R. (2007), 'The short, astonishing history of the National Theatre of Scotland', *New Theatre Quarterly* 23.2, pp. 171–183.

Leask, D. (2014), 'Glasgow University dominates education background of MSPs', *The Herald*, 31 March.

Leask, D. (2016), 'Revealed: MSPs five times more likely to be privately educated than average Scot', *The Herald*, 7 June.
Leith, M. S. (2006), *Nationalism and national identity in Scottish politics*, PhD thesis, University of Glasgow.
Leith, M. S. (2009), 'Governance and identity in a devolved Scotland', Parliamentary Affairs 63.2, April 2010, pp. 286–301.
Leith, M. S. and Sim, D. (2012), 'Second generation identities: the Scottish diaspora in England', *Sociological Research Online* 17.3, www.socresonline.org.uk/17/3/11.html (accessed 2 December 2019).
Leith, M. S. and Sim, D. (eds) (2014), *The modern Scottish diaspora: contemporary debates and perspectives*, Edinburgh: Edinburgh University Press.
Leith, M. S. and Sim, D. (2016), 'Les Écossais en France: a modern diaspora?', *Social Identities*, doi: 10.1080/13504630.2016.1186533.
Leith, M. S. and Sim, D. (2019), 'The Scots in England: a different kind of diaspora?', *National Identities*, 21.2, pp. 119–134, doi: 10.1080/14608944.2017.1397617.
Leith, M. S. and Soule, D. (2011), *Political discourse and national identity in Scotland*, Edinburgh: Edinburgh University Press.
Leonard, T. (1984), *Intimate voices*, Newcastle: Galloping Dog Press.
Lindsay, I. (1997), 'The uses and abuses of national stereotypes', *Scottish Affairs* 20, pp. 133–148.
Lindsay, I. (2006), *Civil society in Scotland*, Glasgow: University of Strathclyde, https://strathprints.strath.ac.uk/1373 (accessed 8 October 2018).
Linklater, M. and Denniston, R. (eds) (1992), *Anatomy of Scotland: how Scotland works*, Edinburgh: Chambers.
Livingstone, K. (2011), 'In praise of multicultural London', in Mahamdallie, H. (ed.), *Defending multiculturalism*, London: Bookmarks, pp. 26–37.
Long, P. (1999), *The Scottish Colourists 1900–1930*, Edinburgh: National Galleries of Scotland.
Lorimer, H. (1997), '"Happy hostelling in the Highlands": nationhood, citizenship and the inter-war youth movement', *Scottish Geographical Magazine* 113.1, pp. 42–50.
Lowndes, S. (2010), *Social sculpture: the rise of the Glasgow art scene*, Edinburgh: Luath.
Lyall, S. (2006), 'An artist loved by no one but the public', *New York Times*, 23 February, www.nytimes.com/2006/02/23/arts/design/23vett.html?8hpib&_r=0 (accessed 2 December 2019).
Lynch, P. (1999), *SNP: the history of the Scottish National Party*, Cardiff: Welsh Academic Press.
Maan, B. (1992), *The new Scots: the story of Asians in Scotland*, Edinburgh: John Donald.
Maan, B. (2014), *Muslims in Scotland*, Edinburgh: Argyll.
McArthur, A. and Long, H. K. (1935), *No mean city*, London: Longmans Green.
MacAskill, K. and McLeish, H. (2007), *Wherever the saltire flies*, Edinburgh: Luath.
McCarry, M. (2010), 'Becoming a "proper man": young people's attitudes about interpersonal violence and perceptions of gender', *Gender and Education* 22.1, pp. 17–30.
McCarthy, A. (2007), 'The Scots' society of St Andrew, Hull, 1910–2001: immigrant, ethnic and transnational association', *Immigrants and Minorities* 25.3, pp. 209–233.
McCormick, J. (2017), *Commission on parliamentary reform*, https://test123582.files.wordpress.com/2016/10/commissiononparliamentaryreformreport-june2017.pdf (accessed 9 October 2018)
McCrone, D. (1998), *The sociology of nationalism*, London: Routledge.
McCrone, D. (2001), *Understanding Scotland: the sociology of a nation* (2nd ed.), London: Routledge.

McCrone, D. (2002), 'Who do you say you are? Making sense of national identities in modern Britain', *Ethnicities* 2.3, pp. 301–320.
McCrone, D. (2017), *The new sociology of Scotland*, London: Sage.
McCrone, D. and Bechhofer, F. (2010), 'Claiming national identity', *Ethnic and Racial Studies* 33.6, pp. 921–948.
McCrone, D. and Bechhofer, F. (2012), 'Coming home: return migrants in twenty-first century Scotland', in M. Varricchio (ed.), *Back to Caledonia*, Edinburgh University Press, pp. 262–280.
McCrone, D. and Bechhofer, F. (2015), *Understanding national identity*, Cambridge: Cambridge University Press.
McCrone, D., Brown, A., Surridge, P. and Thomson, K. (1997), *British general election study: Scottish election survey*, Ann Arbor, MI: Inter-University Consortium for Political and Social Research.
McCrone, D. and McPherson, G. (2009), 'Introduction', in McCrone, D. and McPherson, G. (eds), *National days: constructing and mobilising national identity*, Basingstoke: Palgrave Macmillan, pp. 1–9.
McCrone, D., Morris, A. and Kiely, R. (1995), *Scotland – the brand: the making of Scottish heritage*, Edinburgh: Edinburgh University Press.
McCrone, G. (1969), *Regional policy in Britain*, London: Allen & Unwin.
McDiarmid, H. (1943), *Lucky poet*, London: Methuen.
Macdonald, C. M. M. (2009), *Whaur extremes meet: Scotland's twentieth century*, Edinburgh: John Donald.
Macdonald, C. M. M. (2012), 'Imagining the Scottish diaspora: emigration and transnational literature in the late modern period', *Britain and the World*, 5.1, pp. 12–42.
McEwan, N. (2006), *Nationalism and the state: welfare and identity in Scotland and Quebec*, Brussels: Presses interuniversitaires europennes/Peter Lang.
McGarvey, D. (2017), *Poverty safari: understanding the anger of Britain's underclass*, Edinburgh: Luath.
McGarvey, N. (2008), 'Devolution in Scotland', in Bradbury, J. (ed.), *Devolution, regionalism and regional development: the UK experience*, London: Routledge, pp. 25–44.
McGlynn, M. (2002), '"Middle-class wankers" and working-class texts: the critics and James Kelman', *Contemporary Literature* 23.1, pp. 50–84.
MacGregor, G. (1980), *Scotland: an intimate portrait*, Boston: Houghton Mifflin.
McHarg, A., Mullen, T., Page, A. and Walker, N. (eds) (2016), *The Scottish independence referendum: constitutional and political implications*, Oxford: Oxford University Press.
MacInnes, J. (1992), 'The press in Scotland', *Scottish Affairs* 1, pp. 137–149.
MacInnes, J. (1998), 'The myth of the macho Scotsman: attitudes to gender, work and the family in the UK, Ireland and Europe', *Scottish Affairs* 23, pp. 108–124.
MacInnes, J. (2005), 'Research note: gender role attitudes in Scotland', *Scottish Affairs* 51, pp. 107–112.
McIntosh, I., Sim, D. and Robertson, D. (2004), '"We hate the English except for you, cos you're our pal": identification of the "English" in Scotland', *Sociology* 38.1, pp. 43–59.
Macintyre, J. (2011), 'The curse of victory', *Prospect Magazine*, 25 May.
McIvor, A. (1996), 'Gender apartheid: women in Scottish society', in Devine, T. and Finlay, R. (eds), *Scotland in the twentieth century*, Edinburgh: Edinburgh University Press, pp. 188–209.
Mack, D. S. (2006), *Scottish fiction and the British Empire*, Edinburgh: Edinburgh University Press.

Mackay, F. (1996), 'The zero tolerance campaign: setting the agenda', *Parliamentary Affairs* 49.1, pp. 206–220.

Mackay, F. and Bilton, K. (2001), *Equality proofing procedures in drafting legislation: international comparisons*, Edinburgh: Scottish Executive Central Research Unit.

Mackenzie, J. M. (1999), '"The second city of the empire": Glasgow – imperial municipality', in Driver, F. and Gilbert, D. (eds), *Imperial cities: landscape, display and identity*, Manchester: Manchester University Press, pp. 215–237.

McLaren, L. and Johnson, M. (2007), 'Resources, group conflict and symbols: explaining anti-immigration hostility in Britain', *Political Studies* 55.4, pp. 709–732.

McLay, F. (1988), *Workers' city: real Glasgow stands up*, Glasgow: Clydeside Press.

McLean, F. and Cooke, S. (2003), 'Constructing the identity of a nation: the tourist gaze at the Museum of Scotland', *Tourism Culture & Communication* 4, pp. 153–162.

MacLellan, R. and Smith, R. (eds) (1998), *Tourism in Scotland*, London: International Thomson Business Press.

McLellan, R. S. (1956), *Anchor Line 1856–1956*, Glasgow: Anchor Line.

MacLeod, C. (2017), *The future of community land ownership in Scotland. A Discussion Paper*, Edinburgh: Highlands and Island Enterprise.

MacLeod, L. and Smith-Christmas, C. (2018), *Gaelic in contemporary Scotland*, Edinburgh: Edinburgh University Press.

McMillan, J. (2010), 'Arts budget hardly deserves to "share the pain" of country's cuts', *Scotsman* 23 July, www.scotsman.com/lifestyle/culture/joyce-mcmillan-arts-budget-hardly-deserves-to-share-the-pain-of-country-s-cuts-1-818526 (accessed 2 December 2019).

MacRae, M. and Wight, M. (2011), *The role of home organizations in home countries: Globalscot and Scottish Enterprise*, Washington, DC: World Bank, http://siteresources.worldbank.org/EDUCATION/Resources/278200-1126210664195/1636971-1126210694253/Role_Bridge_Organizations.pdf (accessed 2 December 2019).

MacRaild, D. M. (2011), *The Irish diaspora in Britain, 1750–1939*, Basingstoke: Palgrave Macmillan.

McRury, I. and Poynter, G. (2010), '"Team GB" and London 2012: the paradox of national and global identities', *International Journal of the History of Sport* 27.16–18, pp. 2958–2975.

McTavish, D. (ed.) (2016), *Politics in Scotland*, London: Routledge.

McTavish, D. (2017), 'Redefining the role of the state', *Public Money and Management*, 37.2, pp. 76–78.

Macwhirter, I. (2002), 'The new Scottish political classes', in Hassan, G. and Warhurst, C. (eds), *Anatomy of the new Scotland*, Edinburgh: Mainstream, pp. 27–36.

Maguire, J., Jarvie, G., Mansfield, L. and Bradley, J. (2002), *Sport worlds: a sociological perspective*, Champaign, IL: Human Kinetics.

Maguire, J. and Tuck, J. (1998), 'Global sports and patriot games: rugby union and national identity in a united sporting kingdom since 1945', *Immigrants and Minorities* 17.1, pp. 103–126.

Mahamdallie, H. (ed.) (2011), *Defending multiculturalism*, London: Bookmarks.

Maloney, P. (2010), '"Wha's like us? Ethnic representation in music hall and popular theatre, and the remaking of Scottish urban society', in Brown, I. (ed.), *From tartan to tartanry: Scottish culture, history and myth*, Edinburgh: Edinburgh University Press, pp. 129–150.

Marmot Review (2010), *Fair society, healthy lives: strategic review of health inequalities in England post 2010*, www.ucl.ac.uk/marmotreview (accessed 2 December 2019).

Martin, M. (1695), *A description of the Western Islands of Scotland*, Edinburgh: Birlinn.

Martine, R. (2001), 'The power pack', *Caledonia*, February.

Martine, R. (2002), 'The Scottish aristocracy', in Hassan, G. and Warhurst, C. (eds), *The anatomy of new Scotland: power, influence and change*, Edinburgh: Mainstream, pp. 234–245.

Matheson, C. (2010), 'Legacy planning, regeneration and events: the Glasgow Commonwealth Games', *Local Economy* 25.1, pp. 10–23.

Maxwell, S. (2012), *Arguing for independence: evidence, risk and the wicked issues*, Edinburgh: Luath.

Mehew, E. (ed.) (1997), 'Letter of 28/29 July 1873', in Mehew, E. (ed.), *Selected letters of Robert Louis Stevenson*, New Haven, CT and London: Yale University Press, pp. 37–38.

Melling, J. (1983), *Rent strikes: people's struggle for housing in west Scotland, 1890–1916*, Edinburgh: Polygon.

Milburn, A. (2014), 'Breaking the link between demography and destiny in Scotland', www.gov.uk/government/speeches/breaking-the-link-between-demography-and-destiny-in-scotland (accessed 2 December 2019).

Miles, R. (1982), *Racism and migrant labour*, London: Routledge and Kegan Paul.

Millar, J. (2005), 'The Lithuanians', in Beech, J., Hand, O., Mulhern, M. and Weston, J. (eds), *Scottish life and society: a compendium of Scottish ethnology. Vol. 9 The individual and community life*, Edinburgh: John Donald, European Ethnological Research Centre and National Museums of Scotland, pp. 514–534.

Miller, P. (2013), 'BBC does not reflect our lives say half of Scots', www.pressreader.com/uk/the-herald-1130/20130717/281852936173808 (accessed 19 December 2019).

Miller, W. (1981), *The end of British politics? Scots and English political behaviour in the Seventies*, Oxford: Clarendon.

Mitchell, J. (1995), 'Lobbying Brussels: the case of Scotland Europa', *European Urban and Regional Studies* 2.4, pp. 287–298.

Mitchell, J. (2014), *The Scottish question*, Oxford: Oxford University Press.

Mitchell, J. (2017), Hamilton 1967: the by-election that transformed Scotland, Edinburgh: Luath.

Mitchell, J., Bennie, L. and Johns, R. (2012), *The Scottish National Party: transition to power*, Oxford: Oxford University Press.

Modood, T. (2007), *Multiculturalism*, Cambridge: Polity.

Moir, J. (1991), 'National parks: north of the border', *Planning Outlook* 34.2, pp. 61–67.

Mooney, G. (2004), 'Cultural policy as urban transformation? Critical reflections on Glasgow, European city of culture 1990', *Local Economy* 19.4, pp. 327–340.

Mooney, G. and Scott, G. (eds) (2005), *Exploring social policy in the 'new' Scotland*, Bristol: Policy Press.

Mooney, G. and Scott, G. (eds) (2012), *Social justice and social policy in Scotland*, Bristol: Policy Press.

Moore, L. (2006), 'Education and learning', in Abrams, L., Gordon, E., Simonton, D. and Yeo, E. (eds), *Gender in Scottish history since 1700*, Edinburgh: Edinburgh University Press, pp. 110–139.

Moore, T. and McKee, K. (2014), 'The ownership of assets by place-based community organisations; political rationales, geographies of social impact and future research agendas', *Social Policy and Society* 33.4, pp. 521–533.

Moreno, L. (1988), 'Scotland and Catalonia: the path to home rule', in McCrone, D. and Brown, A. (eds), *The Scottish government yearbook*, Edinburgh: Unit for the Study of Government in Scotland, pp. 166–181.

Moreno. L. (2006), 'Scotland, Catalonia, Europeanization and the "Moreno question"', *Scottish Affairs* 54, pp. 1–21.

Morgan, N., Pritchard, A. and Piggott, R. (2002), 'New Zealand, 100% pure: the creation of a powerful niche destination brand', *Journal of Brand Management* 9.4–5, pp. 335–354.

Morrow, S. (2005), 'Continuity and change: the planning and management of long-distance walking routes in Scotland', *Managing Leisure* 10, pp. 237–250.

Morrow, S. (2006), 'Scottish football: it's a funny old business', *Journal of Sports Economics* 7.1, pp. 90–95.

Morton, G. (2012), *Ourselves and others: Scotland 1832–1914*, Edinburgh: Edinburgh University Press.

Mullen, S. (2009), *It wisnae us: the truth about Glasgow and slavery*, Edinburgh: Royal Incorporation of Architects in Scotland.

Mulvey, G. (2013), *In search of normality: refugee integration in Scotland*, Glasgow: Scottish Refugee Council.

Munro, A. (1991), 'The role of the School of Scottish Studies in the folk music revival', *Folk Music Journal* 6.2, pp. 132–168.

Munro, M. and Madigan, R. (1989), 'Do you ever think about us?', *Architects Journal* 190.25, p. 58.

Museums Galleries Scotland (MGS) (2012), *Going further: the national strategy for Scotland's museums and galleries*, Edinburgh: MGS.

Mycock , A. (2014), 'Invisible and inaudible? England's Scottish diaspora and the politics of the Union', in Leith, M and Sim, D. (eds), *The modern Scottish diaspora*. Edinburgh: Edinburgh University Press, pp. 99–117.

Nagel, J. (1994), 'Constructing ethnicity: creating and recreating ethnic identity and culture', *Social Problems* 41, pp. 1001–1026.

Nairn, T. (1968), 'The three dreams of Scottish nationalism', *New Left Review* 1, p. 49.

Nairn, T. (1977), *The breakup of Britain*, London: New Left Books.

Nairn, T. (1980), *The breakup of Britain* (2nd ed.), London: Verso.

Nairn, T. (2000), *After Britain: New Labour and the return of Scotland*, London: Granta.

National Records of Scotland (2013), *2011 census: key results on education and labour market in Scotland – release 2B*, Edinburgh: NRS.

National Records of Scotland (2016), *Scotland's census: shaping our future*, Standard Outputs, www.scotlandscensus.gov.uk/ods-web/standard-outputs.html (accessed 2 December 2019).

National Records of Scotland (2017), *Projected population of Scotland (2016 based)*, Edinburgh: NRS.

National Records of Scotland (2018), *Scotland's population: the Registrar-General's annual review of demographic trends 2017*, Edinburgh: NRS.

National Records of Scotland (2019), *Mid-year population estimates Scotland, mid-2018*, Edinburgh: NRS.

Nenadic, S. (1994), 'Museums, gender and cultural identity in Scotland', *Gender and History* 6.3, pp. 426–434.

Netto, G. (2011), 'Identity negotiation, pathways to housing and "place": the experience of refugees in Glasgow', *Housing Theory and Society* 28.2, pp. 123–143.

Newland, K. and Taylor, C. (2010), *Heritage tourism and nostalgia trade: a diaspora niche in the development landscape*, Washington, DC: Migration Policy Institute.

Newton, M. (2015), 'The Gaelic diaspora in North America', in Leith, M and Sim, D. (eds), *The modern Scottish diaspora*, Edinburgh: Edinburgh University Press, pp. 136–152.

Nicholson, R. (2005), 'From Ramsay's *Flora MacDonald* to Raeburn's *MacNab:* the use of tartan as a symbol of identity, *Textile History* 36.2, pp. 146–167.

Nicoll, R. (2003), 'Clubbable rogues', *The Observer*, 23 February.

Nock, O. S. (1950), *Scottish railways*, London: Nelson.

Novak, M. (1971), *The rise of the unmeltable ethnics: politics and culture in the seventies*, New York: Macmillan.

Oakley, A. (1974), *The sociology of housework*, Oxford: Martin Robertson.

O'Connor, A. (2017), *Scotland's employment by industry and geography*, SPICe Briefing SB 17–71, Edinburgh: Scottish Parliament.

Office for National Statistics (ONS) (2015), *Nomis official labour market statistics*, www.nomisweb.co.uk/census/2011/ukmig008 (accessed 2 December 2019).

Oil and Gas UK Ltd (2018), *Workforce report 2017*, London: Oil and Gas UK.

Oliver, J. (2005), 'Scottish Gaelic identities: contexts and contingencies', *Scottish Affairs* 51, pp. 1–24.

Olusoga, D. (2016), *Black and British: a forgotten history*, London: Macmillan.

Organisation for Economic Cooperation and Development (OECD) (2011), *Government at a glance 2011*, Paris: OECD, www.oecd-ilibrary.org/governance/government-at-a-glance-2011_gov_glance-2011-en (accessed 4 December 2019).

Organisation for Economic Cooperation and Development (OECD) (2015), *Improving schools in Scotland: an OECD perspective*, Paris: OECD.

Ormond, R. (2005), *The Monarch of the Glen: Landseer in the Highlands*, Edinburgh: National Galleries of Scotland.

Orr, J. (2008), 'Instrumental or intrinsic? Cultural policy in Scotland since devolution', *Cultural Trends* 17.4, pp. 309–316.

Orwell, G. (1937), *The road to Wigan pier*, London: Victor Gollancz.

Özkirimli, U. (2010), *Theories of nationalism: a critical introduction*, London: Palgrave Macmillan.

Özkirimli, U. (2017), *Theories of nationalism: a critical introduction* (3rd ed.), London: Palgrave Macmillan.

Parutis, V. (2014), '"Economic migrants" or "middling transnationals"? East European migrants' experiences of work in the UK', *International Migration* 52.1, pp. 36–55.

Paterson, L. (1994), *The autonomy of modern Scotland*, Edinburgh: Edinburgh University Press.

Paterson, L. (2003a), *Scottish education in the twentieth century*, Edinburgh: Edinburgh University Press.

Paterson, L. (2003b), 'The survival of the democratic intellect: academic values in Scotland and England', *Higher Education Quarterly* 57.1, pp. 67–93.

Paterson, L., Brown, A., Curtice, J. and Hinds, K. (eds) (2001), *New Scotland, new politics?* Edinburgh: Polygon.

Paterson, L. and Iannelli, C. (2006), 'Religion, social mobility and education in Scotland', *British Journal of Sociology* 57.3, pp. 353–377.

Patrick, A. (1997), 'Boy trouble: some problems resulting from "gendered" representation of Glasgow's culture in the education of women artists and designers', *International Journal of Art and Design Education* 16.1, pp. 7–16.

Patrick, J. (1973), *A Glasgow gang observed*, London: Eyre Methuen.

Payne, P. L. (1996), 'The economy', in Devine, T. and Finlay, R. J. (eds), *Scotland in the twentieth century*, Edinburgh: Edinburgh University Press, pp. 13–45.

Peden, G. C. (2005), 'The managed economy: Scotland 1919–2000', in Devine, T., Lee, C. H. and Peden, G. C. (eds), *The transformation of Scotland: the economy since 1700*, Edinburgh: Edinburgh University Press, pp. 233–265.

Penrose, J. and Howard, D. (2008), 'One Scotland, many cultures: the mutual constitution of anti-racism and place', in Dwyer, C. and Bressey, C. (eds), *New geographies of race and racism*, Aldershot: Ashgate, pp. 95–111.

Phillips, D. (1998), 'Black minority ethnic concentration, segregation and dispersal in Britain', *Urban Studies* 35.10, pp. 1681–1702.

Phillips, T. and Phillips, M. (2009), *Windrush: the irresistible rise of multi-racial Britain*, London: Harper Collins.

Pieri, J. (2005), *The Scots-Italians: recollections of an immigrant*, Edinburgh: Mercat Press.

Pittock, M. (1998), *Jacobitism*, Basingstoke: Macmillan.

Pittock, M. (2008), *The road to independence? Scotland since the sixties*, London: Reaktion.

Pittock, M. (2010), 'Plaiding the invention of Scotland', in Brown, I. (ed.), *From tartan to tartanry: Scottish culture, history and myth*, Edinburgh: Edinburgh University Press, pp. 32–47.

Pocock, D. C. D. (1960), 'The migration of Scottish labour to Corby new town', *Scottish Geographical Magazine* 76.3, pp. 169–171.

Pollard, N., Latorre, M. and Sriskandarajah, D. (2008), *Floodgates or turnstiles? Post-EU enlargement migration flows to (and from) the UK*, London: IPPR.

Porter, L. (2009), 'Planning displacement: the real legacy of sporting events', *Planning Theory and Practice* 10.3, pp. 395–418.

Powley, A. and Gillan, R. (2015), *Shankly's village*, Durrington: Pitch Publishing.

Poynter, G. (2009), 'The 2012 Olympic Games and the reshaping of east London', in Imrie, R, Lees, L. and Raco, M., *Regenerating London: governance, sustainability and community in a global city*, London: Routledge, pp. 132–150.

Prentice, R. and Andersen, V. (2003), 'Festival as creative destination', *Annals of Tourism Research* 30.1, pp. 7–30.

Prentis, M. (2008), *The Scots in Australia*, Sydney: University of New South Wales Press.

Public Health England (2015), *A guide to community-centred approaches for health and wellbeing: full report*, London: Public Health England and NHS England.

Quirk, B. (2007), *Making assets work: the Quirk Review of Community Management and Ownership of Public Assets*, London: Stationery Office.

Rahman, M. (2004), 'The shape of equality: discursive deployments during the Section 28 repeal in Scotland', *Sexualities* 7.2, pp. 150–166.

Ratcliffe, P. (2004), *'Race', ethnicity and difference: imagining the inclusive society*, Maidenhead: Open University Press.

Ray, C. (2001), *Highland heritage: Scottish Americans in the American South*, Chapel Hill: University of North Carolina Press.

Reay, D. (2006), 'The zombie stalking English schools: social class and educational inequality', *British Journal of Educational Studies* 54.3, pp. 288–307.

Reid, I. A. (1998), 'Shinty, nationalism and Celtic politics 1870–1922', *Sports Historian* 18.2, pp. 107–130.

Reid, I. A. (2010), '"The stone of destiny": Team GB curling as a site for contested national discourse', *Sport in Society* 13.3, pp. 399–417.

Renan, E. [1882] (2010), *Qu'est-ce qu'une nation?* Whitefish: Kessinger.

Renan, E. (1996), 'What is a nation?' in Eley, G. and Suny, R. G. (eds), *Becoming national: a reader*, New York and Oxford: Oxford University Press, pp. 41–55.

Richards, E. (1999), *Patrick Sellar and the Highland Clearances: homicide, eviction and the price of progress*, Edinburgh: Polygon.

Richards, E. (2000), *The Highland Clearances: people, landlords and rural turmoil*, Edinburgh: Birlinn.

Riddell, S., Weedon, E. and Minty, S. (2015), *Higher education in Scotland and the UK: diverging or converging systems?* Edinburgh: Edinburgh University Press.

Riddoch, L. (2015), *Wee white blossom: what post-referendum Scotland needs to flourish*, Edinburgh: Luath.

Roberts, D. (1999), 'Your clan or ours?' *Oxford American* September–October, pp. 24–30.

Robinson, V. and Hale, S. (1989), *The geography of Vietnamese secondary migration in the UK*, Warwick: Centre for Research in Ethnic Relations.

Rodgers, M. (1980), 'The Lanarkshire Lithuanians', in Kay, B. (ed.), *Odyssey: voices from Scotland's recent past*, Edinburgh: Polygon, pp. 18–25.

Rolfe, H. and Metcalf, H. (2009), *Recent migration into Scotland: the evidence base*, Edinburgh: Scottish Government Social Research.

Rosie, G. (2002), 'Network Scotland: the power of the quango state', in Hassan, G. and Warhurst, C. (eds), *The anatomy of new Scotland: power, influence and change*, Edinburgh: Mainstream, pp. 124–132.

Roy, K. (2018), 'A change of leadership at GSA?', *Scottish Review*, 27 June.

Runnymede Trust (2016), 'Shadow report: submission to the UN Committee on the Elimination of Racial Discrimination with regard to the UK government's 21st to 23rd periodic reports', www.ukren.org/uploads/images/CERD%20Civil%20Society%20Report%20UKfinal.pdf (accessed 2 December 2019).

Rutherford, A. (2009), *Engaging with the Scottish diaspora: rationale, benefits and challenges*, Edinburgh: Scottish Government.

Sales, R. (2007), *Understanding immigration and refugee policy: contradictions and continuities*, Bristol: Policy Press.

Salmond, J. B. (1934), *Wade in Scotland*, Edinburgh: Moray Press.

Sampson, A. (1962), *Anatomy of Britain*, London: Hodder & Stoughton.

Sarup, M. (1996), *Identity, culture and the postmodern world*, Edinburgh: Edinburgh University Press.

Savage, M. (2015), *Social class in the 21st century*, London: Pelican.

Scarles, C. (2004), 'Mediating landscapes: the processes and practices of image construction in tourist brochures of Scotland', *Tourist Studies* 4.1, pp. 43–67.

Schlesinger, A. M. Jr. (1991), *The disuniting of America*, Knoxville, TN: Whittle.

Schlesinger, P., Miller, D. and Dinan, W. (2001), *Open Scotland? Journalists, spin doctors and lobbyists*, Edinburgh: Polygon.

Scott, P. H. (1999), *The boasted advantages: the consequences of the Union of 1707*, Edinburgh: Saltire Society.

Scottish Borders Council (2018), 'Proposal for a single public authority in the Scottish Borders, report by the chief executive', 25 September, https://scottishborders.moderngov.co.uk/documents/s30944/Item%20No.%2013%20-%20Proposal%20for%20a%20Single%20Public%20Authority.pdf (accessed 28 November 2019)

Scottish Council of Independent Schools (2018), 'Facts and figures', www.scis.org.uk/facts-and-figures (accessed 24 January 2019).

Scottish Diaspora Tapestry (n.d.), www.scottishdiasporatapestry.org (accessed 24 January 2019).

Scottish Enterprise (2016), *Scottish key facts*, Glasgow: Scottish Enterprise.

Scottish Executive (2000), *Creating our future, minding our past: Scotland's national cultural strategy*, Edinburgh: Scottish Government.

Scottish Executive (2001), *Scotland: a global connections strategy*, www.scotland.gov.uk/Resource/Doc/158429/0042932.pdf (accessed 24 January 2019).

Scottish Executive (2003), *Preventing domestic abuse: a national strategy*, Edinburgh: Scottish Executive.

Scottish Executive (2007), *All our futures: planning for Scotland with an ageing population*, Edinburgh: Scottish Executive.

Scottish Fiscal Commission (2018), *Scotland's economic and fiscal forecasts December 2018*, Edinburgh: SFC.

Scottish Funding Council (2017), *Gender action plan: annual progress report 2017*, Edinburgh: SFC.

Scottish Funding Council (2018), *Higher education students and qualifiers at Scottish institutions 2016–17*, Edinburgh: SFC.

Scottish Government (2010), *Diaspora engagement plan: reaching out to Scotland's international family*, Edinburgh: Scottish Government.

Scottish Government (2011), *2020 route map for renewable energy in Scotland*, Edinburgh: Scottish Government.

Scottish Government (2013a), *Equality outcomes: ethnicity – evidence review*, Edinburgh: Scottish Government Social Research.

Scottish Government (2013b), *Scotland's future*, Edinburgh: Scottish Government.

Scottish Government (2013c), *Scottish government equality outcomes: gender: evidence review*, Edinburgh: Scottish Government Social Research.

Scottish Government (2014a), *The public bodies (joint working) (national health and wellbeing outcomes) (Scotland) regulations*, Edinburgh: Scottish Government.

Scottish Government (2014b), *Women on board: quality through diversity*, Edinburgh: Scottish Government.

Scottish Government (2015), *Community Empowerment (Scotland) Act 2015*, www.legislation.gov.uk/asp/2015/6/contents/enacted (accessed 3 October 2018).

Scottish Government (2016a), *New perspectives on the gender pay gap: trends and drivers*, Edinburgh: Scottish Government.

Scottish Government (2016b), *Scottish government policy paper on BBC Charter renewal*, Edinburgh: Scottish Government.

Scottish Government (2017a), *Gaelic language plan 2016–2021*, Edinburgh: Scottish Government.

Scottish Government (2017b), *Export statistics Scotland 2015*, Edinburgh.

Scottish Government (2018), *Regional employment patterns in Scotland*, Edinburgh, https://beta.gov.scot/publications/regional-employment-patterns-scotland-statistics-annual-population-survey-2017 (accessed 24 January 2019).

Scottish Parliament (2015), *The economic impact of the film, TV and video games industries*, Edinburgh: Scottish Parliament.

Scottish Refugee Integration Forum (2003). *SRIF action plan*. Edinburgh: SRIF.

Scottish Renewables (2018), www.scottishrenewables.com/sectors/renewables-in-numbers (accessed 24 January 2019).

Scottish Tourism Alliance (2012), *Tourism Scotland 2020: the future of our industry in our hands*, Edinburgh: STA.
Scottish Tourism Alliance (2017), *Tourism Scotland 2020: 2017 yearly review*, Edinburgh: STA.
Seaton, A. V. (1998), 'The history of tourism in Scotland: approaches, sources and issues', in MacLellan, R. and Smith, R. (eds), *Tourism in Scotland*, London: International Thomson Business Press, pp. 1–41.
Seaton, A. V. (1999), 'Book towns as tourism developments in peripheral areas', *International Journal of Tourism Research* 1, pp. 389–399.
Seenan, G. (2005), 'The Guardian profile: the Scottish Raj', *Guardian*, www.theguardian.com/politics/2005/mar/18/uk.scotland (accessed October 2016).
Short, D. and Stockdale, A. (1999), 'English migrants in the countryside: opportunities for rural Scotland?', *Scottish Geographical Journal* 115.3, pp. 177–192.
Silk, H. (2014), 'Corby's hopes and fears for Scottish independence', *Northamptonshire Telegraph*, 12 September.
Sim, D. (2011a), *American Scots: the Scottish diaspora and the USA*, Edinburgh: Dunedin Academic Press.
Sim, D. (2011b), 'The Scottish community and Scottish organisations on Merseyside: development and decline of a diaspora', *Journal of Scottish Historical Studies* 31.1, pp. 99–118.
Sim, D. (2015), 'Refugee onward migration and the changing ethnic geography of Scotland', *Scottish Geographical Journal* 131.1, pp. 1–16.
Sim, D., Barclay, A. and Anderson, I. (2009), 'Migrant worker experiences in Scotland: integration or exclusion?', *Scottish Affairs* 69, pp. 85–105.
Sim, D. and Bowes, A. (2007), 'Asylum seekers in Scotland: the accommodation of diversity'. *Social Policy and Administration* 41.7, pp. 729–746.
Sim, D. and Leith, M. S. (2013), 'Diaspora tourists and the Scottish Homecoming 2009', *Journal of Heritage Tourism* 8.4, pp. 259–274.
Sim, D. and Leith, M. S. (2014), 'Scottish diasporic identities in the Netherlands', *National Identities* 16.2, pp. 139–155.
Sim, D. and McIntosh, I. (2007), 'Connecting with the Scottish diaspora', *Scottish Affairs* 58, pp. 78–95.
Simpson, L. and Smith, A. (2014), *Who feels Scottish? National identities and ethnicity in Scotland*, Manchester: University of Manchester Centre on Dynamics of Ethnicity, http://hummedia.manchester.ac.uk/institutes/code/briefings/dynamicsofdiversity/code-census-briefing-national-identity-scotland.pdf (accessed 2 December 2019).
Smith, A. (1996), 'Memory and modernity: reflections on Ernest Gellner's theory of nationalism', *Nations and Nationalism* 2.3, pp. 371–388.
Smith, A. (1998), *Nationalism and modernism*, London: Routledge.
Smith, A. (2000), *The nation in history: historiographical debates about ethnicity and nationalism*, Cambridge: Polity.
Smith, A. (2003), *Chosen peoples*, Oxford: Oxford University Press.
Smout, T. C. [1972] (1998), *A history of the Scottish people 1560–1830*, London: Fontana.
Smout, T. C. [1986] (2010), *A century of the Scottish people 1830–1950*, London: Collins.
Smout, T. C. (1991), Scottish voices, London: Fontana.
Smout, T. C. (1994), 'Perspectives on the Scottish identity' *Scottish Affairs* 6, pp. 101–113.
Smout, T. C. (1995), 'The culture of migration: Scots as Europeans 1500–1800', *History Workshop Journal* 40, pp. 108–117.

Social Mobility and Child Poverty Commission (SMCPC) (2014), *Elitist Britain?* London: UK Government.

Social Mobility and Child Poverty Commission (SMCPC) (2015), *Elitist Scotland?* London: UK Government.

Social Research (2016), *Programme for international student assessment (PISA) 2015: highlights from Scotland's results*, Edinburgh: Scottish Government, www.gov.scot/Resource/0051/00511095.pdf (accessed 2 December 2019).

Solomon, J. (2003), *Race and racism in Britain*, London: Macmillan.

Sosu, E. and Ellis, S. (2014), *Closing the attainment gap in Scottish education*, York: Joseph Rowntree Foundation.

Spence, A. (1977), 'Boom baby', in Royle, T. (ed.), *Jock Tamson's bairns: essays on a Scots childhood*, London: Hamish Hamilton, pp. 14–28.

Spencer, S., Ruhs, M., Anderson, B. and Rogaly, B. (2007), *Migrants' lives beyond the workplace: the experiences of Central and East Europeans in the UK*, York: Joseph Rowntree Foundation.

Sriskandarajah, D. and Drew, C. (2006), *Brits abroad: mapping the scale and nature of British emigration*, London: Institute for Public Policy Research.

Steinberg, S. (1981). *The ethnic myth: race, ethnicity and class in America*, New York: Atheneum.

Stevenson, D. (2014), 'Tartan and tantrums: critical reflections on the creative Scotland "stooshie"', *Cultural Trends* 23.3, pp. 178–187.

Stevenson, R. (2002), 'Border warranty: John McGrath and Scotland', *International Journal of Scottish Theatre* 3.2, https://ijosts.ubiquitypress.com/articles/222 (accessed 2 December 2019).

Stewart, E. S. (2012), 'UK dispersal policy and onward migration: mapping the current state of knowledge', *Journal of Refugee Studies* 25.1, pp. 25–49.

Stillwell, J. and Phillips, D. (2006), 'Diversity and change: understanding the ethnic geographies of Leeds', *Journal of Ethnic and Migration Studies* 32.7, pp. 1131–1152.

Stirbu, D. S. (2011), 'Female representation beyond Westminster: lessons from Scotland and Wales', *Political Insight* 2.3, pp. 32–33.

Strathern, A. and Stewart, P. J. (2001). *Minorities and memories: survivals and extinctions in Scotland and Western Europe*, Durham: North Carolina Academic Press.

Sullivan, K. (2009), 'A diaspora of descendants? Contemporary Caledonian Society members in Melbourne, Australia – a case study', in Fernandez, J. (ed.), *Diasporas: critical and inter-disciplinary perspectives*, Oxford: Inter-disciplinary Press, pp. 127–138.

Sullivan, K. (2014), 'Scots by association: clubs and societies in the Scottish diaspora', in Leith, M. and Sim, D. (eds), *The modern Scottish diaspora: contemporary debates and perspectives*, Edinburgh: Edinburgh University Press, pp. 47–63.

Sunday Times (2005), 'Paxman blasts Scottish Raj', 13 March.

Te Ara [The Encyclopaedia of New Zealand] (n.d.), www.teara.govt.nz/en/scots (accessed 21 February 2017).

Thomson, D. S. (1992), 'Scottish Gaelic literature', in Price, G. (ed.), *The Celtic connection*, Gerrards Cross: Colin Smythe, pp. 131–153.

Tilly, L. A. and Scott, J. W. (1987), *Women, work and family*, London: Routledge.

Timothy, D. (2011), *Cultural heritage and tourism: an introduction*, Bristol: Channel View.

Tinklin, T., Croxford, L., Ducklin, A. and Frame, B. (2005), 'Gender and attitudes to work and family roles: the views of young people at the millennium', *Gender and Education* 17.2, pp. 129–142.

Torrance, D. (2006), *The Scottish secretaries*, Edinburgh: Birlinn.

Torrance, D. (2009), *'We in Scotland': Thatcherism in a cold climate*, Edinburgh: Birlinn.
Trebeck, K. and Stuart, F. (2013), *Our economy: towards a new prosperity*, Oxford: Oxfam Scotland.
Trevor-Roper, H. (2008), *The invention of Scotland: myth and history*, New Haven, CT: Yale University Press.
Tucker, M. (2008), 'The cultural production of cities: rhetoric or reality? Lessons from Glasgow', *Journal of Retail and Leisure Property* 7, pp. 21–33.
Twain, M. (1869), The *innocents abroad*, Hartford, CT: American Publishing.
Umney, C. (2018), *Class matters*, London: Pluto Press.
VisitScotland (2016), *Insight Department: trends 2017*, Edinburgh: VisitScotland.
VisitScotland (2018), *Tourism in Scotland 2017: summary*, Edinburgh: VisitScotland.
Walls, P. and Williams, R. (2003), 'Sectarianism at work: accounts of employment discrimination against Irish Catholics in Scotland', *Ethnic and Racial Studies* 26.4, pp. 632–661.
Wanner, L. (2015), *Tartan noir: the definitive guide to Scottish crime fiction*, Glasgow: Freight.
Warren, C. R. and Birnie, R. V. (2009), 'Re-powering Scotland: wind farms and the "energy or environment" debate', *Scottish Geographical Journal* 125.2, pp. 97–126.
Waters, M. C. (1990), *Ethnic options: choosing identities in America*, Berkeley: University of California Press.
Watson, F. (2006), *Under the hammer: Edward I and Scotland 1286–1307*, Edinburgh: Birlinn.
Watson, M. (2003), *Being English in Scotland*, Edinburgh: Edinburgh University Press.
Webster, D. (2011), *World history of Highland Games*, Edinburgh: Luath.
Weedon, E. (2015), 'Widening access to higher education in Scotland, the UK and Europe', in Riddell, S., Weedon, E. and Minty, S. (eds), *Higher education in Scotland and the UK: diverging or converging systems?* Edinburgh: Edinburgh University Press, pp. 90–109.
Welsh, I. (1993), *Trainspotting*, London: Secker & Warburg.
What Scotland Thinks (2017), http://whatscotlandthinks.org/questions/if-scotland-became-independent-would-england-be-financially-better-off-worse-of#line (accessed March 2017).
Wightman, A. (2002), 'The landed gentry', in Hassan, G. and Warhurst, C. (eds), *The anatomy of new Scotland: power, influence and change*, Edinburgh: Mainstream, pp. 246–252.
Wightman, A., Higgins, P., Jarvie, G. and Nicol, R. (2002), 'The cultural politics of hunting: sporting estates and recreational land use in the Highlands and Islands of Scotland', *Culture, Sport, Society* 5.1, pp. 53–70.
Wilkie, J. (2001), *Metagama: a journey from Lewis to the new world*, Edinburgh: Birlinn.
Wilkins, S., Shams, F. and Huisman, J. (2013), 'The decision-making and changing behavioural dynamics of potential higher education students: the impacts of increasing tuition fees in England', *Educational Studies* 39.2, pp. 125–141.
Wilson, A. (1995), *Irish America and the Ulster conflict 1968–1995*, Belfast: Blackstaff Press.
Wright, R. (2004), *Population ageing and immigration policy*, Stirling and Strathclyde: Universities of Stirling and Strathclyde, Scottish Economic Policy Network.
Wright, V. (2014), 'A woman's industry? The role of women in the workforce of the Dundee jute industry c.1945–1979', *International Journal of Management Concepts and Philosophy* 8.2–3, pp. 110–125.
Yeoman, I., Greenwood, C. and McMahon-Beattie, U. (2009), 'The future of Scotland's international tourism markets', *Futures* 41, pp. 387–395.
Yinger, J. M. (1981), 'Toward a theory of assimilation and dissimilation', *Ethnic and Racial Studies* 4.3, pp. 249–264.

YouGov (2017), 'How Britain voted at the 2017 general election', https://yougov.co.uk/topics/politics/articles-reports/2017/06/13/how-britain-voted-2017-general-election (accessed 2 December 2019).

Young, A. (2002), 'The Scottish establishment: old and new elites', in G. Hassan and C. Warhurst (eds), *Tomorrow's Scotland*, London: Lawrence & Wishart, pp. 154–167.

Yule, E. and Manderson, D. (2014), *The glass half full: moving beyond Scottish miserablism*, Edinburgh: Luath.

Ziarski-Kernberg, T. (2005), 'Polish communities in Scotland', in Beech, J., Hand, O., Mulhern, M. and Weston, J. (eds), *Scottish life and society: a compendium of Scottish ethnology. Vol. 9: The individual and community life*, Edinburgh: John Donald, European Ethnological Research Centre and National Museums of Scotland, pp. 497–513.

Zimmer, O. (2003), 'Boundary mechanisms and symbolic resources: towards a process-oriented approach to national identity', *Nations and Nationalism* 9.2, pp. 173–193.

Index

Index

Index

Index

Index